About Island Press

ISLAND PRESS is the only nonprofit organization in the United States whose principal purpose is the publication of books on environmental issues and natural resource management. We provide solutions-oriented information to professionals, public officials, business and community leaders, and concerned citizens who are shaping responses to environmental problems.

In 1994, Island Press celebrated its tenth anniversary as the leading provider of timely and practical books that take a multidisciplinary approach to critical environmental concerns. Our growing list of titles reflects our commitment to bringing the best of an expanding body of literature to the environmental community throughout North America and the world.

Support for Island Press is provided by Apple Computer, Inc., The Bullitt Foundation, The Geraldine R. Dodge Foundation, The Energy Foundation, The Ford Foundation, The W. Alton Jones Foundation, The Lyndhurst Foundation, The John D. and Catherine T. MacArthur Foundation, The Andrew W. Mellon Foundation, The Joyce Mertz-Gilmore Foundation, The National Fish and Wildlife Foundation, The Pew Charitable Trusts, The Pew Global Stewardship Initiative, The Rockefeller Philanthropic Collaborative, Inc., and individual donors.

Land Use and Society

Land Use and Society

Geography, Law, and Public Policy

Rutherford H. Platt

ISLAND PRESS
Washington, D.C. • Covelo, California

Library of Congress Cataloging-in-Publication Data

Platt, Rutherford H.
    Land use and society : geography, law, and public policy/
Rutherford H. Platt.
        p.   cm.
    Includes bibliographical references and index.
    ISBN 1-55963-435-9 (pbk. : acid-free paper)
        1. Land use—Law and legislation—United States.   2. Land use—
    United States.   3. Physical geography—United States.   I. Title.
KF5698.P588   1996   95-39226
                                                            CIP

Printed on recycled, acid-free paper ✿ ∞
Manufactured in the United States of America
10 9 8 7 6 5 4 3 2 1

This book is dedicated with admiration and affection to two staunch friends of this beleaguered planet:

Gilbert F. White and

Anne U. White (1919–1989)

Contents

Preface: Reflections on a
Cross-Country Flight

To geographers and their fellow travelers, there are few greater treats than to fly a considerable distance over land on a clear day with a view unobstructed by the airplane wing. I recently enjoyed such a flight nonstop from San Francisco to Boston. Between the sourdough vendors and live lobster purveyors of those two airports stretches about 2700 miles of air distance. Along this trajectory, the route traverses a succession of geographic regions marked by vivid contrasts in both physical and human characteristics. Even the casual observer can scarcely fail to notice and perhaps to wonder about the diversity of the perceived landscape—its physical landforms, land cover, and patterns of rural and urban land use. If the movie is really boring, the window-gazer may attempt to annotate the passing scene by assigning causative factors and implications—some definite, others hypothetical—to what is seen or imagined in the landscape below. *This is thinking geographically.*

The aircraft ascends over the crowded East Bay cities of Oakland and Berkeley, riddled by seismic faults (where the Nimitz Freeway collapsed in the October 17, 1989 earthquake and 3300 homes burned in the Oakland–Berkeley Hills two years later). The flight continues over the geometric patterns of irrigated fields of the Central Valley (handsomely subsidized by the federal taxpayer) and over the snowy peaks and steep declivities of the Sierra Nevada (where John Muir battled Gifford Pinchot around 1910 over damming the Hetch Hetchy Valley to provide a water supply for San Francisco and where today environmentalists oppose plans for a new flood control dam on the American River upstream from Sacramento).

We streak across the empty, in some places radioactive, wastes of the arid Great Basin. Cities and irrigated agriculture briefly reappear in the Mormon settlements east of Great Salt Lake (which in 1987 was pumped into nearby salt flats to reduce record flood levels). The Wasatch Range, crisscrossed by ski slopes and clearcutting, gives way to the upper Colorado River Plateau, another sparsely inhabited region of high desert, sagebrush, and spectacular landforms. (Downstream on the Colorado River, the one-armed geologist and geographer, John Wesley Powell, made his epic journey through the Grand Canyon in 1869 that stimulated his proposals for large-scale irrigation projects in the arid West.) We pass near Dinosaur National Park, where Echo Park Dam, one of Powell's legacies, was defeated by David Brower in the 1950s at the dawn of the modern environmental movement.

East of the snowcapped Rockies lies the Front Range Urban Corridor, a chain of cities extending from Greeley to Pueblo, Colorado, anchored by smog-bound Denver (where in 1995 the world's largest airport, in land area, finally opened). For the next hour, one flies over the vast checkerboard of the High Plains dominated by green or brown circles of center-pivot irrigated fields within the square quarter-sections laid out under the Federal Land Survey during the 19th century. (On successive flights, it appears that the green circles are increasingly turning brown as irrigation is suspended due to high costs of pumping from the declining Ogallala Aquifer and perhaps also the effect of federal land retirement payments.)

We cross the Missouri River in the vicinity of the fabled "100th Meridian" (which roughly corresponds to the 20-inch average annual rainfall contour) where irrigation yields to rain-dependent agriculture. Towns begin to reappear as "beads on a string" along mainline railroad lines and old section-line highways. The rectangular farmscape increasingly gives way to rectangular cities, all interlaced by interstate highways leading to the really big midwestern cities: Kansas City, Minneapolis–St. Paul, St. Louis, Chicago. The alternation of town and farm across the nation's heartland is a totally human-dominated landscape. Few natural or unused areas of land are observed until the Appalachian Upland is reached in Pennsylvania and New York State.

Flight attendants collect headsets as the aircraft descends in humid summer twilight over the northeastern urban corridor for which geographer Jean Gottmann coined the name "Megalopolis." This "stupendous monument erected by titanic efforts" (in Gottmann's laconic words) is curiously dominated by forests, within which several of the nation's largest cities are situated. The failing daylight permits a glimpse of Quabbin Reservoir, Boston's primary water supply, surrounded by an "accidental wilderness" (as described by the Massachusetts Audubon Society) resulting from the forced abandonment of farms and villages when the state purchased the watershed in the 1930s. The plane swings over "the Nation's Technology Highway" (Massachusetts Route 128) where the arms race fostered the illusion of prosperity during the 1980s. It banks over the built-up coastal barriers south of Boston (where hundreds of homes were damaged in 1978 and again in 1991) and lands at Logan International Airport, which, like our departure point at San Francisco, is constructed on a filled wetland.

The cross section of the North American landscape just described is viewed by thousands of travelers on any clear day, albeit without the running commentary. To many observers, the scene below is a pleasant but seemingly random series of abstract images, like the geometric patterns produced by a kaleidoscope. But patterns of human land use are by no means random. To one with geographic training or interests, the variation in the landscape offers not only aesthetic but intellectual stimulation. The geographer seeks to discern order, process, and coherency in the seemingly haphazard sequence of images.

The perennial question of geography is: *Why* is this place the way it is and like or unlike other places? This leads to additional questions, for example: *What* benefits or costs arise from specific practices or ways of using land, air, and water and to whom do they accrue? *How* can we better manage the use of land and other resources to promote the public welfare, however defined, and reduce social costs—and *Who* should make the necessary decisions? These questions ultimately frame the central question of our time: *How may global resources be managed to sustain a world population that has more than doubled since 1950?*

Global resource crisis is at hand according to the Worldwatch Institute, World Resources Institute, the Smithsonian Institution, the National Academy of Sciences, and a host of international organizations. Global resource problems include widespread deforestation, atmospheric warming and ozone depletion, loss of biodiversity, land degradation, food shortages, energy shocks, accumulating wastes, and surface and groundwater pollution.

Geographers of course do not claim any special monopoly on wisdom, nor do they offer ready solutions to these travails. But they do offer the perspective of the "Why" question. They seek lessons from the experience of the past and present, which may profitably be applied to the exigencies of the future. If we can better understand how we got to where we are in our inhabitation of the earth, or portions of it that we label regions, nations, or communities, we may gain some valuable insights into how to deal with the challenges ahead.

Unlike more narrowly focused disciplines, geographers view the earth and its regions holistically and seek explanations (or solutions) through synthesis of diverse phenomena and the formulation of theories regarding the interaction of these variables. From time to time, certain classes of spatially distributed phenomena have been vested with greater importance than others as explanations of human settlement patterns and uses of resources. In the 1920s, the theory of environmental determinism was proposed to explain human actions in terms of the influence of climate and physical characteristics of regions. In the 1960s, central place theory and gravity models attributed human spatial behavior to economic forces operating through the private land market. In the 1980s and 1990s, the "political economy" has provided a focus for post-modern interpretations of cities and land use.

This book takes a different tack. While not discounting the role of physical, economic, and other spatial variables, the primary focus of this book is the role of *law* as a major factor in the way humans use their resources and design their patterns of settlement. In the phrase of James E. Vance, Jr., law is viewed as a "morphogenetic agent" in the shaping of the human environment.

Of course, law is not entirely an independent variable: Laws are products of institutions reacting to their perceptions of exogenous circumstances such as desire for capitalist profit, for a habitable environment, or fear of fire, flood, drought, famine, pollution, or crime. The rules for human activities established by law differ according to the rule maker's perception of external circumstances (see model described in Chapter 2). The rules often comprise an imperfect, partial, or even counterproductive response to an actual problem. Furthermore, laws established to address one problem may compound others. And laws have a habit of remaining in effect long after changes in circumstances have rendered them moot or even pernicious.

This book, then, is offered as an exploration of the influence of law over human use of land from the perspective of a geographer. The specific rules, doctrines, and practices discussed are drawn from the American context, including its common law roots in England. But the role of law as a factor in the shaping of urban and rural land use, for better or worse, is a phenomenon of global applicability.

This is a completely revised, expanded, and updated edition of my earlier book *Land Use Control: Geography, Law, and Public Policy* (Prentice-Hall 1991). This edition retains the historical flavor and approach of the earlier book but strengthens the discussion of contemporary U.S. land use programs and legal issues. In particular, it updates discussion of "the taking issue" with a review of the recent Supreme Court decisions in *Nollan v. California Coastal Commission, Lucas v. South Carolina Coastal Council,* and *Dolan v. City of Tigard.* It also includes new sections on the Endangered Species Act and urban greenway planning, and it updates the topic of federal flood policies to reflect the experience of the Midwest Floods of 1993 and reports ensuing therefrom. State and regional programs are now combined in a new Chapter 10. Housing and inner city issues are placed with the discussion of constitutional issues in Chapter 8.

This new edition is divided into four parts. Part I, "Preliminaries: Land Uses and Concepts," begins by presenting an overview of the current status of land use in the United States. The second chapter of this part gives some basic background on the fields of geography and law and their interaction with respect to land use planning and management. That discussion concludes with a general model used at various points later in the book to help explain the evolutionary process of societal response to the failure or inadequacy of existing land use practices.

Part II, "From Commons to Cacophony: Dispersion of Control over Land," considers the origins and present status of such fundamental concepts as "property rights" and "municipal corporations." In Chapter 3, we revisit some early English history beginning with feudalism, the rise of the medieval city as a chartered corporation, and the evolution into the Baroque era of town planning, dramatized by the Fire of London of 1666 and the Act for Rebuilding London which followed it. Chapters 4 and 5, respectively, summarize the legal and geographic nature of property ownership and local governments in the United States. "Cacophony" of course refers to the fragmentation of control over land use into ever-smaller units of ownership and government, whose respective voices have become increasingly strident lately.

Part III, "Reinventing Cities: Testing the Limits of Intervention," includes four chapters that focus on techniques and experience with urban planning and redevelopment. Chapter 6 resumes the historical thread from the end of Chapter 3 with the advent of rapid growth of newly industrializing cities beginning in the late 18th century. Public response to the squalor and public health threats resulting from that growth is considered under three primary headings: (1) regulation; (2) redevelopment, and (3) relocation. From their origins in the 19th century, these areas have served as the fundamental instruments of urban policy in the 20th century (at least until the 1970s when cities were essentially abandoned in national policy). Chapter 7 summarizes the origins and operations of "Euclidean Zoning." Chapter 8 reviews the constitutional basis for that institution and comparable uses of the regulatory power in American urban planning, including its highly questionable uses to promote suburban exclusivity. Chapter 9 moves "beyond zoning?" to examine other modern techniques available to local governments to manage land use, including subdivision regulation, growth management, floodplain and wetlands regulations, and greenway programs.

Part IV, "The Search for Broader Land Use Policies," examines recent experience in land use management at higher levels of government in the United States. Chapter 10 includes a variety of topics on state and regional planning, including case studies of the Pinelands Commission in New Jersey and the Appalachian Regional Commission. Chapter 11 reviews the tumultuous history and current management issues of the one-third of the United States owned and managed by federal agencies. Finally, Chapter 12, "Congress and Land Use," is virtually a book within a book on recent federal initiatives on environmental impact assessment, coastal zone management, floodplains, wetlands, agricultural land, and hazardous wastes.

The book thus spans a vast spectrum "from feudalism to federalism." In the 1990s, as past approaches are challenged and threatened with repeal at the hands of "property rights advocates," this book hopefully will inform those debates with an appreciation of past experience, legal basis, and geographic realities of society's long-standing efforts to manage land use. Public intervention to control externalities, avoid economic costs and personal harm, and to achieve a physically and emotionally healthy environment is not an ideology. It is the mark of an organized and socially responsible society. And without it, private property rights are extinct.

Part I / *Preliminaries: Land Uses and Concepts*

CHAPTER 1

Land Resources and
Issues in the United States

Introduction: What Is Land?

For the Lord thy God bringeth thee into a good land. A land of
wheat , and barley, and vines, and fig trees, and pomegranates; a
land of oil olive, and honey; a land wherein thou shalt eat bread
without scarceness, thou shalt not lack any thing in it; a land whose
stones are iron, and out of whose hills thou mayest dig brass.

Book of Deuteronomy 8:7–9.

It is a comfortable feeling to know that you stand on your own
ground. Land is about the only thing that can't fly away.

Anthony Trollope: *The Last Chronicle of Barset*, 1867.

When the federal government denies a private property owner the
right to use his or her own land for a harmless activity, I believe a
'taking' has occurred. It's wrong—morally and legally.

W. J. (Billy) Tauzin, Congressman from Louisiana,
Op-Ed column in *The Christian Science Monitor*, August 15, 1994.

From the Old Testament to the "Contract with America," the subject of
land arouses emotions—a vision of hope and faith, a source of wealth and
social status, a subject of indignant political reform, and so on. It seems
appropriate at the outset of a book on "Land Use and Society" therefore
to ask: What really is "land"?

Land is one of the key constituents of life on earth, along with water, carbon, oxygen, and sunlight. Lacking any of these would make it unnecessary and in fact impossible for life to exist as we know it. Daniel Hillel (1994, 20) observes that since three-quarters of our planet is covered by oceans, it should be called "Water" rather than "Earth." True, but those who did the naming happened to stand on "terra firma." Water of course, especially in nonsaline form, is indispensable to the use of land and therefore to terrestrial life. But without land capable of benefiting from the application of water, either through natural precipitation or artificially, life on the planet would be all wet, so to speak.

Land, unlike water, cannot be summarized by a convenient chemical formula such as H_2O. In fact, it is not easily summarized at all. It is many things simultaneously. First, it is the physical stuff under our feet (terra firma). It is the diverse resources that make up the physical earth within reach of human and nonhuman species: soils, minerals, oil and gas, sand and gravel, diamonds, coal, gold, silver, lead, uranium, and so on. Water itself, especially percolating through subsurface aquifers, may be viewed as part of "the land" for some purposes. (See Figure 4-1 and further discussion in Chapter 4.)

The concept of land as the stuff of which it is made was reflected in the English medieval practice of symbolizing ownership of land by a clod of earth from it that the seller physically delivered to the buyer (known quaintly as "livery of seisin"). Nowadays, legal documents perform that role.

Land as "physical stuff" also includes the produce of the soil. The biblical "pomegranates, oil olive, and honey" were part of the "promised land." Both natural and cultivated plants physically define the "landscape" and thus the nature of land, as for instance the giant Sequoia of the mid-California coast, the spruce-fir forest of coastal Maine, the yellow pine of Texas and the Southeast, the corn and soybeans of the Midwest, the prairie wheat, and the cranberries of Plymouth County, Massachusetts. Clearly, vegetation grown on land is part of the land, perceptually, functionally and, in many cases, legally.

Second, land may be reduced to a "parcel" of real estate, comprising an area of the earth's surface that defines a volume extending both upward and downward. Within this space or volume, human activities may be conducted, either out in the open or within structures enclosing interior space against the weather and intruders. As discussed in Chapter 4, the conversion of land from essentially resource-based uses, such as agriculture, to space-enclosing uses, such as homes, office parks, and shopping centers, is a critical and essentially irreversible step in the evolution of "urbanization." The timing and results of taking this step are strongly influenced by relative location, applicable laws, and only secondarily (if at all) by the physical nature of the site itself.

Third, this leads to another concept of land, namely as an object of capital value capable of being "owned" and used by its owner to maximize economic return. Land in this sense is a bundle of legal rights and obligations, both defined (often vaguely) and protected (sometimes uncertainly) by due process of law. In its most abstract form, land is purely an investment to be bought and sold like government bonds, corn futures, or pork bellies. Billions of dollars may be spent on land or structures attached to it with the investors never visiting the site, never getting their shoes muddy, never watching the sunset from its highest point.

Fourth, land may also have noneconomic value, a "sense of place" defined by collective or individual experience and values. Ceremonial grounds of native peoples, a New England commons, battlefields, burial grounds, England's Runnymede, or Woodstock, New York—all exemplify places whose cultural importance transcends their physical, legal, or locational characteristics. Sense of place was perhaps best expressed by Scarlet O'Hara in *Gone with the Wind:* "There will always be [the land of] Tara."

Since the 1960s, many natural places have joined historical and other cultural sites as objects invested with special importance by numbers of people. Beginning perhaps with John Muir's campaign to save the Hetch Hetchy Valley from becoming a reservoir around 1910, campaigns to protect natural areas of scenic, geologic, or biotic significance have been rife in the United States and throughout the world. And as Muir proved, passion can be aroused on behalf of a sense of place even among people who have not the slightest prospect ever to visit the site.

These efforts have in turn spread from truly extraordinary sites, such as the Grand Canyon, which was threatened with a dam in the 1960s, to less auspicious lands that harbor endangered species, offer scenic and recreational amenities, or contribute to the biological integrity of a larger ecosystem. Lengthy and sometimes bitter campaigns have ensued to protect habitat for the Coachella Valley lizard in southern California, the northern spotted owl of the Pacific Northwest, or a small salamander in

Amherst, Massachusetts. All of these ultimately are related to the character, function, and value of land. A collective sense of "stewardship" of the planet's remaining natural areas confronts the more traditional resource-based and investment meanings of land. Who really "owns" the land is the question resounding in the legislatures, the courts, and the news media in early 1995. The debate is as fundamental as land itself.

How Much Land Do We Have?

In the United States there is more land where nobody is than where anybody is. This is what makes America what it is.

Gertrude Stein: *The Geographical History of America*, 1936.

Three decades ago, the noted resource economist Marion Clawson (1963, 1) observed that the total land area of the United States, about 2.1 billion acres, theoretically amounted to a "share" of 12.5 acres for every living American at that time. In 1920, this figure stood at 20 acres per capita; it would further decline, in Clawson's estimate, to 7.5 acres in the year 2000. Clawson's prediction is on track. In 1984, U.S. land area per capita was 9.3 acres and shrinking. It nevertheless remained 14 times higher than that of the world as a whole and was at least three times the total for most other industrialized nations (Conservation Foundation 1984, 144).

Acreage per capita, however, is not a very meaningful figure. In the first place, it masks regional variation and is a poor measure of social well-being. At a state level, the citizens of Connecticut have one acre per capita (dividing its land area by its population) and New Jerseyites have only two-thirds of an acre each, while the 686,000 residents of North Dakota "claim" 64 acres apiece. But does this mean that the people of North Dakota are better off than those of Connecticut? Clearly not in economic terms: Connecticut ranks second in income per capita while North Dakota ranks 33rd. In terms of quality of life, that is a matter of personal judgment: windy open spaces versus the pains and pleasures of Megalopolis.

Second, a large proportion of the nation's wealth of land resources is distant from the everyday habitat of most of us. Three-quarters of the U.S. population (192 million in 1990) live in the nation's 341 metropolitan statistical areas (MSAs) that have been designated by the U.S.

Bureau of the Census. (See discussion of MSAs later in this chapter.) MSAs occupy about 16 percent of the nation's land area and have an average density of 2.1 acres per capita. But even within MSAs most of the population that does not live at the urban–rural fringe feels remote from "the country," which is apt to be privately owned and inaccessible in any case. Most metropolitan area residents live, work, and seek nearby recreation under conditions of extreme and worsening crowding, particularly on highways and in public parks.

A third limitation of the acres-per-capita measure of land wealth is the diversity of physical capabilities and use categories into which land resources may be classified. Overall totals of land area reveal little about the sufficiency of land for particular purposes such as production of food and fiber, forest products, water resources, recreation, natural habitat, and urban uses. Figure 1-1 depicts broad categories of land uses over time. Even these raw data reveal little about the sufficiency of land for the purposes listed. Assessments must be tempered by the potential for interchange among various categories, that is, the degree of reversibility of land use changes. Also, the growing importance of the global economy, the rise of the U.S. trade deficit, the effect of currency exchange rates, and the flow of commodities and people across national borders vastly complicate the task of appraising the adequacy of U.S. land resources.

Finally, land differs as to its ownership status. About one-third of the U.S. land area is owned by the federal government and is thus removed from the operation of the private land market, although federal lands do accommodate a variety of private activities (Figure 1-2). (Federal lands are the subject of Chapter 11.)

With these qualifications in mind, the rest of this chapter briefly reviews the status of land usage and related issues according to the major categories represented in Figure 1-1. This discussion also serves as a synopsis of several topics treated in more detail in later chapters.

Classes of Land Use

About three-quarters of the total U.S. land area is devoted to three primary categories of rural land usage: (1) cropland, (2) grazing land (including pasture and range), and (3) forest land. Each of these represents a productive and economically beneficial class of land resource,

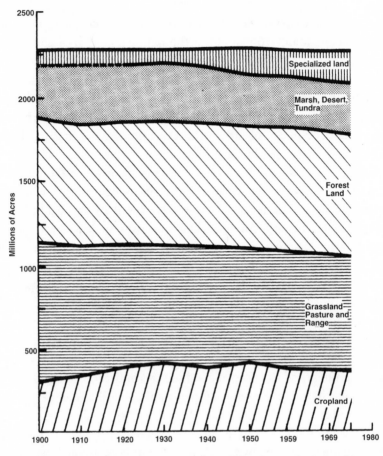

Note: *Forest Land* excludes reserved forest land in parks, wildlife refuges, and other special-use areas. *Specialized Land* is urban and built-up areas (e.g., cities and towns, rural highway and road rights-of-way, railroads, airports, and public institutions in rural areas) and nonurban special-use areas (e.g., federal and state wildlife refuges and parks, as well as other rural parks; recreational areas; national defense sites; flood-control areas; federal industrial areas; farmsteads; and farm roads).

FIGURE I-I   Major uses of land in the United States: 1900–1974. *Source:* U.S. Council on Environmental Quality, 1979.

although the more remote forests and more arid grazing lands may seldom be exploited and are left relatively untouched by human activities. About 40 million acres of federal forest, desert, and mountainous lands are designated as "wilderness areas" under the 1964 Wilderness Act. Other portions of our undeveloped land resources are managed for specialized purposes, including wetlands, recreation areas, and wildlife sanctuaries.

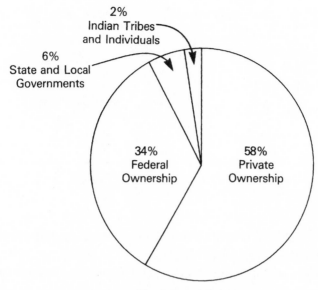

2%
Indian Tribes
and Individuals

6%
State and Local
Governments

34%
Federal
Ownership

58%
Private
Ownership

Total Area 2.3 Bil. Acres

FIGURE I-2   Land ownership in the United States, 1969; 94 percent of federal
ownership is in the 11 westernmost states and Alaska (about 50
percent is in Alaska). *Source:* U.S. Department of Agriculture,
1974.

At the other extreme, a small but critical proportion of our nation's
land resources is devoted to urban uses, including housing, commercial,
industrial, and transportation facilities. Most Americans live out their
lives in these metropolitan and urbanized areas.

Cropland

Cropland is the most sensitive and valuable of the nation's rural land
resources. The protection of the cropland base, especially those portions
of it deemed "prime land," has been the subject of lively discussion and
debate over the past two decades, both among scholars and in the public
media (Platt 1985). Both total cropland and harvested cropland fluctu-
ate considerably from year to year (Table 1-1). Observing that total cropland in 1980 was nearly the same as in 1959, and that harvested cropland was greater in 1992 than in 1970, it cannot be concluded from such
data that cropland has been significantly "lost" to urbanization or other
conversions. The ups and downs in harvested cropland in particular are

TABLE I-I   U.S. Cropland Resources from 1959 to 1992
(in millions of acres)

Year	Total Cropland	Harvested Acreage	Irrigated Acreage
1959	392	N.A.	31
1970	332	289	
1980	382	342	49 (1982)
1985	372	334	46 (1987)
1990	341	310	
1992	340	308	

Source: Statistical Abstract of the U.S.: 1994, Tables 1111 and 1082
(based on U.S. Department of Agriculture data).

functions of weather, market prices, and government subsidies, not necessarily related to conversion to other uses.

Moreover, the average productivity of U.S. agriculture has risen by 54 percent from a farm output index of 76 in 1960 to 117 in 1990, according to the U.S. Department of Agriculture. This increase, which has been achieved through the massive use of fertilizers, pesticides, irrigation water, and genetic research (the "Green Revolution"), has expanded U.S. agricultural production by more than the equivalent of an additional 186 million acres of cropland. Indeed, the rising productivity of American agriculture has had the ironic result of achieving such an abundance of farm commodities that low prices prevailed during the 1980s, causing farmers to suffer widespread economic distress. Government price supports paid to farmers reached a peak of $25 billion in 1986.

Despite the apparent sufficiency of cropland, the need for careful stewardship of this resource remains a public policy concern. In the first place, annual estimates of harvested cropland are not totally reliable (as is the case with most land use data at a national scale). Such estimates are obtained from individual agricultural extension agents in most of the nation's 3041 counties and equivalent units. There is thus a considerable margin of error due to variability in the accuracy of individual cropland estimates. Also, the inventories for different years are not strictly comparable due to changes in definitions, sampling techniques, and data management. Microcomputers were virtually unknown before the 1980s.

A second important qualification is that totals of harvested cropland give no indication of the *average quality* of land under cultivation. As documented by the U.S. Soil Conservation Service (1977), much land is converted from one rural category to another, as well as into urban and built-up status over time (Figure 1-3). The 1982 National Resources Inventory indicated that about 900,000 acres per year are converted to urban and built-up purposes, essentially an irreversible process (U.S. Council on Environmental Quality 1984, 283). Since harvested cropland has remained relatively constant for three decades, it is apparent that replacement land for cultivation has been drawn from other rural categories—for example, forest, range, pasture, and wetlands. The U.S. Department of Agriculture estimated in 1982 that some 127 million acres of potential cropland could be found in these other categories of land use.

But replacement land is not necessarily equivalent in quality to the cropland converted to nonagricultural purposes. Heavier application of irrigation water, chemical fertilizers and pesticides, and labor is required to render such marginal lands productive in cultivation. Furthermore, the continued drainage of wetlands for agriculture in the south central states, Florida, and California—once consistent with national policy— now is viewed as threatening to the ecological values and functions of wetlands in their natural state.

There is growing evidence that increased use of *fertilizer* has reached a point of diminishing returns. Crosson and Brubaker (1982) estimated that an actual increase of 64 million acres of cropland will be required to meet agricultural demand by 2010.

> Per-acre applications of fertilizer grew much more slowly after 1972 as farmers moved toward more land-using technologies after that date. . . . The slower increase in per-acre applications of fertilizer after 1972 was consistent with the post-1973 slowdown in yield growth. Correspondingly, our belief that the trend of yields to 2010 will more nearly resemble the post- than the pre-1972 experience is based in good part on our belief that per-acre applications of fertilizer will grow more slowly.   Crosson and Brubaker 1982, p. 68.

Similarly, the use of *irrigation* to reclaim arid lands for cultivation may also have peaked. Between 1959 and 1982, irrigated land in 17 arid western states plus Louisiana increased by 35 percent from 31 million to 42 million acres. In the latter year, the national total of irrigated land was 49.4 million acres, which represented 15 percent of total cropland.

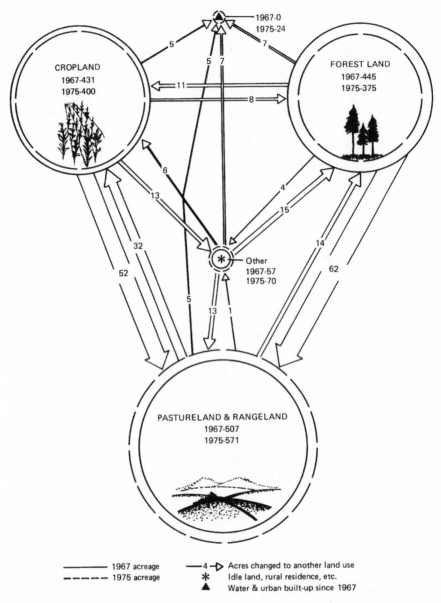

CROPLAND
1967-431
1975-400

FOREST LAND
1967-445
1975-375

1967-0
1975-24

Other
1967-57
1975-70

PASTURELAND & RANGELAND
1967-507
1975-571

5   7
5   7
11
8
6
13
4
15
32
14
52
62
5
13 1

———— 1967 acreage   ——4—▷ Acres changed to another land use
– – – – 1975 acreage   ✳ Idle land, rural residence, etc.
                             ▲ Water & urban built-up since 1967

FIGURE I-3   Land use conversion between 1967 and 1975 (million acres).
Source: U.S. Soil Conservation Service, 1977.

Continued expansion of the area under irrigation is doubtful, as new ground and/or surface water supplies are increasingly difficult and expensive to develop. Unless irrigated land is properly drained, salts in irrigation water will contaminate the soil zone ("salinization"), leading to destruction of the land's fertility (Hillel 1994). Environmental objections and economic costs have deterred the further expansion of irrigation facilities in recent years. Furthermore, the mining of groundwater in the Ogallala Aquifer of the High Plains and the salinization of groundwater supplies in the Colorado Basin threaten to reduce the acreage presently receiving irrigation water.

Soil erosion is another source of concern about the future adequacy of the nation's cropland base. The USDA estimates that 44 percent of all cropland nationally is eroding at rates exceeding the normal rate of replacement through natural processes (which differ from one location to another). Especially high levels of soil erosion, ranging from 5 to 14 tons of soil per acre per year, were identified in most of the north central region—the Corn Belt—as well as in dissected uplands of the Southeast, Texas, and the Southwest (U.S. Council on Environmental Quality 1984, fig. 5-10). The precise effects of soil erosion are difficult to quantify but represent a long-term loss of natural soil productive capacity.

The available supply of cropland is more than adequate for the present domestic and export needs of the nation. However, reliance on technological inputs and the use of marginal land for cultivation may be nearing the point of diminishing returns. Environmental objections to the use of certain chemicals, shortage of water for irrigation, and declining soil quality due to erosion all suggest the need for wise management of land naturally suited to cultivation of crops. (See further discussion in Chapter 12.)

Forest Land

Total forest land, according to the U.S. Forest Service appeared to increase from 664 million acres in 1952 to 737 million acres in 1992 (Table 1-2). But "timberland" has remained relatively constant, with the 1992 total only 19 million acres less than in 1952. Most of the increase in total forest land is actual—due to reforestation of abandoned farmlands, as in New England and the upper Midwest. Conversely, some forest land has been cleared for cropland usage as depicted in Figure 1-3.

TABLE 1-2   U.S. Forest and Timberland Resources: 1952–1992 (in millions of acres)

Year	Total Forest Land	Total Timberland[a]	Private Timberland	% Private Timberland
1952	664	509	356	70.0%
1962	759	515	363	70.4
1970	754	504	354	70.2
1977	737	491	347	70.6
1987	731	483	347	71.8
1992	737	490	358	73.0

Source: Statistical Abstract of the U.S.: 1994, Table 1130 (based on U.S. Forest Service data).

[a] Timberland is forest land that is producing or is capable of producing crops of industrial wood and not withdrawn from timber utilization by statute or administrative regulation.

Still other forest land was converted to water bodies, highways, and urban development. The exact extent of these conversions is unknown.

About three-fourths of forested land is classified by the U.S. Forest Service as "commercial timberland," which is defined as being capable of yielding at least 20 cubic feet per acre per year of commercial wood products and is not closed to cutting by governmental prohibition (for example, wilderness status). Contrary to popular impression, 76 percent of New England is forested and all but 5 percent of this is designated as commercial timberland, although much of it is unmanaged. The preponderance of noncommercial forest lands is in the West and Alaska.

During the 19th century, most of the major forest lands accessible to loggers were cleared without consideration of adverse effects such as soil erosion, forest fires, and loss of regeneration capability. Out of concern for maintaining adequate forests for the nation's future needs, the National Forest System was initiated in 1891 at the urging of Gifford Pinchot, who was appointed by President Theodore Roosevelt as the first Director of the U.S. Forest Service in 1905. The national forests now comprise a total land area of 230 million acres, which has barely changed in the past 40 years. (About 190 million acres are actually forested.) National forests are managed to ensure a sustained yield of forest products while serving other public needs such as water supply, natural habitat, recreation, and mining.

There appears to be little cause for concern about the adequacy of forest land to meet both domestic and export demand for forest products. Regardless of the adequacy of potential domestic production, imported forest products, particularly from Canada, are highly competitive. In 1989, the United States imported about one-quarter of its demand for lumber and 40 percent of its pulpwood needs (although it also exported one-fourth of its domestic pulpwood production, primarily to Asia).

There is, however, some imbalance between hardwood stocks in the Northeast, which are increasing rapidly in relation to harvesting levels, and softwoods of the South and West, for which growth is about equivalent to cutting. Also, there are serious regional problems with insect pests such as the gypsy moth, which has been identified in 30 states, and the spruce budworm, which has caused much damage to the pulp forests of Maine. In Oregon and northern California, cutting of old-growth timber has been adamantly opposed by wildlife activists, who have invoked the Federal Endangered Species Act to protect natural habitat for the northern spotted owl. The U.S. Department of the Interior has sought to broker a compromise plan to satisfy both logging and environmental interests with respect to these forests.

Grasslands

Grasslands suitable for grazing have remained relatively unchanged over the past three decades and in 1982 amounted to about 662 million acres, the largest single land use category. Grasslands include two very different subclasses: (1) cropland used for pasture and (2) rangeland. While the former comprises only 10 percent of total grazing lands, it is generally located in the more humid regions of the country and yields a very large share of total forage production (U.S. Department of Agriculture 1974, 8). Rangeland is substantially located in the Mountain and High Plains states and receives rainfall of only 10–20 inches annually. Such lands produce very little forage and must be grazed on a very land-extensive basis.

Ownership of western range lands is split among the federal government, states, and private owners. Federal grasslands total about 160 million acres, of which 130 million acres are administered by the Bureau of Land Management (BLM) and the remainder by the U.S. Forest Service

(USFS). Grazing in the West has always involved joint usage of both private and public lands by ranchers. Before 1934, private use of federal range was generally unregulated, illegal, and the source of disputes among competing interests—for example, cattlemen versus sheep raisers and "sod busting" versus grazing. The Taylor Grazing Act of 1934 authorized the establishment of federal grazing districts under the general land office and the issuance of permits for private grazing rights on such lands, bringing a semblance of order to the prior chaos. Since 1950, both BLM and USFS have sought to reduce grazing pressure on federal rangelands to protect their productive capacity over the long term (Clawson 1983, 67). In the 1990s, private property interests are demanding greater access to and authority over federal grazing and timberlands.

Recreational Land

It is difficult to estimate the total amounts and trends in the supply of recreational land. In 1989, the National Park System comprised about 76 million acres, but about half of those lands are in Alaska and virtually inaccessible. Additional federal lands administered by BLM and the USFS are managed for multiple use, including recreation. (See Chapter 11.) Similarly, water resource projects of the Army Corps of Engineers, the Tennessee Valley Authority, and the Bureau of Reclamation all involve provision for recreation. Much of the recreational benefit provided by these facilities is in the form of water-based activities, including boating, swimming, and fishing, for which land acreage data are not an adequate measure. State park systems total about 11 million acres, with county, regional, and municipal parks comprising perhaps another 10 million acres.

A large but unquantifiable amount of private land is devoted to commercial recreation. This would include intensive-use facilities such as golf courses, ski resorts, tennis clubs, and private campgrounds, as well as more extensive facilities such as private nature sanctuaries and membership camping and hiking parks. Schools and colleges provide additional recreational land on their grounds.

Acreage data, of course, do not adequately measure the potential value of a recreational site. Location, site design, amenities, and natural characteristics are usually more important than mere size in determining the functional utility of recreational land.

Wetlands

Wetlands comprise an important subset of the total land and water resources of the United States. Wetlands are generally characterized by (1) the presence of water at or close to the surface, (2) predominance of saturated hydric soils, and (3) prevalence of vegetation adapted to wet conditions (Mitsch and Gosselink 1986, 15–16). Depending on their physical nature, size, and location, wetlands perform various natural functions such as providing natural habitat, flood storage, concentration of nutrients, absorption of pollutants, buffering of coastlines from storm waves, recharge of groundwater aquifers, and scenic amenity.

The National Wetlands Inventory, conducted by the U.S. Fish and Wildlife Service, estimated total wetlands in the early 1980s to comprise about 99 million acres nationally (Frayer et al. 1983). A study by the U.S. Department of Agriculture (1981) estimated nonfederal wetlands to amount to 70.5 million acres, with an apparent loss of 14 percent between 1956 and 1980. Average annual loss of wetlands nationally due to dredging, filling, drainage, and conversion to agricultural or urban purposes is roughly estimated to be 290,000 acres (Dahl and Johnson 1991). About 87 percent of the wetlands losses between the 1950s and 1970s were due to agricultural drainage (which is not subject to regulation under the federal Clean Water Act). The remaining 13 percent of losses were due to urbanization and other development (Tiner 1984, 31). But between the mid-1970s and the mid-1980s, agricultural drainage accounted for only 54 percent of the total loss of 2.6 million acres during that period, of which 95 percent were freshwater wetlands and the remainder coastal wetlands (Dahl and Johnson, 1991). Coastal Louisiana has been losing extensive areas of estuarine and freshwater wetlands annually due in part to land subsidence related to agriculture as well as to sea level rise. (See further discussion of wetlands in Chapters 7 and 12.)

Urban Land

Estimation of urban land usage nationally is difficult. Rural land categories—farming, forestry, grazing, and barren lands—tend to occur in sizable, relatively homogeneous spatial units that are easy to identify. The urban landscape by contrast is a finely variegated mosaic of buildings, paved areas, parks, vacant land, private yards, and even residual agriculture. How much of this crazy-quilt pattern of land use is "urban"? Drawing a boundary between urban and nonurban areas is a matter of definition and subjective judgment.

Another problem is the scarcity of national-level data on urban land usage. In the case of agriculture and forestry, large federal agencies are charged with administering programs that require accurate and frequently revised data on the nature and extent of those land uses. By contrast, the federal government, particularly since the 1970s, has been less involved with urban land planning, leaving it to states, regional, and municipal authorities. Accordingly, the federal government does not assemble or publish detailed statistics on urban land as it does for rural natural resource regions. Even the U.S. Department of Housing and Urban Development (HUD), which administers urban housing assistance programs, devotes little attention to the growth of urban areas (notwithstanding the second part of its title).

By any estimate, urban and built-up areas comprise a very small proportion of the nation's total land resources. The 1982 National Resources Inventory (NRI) conducted by the U.S. Soil Conservation Service (undated) estimated urban and built-up areas to total 47 million acres, or about 2 percent of the total U.S. land area. This figure in fact comprised a reduction from 69 million acres of urban land estimated in the 1977 NRI, also conducted by the SCS. This reduction of course does not mean that urban areas diminished between 1977 and 1982. Instead, the latter estimate was based on "better maps, more time for data collection, many more sample points, and better quality control" (U.S. Council on Environmental Quality 1984, 283).

Far more important than the absolute amount of land devoted to urban usage at a given time is the rate of growth of urban areas. Clearly, the NRI data do not support such an intertemporal comparison. The U.S. Bureau of the Census has developed two sets of spatial units to measure changes in urban land use and other spatially variable data over time: (1) Metropolitan Statistical Areas (MSAs) and (2) Urbanized Areas (UAs).

Metropolitan growth involves the spatial expansion of older urbanized cores into surrounding rural areas. Over time, such expanding urban areas tend to coalesce with their neighbors to form even larger metropolitan areas, encompassing multiple central cities together with their suburbs and nearby urban fringe areas. The political geography of such urbanizing regions thus reflects several kinds of local jurisdictions: (1) central cities, (2) incorporated suburbs, (3) nearby unincorporated areas under county jurisdiction that are likely to be developed soon, and (4) special districts of various types and sizes. (See Chapter 5.)

To assess regional trends in population, housing, land use, and other variables, without having to add up all the separate jurisdictions, the Bureau of the Census since 1950 has designated *metropolitan statistical areas*, for which it publishes a variety of data approximately every 10 years (Figure 1-4). Since 1980, metropolitan statistical areas have been defined to include:

1. A core area consisting of either (a) one or more cities of at least 50,000 inhabitants or (b) a Census Bureau-defined "urbanized area" of at least 50,000 (with additional requirements of MSA population)

2. The county or counties that contain such core area(s)

3. Adjoining counties, if any, with at least 50 percent of their population in the urbanized area

4. Any additional counties that meet specified requirements of commuting to the central counties and of metropolitan character. (In New England, MSAs are defined in terms of clusters of cities and towns rather than counties.) (U.S. Bureau of the Census 1994, Appendix II)

The number of metropolitan units designated by the Bureau of the Census has grown from 169 in 1950 to 323 in 1990. Of those 323 areas, 73 are designated "primary metropolitan statistical areas" (PMSAs), which comprise 18 "consolidated metropolitan statistical areas" (CMSAs). The latter reflect the coalescence of many smaller metropolitan areas into the nation's largest urban regions. A wealth of demographic, economic, social, and land use data are compiled and published for each of these metropolitan area units.

Total metropolitan population has increased from 84 million (55% of U.S. population) in 1950 to 197.7 million in 1990 and 203.1 million (79.7%) in 1992 (Table 1-3a). Recent data cannot be strictly compared with earlier census enumerations, however, since the number of MSAs and the area included within them has changed periodically. MSAs are

FIGURE 1-4   Metropolitan Statistical Areas, 1979. *Source:* U.S. Bureau of the Census.

TABLE 1-3A   U.S. Metropolitan and Nonmetropolitan Population:
1980–1992 (in millions)

Year	Metro Pop.[a] (% of U.S.)	% Change 1980–1992	Nonmetro Pop. (% of U.S.)	% Change 1980–1992
1980	172.6 (78.1%)		49.6 (21.9%)	
1990	197.7		50.9	
1992	203.1 (79.7%)	14.9%	51.9 (20.3%)	4.5%

TABLE 1-3B   Metropolitan Statistical Areas by Size, 1990

Size Class	Number[a]	Pop. (mill.)	% of Metro Pop.	% Change 1980–1990
2.5 mill. +	13	58.2	29%	11.6%
1.0–2.5 mill.	38	60.5	31	12.7
500,000–1.0 mill.	41	29.4	15	12.6
250,000–500,000	78	27.5	14	16.1
100,000–250,000	130	20.1	10	9.2
<100,000	23	2.0	1	5.5
Total	323	197.7	100	11.7

Source (both tables): Statistical Abstract of the U.S.: 1994, Tables 39, 40, and 41.

[a] Includes 323 MSAs and PMSAs defined by the Bureau of the Census as of June 30, 1993.

often enlarged by adding counties (or New England towns) to reflect ongoing growth, so care must be taken to hold area constant in making statistical comparisons from one census to another.

Metropolitan population is very unevenly distributed among metro areas of different sizes (Table 1-3b), with consequent wide variation in the meaning and land use implications of the term "metropolitan." Sixty percent of metropolitan residents, and nearly half the nation's entire population, live in MSAs of more than one million inhabitants. The fastest growing class of MSAs is the 250,000 to 500,000 group, with a 1980–1990 growth rate of 16.1 percent compared with 11.7 percent for metro areas as a whole.

Population constantly shifts within metro areas, among different metro areas, and between metro and nonmetro areas. In 1992, metro areas accounted for about 80 percent of the U.S. population, with the other 20 percent living in "the rest of the nation, in nonmetro smaller cities, towns, on farms, and in the country." Despite a much publicized resurgence in nonmetro population during the 1970s, due apparently to "back to the land" sentiments among some urbanites, the proportion of the nation living in metro areas continues to gradually rise.

Within metro areas, the prevalent trend has been a rapid increase in suburban portions of MSAs with a concomitant decline of central cities. Figure 1-5 illustrates this trend between 1960 and 1980. The 1990 census did not retain the differentiation between central city and suburban areas because some newer MSAs have been designated with an urbanized area rather than a central city as their core. Shifts in population from central cities to suburbs of course have long been reflected in the spread of lower density residential and office construction in outlying areas, oriented to interstate highways, with a corresponding decline of existing housing and neighborhoods in central cities. An exception to this trend has been the process of "gentrification," whereby well-located urban neighborhoods such as Capitol Hill in Washington, D.C. and Back Bay in Boston are revitalized for more affluent residents. Also, Edge Cities" of the past two decades comprise high-density clusters in scattered locations oriented to highway intersections rather than central cities.

Land area within metropolitan units has risen from about 207,000 square miles in 1950 (6 percent of the United States) to over 650,000 square miles (19 percent) in 1992. The total area shown for metropolitan

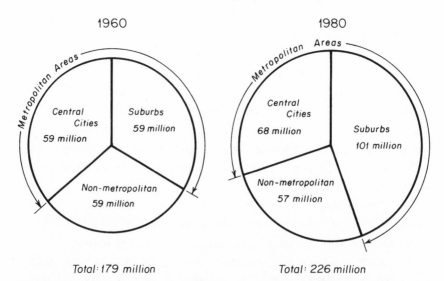

FIGURE 1-5   Distribution of U.S. population, 1960 and 1980.

land, however, vastly overstates the quantity of land actually devoted to urban purposes. MSAs, being defined according to county jurisdictions, contain extensive areas of still-undeveloped, rural land. The U.S. Department of Agriculture (1987, 3–12) has estimated that metropolitan areas contain 20 percent of the nation's cropland and 20 percent of the land with high and medium potential for conversion to cropland (currently in forest, pasture, or other rural use).

Urbanized Areas (UAs), unlike MSAs, are not based strictly on county or municipal units, but instead are drawn to conform approximately to the actual urban or built-up area within and surrounding a core city. According to the U.S. Bureau of the Census (1984, 5): "A UA comprises an incorporated place and adjacent densely settled surrounding area that altogether have a minimum population of 50,000." Political units are divided where necessary to distinguish urban and nonurban land. Inevitably, designated boundaries err in both over- and underinclusion of urban land. Nevertheless, the UA is the best national-level estimate of the extent and rate of increase of urbanized land in the United States.

As shown in Table 1-4, between 1920 and 1960, UAs exceeding 50,000 inhabitants doubled in number, grew from about 40 million to 100 million in population, and nearly quadrupled in land area (Pickard 1967). This was accompanied by a decline in average density from 6160 to 4090 persons per square mile. By 1980, there were 366 UAs, which collectively contained 139 million inhabitants and covered 52,000 square miles. Average density by then had fallen to only 2177 persons per square mile.

TABLE 1-4   Urbanized Areas Exceeding 50,000: 1920–1990

Year	No. of UAs	Population (millions)	Land Area (sq. miles)	Average Density
1920	131	38.9	6,318	6,160
1940	190	58.1	10,452	5,560
1960	269	98.7	24,111	4,090
1980	366	139.1	52,017	2,675
1990 Total	396	158.0	61,014	2,589
central places		78.1	40,388	3,320
urban fringe		79.2	26,191	2,130

Sources: Pickard 1967; Bureau of the Census 1984, 1994.

Thus, between 1960 and 1980, 41 million persons were added to UAs of more than 50,000 inhabitants, while the total land area of such UAs expanded by 27,906 square miles. This amounts to an average density of 1469 persons per square mile, or 2.2 persons per acre. Each new UA resident therefore accounted for 0.45 acre of additional urbanized land (including residential, nonresidential, and transportation uses).

To estimate future urban land demand, let us assume for the sake of discussion that the population of the United States will level off at about 289 million early in the next century, as reported in 1987 by Lester Brown of the Worldwatch Institute. This would represent an increase in total population of 63 million above the 1980 level. Assuming conservatively that the proportion of this increase that will accrue to UAs is the same as in 1980 (61% of total population), this would represent an increase of 38.4 million UA residents. Applying the 1960–1980 rate of land consumption per additional UA resident of 0.45 acre, this new population would require about 17 million additional acres of urbanized land or about 27,000 square miles, raising the total UA land area to about 79,000 square miles (about 50 million acres). This would represent an addition of new urban land of 24,111 square miles between 1980 and the year we reach a stable population *that exceeds the total area of UAs in 1960*. That also is about equivalent to the increase in UA area between 1960 and 1980 (27,906 square miles). In other words, the total land area of UAs exceeding 50,000 inhabitants in 1960 actually doubled over the following 20 years and will have *tripled* by the time the nation reaches a stable population growth of about 289 million.

Of course, this probably underestimates future urban land needs, because the nation may well have grown far beyond 289 million if current immigration trends continue. Also, the proportion living in urban areas may increase over the level shown for 1980. Barring economic collapse or other calamity, the United States appears to be well on its way to at least replicating for a second time the total area of land urbanized by 1960.

Even the achievement of a stable population would not end the expansion of all urbanized areas. Both intra- and interregional shifts of population, which were prominent in the 1970s and 1980s, may be expected to continue. Thus, while net national population may level off, some UAs will continue to attract migrants from other regions. Urban land requirements in such growing regions as Tampa, Phoenix, and San

Diego would continue to rise, but land already urbanized in UAs that are losing population, such as New York, Cleveland, and Detroit, would remain urbanized, albeit underutilized. Thus, total urbanized land could continue to expand indefinitely.

The rate of such future expansion is difficult to predict. Earlier discussion simply extrapolated from rate of land consumption per additional UA resident in 1980 (0.45 acre). This rate might prove to be too high in light of the trend toward smaller household size (including single parent households) and toward multiple-family construction (rental and condominium) in place of single-family houses. A recurrence of the 1970s oil shocks coupled with the substantial completion of the federal Interstate Highway System also might suggest a lower rate of urban land expansion in the future.

Problems of undercounting and overcounting may be expected. Infilling of residual pockets of undeveloped land already included in UAs would not add to the statistical size of such units, even though appreciable effects from such conversions might be experienced at a local or metropolitan scale. On the other hand, population growth in smaller towns and cities, which presently do not qualify as UAs of more than 50,000 inhabitants, will promote many of them to that status. At that point, their entire land areas would be added to the national UA total. That would overstate the amount of newly urbanized land since long-urbanized land in newly recognized UAs would be included as well.

A number of issues for public policy arising from the urbanization of land may be identified in general terms at this point, with more detailed consideration of some of them deferred until later chapters.

INEFFICIENT USE OF LAND

- waste of cropland
- loss or pollution of wetlands
- overextension of public services
- visual blight

ENERGY WASTE

- lengthy journeys to work
- traffic congestion
- decline of public transportation
- heating and air conditioning of small structures

NATURAL HAZARDS

- urban flooding
- seismic risk
- soil and slope instability
- coastal storm hazards

SOLID WASTES

- rising volume of wastes
- shortage of landfill capacity
- siting of new landfills and incinerators

PUBLIC RECREATION AND OPEN SPACE

- spatial imbalance of supply and demand
- multiple functions and constituencies
- deterioration of older facilities

AFFORDABLE HOUSING

- exclusionary zoning
- inadequate public financing
- conversion of rental units to condominiums
- deterioration of older housing

Conclusion

This chapter has summarized the status and usage of land resources in the United States as of the mid-1990s. A clear dichotomy exists between rural land uses on the one hand and urban and built-up uses on the other. Rural land, predominantly used for cropland, grazing, or forestry, is abundant in quantity to meet anticipated domestic needs. Adequacy in terms of international demand is difficult to assess in light of fluctuating currency exchange rates and global trade patterns. The overriding goal of public policy toward rural land should be to preserve the productive capacity or "sustainability" of such resources to meet future domestic and foreign demand. In particular, those lands deemed most or least suitable for specific uses should be identified, designated, and used accordingly by public and private land managers. Reversible conversion of rural land from one use to another is a normal response to changing economic circumstance. Irreversible transformation of productive rural land, either to a degraded condition (due to soil erosion, salinization, or inundation) or to an urban or built-up condition, poses important public policy issues.

The spatial growth of urban land is the mirror image of the loss of rural land to development. But the implications of such growth are not limited to the loss of productive or potentially productive rural land. Urbanization involves a spectrum of public issues including environmental quality, adequacy of water supply, equity in housing and economic opportunity, energy consumption, traffic congestion, visual blight, natural hazards, and rising public costs per capita for providing utilities and services to a vastly expanded region of urban habitation.

References

Brown, L., et al. 1987. *State of the World–1987*. New York: Norton.

Clawson, M. 1963. *Land for Americans: Trends, Prospects, and Problems*. Chicago: Rand McNally.

———. 1983. *The Federal Lands Revisited*. Baltimore: Johns Hopkins Press.

Conservation Foundation. 1984. *State of the Environment: An Assessment at Mid-Decade*. Washington: Conservation Foundation.

Crosson, P.R., and S. Brubaker. 1982. *Resource and Environmental Effects of U.S. Agriculture*. Washington: Resources for the Future.

Dahl, T.E., and C.E. Johnson. 1991. *Status and Trends of Wetlands in the Coterminous United States, mid-1970s to mid-1980s*. Washington: U.S. Department of the Interior, Fish and Wildlife Service.

Frayer et al. 1983. *Status and Trends of Wetlands and Deepwater Habitats in the Conterminous United States: 1950s to 1970s*. St. Petersburg, FL: U.S. Fish and Wildlife Service.

Hillel, D. 1994. *Rivers of Eden: The Struggle for Water and the Quest for Peace in the Middle East*. New York and Oxford: Oxford University Press.

Mitsch, W.J., and J.G. Gosselink. 1986. *Wetlands*. New York: Van Nostrand Reinhold.

Pickard, J.P. 1967. *Dimensions of Metropolitanism*. Research Monograph 14. Washington: Urban Land Institute.

Platt, R.H. 1985. "The Farmland Conversion Debate: NALS and Beyond." *Professional Geographer* 37(4): 433–442.

Tiner, R.W., Jr. 1984. *Wetlands of the United States: Recent Status and Trends*. Washington: U.S. Government Printing Office.

U.S. Bureau of the Census. 1984. *Population and Land Area of Urbanized Areas–1980 and 1970.* Supp. Report. Washington: U.S. Government Printing Office.

———. 1985. *Statistical Abstract of the U.S.: 1986.* Washington: U.S. Government Printing Office.

———. 1994. *Statistical Abstract of the U.S.: 1994.* Washington: U.S. Government Printing Office.

U.S. Council on Environmental Quality. 1979. *Environmental Quality: 1979.* Washington: U.S. Government Printing Office.

———. 1984. *Environmental Quality: 1984.* Washington: U.S. Government Printing Office.

U.S. Department of Agriculture. 1974. *Our Land and Water Resources.* Misc. Pub. no. 1290. Washington: Economic Research Service.

———. 1981. *America's Soil and Water Conditions and Trends.* Washington: U.S.D.A.

———. 1987. *The Second RCA Appraisal: Soil, Water, and Related Resources on Nonfederal Land in the U.S.* (Review draft) Washington: U.S.D.A.

U.S. Soil Conservation Service. 1977. *Potential Cropland Study.* Stat. Bull. no. 578. Washington: U.S. Government Printing Office.

———. Undated. "Preliminary Data, 1982 National Resources Inventory: Executive Summary." (mimeo)

CHAPTER 2

The Interaction of
Geography and Law

Introduction

The fields of geography and law to some people may seem to have as much in common as astronomy and neurology, or mathematics and poetry. But as applied to problems of managing land resources, the two fields are logical and necessary allies, with much to contribute to each other. If geography is defined as the science of spatial organization of human activities, land use geography seeks to explain the functional interrelationships of units of land area to each other and to larger systems of land use—for example, communities, regions, nations, and the Earth. In other words, geography asks *what* land is like, *why* it is used in a particular way, and whether it could be better utilized to achieve specified goals (e.g., housing, food supply, environmental sustainability).

Land use law, on the other hand, addresses *how* desirable uses of land may be achieved, and *who* has the authority to decide among competing uses. Law is concerned with the process by which land is allocated for various purposes through the recognition and exercise of private rights and public powers to influence the use of land. A primary purpose of an organized society is to use law to facilitate the efficient and productive use of land. According to the philosopher John Locke (1689/1952, 71):

> I cannot count upon the enjoyment of that which I regard as mine, except through the promise of the law which guarantees it to me. It is law alone which permits me to forget my natural weakness. It is only through protection of law that I am able to enclose a field, and

to give myself up to its cultivation with the sure though distant hope of harvest.

Law thus confirms property rights in a capitalist society. If Locke had lived in the 20th century rather than the 17th, he would surely have mentioned the additional role of law as a means to control harmful externalities among users of land. Both of these functions of law—facilitating productive use of land and abating externalities—are fundamentally influenced by the geographical context of the land in question.

This book examines the interactive nature of geography and law as reflected in the evolution of social controls over land use. Law is viewed both as a product of societal perception of the physical environment and as an independent variable that itself shapes that environment in sometimes unexpected ways. The model that describes this interactive relationship is discussed later in this chapter. First, however, the opening section contrasts some fundamental differences between the two fields that have impeded recognition of their interdependence. After that, we consider the role of law in the shaping of land use patterns or morphology and briefly summarize the nature and powers of land use managers (which will be considered in more detail in later chapters).

The Geographical Landscape

The field of geography is inherently eclectic. Its two major branches, physical and human geography, are in turn subdivided into a number of subfields that respectively contribute to an understanding of the nature and use of land resources. These subfields include on the physical side, geomorphology, hydrology, biogeography, and climatology; and on the human side, urban, political, economic, cultural, and social geography, among other specialties. Some geographical topics bridge the physical–human dichotomy, as in studies of human response to natural hazards (James and Martin 1981).

It is sometimes charged that geographers have more in common with their colleagues in cognate disciplines (geology, economics, political science, urban planning) than they do with one another. Geographers have sometimes wondered if they have a field of their own. In the role of devil's advocate, the noted geographer Richard Hartshorne (1939, 125) has written: "Defined not in terms of a particular set of facts, but in terms of causal relationships presumed to exist, [the field of geography] could have but a parasitic character."

Its interest in causal relationships (the perennial "Why"), however, as Hartshorne went on to argue, indeed defines geography as a separate discipline. Certain organizing themes, models, and concepts characterize the geographic perspective and method. For present purposes, the following concepts are pertinent:

1. spatial organization

2. scale

3. function

4. externalities

Spatial Organization

A common denominator that unites geographers of all specialties is a fundamental concern with the organization or distribution of diverse phenomena in space (James and Martin 1981, chapter 15). Spatiality is to geography what spirituality is to the ministry and health is to the physician. The identification, delineation, and interpretation of spatial patterns of diverse phenomena, notably including land usage, are long-standing geographical pursuits (Morrill 1970). To identify, spatial data are derived from field surveys, interviews, government reports, remote sensing, and other sources. To delineate, geographers utilize maps, photographs, graphs, and other means of representing spatial data. Cartography, the development and preparation of maps suitable for particular tasks, is itself a subfield of geography and is now of course primarily computer-based. To interpret perceived spatial patterns of phenomena requires the application of various sources of inference including statistical analysis, computerized geographic information systems (GIS), modeling, and scholarly intuition. Geographical analysis often involves the identification of cross-relationships among different systems of spatial data.

Spatial patterns of land use may be broadly analyzed in terms of the interaction of three overlapping categories or macrosystems of spatial data: (1) physical phenomena, (2) human socioeconomic activities (referred to by geographers as cultural phenomena), and (3) patterns of legal and political authority over land. (See Figure 2-5 and accompanying discussion later in this chapter.)

The *physical geography* of a specified site, locality, or region may be described and interpreted in terms of the spatial characteristics of bedrock and landforms, soils, hydrology, natural vegetation, wildlife, and climate. Each of these subclasses of physical data represents a major branch of natural science. The geographer draws on the findings of the appropriate field to the level of detail necessary to resolve the problem under consideration.

The geography of *human activity patterns* includes systems of rural land use—agriculture, forestry, and mining—as well as urban settlements ranging from hamlets to metropolitan regions. Aggregate human activity patterns reflect systems of economic enterprise. It has been argued that human geography is basically economic geography (Hartshorne 1939). The spatial analysis of economic systems involves the identification of "nodes" or points of activity and "linkages" or connections between nodes—for example, transportation corridors, pipelines, and communications networks. Such linkages serve as conduits between activity nodes for a variety of dynamic commodities—for example, people, materials, nutrients, energy, goods, information, and capital.

The geography of *legal and political authority* may be described as a series of jurisdictional templates overlying land, representing the layers of land managers who play a role in determining the use of land in the United States:

- Ownership (private or public)

- Minor civil divisions (municipalities, special districts, counties)

- States

- The federal government

Units of authority at each level in the hierarchy (Figure 2-1) are bounded by precise, if irregular, territorial limits that define the geographic reach of their legal power over land. Moreover, units at different levels in the hierarchy influence the use of land within their jurisdictions in different ways according to their respective legal, political, and fiscal

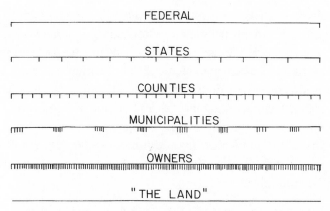

FIGURE 2-1   Diagram of hierarchy of land use managers.

capabilities. The use of individual parcels of land thus reflects a complex interaction among the various levels of land managers who share jurisdiction over a given site. Broader patterns of land use result from the aggregation of use characteristics of individual parcels.

Legal and political boundaries of course are invisible to observation unless marked by a sign, fence, or other visual indicator. But the presence of institutional boundaries may often be inferred from observation of abrupt changes in land use patterns, as from a high-income, low-density residential district to an adjoining area of congestion, commerce, clutter, and blight. The haphazard location of legal and political boundaries often exerts substantial influence on the arrangement of human activities and perceived land use patterns (Whittlesey 1935; Cohen and Rosenthal 1971; Clark 1985). Of course, institutional patterns are not totally independent variables. Particularly in the case of recently established suburban jurisdictions, political boundaries tend both to reflect and in turn to reinforce the spatial arrangement of housing markets, economic activity, and locational preferences of the elite.

Scale

Fundamental to geographic analysis of spatial organization is the concept of scale or hierarchy. Certain kinds of spatial variability may be classified according to position within a hierarchy of nested subsets of phenomena that comprise the overall spatial system under consideration. A river drainage system, for instance, is physically organized into a hierarchy of main stem, major tributaries, subtributaries, and headwaters, each with its associated watershed (area of surface drainage). For purposes of land planning and water management, the position of a tract of land in relation to this hierarchy of drainage is significant in terms of quality and quantity of surface flow past the site and degree of flood risk to which it is exposed.

Patterns of economic activity and human settlement are also hierarchical. Commercial centers may be classified in terms of size and complexity; for example:

1. Primary metropolitan center (such as New York, Chicago, San Francisco)

2. Super-regional mall

3. Regional shopping center

4. Medium-sized city center

5. Neighborhood shopping center or mini-mall

6. Traditional village center

7. Crossroads gas pump and convenience store

The status of a particular commercial center in this hierarchy is not accidental. Geographers have developed numerous theories and models to account for the spatial organization of urban and economic systems. Central place theory, in particular, relates the size and spacing of commercial centers to the distance consumers are willing to travel to obtain certain goods and services. Thus, beer, bread, and milk are purchased from the nearest among a myriad neighborhood or convenience outlets. New cars and banking, legal, and health services are obtained from larger ("higher order") centers, while rare art objects, fur coats, large-scale financing, and open heart surgery are likely to be sought in a major metropolitan city. Commercial centers at each higher level thus provide a wider array of goods and services to consumers from a broader geographic "hinterland." Concomitantly, the size and diversity of a commercial center are limited by its proximity to competing centers of the same or higher order. (For further discussion see Berry and Garrison 1958; Berry 1967; or Palm 1981, chapter 8.)

The geographic location of a tract of land in relation to the hierarchy of urban places, like its position in a drainage system, bears an important relationship to its suitability for particular uses. The history of American land settlement is rife with examples of speculative land ventures that failed to achieve the shining prosperity predicted by their promoters, in part because they were too close to a better situated place that attracted available settlers and commerce in that region. For every successful Chicago or St. Louis, there have been many a disappointed Michigan City, Indiana, or Cairo, Illinois, that was eclipsed by its more prosperous (and better located) rival. Today's counterpart is the proliferation of regional shopping centers and office parks, regardless of the need or economic viability of such facilities in a particular location.

Function

A closely related notion to that of scale is the concept of function. The raison d'etre of a settlement and its size and rank in the central place hierarchy are directly related to the function(s) that it performs. An urban place without a function is a virtual nullity, regardless of what laws or promoters may say. Colonial legislatures of Virginia and Maryland attempted to encourage the growth of towns by laying out sites adjoining rivers and granting them special port privileges. The region, however, shipped its products directly from river landings at each plantation and needed no port towns. In the pithy words of Thomas Jefferson (1784/1944, 227), a geographer among his many talents: "The laws have said there shall be towns; but nature has said there shall not, and they remain unworthy of enumeration."

Urban economic functions may be primary (agriculture, forestry, mining); secondary (manufacturing); or tertiary (retail and service) activities, or a combination of them. Some urban places are characterized by a single dominant function, as in the case of sea or lake ports, transportation hubs, governmental centers, academic towns, recreational resorts, and retirement communities. Larger cities usually encompass more than one major function, in addition to a variety of subsidiary activities (for example, shopping, banking, medical care, car sales). Urban functions change over time with technological innovation, patterns of economic investment (both domestic and international), demographic and lifestyle trends, shifts in political power, and changing popular perception. Thus urban places may lose or gain in their range of functions and correspondingly in their size and importance within the national system of settlements. "Smokestack cities" like Detroit and Cleveland lost much of their population and commercial importance during the 1980s, while "sunbelt/leisure" cities like Orlando and San Diego boomed.

The notion of function may also be applied to individual parcels of land or real property. This concept relates each discrete unit of land to the larger physical and human spatial systems of which it is a component. In ecological terms, land in its natural state may facilitate recharge of groundwater, store surface runoff in soil moisture or ponding, support vegetation, concentrate energy through photosynthesis, and provide habitat for wildlife. Land within the agricultural system functions as cropland, pasture, fallow, horticulture, or farmstead. Urban land functions as sites for residential, commercial, industrial, institutional, or public activities.

Function is related to, but not synonymous with, *land use.* Function refers to the relationship between a parcel of land and the wider physical and socioeconomic spatial systems to which it belongs. Even vacant land that is unused in a market sense may function in a physical and socioeconomic sense, and such functions may be either positive or negative with respect to the surrounding area. Thus, a vacant urban lot may have no formal economic use but may function as a visual amenity, a perceptual buffer between neighborhoods, a play space for children, an informal parking area, or a habitat for wildlife. Negatively, it may serve as a dumping site for trash, junk cars, or hazardous wastes, or as a refuge for drug abusers or other illicit activities.

Externalities

The concept of function suggests that no parcel of land is an island unto itself. The use or condition of any unit of land may generate external effects or "externalities" on surrounding areas. Such effects, which may be either positive or negative, result from noncongruity of the geographical patterns of the land use variables—physical, socioeconomic, and legal/political. While the authority of land managers is confined to the geographic space defined by their jurisdictional boundaries, the physical and socioeconomic consequences of their actions are distributed according to the spatial pattern of the variable considered (Figure 2-2).

Physical externalities take such forms as air and water pollution; flooding; impacts on fisheries, birds, and other wildlife; depletion of water supplies; littering and dumping of wastes; noise; and visual blight. Socioeconomic externalities due to spatial shifts in economic activity result in loss of jobs, retail sales, and taxes and increased burdens on schools and other public services in adversely affected jurisdictions. Traffic congestion in neighboring jurisdictions is a frequent concomitant of a development decision.

While the nature, extent, and economic consequences of externalities vary according to the scale at which they arise, the fundamental problem is the same: How can favorable externalities be encouraged and adverse externalities suppressed or mitigated? Furthermore, some externalities are "serious enough" to justify governmental intervention (flagrant air pollution) while others are simply left to the victim to endure (loss of local tax revenue). The determination of which is which poses legal and political questions. The geographer, having framed the problem, refers its solution to the law.

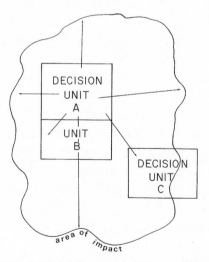

FIGURE 2-2   Diagram of spatial impacts of externalities on adjacent and nonadjacent land.

The Legal Landscape

The legal landscape is very different from that of the geographer. While the latter is a composite of several interacting types of spatial phenomena—physical, economic, social, and institutional—the law is primarily concerned with the last category, legal and political authority over land, and only secondarily with the others. Where the geographical model of the land economy identifies systems of nodes, linkages, flows, hierarchies, and functions, the legal counterpart may best be described as a "battlefield" on which private property interests struggle against each other (the private law context) as well as against governmental constraints imposed on behalf of the "public interest" (the public law context). This landscape is crisscrossed with earthworks of entrenched legal interests and is littered with the shell craters of past legal salvos.

The adversarial and pragmatic perspective of law contrasts with the positivist orientation of geography. Land use patterns to the lawyer are the collective outcome of a myriad individual cases, conflicts, appeals, administrative rulings, and political actions to which geographical notions of scale, function, and central place theory may seem irrelevant abstractions. The holistic, systematic perspective of geography yields to the particularistic, adjucative focus of the law. To the latter, substantive outcomes, particularly broad-scale, long-term applications, are secondary to constitutional issues of fairness and reasonableness of the process by which conflicts are resolved. As will be discussed in Chapter 8, however, the constitutionality of public land use measures is strongly related to the reasonableness of their impacts, which raises geographical questions.

A fundamental dichotomy in land use law lies between concepts of *ownership* (either private or public) and *jurisdiction* (public). The former represents a set of rights and duties that inure to the party(ies) that hold a legally recognized interest in specific real property. The latter represents the power of a governmental body to regulate private activities including land usage within its political boundaries. Confusingly, both the public authority and the geographic territory within which it is exercised are referred to as "jurisdiction."

The recognition of competing interests is itself an important difference between geography and law. The former identifies spatially differentiated "clusters" of common interest defined by diverse criteria (for example, immediate neighbors, neighborhood, ethnic community, business district, watershed, metropolitan housing market, and so on). In contrast to this open-ended approach, the law focuses on "parties in interest" who possess legal "standing" that qualifies them to seek legal redress. Classes of parties with legal standing in land use disputes normally include property owners directly affected by a decision, their immediate neighbors, and any governmental body having jurisdiction over the site in question. Other geographically relevant constituencies such as the neighborhood, downstream residents, or the metropolitan region lack legal standing except to the extent that an organizational surrogate may successfully claim to represent affected interests.

Environmental and civil rights organizations and other interest groups have been fairly successful in asserting standing on behalf of their constituencies in lawsuits since the 1970s. Also "class actions" have been another means of asserting standing on behalf of a large number of similarly affected individuals, as in product liability cases. The rigidity of traditional legal rules regarding "standing" has thus somewhat eased in tacit recognition of geographically diffuse "parties in interest."

The complex hierarchies of political geography however are collapsed into a monolithic "public" for purposes of land use litigation that commonly takes the form of private property owner versus "the public." This blurs or erases geographical distinctions between diverse "publics" with very different interests—neighbors, community, region, state, nation, globe.

Three classes of typical land use disputes may be identified: (1) owner versus owner, (2) owner versus public, and (3) public versus public. Disputes of the first type are usually settled by a court through application of common law doctrines such as nuisance and trespass derived from past judicial decisions in the United States and Great Britain (see Chapters 3 and 4). The second class of disputes involves *constitutional* issues governing the respective rights and powers of private and governmental interests (Chapter 8). The third category may involve disputes either between peer units of government on the same level ("horizontal") or between units at different levels ("vertical"). Disputes between the federal government and one or more states present issues of *federalism*, while disputes between a state and a local government involve the extent of municipal autonomy under express or implicit grants of state authority or *home rule* (Clark 1985). (See Chapter 5.) Federal–local disputes also arise in connection with enforcement of federal environmental, civil rights, and other action-forcing legislation.

Land use disputes of all three classes listed above are prevalently concerned with harmful externalities inflicted by one land use manager on one or more other units (of the same or different level). Like private owners, units of public authority seek to minimize internal benefits of land use within their own jurisdiction, to ignore adverse externalities inflicted on neighbors, and to resist such adverse impacts being inflicted on themselves. In this "beggar thy neighbor" game, there is no real "public interest," regardless of constitutional rhetoric. There are only the competing interests of the parties to the litigation. In the absence of a representative of a genuine public interest, courts are often at a loss to determine who to protect—for example, the private owner, the municipality, or a larger region. (As an example, compare the geographical perceptions of the Federal District Court and U.S. Court of Appeals in the *Petaluma* case discussed in Chapter 9.)

With all the contrasts indicated above, can it be said that land use geography and law occupy any common ground? The answer is strongly affirmative. It was suggested above that the problem of externalities is an area of overlap between the geographical and legal frames of reference. Externalities, which represent friction among components in the geographer's macro view of the land economy, are in fact the central concern of the lawyer's micro view. If there were no externalities among land use management units, there would be no need for land use law. *The central problem of land use law is that of externalities, and that problem is fundamentally geographical.*

The Legal Process

Before proceeding further, it is important that the nonlegal reader understand the context in which the American law of land use is articulated. In the Anglo-American legal tradition, first came the "common law." As discussed in Chapter 3, relations among private owners are defined according to principles of common law articulated in past court decisions dating back in some cases to medieval England.

The U.S. Constitution—the "supreme law of the land"—and its state counterparts establish fundamental principles governing the relationship between government (federal, state, local) on the one hand, and the private individual on the other. Of particular importance to the land use context, the Fifth Amendment to the U.S. Constitution declares: "No person shall be . . . deprived of life, liberty, or property without due process of law, nor shall private property be taken for public use without just compensation." (In 1995, the "taking" issue based on the last phrase of this provision is a hot topic. See Tauzin quote at beginning of Chapter 1 and discussion in Chapter 8.)

Responsibility for the establishment of laws concerning land use lies with the individual states, which in turn have delegated most of their authority to local governments. The latter may adopt land use zoning laws and other measures regulating private use of land. In recent years, many states have also adopted state-level regulations for particular types of sensitive or significant areas such as floodplains, wetlands, historic sites, or agricultural land (Kusler 1985; DeGrove and Stroud 1987). State and municipal laws may further delegate authority to administrative bodies to promulgate specific rules that elaborate on the broader provisions of the statute.

Statutes and administrative regulations concerning land use are subject to review by courts ("judicial review"). Lawsuits may be filed in either the relevant state court system or in the federal court system where a federal constitutional or legal question is involved. In either case, courts are asked to resolve whether the measure is constitutional and fairly applied to the challenging party ("plaintiff") by the relevant unit of government ("defendant"). Many suits are decided on procedural grounds without reaching the merits of the case. Others are found to be "fairly debatable" on their merits and courts then normally apply a presumption that the public action is valid. In a third set of decisions, courts are persuaded by the plaintiff that the public measure is "discriminatory, arbitrary, or capricious" and the measure is held invalid, at least as applied to the plaintiff.

Very few land use disputes actually reach the courts and even fewer are appealed by the losing party to a higher ("appellate") court. Cases of major significance are occasionally accepted for review by the U.S. Supreme Court, which has issued about 10 land use opinions since 1985 (see Chapter 8). The state supreme courts collectively account for most significant decisions in the field of land use. Their decisions apply directly only to the state in which they arise but are published nationally to provide guidance to courts elsewhere.

Published decisions on land use cases in the state and federal court systems comprise a rich archive of judicial perspectives on the relationship of law and geography. Judicial opinions result from the application of legal authorities (examples are prior case law, statutes, principles of "black letter law," learned treatises) to the facts of the case. It is the role of the attorneys for each party to portray applicable legal authority and the facts of the case favorably to their respective positions. The court in turn forms its own opinion of the state of the law and the facts of the case and reaches a decision accordingly. *The legal outcome therefore reflects in part the court's perception of the geographic context.*

Judges, being human, do not necessarily view the circumstances of a land use issue in the same way (Clark 1985). Judicial disagreement may arise (1) between individual judges on a multijudge court (as expressed in dissenting opinions); (2) between a lower and higher court reviewing the same case; (3) between courts in different states or federal jurisdictions reviewing similar cases; and (4) between courts considering a similar issue at different points in time. The last category is particularly important in weighing the role of geographical perspective in the judicial process. Law is a flexible and dynamic institution. The adjudicative process permits reinterpretation of legal principles over time in response to actual or perceived changes in society and its needs. As stated by the U.S. Supreme Court in *Village of Euclid v. Ambler Realty Co.* (272 U.S. 365, 1926):

> . . . while the meaning of the constitutional guarantees never varies, the scope of their application must expand or contract to meet the new and different conditions which are constantly coming within the field of their operation. (272 U.S., at 386).

Leading decisions on similar land use issues over time may thus reflect shifts of legal response to new and different conditions among which geographical circumstances loom large.

Law as an Agent of Urban Form

The influence of law in the pattern or morphology of landscape was noted by the Harvard geographer Derwent W. Whittlesey (1935, 85):

A Note on Legal Citations in This Book

Many statutes and judicial opinions are cited in this book, particularly in Chapters 8, 9, 10, 11, and 12. For law review articles, legal briefs, and treatises, the standard forms of legal citations are set forth in A Uniform System of Citation ("Blue Book") available in any law library. In the interest of simplification, this book does not adhere strictly to those rules of style. Federal statutes are usually cited by their Public Law (P.L.) number, which refers to the text of a law as originally adopted. For example, the National Environmental Policy Act of 1969 (P.L. 91-190) was the 190th act to be passed by the 91st Congress. Public Laws are published in two forms: the U.S. Code Congressional and Administrative News (an annual series of very large volumes found in any law library) and Statutes at Large (less frequently used and sometimes not available).

The Public Law form of a statute of course does not reflect earlier statutes that it may have amended or subsequent laws that amend it. The current version of a federal law, reflecting all additions and deletions by various public laws passed at different times, is "codified" by subject matter in the *U.S. Code* (U.S.C.) and *U.S. Code Annotated* (U.S.C.A.). The former contains only the statutes themselves, while the latter provides a wealth of additional information on legislative history, changes in language, court decisions, and law review articles that discuss the statute, and so on.

Discussion in this book is primarily historical, focusing on the evolution of public response to perceived environmental needs. The use of Public Law citations is appropriate for this purpose, since we are interested in the language of a law as adopted at a particular moment in time. But for anyone who wishes to research the current status of a federal law, the U.S.C. or U.S.C.A. are indispensable. [State laws follow the same twofold form of citation: (1) by order of adoption and (2) codified by subject matter.]

Judicial opinions (court decisions) are published in a series of "reporters" by West Publishing Co., which are available in law libraries. The standard form of citation used in this book is as follows:

Plaintiff v. Defendant, Vol. no., Reporter, First Page no. (State, Year).

For example, *Just v. Marinette County,* 201 N.W.2d 761 (Wis., 1972).

(N.B. "N.W.2d" refers to the Northwest Reporter, Second Series. Consult a law librarian for explanation of other reporter abbreviations.)

Political activities leave their impress upon the landscape, just as economic pursuits do. Many acts of government become apparent in the landscape only as phenomena of economic geography; others express themselves directly. Deep and widely ramified impress upon the landscape is stamped by the functioning of effective central authority.

The "impress" of law, however, differs from place to place, from one historical period and social order to another, and among different types of land use. As will be illustrated in the case of Boston, Massachussetts, the role of law may be discerned in different ways among districts of the same city built at different periods of social and economic development. The urban geographer James E. Vance, Jr. (1977, 24) distinguishes between "organic cities," which reflect individual rather than centralized control over their origin and growth, and "preconceived cities," which reflect the "impress" of an imposed land use plan. These two archetypes may be viewed side by side in Edinburgh, Scotland, which retains the disorderly but picturesque medieval "Old Town" just across a park from the elegant baroque symmetry of James Craig's "New Town," laid out in 1766 (Figure 2-3).

Most urban landscapes lie somewhere between these two extremes, as preconceived plans and individual preferences mingle in ever-shifting combinations with physical site, economic context, and culture to produce the cities of the world. Law as an instrument of both private rights and public authority is a subtle but ubiquitous agent in the evolution of urban form, and is often discernible in the rural landscape as well.

To further illustrate this point, the following discussion first considers the most conspicuous and familiar example of a preconceived or imposed land use pattern: the orthogonal or "grid" street plan. It then takes a longitudinal look at the evolution of a particular city, Boston, in terms of the relative influence of law over time.

Imposed Plans: The Ubiquitous Grid

The use of the grid as a basis for land allocation and street layout has been traced back to the third millennium B.C. in the Indus Valley by

FIGURE 2-3 Edinburgh, Scotland: medieval Old Town and Craig's baroque New Town, 1766. Reproduced by permission of the Scottish Records Office.

geographer Dan Stanislawski (1946), who cites such a plan, wherever found, as evidence of centralized control:

> This pattern is not conceivable except as an organic whole. If the planner thinks in terms of single buildings, separate functions, or casual growth, the grid will not come into being; for each structure considered separately the advantage lies with irregularity. History is replete with examples of the patternless, ill-formed town that has been the product of growth in response to the desires of individual builders.

Similarly, Castagnoli (1971, 124) stresses the influence of governing authority in establishing a preconceived pattern of land allocation and usage:

> The regularity or irregularity of town forms depends entirely on the presence or absence of spontaneity in their birth and growth. The irregular city is the result of development left entirely to individuals who actually live on the land. If a governing body divides the land and disposes of it before it is handed over to users, a uniformly patterned city will emerge.

The grid plan serves several administrative goals: equitability of land allocation, convenience of survey and house numbering, and ease of expansion into later settled areas. Its disadvantages include incompatibility with irregular terrain, problems of defensibility, excessive street length in relation to built-up land, and (to contemporary observers at least) monotonous regularity.

Grid street plans have been employed in diverse sociocultural contexts and periods of urban history. Beijing, Kyoto, Mexico City, Berlin, Buenos Aires, New York, and most North American cities are orthogonal, at least in part. The grid was particularly suited to the layout of colonial outposts and new settlements, from the cardo and decumanus of Roman enclaves in conquered territories (Grimal 1954/1983), to 13th century bastide towns in France, Wales, and Ireland (Beresford 1967), to Spanish and French settlements in the New World following Roman standards established by Vitruvius (Stanislawski 1947). The grid also appears where a newly planned sector has been added to an earlier, unplanned city, as in James Craig's 1766 plan for Edinburgh's New Town

(Figure 2-3). London's 17th and 18th century West End estate developments starkly contrast with the unplanned clutter of the older City of London (much of which burned in 1666). Pombal's formal baroque reconstruction of central Lisbon following its 1755 earthquake similarly contrasts with the delightful informality of the adjoining Alfama district that survived that disaster (Mullin 1992).

The grid served as a standard pattern for new settlements established by land proprietors in colonial America such as William Penn's 1686 checkerboard plan for Philadelphia, James Oglethorpe's 1733 plan for Savannah, and the 1820 Mount Auburn subdivision in Boston (Reps 1969). The pervasive rectangularity of rural and urban land use in the United States west of the Appalachians resulted from one of the first acts of the new national government upon its assumption of sovereignty: the federal cadastral survey initiated in the Land Ordinance of 1785 (Clawson 1983, 20).

The grid plan thus unmistakably reflects the influence of supervening authority—crown, military governor, proprietor, national or local government—on the use of land by individuals. So also do other geometric urban forms that conspicuously reflect an imposed plan, as in the case of round cities of the Renaissance (Johnston 1983) and baroque cities (Sitte 1945). Washington, D.C. is a composite of a grid street plan and a baroque pattern of radial avenues, as designed by the French engineer Pierre Charles L'Enfant in 1792. (It is ironic that the plan for the capital of democracy was inspired by the absolute monarch Louis XIV's palace and grounds at Versailles.)

But the urban-shaping role of law is not necessarily as obvious or as areally extensive as in these cases. It may operate more subtly and prosaically, as for instance in the width of streets; the size, spacing, construction, and use of buildings; and in the balance of built and unbuilt space. How are physical differences among sections of the same city explained? To paraphrase landscape architect Grady Clay (1973), we must "read the city" in terms of legal and institutional influences as well as economic, cultural, and geomorphic factors.

Evolution Over Time: Boston

A short walk across central Boston traverses an archive of different stages of public involvement in the city-shaping process (Figure 2-4). Starting in the vicinity of the waterfront on Boston Harbor, one wanders through the

North End and financial district whose irregular street pattern dates from the mid-17th century. (It is Boston folklore that these streets originated as cow paths.) These lead eventually to the city's open core, the Boston Common and the Public Garden, set aside from private development by public action respectively in the 1630s and the 1830s. Adjoining the Public Garden to the west are the rectilinear streets and bowfront brick row-houses of Back Bay, Boston's mid-19th century expansion onto newly filled land bordering the Charles River. Crossing Boyleston Street from Back Bay, one enters the high-rise complex of multiple-use structures in Prudential Center and adjacent areas (Figure 2-5).

How does one account for the perceived differences in urban form between the North End, Back Bay, and Prudential Center? Contrasts between the three districts may be conventionally explained in terms of their functional relationships to the economic circumstances of Boston and the demand for land at the time of their development. Thus, the North End and financial district originally served as the core of a crowded, mercantile settlement oriented chiefly to its wharves (McManis 1975, 81–82). Back Bay originated, and in part still serves, as an elite residential quarter reflecting Boston's 19th century prominence as a center of education, finance, and culture (Whitehill 1968). The Prudential Center involved the revitalization of a blighted site to enhance Boston's function as a corporation headquarters and convention site (Conzen and Lewis 1976, 50).

One may also interpret the outward differences among the three districts in terms of changes in transportation technology, from foot and sailing vessel in the 17th century, to carriage and streetcar in the 19th century, to automobile and elevator in the 20th century. In terms of construction technology, one moves from the era of clapboard and shingle, to brick and slate, to reinforced concrete, glass, and steel.

But there is an additional explanation for the contrasting patterns of the three districts, namely *the extent and form of public intervention in the private building process*. Boston's early growth was largely organic. Actions by the town selectmen to constrain individual freedom in building were limited to measures concerned with fire, as in specifying materials to be used in roofing and chimneys and in requiring the possession by householders of fire-fighting implements (Bridenbaugh 1964, 55–61). Otherwise, the town placed few restrictions on the layout and consstruction of individual structures.

FIGURE 2-4   Three eras of legal geography in Boston, Massachusetts: (1) the North End, (2) Back Bay, and (3) Prudential Center.

FIGURE 2-5   Aerial view of Back Bay (lower part) and Prudential Center in Boston.

Back Bay, by contrast, was a totally preconceived expansion of Boston. New land created through filling of the malodorous fens vested legally in the Commonwealth of Massachusetts, which historically holds tidelands in trust for the public. In 1856, a multipartite agreement to govern the filling and development of the fens was executed between the Commonwealth, the City of Boston, and various private proprietors (Whitehill 1968, 151). Pursuant to this agreement, the Commissioners on the Back Bay, a legal entity created by the legislature in 1852, exercised total control over the layout of streets and disposition of parcels. Purchasers of building lots were required to accept deed restrictions limiting the use, height, and external appearance of structures. Municipal land use zoning would not appear in Boston until after World War I. Meanwhile, private deed restrictions provided strict legal control to ensure harmonious development of Back Bay.

Prudential Center legally resembles the Back Bay project to the extent that public authorities promoted the development of an underutilized site (in this case a railroad yard) and controlled its form and usage through deed restrictions. But Prudential Center involved other legal devices as well. The site (including the newly recognized property interest in "air rights") had to be acquired from the private owner using public eminent domain power. It was then reconveyed at a lower cost to the redevelopment corporation. The latter was required to provide an auditorium and convention hall, as well as public ways and parking spaces, as a condition to constructing private commercial space. A special state law deferred certain real estate taxes for up to 45 years as a subsidy to the development's future profitability (Haar 1963, 181–182). Prudential Center thus resulted from a complex interaction of public and private initiatives characteristic of much contemporary metropolitan development (Platt 1994).

Legal influences on land use assume many forms and operate in subtle and sometimes contradictory ways. These interact with nonlegal constraints, such as site and situation, economic conditions, culture, and technology, in various combinations. The relative influence of legal and other constraints differs from one time period to another and from site to site. A further tour along the Boston waterfront, for instance, reveals a highly differentiated pattern of selective public intervention and private investment as one proceeds from the revitalized Faneuil Hall Market complex toward Charlestown or South Boston. Historic restoration tax credits, flexible zoning provisions, tidelands building lines, National Park Service programs, accelerated depreciation, urban development action grants–these and many other legal measures interact with physical and economic factors to shape the urban landscape of the Boston waterfront. For example, the Massachusetts Supreme Judicial Court in *Boston Waterfront Development Corp. v. Commonwealth* 393 N.E.2d 356 (1979) revived the doctrine of public trust based on the Massachusetts Bay Colonial Ordinance of 1641 and various 19th century court decisions. Pursuant to *Boston Waterfront*, the state now requires public walkways and other forms of access for any construction on present or former tidelands.

A General Model of Land–Law Interaction

The complexity of land use management, in terms of the types of decision makers, the powers they exert, and the interactions between them, tends to impede perception of an overall process: The forest cannot be seen for the trees. Furthermore, the legal perspective on land use, as stated earlier, views the decision process as adversarial between private and public interests. In fact, both private and public managers may be viewed as "partners in equity" (to use a term suggested by resource economist Mason Gaffney) which jointly, although not necessarily amicably, determine for better or worse the way in which a society puts its land resources to use.

Figure 2-6 depicts a simple model in which all relevant decision makers, public and private, are represented holistically by the "legal" circle. The other two circles represent the "physical" resource systems and "cultural" or human activity systems. Each circle thus depicts a different set of spatially distributed phenomena or geographies–of the land itself, of human activities on the land, and of legal/political authority that directs those activities. Each circle may be thought of as a template overlying the land surface. For any given location on that surface, a specific set of physical, cultural, and legal characteristics apply. And these are interrelated with each other as suggested by the vectors in the model.

The most important vector for purposes of the present discussion is labeled "resource management," a term that includes but is not limited to *land use control*. (Air and water management also fall within the broad

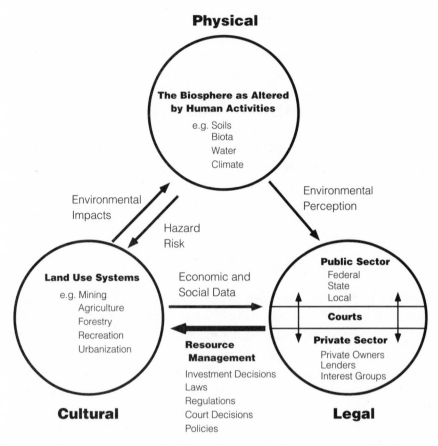

FIGURE 2-6   A general model of land–law interaction.

parameters of the model.) This vector represents the aggregate influence of public and private authority over land use as expressed through the various management instruments available to each type of decision maker. The nature and form of human activity systems such as urbanization are determined by the collective guidance of private and public decisions articulated via the "resource management" vector.

Two inputs to the "legal" circle inform the decision makers and thus influence the resource management output. One of these is "environmental perception." This term is used broadly here to refer to the flow of information or cues concerning the state of the physical resource as perceived by managers relevant to their respective areas of property rights or jurisdiction. Environmental cues include data concerning the sustainability of particular land uses, risks posed by natural or technological hazards, and, in general, the positive and negative implications of particular ways of using land.

Environmental perception applies both to cues originating within the land area of direct interest and to cues derived from activities external to such land area (externalities). By definition, harmful externalities tend to be ignored by the manager (usually the owner) that generates them, unless forced by the victims to abate them (for example, through a nuisance action) or by higher public authority through administrative or judicial intervention. The resource management vector represents the net effect of all these various signals issued by different managers having a legal interest in the use of land in question.

The other input vector, "economic and social data," represents feedback on the functioning of each activity system to responsible or affected decision makers. Environmental and socioeconomic inputs are interpreted in terms of the goals or expectations of each manager. Different types and levels of managers may differ in their objectives. Furthermore, different public agencies of municipal, state, or federal governments may seek different objectives, for example, economic development versus environmental quality. Also, each manager differs with respect to receptivity to environmental cues in relation to the second set of inputs—economic and social data derived directly from the activity systems themselves. The relative weight of these two vectors may change over time. Until the 1960s, economic profitability prevailed over resource degradation in determining resource management actions. With the rise of the environmental movement in the late 1960s, the "environmental perception" vector gained greater weight. In the 1990s, the economic signals are gaining renewed influence.

Clearly the processing of environmental and socioeconomic inputs within the "legal" circle and the interaction of resultant management outputs or signals is very complex. The latter may include conflicting signals from different levels or agencies of government that modulate in different ways the management actions of individual users of land. Also, the use of land is modified in response to changes in official or social priorities over time. For example, the design of cities has historically been influenced by many objectives. From time to time and from place to place, these have included such goals as military defensibility, religious piety, royal or imperial vanity, colonial orderliness, public healthfulness, civic attractiveness, functional efficiency, and environmental sustainability.

The interactive loop of the model is completed by the vector labeled "environmental impact": the modification of the physical resource by human activities. In the agricultural context, row cropping on hilly terrain hastens soil erosion and causes sedimentation and pollution of downstream water bodies; irrigation may lead to salinization of the soil mantle or, where based on groundwater, to a lowering of aquifer levels. Such practices, if continued unchecked, may lead to a loss of productivity in the areas affected, and eventually to a destruction of a portion of the physical resource. If and when the counterproductive tendency of existing practices is environmentally perceived by a legal entity having jurisdiction over the area in question, new resource management signals may be issued to modify the status quo. In the case of soil erosion, for instance, Congress has twice acted to modify the destructive practices of farm operators: first, in the establishment of the Soil Conservation Service in 1935 and, second, in the creation of a "conservation reserve" in the Food Security Act of 1985. (See Chapter 12.)

Thus the model depicts a dynamic process whereby the way in which land is used in human activity systems may be modified by a new set of resource management signals emitted by the "legal" circle in response to new awareness of the impacts of existing practices on the physical resource. This new awareness may result from a single dramatic catastrophe, which instantly leads to revision of the prevailing rules, as when the Fire of London in 1666 led to a dramatic reform of building practices in the Act for Rebuilding London of 1667 (as discussed in Chapter 3). Or it may result from a change in social values regarding an existing state of affairs which, previously acceptable or ignored, becomes intolerable and leads to legislative reform. Thus, the Sanitary Reform Movement of the 1840s and the Progressive Movement in the early 20th century focused public attention on conditions of urban squalor and overcrowding and prompted the adoption of sanitary codes and zoning laws, respectively. (See Chapters 5 and 6.)

The past two decades have witnessed a proliferation of new environmental laws and programs in response to the perception of environmental deterioration inspired by the writings of Rachel Carson, Barry Commoner, Joseph Sax, William H. Whyte, Gilbert F. White, and many others beginning in the 1950s. At this writing, the feedback loop of our model is laboring to formulate legal response to the growing recognition of new threats to the biosphere in the form of global warming, stratospheric ozone depletion, and deforestation. As in the past, the development of new institutions—additions to the "legal" circle—may be required to supply the needed resource management signals to modify human actions.

A number of writers have commented on the relationship of law and society in terms consistent with this model. For example, Whittlesey (1935) has written:

Laws affect both the tempo and the direction of settlement in all new countries, although in the process the law itself is much modified, or where it conflicts too stridently with its new-found environment, abrogated.

As illustration, Whittlesey cited the evolution of the appropriation doctrine of water rights in the arid western parts of the United States in place of the common law riparian doctrine that applies in the humid eastern states. He further noted the appearance of land redistribution laws in the wake of social revolution. Thus, alteration of objectives through political or social upheaval may precipitate drastic modification of the legal status quo.

Relocation of an organized social community to a new physical environment may prompt alteration of legal institutions inherited from the country of origin. Concerning the Puritan migration to New England in the 1630s, McManis (1975, 41) writes:

. . . Old World ways-of-doing were almost immediately modified as the colonists adopted native practices or adjusted to local soils and climatic conditions. . . . The individuality of colonial development was encouraged by the selective transfer of English practices to the colonies and by the relative freedom . . . from restraints of English traditions such as feudal rights and land entailments, from English local government which was a combination of feudalism and later innovation, and from many contemporary actions of the central government that were reshaping the landscape of Britain.

A case in point was the initial establishment of the open field system of land tenure in certain towns such as Sudbury, Massachusetts, by settlers from areas of England where that practice still prevailed. Under pressure from population growth and scarcity of arable land, however, such open field settlements soon evolved into a proprietary form of land tenure (Powell 1963).

Gradual, as opposed to sudden, social change may also be expressed in, and in turn furthered by, modification of legal doctrines concerning land, as in the case of the abolition of primogeniture in England in 1926. The long persistence of this doctrine, according to Cohen and Rosenthal (1971, 9):

> ... maintained intact the great estates that were the source of wealth and power, not just for the landed nobility but for their familial offshoots who were impelled, encouraged, and assisted to apply their energies to the Church, the military, or the colonial service. ... Without primogeniture, more farmers would have remained on the land but in less affluent conditions, and the early enclosure laws could not have been used to transform agriculture from row crops to livestock.

Physical catastrophe, whether or not accompanied by social upheaval, may also serve as a catalyst to legal innovation in managing the redevelopment process. The Act for Rebuilding London after the Great Fire of 1666 involved no change of government but a major change in official policy regarding urban development. The 1755 Lisbon earthquake precipitated both a social revolution and a novel approach to the management of the city's reconstruction (Mullin 1992).

On the other hand, Hohenberg and Lees (1985, 36) suggest that institutional inertia impaired the viability of the late medieval city:

> A key to the declines that dogged cities through the postplague years and periodically for centuries beyond that is their inability to change when the environment did. In modern terms, medieval cities were institutionally closed systems, poorly attuned to changes in the external environment.

Over time, specific legal institutions and measures have thus emerged in response to the prevailing coalescence of political, social, and economic objectives regarding land use. As societal conditions and expectations changed, however, the broad legal concepts did not necessarily vanish, although specific applications may have been superseded. Like the woodstove and the windmill, the legal approaches of earlier eras remain available for subsequent rediscovery and reuse.

References

Beresford, M. 1967. *New Towns of the Middle Ages*. New York: Praeger.

Berry, B.J.L. 1967. *Geography of Market Centers and Retail Distribution*. Englewood Cliffs, N.J.: Prentice-Hall.

——, and W.L. Garrison. 1958. "The Functional Bases of the Central Place Hierarchy." *Economic Geography* 34: 145–154.

Bridenbaugh, C. 1964. *Cities in the Wilderness: Urban Life in America 1625–1742*. New York: Capricorn Books.

Castagnoli, F. 1971. *Orthogonal Town Planning in Antiquity*. Cambridge: The M.I.T. Press.

Clark, G.L. 1985. *Judges and the Cities*. Chicago: University of Chicago Press.

Clawson, M. 1983. *The Federal Lands Revisited*. Baltimore: The Johns Hopkins Press for Resources for the Future.

Clay, G. 1973. *Close-Up: How to Read the American City*. Chicago: University of Chicago Press.

Cohen, S.B., and L.D. Rosenthal. 1971. "A Geographic Model for Political Systems Analysis." *Geographical Review* 61: 5–31.

Conzen, M.P., and G. Lewis. 1976. *Boston: A Geographical Portrait*. Cambridge: Ballinger.

DeGrove, J.M., and N.E. Stroud. 1987. "State Land Planning and Regulation: Innovative Roles in the 1980s and Beyond." *Land Use Law* (March): 3–8.

Grimal, P. 1954/1983. *Roman Cities*. (G.M. Woloch, trans. and ed.). Madison: University of Wisconsin Press.

Haar, C.M. 1963. "The Social Control of Urban Space." In *Cities and Space* (L. Wingo, Jr., ed.). Baltimore: Johns Hopkins Press.

Hartshorne, R. 1939. *The Nature of Geography*. Lancaster, PA: Association of American Geographers.

Hohenberg, R.M., and L.H. Lees. 1985. *The Making of Urban Europe: 1000–1950*. Cambridge: Harvard University Press.

James, P. E. and G. J. Martin. 1981. *All Possible Worlds: A History of Geographical Ideas* (2nd ed.). New York: Wiley.

Jefferson, T. 1784/1944. "Notes on Virginia." In *The Life and Selected Writings of Thomas Jefferson* (A. Koch and W. Peden, eds.). New York: The Modern Library.

Johnston, N.J. 1983. *Cities in the Round.* Seattle: University of Washington Press.

Kusler, J.A. 1985. "Roles Along the Rivers: Regional Problems Meet National Policy." *Environment* 27(7): 18–20; 37–44.

Locke, J. 1689/1952. *Second Treatise of Government.* New York: The Liberal Arts Press.

Matthews, O.P. 1984. *Water Resources: Geography and Law.* Washington: Association of American Geographers.

McManis, D.R. 1975. *Colonial New England: A Historical Geography.* New York: Oxford University Press.

Morrill, R.L. 1970. *The Spatial Organization of Society.* Belmont, CA: Wadsworth.

Mullin, J.R. 1992. "The Reconstruction of Lisbon Following the Earthquake of 1755: A Study in Despotic Planning." *Planning Perspectives* 7: 157–179.

Palm, R. 1981. *The Geography of American Cities.* New York: Oxford University Press.

Platt, R.H. 1994. "Commentary on 'The Entrepreneurial City': Fabricating Urban Development in Syracuse, New York." *The Professional Geographer* (May) 46(2): 250–251.

Powell, S.C. 1963. *Puritan Village: The Formation of a New England Town.* Middletown, CT: Wesleyan University Press.

Reps, J. 1969. *Cities of the American West: A History of Frontier Urban Planning.* Princeton: Princeton University Press.

Sitte, C. 1945. *City Planning According to Artistic Principles.* New York: Random House.

Stanislawski, D. 1946. "The Origin and Spread of the Grid-Pattern Town." *Geographical Review* 36(1): 105–20.

———. 1947. "Early Spanish Town Planning in the New World." *Geographical Review* 37(1): 94–105.

Vance, J.E., Jr. 1977. *This Scene of Man.* New York: Harpers College Press.

Whitehill, W.M. 1968. *Boston: A Topographical History.* 2nd ed. Cambridge: Harvard University Press.

Whittlesey, D.W. 1935. "The Impress of Effective Central Authority upon the Landscape." *Annals of the Association of American Geographers* 25: 85–97.

Part II | *From Commons to Cacophony: Dispersion of Control over Land*

CHAPTER 3 / English Roots of Modern
Land Use Controls

Introduction

The history of social organization of land use in the United States has been profoundly influenced by English precedents and practice. In part this derives from the transplanting of the common law of England to the American colonies during the 17th and 18th centuries. Judicial precedents from the courts of the mother country were thus directly applicable in the colonies, and most American states today still adhere to the common law tradition in matters relating to land. (A few states such as Louisiana, Florida, Texas, New Mexico, and California retain elements of the civil law imported from France or Spain.) After American independence, England continued to influence the development of new legal concepts affecting land use in the United States, as with the Chadwick Report on Sanitary Reform in the 1840s, Ebenezer Howard's garden cities idea at the turn of the century, and the post-World War II New Towns Movement.

This chapter reviews the evolution of English legal practice concerning land use from its origins in feudalism predating the Norman Conquest of 1066 through the appearance of building codes, private deed restrictions, and the improvement commission in the 17th and 18th centuries. This will set the stage for the next chapter to survey the expansion of urban institutions in response to the explosive growth of European and American cities in the 19th century.

The Feudal Commons

Private ownership of land is characteristic of a mature capitalistic society. In England and most other capitalist nations, the division of land into separately owned units replaced an earlier system of social control over land that we refer to as *feudalism*, whose hallmark was the holding ("tenure") of land in common rather than in individual ownership.

Common rights in land differ markedly from private rights. In a commons, no individual has exclusive and permanent control over any particular land. Instead, rights to use available land are shared or exercised in common on a group basis (Figure 3-1). The group, ideally, is small and clearly defined, such as the inhabitants of a feudal village. But the "group" may also be large and diffuse—for example, the population of the world, which shares the common oceans and atmosphere. Clearly, the size and specificity of the group sharing a common resource affect the feasibility of imposing collective rules on members of the group to manage the resource for the sustained benefit of all.

The biologist Garrett Hardin (1968) has formulated the gloomy axiom of "the tragedy of the commons." According to Hardin's proposition, if shared resources are not regulated through group self-restraint, individual users will inevitably maximize their own gains to their eventual mutual detriment:

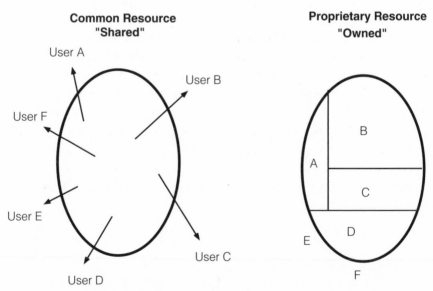

FIGURE 3-1 Diagram of common and proprietary forms of land tenure.

Ruin is the destination toward which all men rush, each pursuing his own best interest in a society that believes in the freedom of the commons. Freedom in a commons brings ruin to all.

Since the publication of this seminal article in 1968, the notion of the "commons" has been associated with the threat of environmental disaster, global warming, or nuclear war. But despite its contemporary implications, the commons proved to be a durable and sustainable means of organizing land use under feudalism. In England, the feudal commons originated deep in the Dark Ages (perhaps ca the 8th century A.D.) and continued to thrive until approximately the 1400s. Thereafter it was eroded by the process of enclosure but persisted in some locations until well into the 19th and even the 20th centuries. An institution for land use control that lasts a thousand years deserves closer scrutiny.

The system of mutual interdependence known as the feudal commons arose, not from fiat or statute, but from practical necessity. The collapse of Roman urbanism, trade, and military protection after the 6th century caused a general reversion to a precarious agrarian existence. Mere survival against starvation, freezing weather, and hostile attack assumed paramount importance. In the words of Lewis Mumford (1961, 249): "From the eighth century to the eleventh, the darkness thickened; and the early period of violence, paralysis, and terror worsened with the Saracen and the Viking invasions. Everyone sought security. . . ."

Security was achieved, to the extent possible, through the evolution of the feudal hierarchy of authority. Petty monarchs and local warlords assumed transient control over particular districts only to be overthrown from time to time by invading barbarian hordes or jealous neighbors. To sustain continuous preparations for war and to indulge in the pleasures of riotous living during peacetime, each local princeling exacted tribute from the inhabitants of his realm. "Tribute" typically included a portion of the food and fiber produced in each local area, as well as monetary payments and manpower for military service. As feudalism developed in Saxon England, local lords or barons typically exercised authority within their fiefdoms by the grace of a higher overlord who assured the baron's status in exchange for rendition of a portion of his tribute. The overlord in turn had to secure his own position by rendering tribute to the Crown.

Thus feudalism was a pyramid with the king at the apex, the peasantry at the bottom, and miscellaneous local lords and overlords in between. Essentially, feudalism was an ancient version of modern organized crime. Then, the price of security was the surplus product of the land. Today, it requires monetary payoffs and kickbacks.

But feudalism worked. Its success relied on the development of a socioeconomic institution that would ensure that land would be productively utilized to sustain both the local population and the superstructure of nobility. The institution that served this purpose was the *feudal manor* within which the commons prevailed.

The manor and commons were well established in Saxon England at the time of the Norman Conquest in 1066. William the Conqueror consolidated his political control by replacing Saxon overlords with his own principal followers, thus installing himself at the apex of the feudal pyramid. Yet he did not tamper with the equilibrium of the manor and commons, which were essential to the viability of the entire system. Instead, he inventoried the assets and resources of all manorial units within his realm in the "Domesday Book" of 1086 (Trevelyan 1953, 171 ff).

The manor was the fundamental economic, political, and social unit of English feudalism. It typically consisted of an extensive tract of land divided into (1) arable or cropland; (2) rough pasture or meadows; and (3) waste, including woods, ponds, wetlands, and uplands (Figure 3-2). The nucleus of the manor was a village settlement. This was no borough or town, but merely a cluster of dwellings huddled near the baron's hall, a parish church, and a water-powered mill. The manorial village had no legal or corporate status but served as the domicile and socioeconomic nexus of the baron and peasantry. (The latter consisted of two classes: the free "yeomenry" and the "villeins" or unfree tenants.) The baron's hall served as gathering place and occasionally as court for the village (Trevelyan, 199 ff.).

The feudal manor in its ideal form represented a balance between population and resources. Use of the land required the limitation of individual greed and desire for short-term gain in the interest of long-term productivity. This in turn required a state of legal equilibrium in which all parties, baron and peasantry alike, were bound by customary rules and constraints in the use of manorial resources. Without such constraints, the "tragedy of the commons" would soon have ensued. With constraints, the system proved to be sustainable.

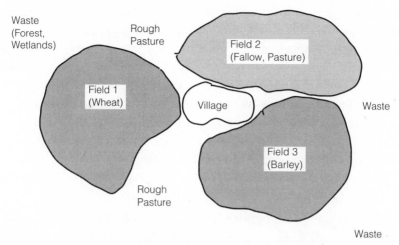

FIGURE 3-2   Diagram of land allocation in an English feudal manor.

The degree of control differed among the three classes of manorial lands—cropland, pasture, and "waste." Apparently little regulation was needed regarding the use of waste. As long as population pressure was low, there was adequate fish, game, and firewood (although the killing of wildlife in protected royal forests was a capital offense). Pasture ("green common") was normally subject to limitations on the number of livestock that each household, including the baron's, could graze.

Management of the cropland ("arable") was more complicated. A manor's cropland was usually divided into three large open fields. These three fields were rotated annually among wheat, oats, and fallow. This customary cycle allowed the soil to restore itself to ensure long-term productivity. Fertility was also maintained through the application of human and animal wastes. In its fallow year, a field was grazed by livestock to restore its soil nutrients, and "night soil" (human waste) was regularly deposited on all the fields.

Each open field was internally divided into strips of approximately one acre each. Certain strips were reserved to support the baron's household and provide tribute to the higher nobility. The remaining strips were allocated among the tenants as *commoners*. Each commoner household was assured the use of about 30 one-acre strips, from which it derived food and fiber for its own sustenance and for tribute to the baron. (Commoners also had to cultivate the baron's strips.) Allotments of strips within the open fields were interspersed side by side and end to end rather than being clustered in blocks under a single landholder. What this fragmentation lacked in productive efficiency, it gained in equity:

> It is probable that the strips were scattered in this way in order to give each owner a little bit of the good land, a little bit of the indifferent, and a little bit of the bad. To allot to each owner a continuous area, compensating by extent of area for deficiency in quality, was beyond the powers of a primitive community.
>
> Holdsworth 1927, p. 39.

Although internally apportioned, the open field was a species of commons. Individual strips were not fenced and were separated only by low ridges that served as both boundaries and foot paths. During the fallow cycle, animals could be pastured without the need to be tethered within particular strips. Undoubtedly conflicts arose regarding trespass, vandalism, or encroachment on each other's strips. These were settled in a peculiarly feudal institution: the manorial court. Herein was an important antecedent to the future courts of equity in England and its colonies (Trevelyan, 173–176).

Land management in feudal England was thus dominated by the commons. Much of the manorial land was literally shared in common, and even allocated cropland in open fields was subject to a high degree of collective mutual involvement. The use of one's own strips was dependent on the compatible use of surrounding land. No one, not even the baron, was free to break out of this system and introduce new crops or fence in his holdings. In the fanciful description of the English legal historian F.W. Maitland (1898, 32):

> Even in the boroughs, the common bell called the commons to the town from the common streets and the green commons to the common hall and in common hall assembled a common seal to release their common land, for which a fine is paid into their common chest. All is common; nothing is public.

The last sentence of this quotation is vital to understanding the early development of land use control. Under feudalism, there was no "public" regulation or management of land. The manorial system was symbolically subject to the power of lord, overlord, and crown. But, in fact, none of these could tinker with the manorial system of open fields and commons without toppling the entire delicately balanced structure. This system was perhaps the best example in all history of a land management system that was self-perpetuating and sustainable. Again, Maitland:

> We underrate the automatism of ancient agriculture. . . . So far as the arable land is concerned, the common-field husbandry, when once it has been started, requires little regulation. . . . [By 1803 in Cambridge], for some centuries the common-field husbandry had needed no regulation; it had been maintaining itself (p. 25).

Why was the commons so durable as a land management institution? In earlier times, prior to the 17th century, there was no feasible alternative to the commons as a means of organizing land use to supply a reliable, if not necessarily optimal, supply of food: "Common rights . . . were a necessary element in agricultural systems, they were involved in the ownership and cultivation of the land, and they were largely the source of the profits obtained from the land, the means of rendering its cultivation effective" (Gonner 1966, 4).

But stability does not necessarily imply efficiency or vitality. The stifling conformity of feudalism discouraged innovation and creativity both in the use of land and intellectually. Beginning with the depopulation of the rural manors due to the Black Death in the 14th century, changing demographic and technological conditions placed increasing pressure on the ancient ways of using land. And concurrently, as discussed below, the revival of towns attracted the more enterprising who fled from toil on the land. Trade with the continent and the rise of the wool staple simultaneously stimulated private commerce and motivated the landed nobility to fence off ("enclose") common lands for sheep raising.

Since common rights were protected by common law, they could be legally abridged only by statute. Beginning as early as 1235, Parliament adopted a long series of special acts authorizing specified tracts of land to be enclosed or "privatized" to the exclusion of commoners, who were forced to choose between working as hired laborers or seeking employment elsewhere (Gonner, 43 ff.). The commoners resisted this erosion of their livelihood and security as best they could, sometimes resorting to open violence, but with little success. The enclosure movement represented a gradual but distinct social and legal revolution in which common rights in land were slowly extinguished and replaced with the modern system of private rights in real property. In towns, feudalism yielded to new institutions of municipal self-governance. These processes were consistent with the general model of land–law interaction proposed in Chapter 2.

The 17th century settlement of New England coincided with the last stage of the open field or commons system of land tenure in certain parts of England. Settlers originating in various districts of England initially established the system of land tenure that prevailed in their place of origin, either open field or private proprietorship. Thus, Sudbury, Massachusetts followed the open field practice of Sudbury, England for its first few decades (Powell 1963). Each family was granted by the original proprietors a small house lot and garden for its personal use, together with rights to plant crops and graze livestock on the town's open or common fields. Eventually in Sudbury and in other towns, the open field system, a legacy of the vanishing feudal manor, yielded to private ownership of farmland, as was the trend in England.

A type of commons persists to the present time in England and the northeastern United States in the form of patches of open space in the centers of old towns. But could a citizen of Boston today cut firewood or graze a cow on Boston Common? Clearly the legal status, purposes, and usage regulations of these open space legacies have changed. The village common is no longer common property of the inhabitants, but instead is owned and managed by the local municipal government for such allowed uses as recreation, carnivals, and parking.

In a different sense, however, the modern world is awash in common resources: the oceans, major rivers and lakes, the atmosphere, outer space. In our cities, streets, parks, subways, and schools have elements of the commons and are vulnerable to "tragedy" if not properly managed. As society attempts to manage the use of these contemporary common resources, the feudal experience provides useful inspiration. During its period of ascendancy, the feudal commons was a long-lived land management institution that, as long as population was limited, persisted in harmony with the demands upon it, both human and ecological.

Medieval Cities—Advent of the Municipal Corporation

The feudal commons, however, was ill-suited to the governance of *urban* communities. As Maitland so vigorously stated, the commons involved no concept of "public." All transactions were based on custom and personal status, not laws adopted by a few on behalf of the many. The revival of towns and cities in England and the continent starting in the 11th century called for the development of a new institution more suited to the governance of closely built, nonagricultural settlements—the municipal corporation.

Conditions for Urban Revival

For centuries after the Fall of the Roman Empire, feudalism blanketed England and Europe like a miasma, smothering commercial and artistic exuberance and confining most of the population to a short, ignorant, pastoral existence. Only the Christian Church through its far-flung network, and Islamic sanctuaries in Southern Europe and Africa, could preserve literacy and promote artistic impulse. The great cathedrals erected between 1100 and 1400 attest to the creative genius and the wealth at the disposal of the Church. Similarly, the advent of universities in the Middle Ages such as Oxford, Cambridge, Paris, and Heidelberg reflected the survival of classical learning and scholarship within the walls of monasteries and abbeys throughout Europe.

Towns would not forever remain moribund, inhabited by monks, cats, and Roman ghosts. By the 11th century, hints of a coming urban revival could be detected. According to Pirenne (1952), the prerequisite to this process was the revival of trade between regions, giving rise to the need for markets. This in turn would lead to the regrowth of a merchant class that would inhabit towns and give them political as well as functional importance. Broadly speaking, the urban revival was characterized by (1) an increase in urban populations largely due to migration from rural areas; (2) reappearance of a middle class engaged in manufacturing and commerce; (3) physical growth of towns as reflected in new building, both within and outside the old fortified areas; (4) the emergence of the municipality as a new legal institution independent of feudalism; and (5) the onset of urban problems such as water supply, disease, and fire.

The market function of towns involved both a physical space and a legal climate within which it could flourish. The physical marketplace was a central open space at the heart of the old walled city. Often the marketplace was surrounded by the cathedral, town hall, guild hall, and other civic buildings. The marketplace was multifunctional: Besides its commercial role, it provided open space for ecclesiastic and civic ceremonies, social interaction, and games (Mumford 1961). (Today, many European marketplaces retain these functions, plus outdoor cafes, political demonstrations, street life, and parking.)

For a marketplace to function, it had to be accessible. Streets leading from the city gates to the market had to be wide enough for people, animals, and carts to squeeze past each other. Given the scarcity of buildable land within the walls, streets and the marketplace itself were subject to chronic pressure of encroachment by adjoining property owners. This pressure was opposed, not by building laws, which were rarely effective where they existed at all, but literally by the throng of humanity and traffic. According to Saalman (1968, 30): "Streets will be as narrow as they can be while allowing for transit of goods and persons" (Figures 3-3 and 3-4).

In many cases, the demand for market space generated by growing trade simply outstripped available land within the city walls. As the threat of hostile attack declined, development of new markets and accompanying houses and workshops appeared outside the gates of many new cities. These areas, known as "faubourgs," were the original suburbs. Pirenne stresses that their commercial functions were not limited to periodic markets or fairs but assumed the continuous nature of modern commercial districts. It is likely that commerce outside the walls was promoted in some cases by a desire to escape the restrictions imposed on trade within the walls.

Municipal Charters

The medieval city was as much a legal as a geographic phenomenon. Seldom of any great size in area or population, medieval cities nevertheless achieved a high degree of self-governance as virtual city-states. Legally independent of the onerous structure of feudalism, ". . . the symbol of the city in the Middle Ages was eventually found in the sworn community that legally assumed the form of a corporation" (Weber 1958, 105).

The origins of this "corporate revolution" are obscure. In England after

FIGURE 3-3   Riverfront view of Frankfurt Am Main, 1646. *Source:* Saalman, 1968.

FIGURE 3-4   Plan of Frankfurt Am Main, 1646, a classic late medieval walled city. *Source:* Saalman, 1968.

the Conquest, certain older towns obtained charters or grants of privileges from the Crown. Charters were either purchased or awarded as a token of royal favor. Some towns claimed the benefit of charters on the grounds that they had been exercising certain powers of self-government "since time out of mind" (a very long time), and therefore such powers could not be abrogated.

The effect of a charter was to release the town and its inhabitants from traditional feudal obligations to render tribute in money, goods, or military service. Municipal courts replaced the whim of crown or overlord in petty judicial matters. Persons attending the weekly market would be excused from paying a market toll to the lord, which was regarded by merchants as a hindrance to trade. In place of these feudal obligations, the town was authorized to appoint its own sheriff, raise revenue from any available sources, and render annual tribute in the form of monetary payment to the Crown:

> Charters appeared at the close of the Eleventh Century and for the next two centuries they increased both in number and in the extent of the privileges granted. The acquisition of charters finally made the majority of towns communities with extensive rights of self-government and helped to make the townsmen a distinct element in the political, social, and economic life of the nation.
>
> Lunt 1956, p. 178.

Broadly speaking, the privileges bestowed by charter included (1) the right to hold a market; (2) the right to organize merchant guilds; (3) freedom from feudal tribute, except certain taxes; and (4) the right to coin money and to regulate weights and measures.

Citizens of towns ("burghers") enjoyed not only commercial freedom but personal freedom as well. Even serfs who fled from their manors and resided in towns for a year and a day were legally released from their feudal bonds and gained the status of freemen:

> The status . . . [of the individual under city law] was one of freedom. It is a necessary and universal attribute of the middle class. Each city established a "franchise" in this respect. Every vestige of rural serfdom disappeared within its walls. Whatever might be the differences and even the contrasts which wealth set up between

men, all were equal as far as civil status was concerned. "The air of the city makes free," says the German proverb. Pirenne, p. 193.

However, the medieval countryside and town maintained a symbiotic, not hostile, relationship. Towns depended on their rural hinterland for the necessities of life as well as products to be traded in their markets. Rural manors needed markets as well as the genteel "night soil" from well-fed burghers. Amicable relations were often preserved with the local nobility and the church as well. In general, this period impresses the modern mind with its high degree of pragmatism and mutual interdependence among manor, aristocracy, church, and town.

Merchant Guilds

Guilds were organizations of merchants or craftsmen that wielded great influence within the medieval town and its economy. The guilds' economic and political power arose from grants of monopoly status conferred on them by the Crown. Thus, the wool traders guild could establish the place and hours of operation, standards of quality, weights and measurement, and terms of credit for all wool trading in the town. Nonmembers of the guild were either prohibited from wool trading in the town or were required to pay exorbitant fees to the guild. In addition, they could sell only to guild retailers: no nonmember middlemen were allowed (Stenton 1962, 178).

London by the early 17th century had over 50 craft guilds ranging from apothecaries to woodmongers, each with its own hall or meeting place. The leading members of the more important guilds were ipso facto leading citizens. The guilds provided a social and cultural dimension; their halls were the scene of banquets, plays, and ceremonies. They also contributed to the physical development of the community. Street maintenance, construction or replacement of bridges, additions to hospitals, repair of fortifications, and most permanent of all, the building of cathedrals—all were among the public-spirited works of guilds (Pirenne 1952, 186). The phrase *public-spirited* is deliberately chosen; for the first time since the fall of Rome, there was emerging a sense of "public."

Ultimately, the influence of the guilds was reflected more enduringly in legal institutions than in bricks or mortar. Over time, medieval cities under their direction assumed a new legal status as "bodies politic" or "municipal corporations." By 1400, English municipal corporations had acquired the following characteristics: (1) perpetual existence; (2) power to own land and buildings; (3) power to establish courts and to sue and be sued; (4) power to adopt ordinances and elect local officials; and (5) the right to formalize documents with a corporate seal (Holdsworth 1927). These legal characteristics of the municipal corporation have remained fairly constant from the Middle Ages to the present time. (Chapter 5 further discusses municipal corporations in the American context.)

Municipal corporations exercise jurisdiction over a specific territory— the walled city in the medieval case. This concept of *jurisdiction* differed from *ownership*:

> A municipal corporation owns a few, but only a few, of the houses in the town. Over the whole town it exercises a certain governmental power. We have here two different ideas; they can be sharply contrasted. . . . There [was] a sort of lordship over the whole town, and of a few houses there will be landlordship.
>
> Maitland, p. 30.

The question logically arises as to what use municipal corporations made of their "lordship" or jurisdiction over land within the city walls. How in particular did they utilize their power to adopt ordinances and to what extent did they attempt to improve the quality of the deteriorating urban environment?

English municipal ordinances of the Middle Ages may be roughly divided into two classes. First were those concerned with public morals, health, and safety in the urban environment. London, for instance, had ordinances dealing with the removal of dung from stables, the lighting of streets, and "sweating houses, whereunto many lewd women resort" (Hearsey 1965, 11). These ordinances were at best unevenly enforced and, at worst, totally ignored.

The second class of regulations dealt with offenses against trade and commerce, such as theft, overcharging, and sale of inferior goods. Penalties for these offenses, which struck directly at the economic welfare of the guilds, were swift and often terrible. One of the lighter punishments, as described by Pendrill (1937, 22), involved a baker caught selling bread of substandard weight who was ". . . strapped to a sort of low cart harnessed to a horse and dragged through the streets, accompanied by the City Minstrels playing on tabors and pipes, and finally brought back and released at his own door." Breaches of the "market peace," for example, theft or disorderly conduct, were subject to far more brutal punishments:

> This city peace was a law of exception, more severe, more harsh, than that of the country districts. It was prodigal of corporal punishments: hanging, decapitation, castration, amputation of limbs. It applied in all its rigor the "lextalionis": an eye for an eye, a tooth for a tooth. Its evident purpose was to repress derelictions, through terror.
>
> Pirenne, p. 200.

Regulation of the urban environment was clearly of lower priority than deterring crimes against property. Petty theft of commercial goods in a public thoroughfare was a breach of the market peace and punished severely. But the permanent encroachment of private buildings into or above the same public way was likely to be ignored (Saalman, 30–31).

The existence of corporate jurisdiction over the medieval city, therefore, did not necessarily mean that such power was used effectively to regulate the placement, height, construction, or use of buildings. The resulting cityscape was characterized by narrow, twisting streets, overhanging upper stories, and prevalent use of wood as a construction material. Just as the casual disposal of human and animal waste and lack of clean water contributed to periodic epidemics, the unregulated crowding of buildings posed a constant and growing danger of citywide fire. As in modern times, reform and progress were the result, not of enlightened foresight, but of bitter hindsight.

The Common Law: Trespass and Nuisance

The 13th century marked the dawn of the modern era of land law in England. The new era was characterized by the gradual replacement of feudal tenure with property ownership or "proprietorship," a process that would extend over the next six centuries. This process has been characterized by legal scholars as a transition from "status" to "estate"

(Dukeminier and Krier 1981, 362). As described earlier, feudal land was not "owned" in the modern sense, but instead was "held" by one party in subservience or "fealty" to another. The holder was essentially entitled only to mere right of usage in exchange for tribute to someone higher in the feudal pecking order. A right of usage did not involve the right to sell, give, or devise the land to one's heirs. Nor, under the management constraints of the commons, could land be converted to nontraditional uses or simply removed from production.

The transition from feudal tenure to freehold ownership of land first appeared in the reviving towns rather than the countryside. The breakdown of feudal control over land was a concomitant of the growth of personal freedom within city walls:

> With freedom of person there went on equal footing, in the city, the freedom of the land. In fact, in a merchant community, land could not remain idle and be kept out of commerce by unyielding and diverse laws that prevented its free conveyance and restrained it from serving as a means of credit and acquiring capital value. This was the more inevitable in that land, within the city, changed its nature–it became ground for building. It was rapidly covered with houses, crowded one against the other, and increased in value in proportion as they multiplied. Thus it automatically came about that the owner of a house acquired in course of time the ownership, or at least the possession of the soil upon which it was built. . . . Cityhold thus became freehold.   Pirenne, pp. 194–195.

Just as freehold was essential to city growth, feudalism had to also break down in the countryside for innovation to flourish and personal (albeit unequal) wealth to be amassed. The transformation of rural land from feudal tenure to proprietorship began with the "Statute Quia Emptores" in 1290. This statute prohibited the practice of "subinfeudation," which was causing proliferation of intermediate lordships and devaluation of tribute received by the Crown. The statute however permitted the substitution of one holder for another, subject to the same obligations to the overlord as the earlier holder. This in effect legitimized conveyance of land from one party to another on a monetary basis, which is the essence of property ownership (Dukeminier and Krier, 358). Over time, intermediate lordships withered away and virtually all land came to be held by individual proprietors directly "of" the Crown. That is the state of land tenure in Great Britain and its remaining colonies today.

By the 18th century, property ownership in both England and the American colonies was solidly established as a sacred institution with which even the Crown was constrained from interfering. The concept that "every man's home is his castle" was most forcefully stated by the jurist William Blackstone in his "Commentaries on the Common Law" in 1768:

> There is nothing which so generally strikes the imagination, and engages the affections of mankind as the right of property; or that sole and despotic dominion which one man claims and exercises over the external things of the world, in exclusion of the rights of any other individual in the Universe.
>
> Blackstone 1768/1863, p. 1.

Although tinged with hyperbole, Blackstone's view of private property stands the feudal tenure system on its head and exalts the proprietor over the Crown.

But as John Locke declared in the quote in Chapter 2, private property is valueless unless the owner is secure in reaping the "harvest" or other benefits of ownership. Blackstone's proposition declares that the owner is protected from the Crown, but what about one's neighbors? The answer lay in the development of the common law doctrines of trespass and nuisance under which an aggrieved property owner could seek the protection of the courts from offensive conduct by other parties.

The *common law* consists of the accumulated wisdom of courts faced with specific disputes to which they apply principles of law, drawn from earlier decisions and other sources, as a basis for decision. The common law evolves on a case-by-case basis and requires the aggrieved party (plaintiff) to bring an action against the alleged offender (defendant) in court. This reliance on past decisions in similar fact situations is referred to as "precedent" and has been the basis for the development of the common law in England and its present and former dependencies, including the United States.

The common law has never been an efficient means of regulating urban land use. It was supplemented (but not replaced) in the 19th and 20th centuries by public land use regulations such as zoning. But before the advent of such regulations, adjudication of disputes between private parties under the common law provided a crude means for redressing flagrant abuses against property ownership in the preindustrial urban community.

The most fundamental protection afforded by the common law was against *trespass*. Without security against physical invasion of the premises, property ownership meant nothing. The essence of trespass was a physical invasion or encroachment by an individual who had no right to enter the property in question. Over time, courts expanded the doctrine of trespass to hold parties liable who allowed livestock or even water to enter on the property of another without permission.

Beginning in the 13th century, trespass was broadly construed as a breach of the criminal law, punishable by fine or imprisonment. No proof of any actual damage was required since invasion of the plaintiff's rights was regarded as wrongful in itself. Furthermore, liability for trespass was imposed regardless of negligence: The defendant was "strictly liable" if proven to have encroached on the plaintiff's property (Prosser 1971, 357–364). The common law doctrine of trespass since medieval times has always reflected the principle that one's home and land are sacred.

The doctrine of *nuisance* afforded additional protection to property owners under the common law. Unlike trespass, nuisance did not require any physical invasion of the premises. Rather, it addressed the externalities of actions taken elsewhere, typically on adjoining land, which injured the beneficial enjoyment of the plaintiff's property. Typical forms of nuisance include blocking off a neighbor's light and air, causing bad odors and air pollution, loud continuing noises, and other externalities that impair the quiet enjoyment of nearby property. The medieval doctrine of nuisance—still cited today—was *sic utere tuo ut alienum non laedas*: use your property so as not to harm that of others.

This "golden rule" of nuisance has always been easier to express than to apply. In deciding nuisance cases, courts have traditionally attempted to "balance the equities," that is, weigh the social benefits, if any, of the conduct complained of against the degree and type of harm suffered by the plaintiff. Courts favor the plaintiff where the harm clearly outweighs the value of the activity. But, with the coming of industrialization, plaintiffs often lost cases in which the defendant was an industrial polluter that happened to supply a useful product and employ many people. Courts gradually became more creative in fashioning orders (injunctions) that limited the harmful effects of a particular enterprise without terminating it entirely. (See further discussion in Chapter 4.)

Building Laws: The Act for Rebuilding London

While medieval municipal corporations attempted to impose rules for building practices in urban areas on a piecemeal basis, most were doomed to futility. Part of the problem lay in the "tragedy of the commons": Each property owner viewed the streets and marketplaces as common property to be encroached on for private gain to the maximum extent possible. Without a clearcut purpose for such restrictions, backed up by a determined enforcement effort, the early attempts to regulate the urban environment were ineffectual. A comprehensive building law did not arrive in London until the late 17th century, and its advent required the bitter experience of a citywide disaster: the Great Fire of 1666.

London Before the Fire

Between 1400 and 1666, London's population grew from 50,000 to about 400,000 inhabitants—an eightfold increase. This demographic expansion reflected both an influx of rural laborers displaced by enclosure of common lands and immigration of persons fleeing persecution on the Continent. It was accompanied by physical expansion of London's housing stock both within and beyond the old Roman city walls. Queen Elizabeth I in 1580 attempted to halt the peripheral sprawl in a famous decree (anticipating the "greenbelt" laws of the mid-20th century) which ordered all persons to:

> ... desist and forbear from any new buildings of any house or tenement within three miles from any of the gates of the said city of London. ...
> Quoted in Rasmussen 1934/1967, p. 68.

This decree was a total failure as indicated by the continued growth of London outside its walls and gates. By 1666, the walled City of London was described as comprising only one-third of the total urbanized area of London: "The great urban spread had begun, and already a number of the better-off preferred to live outside the City where their work or business was" (Hearsey, 2). What is now the chic West End of London was then the rural–urban fringe, with large homes interspersed among residual common fields and districts of small cottages (Rasmussen, ch. 4).

The walled City (now the financial district known simply as "the City") remained in 1666 solidly medieval in character. Pre-fire London was a labyrinth of narrow, twisting streets with pervasive overhanging upper stories. Wood was the usual construction material. Since 1189 exterior walls were required to be of brick or stone, but "the precaution was very partially observed" (Bell 1920/1971, 11). The City was connected to the surrounding countryside by gates on the landward side and by the famous London Bridge across the Thames. The walled City contained 109 parish churches and some 50 guild or livery halls. The ancient gothic pile of St. Paul's Cathedral, the largest in Europe–its tower reached 449 feet and its nave measured 585 feet in length–loomed above the smoky, crowded city (Hearsey, 60).

The Fire

The Great Fire of September 2–7, 1666, was perhaps the first major catastrophe of modern times to be fully described by competent eyewitnesses. Samuel Pepys' "Diary" relates:

> . . . Jane comes in and tells me that she hears that above 300 houses have been burned down tonight by the fire we saw [the night before] and that it is now burning down all Fish-street, by London Bridge. So I made myself ready presently, and walked to the Tower, and there got up upon one of the high places, . . . and there I did see the houses at that end of the bridge all on fire, and an infinite great fire on this and the other side. . . . So down with my heart full of trouble to the Lieutenant of the Tower, who tells me that it begun this morning in the King's baker's house in Pudding-lane, and that it hath burned down St. Magnes Church [the first of 80 churches to be burned] and most part of Fish-street already. So I down to the water-side and there got a boat, and through bridge, and there saw a lamentable fire. . . . Everybody endeavoring to remove their goods, and flinging into the river, or bringing them into lighters that lay off; poor people staying in their houses as long as till the very flames touched them, and then running into boats, or

clambering from one pair of stairs by the water-side to another . . .
and the wind mighty high, and driving it into the City; and everything after so long a drought proving combustible, even the very
stones of the churches. . . .

Pepys 1666/1898, pp. 392–393.

In the absence of an efficient water distribution system, little could be
done to fight such a conflagration. The standard technique of medieval
firefighting was to "pull down houses," thus creating a firebreak to stop
the progress of the flames. The Lord Mayor of London vacillated in using
this technique out of concern for potential liability to the house owners.
An old law required that whoever pulled down a house in London had
to bear the cost of replacing it (Hearsey, 125). In the absence of any effective effort to limit the spread of the fire, it burned unchecked for three
days and consumed most of London within the walls and a considerable
area outside. Within this area 13,200 houses were destroyed in some 400
streets and alleys. Over 100,000 were homeless and left camping miser-
ably in fields outside the city.

In terms of loss of life, the Great Fire of 1666 was vastly overshadowed by an outbreak of plague in London the previous year. While
56,558 persons were reported to have died in the plague, only four
deaths were attributed to the fire out of a population of 400,000. It is perhaps an ironic quirk of human nature that physical destruction such as
occurred in the fire is given a higher place in history than human loss of
life as occurred in the plague. In any event, the fire indeed eliminated
medieval London, though fortunately not its inhabitants.

The First Modern Building Law

The fire epitomized Hardin's axiom: "Freedom in a commons brings
ruin to all." Although London was scarcely a feudal commons, neglect of
the urban environment under four centuries of municipal self-government had yielded disaster. Its public spaces were virtually an unregulated commons, with private structures clogging the narrow lanes and
passageways and blocking access to the Thames River. In the absence of
effective regulation of building size, location, and construction materials, the fire was inevitable. Without access to water, it could not be
halted.

The point was not missed by certain leading minds of the time. While the ruins were still smoking, plans, or at least concepts, for the rebuilding of London were being prepared by Sir Christopher Wren, the city's leading architect, and several others (Bell, ch. 13). Wren's plan proposed to transform the city into a monumental, baroque-style imperial capital, much as Haussmann would later restructure Paris in the mid-19th century. The pre-fire street alignments and property lines were to be abolished where necessary and replaced by an orderly, geometric network of major streets and open plazas with lesser streets leading into them. Churches, company halls, and other important buildings would be situated on the new squares or along the connecting arteries. The Thames embankment would be cleared and reserved for major buildings with open space between and in front of them. Dwellings would be confined to the lesser streets. The city should be rebuilt, according to Wren, along the lines of baroque Renaissance cities in Italy, which he greatly admired.

Such a radical proposal for restructuring the city was incompatible with the political and economic temper of the times. Charles II, the recently restored Stuart monarch, lacked the despotic powers that cost his father Charles I his head. The government could not afford to pay property owners whose private lots would have been taken to implement the plan (a very modern dilemma). The plan would take too long to implement; the City's commercial interests were anxious not to lose time in reestablishing their business activities. Finally, the plan was too grandiose for the English taste (Hearsey, 179).

A week after the fire had subsided, Charles II addressed by proclamation the need for restraint and foresight in the rebuilding process, pending a full investigation of the causes of the disaster. Rasmussen praises this declaration as "astonishingly modern . . . a true piece of town-planning, a programme for the development of the town" (117). In its preamble, the proclamation combined 17th century moralism and 20th century civic boosterism:

> And since it hath pleased God to lay this heavy Judgement upon Us . . . as evidence of His displeasure for Our sins We do comfort Our Self with some hope, that he will . . . give Us life, not only to see the foundations laid, but the buildings finished of a much more beautiful City than is at this time consumed. . . . Quoted in Rasmussen, p. 117.

The proclamation went on to address five practical aspects of the rebuilding process:

1. Stone or brick was to be used for exterior facades in place of wood.

2. The width of streets was to be established in relation to their importance.

3. A broad quay or open area would be maintained along the Thames for access to water for firefighting.

4. Public nuisance activities such as breweries or tanneries should be removed from central London to more suitable locations.

5. Reasonable compensation should be determined and paid to property owners whose right to rebuild was curtailed by public restrictions (Rasmussen, 116–117).

King Charles II then appointed a special investigative commission (like a modern mayor appointing a "blue ribbon committee") to draw up recommendations for future building practices in London. Christopher Wren served on the Commission and was to be a principal figure in the reconstruction of the city. Another interim measure of "the greatest aid in the rebuilding of London" was an act of Parliament that established a Court of Fire Judges to resolve disputes between landlords and tenants and to apportion rebuilding cost equitably between them (Bell, 242–243).

Based on the proclamation and the commission's report, the "Act for Rebuilding London" was adopted February 8, 1667, five months after the fire. What the law lacked in immediacy, it made up in detail. The Act has been described as London's first "complete code of building regulations" (Bell, 251). It was long and detailed:

> [It] covered important aspects of the rebuilding program: first, the rearrangement of some of the worst features of the old plan, with its apparently wayward meanderings, jutting corners, and frequent bottlenecks; second, the partial standardization of the new buildings, particularly with a view to fire resistance; and third, the raising of money for the public . . . buildings by a tax on coal.
>
> Summerson 1962, p. 53.

By far the most indelible of the Act's provisions dealt with the height and construction of dwellings to replace those burned in the fire. These consisted of four classes of structures, ranging from two-story, modest dwellings to houses of "the greatest bigness." The class of home that could be built on a site depended on the location and importance of the street or square on which it faced. The use of stone or brick for exterior walls was required. Thickness of walls, ceiling heights, and other architectural details were also specified. No overhang above the public way would be allowed.

The building provisions of the Act marked a significant departure from medieval style and construction practices, but those had long been abandoned in newer construction for the wealthy. According to Summerson (54), the Act ". . . crystallized the best practice of the time. . . ." It was, in effect, a building code for the redevelopment of the burned area and a guide to new construction in surrounding areas. The Act was farsighted in its administrative provisions for permits and fines, a precedent for modern building codes. And its regulations regarding the banishment of smoky or noxious activities to specified locations anticipated modern zoning laws.

The Act was not uniformly effective, for indeed there was little experience or administrative structure to enforce its requirements in every case. Furthermore, it did not purport to change building patterns or land usage to eliminate overcrowded alleys and courts behind other buildings. Working-class London sprang back to life still densely crowded and deprived of light and air. Such conditions would become increasingly intolerable over the next two centuries.

While the exact influence of the Act is difficult to discern from what might have occurred in its absence, it clearly marked a threshold between the medieval and the modern eras of urban land use control. The lethal combination of overcrowding, use of flammable building materials, and abysmal sanitary conditions produced the twin perils of the medieval city—disease and fire, both of which struck London in tandem in 1665–1666. The fire swept away not only the overhanging wooden houses and the rats they contained, but also the attitude of medieval neglect toward the urban environment. Charles II's moratorium on rebuilding and appointment of an expert investigative commission marked a vast change in governmental process from Elizabeth's useless edict of 1580. The Act of Parliament that resulted from the commission's findings represented the beginning of modern urban planning, although two centuries would elapse before public building codes were widely adopted in England and the United States. The Act for Rebuilding London, based on expert advice and perception of the causes of the disaster, epitomized the operation of our general model (Figures 2-6 and 3-5).

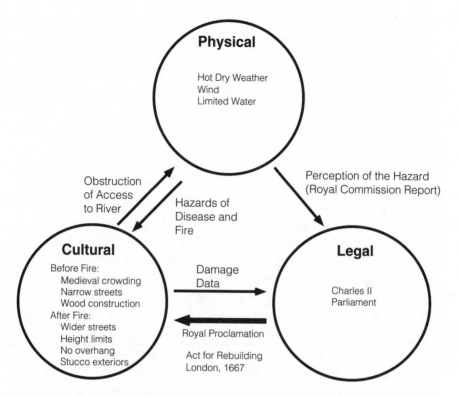

FIGURE 3-5   Model of legal response to Fire of London, 1666–1667.

Private Land Use Restrictions

At the same time that the old walled City of London was being rebuilt under the 1667 Act, the estates beyond the walls were undergoing development for the first time. The building boom north and west of the city proper (including what is now the fashionable West End district) was not subject to the Act, but displayed nevertheless a remarkable uniformity in land use pattern and architectural style. This uniformity was achieved, not through governmental intervention, but through private agreements between the aristocratic owners and occupants of the land in question, as expressed in deed and lease restrictions.

The prototype for the 17th and 18th century London squares was the Place Royale in Paris, commissioned by King Henri IV in 1615 (now the Place des Vosges). The Place Royale consisted of a small park surrounded by townhouses of equal height and similar facades, fronted by a street-level arcade, all subject to deed restrictions imposed by the Crown. This design was soon introduced to London by Inigo Jones in 1630 in his design for Covent Garden. Although the "least English" of London's squares (Zucker 1959, 200), Covent Garden in plan served as a paradigm for two centuries of elegant residential development in London.

The building of "Georgian London" between the 1630s and the 1820s responded to private demand for upper-class housing and residential neighborhoods near the royal court, the clubs, and social life of London (Summerson 1962). Several factors underlay this demand, including: (1) the increased overcrowding of London with its demonstrated hazards of plague and fire; (2) the accumulation of wealth due to the economic success of the City; and (3) the availability of buildable land in large estates at the outskirts of the City (Morris 1979, ch. 8). Some of these estates were held by nobility under feudal grants dating back to the Conquest; others were more recently acquired through the dissolution of monasteries and redistribution of church land by Henry VIII. In either case, the landed nobility were eager for profit.

A quirk of English legal history was to determine the scale and quality of the development of the London West End (Vance 1977, 234). Land tenure was customarily in "fee tail" rather than "fee simple," which meant that land was always inherited (normally by the eldest son) and could not be sold on the open market. This accounts for the customary English practice of leasing land for a long term rather than selling it outright. The land could be productively developed while the underlying ownership was passed from one dissolute male heir to the next. Since ownership remained in a single family, control was retained over the use of the land. This permitted the careful planning and uniform execution of the neoclassic squares and residential terraces that characterize upper-class London to the present day.

The elegant uniformity of exterior appearance that characterized these developments was achieved through private restrictions or *covenants*. A covenant is a promise made by the purchaser or lessee of real estate that the use of the premises will conform to conditions specified by seller or lessor. Thus landlords, with the aid of architects such as Inigo Jones, John Woods, Thomas Cubitt, and John Nash, could absolutely control the use of their property by the lessee. This included the exact locations of streets, squares, and building-lot lines as well as the size, appearance, and sometimes the interior layout of buildings.

The enforceability of covenants over time was seldom an issue where the original lessee or purchaser remained in possession. The landlord always had the legal right to enforce covenants against the party that had accepted them. However, many leases ran for periods of 99 years or longer and transfers from one party to another were common. This practice raised the question of whether the covenants would still be enforceable against subsequent parties in possession who had not specifically accepted the restrictions. The 1848 decision in *Tulk v. Moxhay* (41 Eng. Rep 1143), concerning London's Leicester Square, established the rule that covenants may "run with the land" and bind the use of land indefinitely.

The neoclassical residential districts regulated through private covenants were the antithesis of medieval unplanned growth. They epitomized the "preconceived" as opposed to the "organic" urban pattern. They exuded wealth, conservatism, power, and control in contrast to the irregular, heterogeneous, human scale of older districts. James Craig's 1766 plan for the New Town in Edinburgh stands in startling contrast to the medieval Old Town (see Figure 2-3). Although little of medieval vintage remains today in the Old Town, it retains a mysterious, romantic, and vaguely sinful atmosphere. Across a narrow linear park (formerly a fetid creek), the New Town stands rectilinear, symmetrical, and respectable, graced by its Adam doorways and leafy squares.

In the United States, the English-style residential square inspired several counterparts, notably Louisburg Square in Boston's Beacon Hill, laid out by private developers in 1826, and New York City's Gramercy Park, established in 1832. Both of these today remain private parks with keys available only to owners and tenants of adjacent buildings. (The use of deed restrictions to regulate modern subdivisions is considered in Chapters 4 and 9.)

Improvement Commissions

Private deed restrictions served the needs of the wealthy to implant their concepts of style on their elite quarters. But industrial working-class districts, which began to grow rapidly in the 18th century, were a different story. London doubled from about 400,000 at the time of the fire to 864,000 in 1801 (Ashworth 1954, 9). Other British and Scottish industrial cities, including Manchester, Birmingham, Liverpool, and Glasgow, grew at comparable rates. Most of this population increase, which anticipated even more massive growth in the following century, consisted of migration from the countryside and from Ireland and the Continent to the "satanic mills" of the industrial cities. This caused hideous overcrowding of existing dwellings and a proliferation of cheap, shoddy, unplanned tenement districts within walking distance to the factories and mills.

To make matters worse, the old municipal corporations that nominally governed each city had stagnated by the 18th century. Municipal offices were allocated according to status and privilege, not experience or interest in reform or public service (sound familiar?). The corporations were unresponsive to what Ashworth (50) has termed "the increasingly lethal nature of the swelling towns." The result was a state of anarchy in the town building process throughout the 18th and well into the 19th century.

Not only the municipal corporations but also the courts were largely ineffectual in confronting the new circumstances. In earlier and simpler times, the common law doctrine of nuisance had afforded crude relief to property owners and the public against the more obnoxious abuses of public health, safety, and the common welfare. For instance, a builder could be prevented from blocking the "ancient lights" and ventilation from reaching preexisting structure or from threatening an adjoining structure with collapse. Such actions had earlier provided limited, if cumbersome, protection against unreasonable or dangerous building practices.

But abatement of nuisance through court intervention was limited to case-by-case treatment upon petition of the wronged party. Normally, the harm complained about had to be in existence; it was rare that courts would enjoin a prospective nuisance. And the party seeking a remedy had to own the property, not be a mere tenant. Also legal action was expensive then as it is today. In theory nuisance actions remained available, but in practice, the courts in the 18th and 19th centuries exercised little restraint over the tenement-building process, since the victims seldom were able to complain.

Sydney and Beatrice Webb (1963, 236) in their classic history of English local government provide vivid images of the residential environment of early industrial England; for example:

To begin with the houses–springing up on all sides with mush-room-like rapidity–there were absolutely no building regulations. Each man put up his house where and as he chose, without regard for building-line, width of street or access of light and air.... 'Streets of projecting houses nearly meeting at the top rooms with small windows never meant to open; and dirt in all its glory, excluded every possible access for fresh air'.... The narrow ways left to foot and wheeled traffic were unpaved, uneven, and full of holes in which the water and garbage accumulated. Down the middle of the street ran a series of dirty puddles, which in time of rain became a stream of decomposing filth.

This was mild in comparison with the reports of Edwin Chadwick and other public health reformers of the mid-19th century, as discussed in Chapter 6. But the urban environment, apart from the elite districts, was fast disintegrating during the 18th century.

The ruling elite in this period, however, were dominated by conservatism, distracted by foreign wars, and generally disinterested in the fast-growing squalor within the cities. They simply went to parties and spent much of their time at their country estates. Creative and large-scale measures to address the crisis–for example, public sanitation and building laws, the public parks movement, urban redevelopment, and model planned towns–would not appear until the second half of the 19th century.

However, one simple but practical stopgap was devised in the late 17th century to address the need for better public services: the *improvement commission*. These commissions were statutory bodies established by Parliament to perform certain functions in specified localities. They were the forerunners of contemporary special districts and authorities in England and the United States. Like their modern counterparts, improvement commissions could overlie general-purpose units of government and indeed could serve more than one municipality. The first of these new institutions was the Commissioners of Scotland Yard (1662), which encompassed London and Westminster. This was not a detective agency but rather was empowered to "make new sewers, enlarge old ones and to remove nuisances . . . to appoint public rakers or scavengers, who were to make daily rounds with 'carts, dungpots, or other fitting carriages' ... and to remove encroachments upon public ways and to license hackney coaches" (Webb and Webb, 240).

Improvement commissions proliferated throughout England during the 18th century, numbering some 300 by the early 1800s. These bodies overlapped geographically and functionally with the old municipal corporations (which were substantially reformed by Parliament in 1835). They assumed many of the functions of modern local governments, such as "paving, cleansing, lighting, watching, and regulating" (Webb and Webb, 242). In addition, they engaged in activities of a more regional nature, for example: building bridges and canals, drainage improvement, enclosure of commons, erection of markets and slaughterhouses, water supply, and highway construction.

But like the municipal corporations and courts, the improvement commissions were hampered by institutional constraints in their efforts to stem the deterioration of English cities. They were strictly limited to specified functions and geographic areas as established by Parliament. They had no general jurisdiction or "home rule" authority to address a wider spectrum of urban needs without parliamentary approval. Thus, a commission responsible for paving and lighting in a particular district had no authority to deal with drainage or water supply, no matter how obvious the need. Furthermore, they lacked any authority to plan or regulate new building; they were largely limited to dealing with harmful conditions after the fact, if at all, and never beforehand. By the early 19th century, the improvement commissions:

> ... too often concentrated their attention solely on the middle-class districts of their towns, leaving the greater number of streets inhabited by the poorer classes wholly without essential services. However valiantly the improvement commissioners might struggle to cope with the flood-tide of urbanization—and few of them struggled very valiantly—they were fighting losing battles. [They were] constitutionally, financially, administratively, technically, and ideologically ill-equipped to cope with the frightening immensity of the task. ...
>
> Flinn 1965, p. 17.

Improvement commissions were thus a temporary expedient, a palliative to remedy certain kinds of urban ills on a piecemeal basis until more sweeping public approaches were devised. They totally failed to restrain the continued proliferation of slums and the lethality of the working-class residential environment. But the idea of the improvement commission, like the municipal corporation, was to become a permanent addition to the institutional fabric of urban and metropolitan government in Great Britain, the United States, and elsewhere.

Conclusion

The creativity of the English people and their legal system thus yielded a series of institutional innovations over several centuries to meet perceived needs to better organize and control the use of land. The source of each device differs considerably. Some of the institutions discussed in this chapter, such as the feudal commons and the municipal corporation, arose spontaneously from the "invisible hand" of social necessity. The doctrines of trespass and nuisance and later the recognition of private covenants as restrictions that run with the land were products of the English judicial system. The Act for Rebuilding London and the improvement commissions were created by acts of Parliament. The latter two institutions—the courts and the legislature—have continued to play dominant roles in the fashioning of additional public responses to urban and environmental deterioration in the 19th and 20th centuries.

The two principal decision makers with respect to the use of land in the United States today are each legacies of medieval England—namely the private owner of property and the local municipality. These are respectively the topics of the next two chapters. The historical thread resumes in Chapter 6.

References

Ashworth, W. 1954. *The Genesis of Modern British Town Planning*. London: Routledge and Kegan Paul.

Bell, W.G. 1920/1971. *The Great Fire of London in 1666*. Westport, CT: Greenwood Press.

Blackstone, W. 1768/1863. *Commentaries on the Laws of England* (Second Book). Philadelphia: J.B. Lippincott and Co.

Dukeminier, J., and J. Krier. 1981. *Property*. Boston: Little, Brown.

Flinn, M.W., ed. 1965. *Edwin Chadwick's Report on the Sanitary Condition of the Labouring Population of Great Britain*. Edinburgh: Edinburgh University Press.

Gonner, E.C.K. 1966. *Common Land and Inclosure* 2nd ed. London: Frank Cass.

Hardin, G. 1968. "The Tragedy of the Commons." *Science* 162: 1243–1248.

Hearsey, J.E. 1965. *London and the Great Fire*. London: J. Murray.

Holdsworth, W.S. 1927. *An Historical Introduction to the Land Law*. Oxford: Clarendon Press.

Lunt, W.E. 1956. *History of England*. New York: Harper and Row.

Maitland, F.W. 1898. *Township and Borough*. Cambridge: Cambridge University Press.

Morris, E.E.J. 1979. *History of Urban Form: Before the Industrial Revolution* 2nd ed. New York: Wiley.

Mumford, L. 1961. *The City in History*. New York: Harcourt, Brace and World.

Pendrill, C. 1937. *Old Parish Life in London*. London: Oxford University Press.

Pepys, S. 1666/1898. *Diary*. H.B. Wheatley, ed. London: George Bell and Sons.

Pirenne, H. 1952. *Medieval Cities: Their Origins and the Revival of Trade*. Princeton: Princeton University Press.

Powell, S.C. 1963. *Puritan Village: The Formation of a New England Town*. Middletown, CT: Wesleyan University Press.

Prosser, W.L. 1971. *The Law of Torts* 4th ed. St. Paul: West Publishing Co.

Rasmussen, S.E. 1934/1967. *London: The Unique City*. Cambridge: The M.I.T. Press.

Saalman, H. 1968. *Medieval Cities*. New York: George Braziller.

Stenton, D.M. 1962. *English Society in the Early Middle Ages*. Baltimore: Penguin Books.

Summerson, J. 1962. *Georgian London*. Baltimore: Penguin Books.

Trevelyan, G.M. 1953. *History of England*, Vol. 1. Garden City, NY: Doubleday Anchor.

Vance, J.E., Jr. 1977. *This Scene of Man*. New York: Harper's College Press.

Webb, S., and B. Webb. 1963. *Statutory Authorities for Special Purposes*. Hamden, CT: Archon Books.

Weber, M. 1958. *The City*. New York: The Free Press.

Zucker, P. 1959. *Town and Square. From the Agora to the Village Green*. New York: Columbia University Press.

CHAPTER 4

Property Rights:
The Owner as Planner

Introduction

The property owner is the primary planner of land use. This statement may appear to conflict with the conventional notion that planning and resource management are public functions, to be exercised by government officials, boards, and professional staff. But the public role in the United States is essentially reactive to the decisions of the property owner. It is the owner who determines *how* to utilize his or her land in light of geographic, economic, legal, and personal circumstances. It is also the owner who determines *when* a change in existing land use should occur. It is the owner's decision to change the use of land that triggers the public reactive role.

This chapter is devoted to a summary of the institution of land ownership and the role that the owner plays in the unfolding pattern of land usage. This will set the stage for examination of the various levels of public involvement in the land use decision process in subsequent chapters.

What Is Real Property?

The legal concept of property distinguishes between two classes of property: real and personal. *Real property* includes physical land, improvements such as buildings, vegetation, subsurface minerals, and, in some states, water rights. *Personal property* consists of chattels or movable objects owned by an individual. These may include motor vehicles, livestock, furniture, equipment or inventory, and personal possessions.

Crops are sometimes treated as personal property separate from the land on which they grow. The distinction between real and personal property is important in several ways: (1) They are taxed differently; (2) they are bought and sold with different procedures; and (3) a buyer of real property is not necessarily entitled to personal property located thereon.

The concept of land as real property is three-dimensional. A medieval legal maxim states: "Cujus est solum, ejus est usque ad coelum ad infernos" (roughly translated: "whomsoever owns the soil, owns also to heaven and to hell"). This means that the ownership of real property includes not only the horizontal plane of the land surface within the parcel of land in question, but also vertically downward and upward to the limits of practical or legal feasibility. Thus, real property ownership extends to subsurface rights below, and air rights above the land in question. (See Figure 4-1.)

Another useful legal cliché describes land ownership as a "bundle of green and red sticks." The green sticks represent rights that an owner

FIGURE 4-1 The geography of legal rights in land: Elements of real property ownership.

enjoys in making profitable or pleasurable use of his or her land. Green sticks include the right to build on or above land, the right to till the soil and reap the benefits of its fertility, to cut its timber, to exploit its subsurface minerals, and sometimes to use its water resources. The entirety of such rights is known legally as the *fee simple absolute.*

The red sticks represent the duties of real property ownership that are necessary to enjoy the green sticks. These include principally the duty to pay property taxes, to refrain from creating a nuisance (harmful externalities), and to conform to applicable public laws, such as zoning, building codes, subdivision laws, and sanitary codes. The constitutional question of how far land use regulations may restrict the use and therefore the value of property, "the taking issue," will be considered later in Chapter 8.

Green Sticks: Rights of Real Property Ownership

The principal rights that bestow value on real property are of two types: material and spatial. These reflect the dual nature of land as a wedge of the physical material of the earth and alternatively as a volume that may be enclosed by buildings.

MATERIAL RIGHTS

The material elements of land value are derived from the physical circumstances of the site: its soil fertility; its surface- and groundwater resources; its elevation, slope, and solar exposure; its climate; its minerals and energy resources; its suitability as habitat for flora and fauna; its scenic amenities and potential for outdoor recreation. The location of the site influences the economic feasibility of exploiting any of these characteristics, although remoteness may be overcome where the economic value of the resource is high, for example, oil and gas fields or high-quality ski slopes.

The value of land for agriculture is a complex function of soil type and quality, slope, drainage, location, and rainfall or irrigability (without considering external factors such as world price levels and economic conditions). Mineral development, where economically feasible, normally preempts agricultural use where surface disturbance due to strip mining is necessary. Where mineral or energy resources may be derived with minimal surface disturbance by means of tunnels or gas and oil wells, both farming and mineral extraction may coexist within the same tract of land.

Mineral rights are usually leased or sold to mining companies and thus are severed from ownership of the surface. This may lead to future problems of surface subsidence and collapse due to undermining. Acid mine drainage, which pollutes downstream water, is another harmful externality of surface coal extraction.

Water rights are defined by diverse legal doctrines that apply in different states and regions of the United States. East of the Mississippi and in certain western states, the doctrine of riparian rights prevails. "Riparian" refers to land adjoining a stream, lake, or tidal body of water. Owners of riparian land are vested under long-standing common law doctrine with special rights to use such water. Riparian owners may withdraw water for reasonable use, impound streams for water or hydroelectric power, build a wharf, discharge wastes, collect shellfish, and in other ways make economic use of the water as a resource.

The rights of each riparian owner, however, are constrained by an obligation not to substantially interfere with the enjoyment of similar rights of other riparians upstream and downstream. Riparian law was the customary principle for allocating water rights in areas of ample supply until the early 20th century. With the growth of urban water supply systems and large-scale sources of industrial and urban pollution, riparian law was inadequate for water resource management. Various public programs and policies have largely superseded the riparian doctrine to manage the quantity and quality of water resources (Trelease 1979).

In certain arid western states such as Colorado and Wyoming, water rights have been severed completely from the ownership of land and no riparian rights are recognized. Historically, this resulted from the need to assemble large quantities of water for agriculture and mining in areas that provided inadequate average stream flow and severe annual variations. Thus, landowners in the West must separately purchase the right to water and have no vested interest in streams that happen to flow across or past their land. This doctrine is known as *prior appropriation*. The contrast between eastern and western water rights law has long been recognized as a classic case of law being shaped by geographical context (Whittlesey 1935).

Other valuable material attributes of real property include a variety of natural resources such as timber, fruits, berries, herbs, nuts, maple sap, shellfish, finfish, wildlife, and so on. Hunting and fishing are however limited by state and local laws regarding species, size, season, and size of catch.

SPATIAL RIGHTS

Alternatively, the fee owner may choose to build on the land, that is, to enclose a portion of the air column above the site for usable interior space. Where geology and economics allow, such enclosure may proceed downward as well as upward from the land surface in the form of excavation for a basement, a parking garage, a shopping concourse, or an art gallery. The above-surface air column may be enclosed by a structure built on pilings or stilts so as to retain most of the surface or subsurface for a different purpose such as railroad tracks or a highway. Structures so elevated are referred to as air rights development.

The owner may choose to subdivide a structure into dwelling or commercial units that may be sold individually in fee simple as *condominiums*. In this way, the overall air column may be divided legally as well as physically. Condominiums above the first floor are units of real property that "float" in mid-air supported by the framework of the building. Ownership of a condominium unit ("condo") also involves a proportional ownership of the common elements of the overall building—its basement, exterior walls, roof, stairs, elevators, and the like. Those facilities are maintained by a condominium association whose costs are paid from monthly assessment fees charged to each condo owner.

The exploitation of real property as *space* is thus substantially different from the use of real property as *matter*. Of course, the material character of a site is not totally irrelevant to the type and cost of spatial development to which it is suited. Buildings must be physically situated on or above the land. Many sites are physically hazardous for development—for example, floodplains, coastal hazard areas, seismic faults, wetlands, and unstable slopes. But the private market tends to ignore such limitations, or tries to overcome them through engineering solutions in profitable locations. Thus, Boston's Back Bay, a former marsh, is home to the Prudential and John Hancock office towers, which stand on footings extending to bedrock. Canyons of the San Gabriel Mountains bordering the Los Angeles basin are filled with expensive homes that occasionally are destroyed in chaparral fires or debris flows from upslope (McPhee 1989). The willingness of Californians to risk earthquake hazards in their locational decisions is well known (Palm 1986).

Real property as space is thus an investor's abstraction: physical site limitations are the concern of the engineer and architect. Potential adverse effects on future site occupants, neighbors, community, region, or nation tend to be overlooked by the private market. There are, however, the red sticks.

Red Sticks: Duties of Real Property Ownership

NUISANCE

The most ancient duty of real property ownership in countries sharing the British common law tradition, as discussed in Chapter 3, is to refrain from creating a nuisance that interferes with the rights of adjoining property owners and/or the general public. Nuisance may be either private or public. A "private nuisance" is a harmful externality inflicted primarily on the occupants of neighboring property. Traditional forms of private nuisance include sickening odors, cutting off light and air, overflow of water, accumulation of wastes that harbor vermin and insects, or allowing trash or dust to blow onto neighboring property. Courts in individual lawsuits have recognized certain new forms of nuisance such as recurrent noise, raucous parties, floodlighting, windmill-driven generators, race tracks, and animal feedlots. In 1990, a trial court in Massachusetts held that ringing of a church bell every hour all night long was a nuisance to adjoining homeowners (who had moved there when the clock was inoperative).

A "public nuisance" is one that affects a wider area or the public at large, as in the emission of air or water pollution, conducting an immoral or antisocial business, such as maintaining a "crack house," or dumping hazardous wastes. The borderline between a private or public nuisance is not always clearcut. However, public nuisances may be defined by state or local law and thus comprise criminal offenses (Prosser 1971, ch. 15). Violation of an environmental statute, for example, on hazardous waste disposal, may be both a public and a private nuisance.

Private nuisances may be "enjoined" (prohibited) by a court upon suit of the injured party or parties. Civil nuisance suits, however, involve wide latitude for judicial discretion. The court attempts to "balance the equities" to determine the relative costs to the defendant and society of abating the activity in comparison with the harm to the plaintiff if the activity continues. If the plaintiff moved to the area after the harmful activity was underway, the court may deny relief because the plaintiff "came to the nuisance." Relief may also be denied if the plaintiff waited unreasonably long to file suit against the objectionable activity or is also creating a nuisance.

A Hypothetical Scenario.   When should "the law" step in? Not every harmful externality in a *geographical* sense comprises a *legal* nuisance. Some external harms may simply cut off an external benefit unfairly enjoyed, or may be relatively minor and left to the recipient to simply live with. Another Latin maxim refers to that as "damnum absque injuria"–harm without remedy. Consider the following hypothetical scenario as illustrated in Figure 4-2. Assuming no public zoning or other public regulations are in effect, *when should a court reasonably grant relief against A?*

1. Homeowner B enjoys the proximity of A's woods next door. B benefits from the shade, the privacy, the birdlife, and also the opportunity for his children and pets to cavort in A's woods and to gather firewood there.

2. A, after discovering B's unauthorized use of his property, builds a fence that deprives B's family of their access to the woods. B is thus "harmed" but can he complain legally of being denied the right to trespass?

3. A cuts down his woods, thus additionally depriving B of the external benefits of shade and natural surroundings. Should the law prevent this externality?

4. A constructs a house similar to that of B, who now loses his privacy and whose property declines in value. Should A be prevented from doing so?

5. Instead of a house, A builds an animal hospital that will involve 24-hour floodlighting, incessant barking, vehicular traffic, and the stench of the furnace in which deceased pets are cremated. Does this comprise an unreasonable externality that a court might find to be an actionable nuisance?

Very likely the earlier actions would be considered nonactionable harms–no legal relief would be available to B. Stage 5 however would

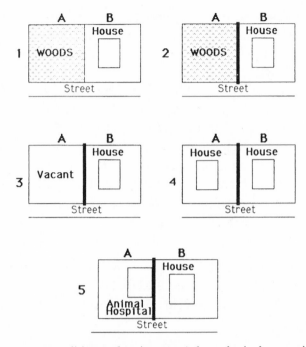

FIGURE 4-2 Externalities and nuisance: A hypothetical scenario. A inflicts externalities upon B. When may B validly claim judicial protection under the doctrine of nuisance?

likely be viewed as an "unreasonable" use of A's land causing damage to B that would be enjoined in a court (provided B files a suit). In the absence of public regulation or legal complaint by B, A would be free to continue the animal hospital. If B sues, however, a court might try to avoid closing the business entirely (such facilities are needed) by ordering changes in the hours of operation, perhaps a landscape buffer, and maybe move the crematorium elsewhere.

PROPERTY TAXES

Another unpleasant duty of a property owner is to pay all taxes and special assessments levied against the real estate. These include ad valorem taxes levied annually by the local municipality, county, and special districts within whose jurisdiction the property is situated. One-time charges in the form of special assessments are also the responsibility of the property owner. Special assessments are often charged for public improvements that benefit the real property in question, as in the case of sidewalk or street reconstruction, new sewers, water lines, or other facilities of localized, as distinct from citywide, benefits. (Taxes are discussed further in Chapter 6.)

PUBLIC REGULATIONS

Beyond nuisance and tax obligations, the landowner is confronted by a bewildering array of further public constraints in the form of land use and building regulations imposed at the local, state, and federal levels. These include, for example, building codes, zoning, subdivision regulations, wetland restrictions, seismic design requirements, floodplain regulations, and public nuisance laws. The rest of the book is largely concerned with such public limitations on private property usage.

Types of Owners and Legal Interests

Land may be owned by many kinds and combinations of owners. These may include individuals, spouses, partnerships, corporations (business or nonprofit); or the owners may be public entities, including federal, state, county, municipal, or special district agencies. Ownership may be divided among multiple parties each holding a fractional interest in the real property. For example, one-third of a parcel of land might be owned by a family partnership, and the other two-thirds by two spouses as *joint tenants* (when one dies, the other succeeds to his or her share). Real property is also subject to various claimants who hold interests less than fee—for example, tenants, lessees of specific rights, and even squatters.

To better appreciate the complexity of ownership, which may plague the best-intentioned plans for the future use of particular land (such as public open space), the following summarizes the types of legal interests that may be encountered.

Fee Simple Absolute

The highest and most complete interest in real property is known as the "fee simple absolute," also known as the fee simple or just the "fee." This concept involves both a geographical and a temporal dimension. As described in the foregoing, a fee simple interest in real property is three-dimensional, extending within the bounds of the parcel perimeter upward and downward, and indefinitely into the future. Land owned in fee may be sold, rented, given away, or devised to heirs by means of a will. According to Moynahan (1962, 29) the fee simple absolute "denotes the maximum of legal ownership, the greatest possible aggregate of rights, powers, privileges and immunities which a person may have in land."

The owner may divide the fee simple in several ways: (1) physical partition, (2) severance of specific usage rights, and (3) division in time. Physical partition of the land into two or more parcels allows a portion to be sold or given away and the rest retained. Farmers sometimes split off roadside building lots to raise cash, or may give them to offspring as homesites or for resale. This lowers the eventual inheritance taxes on the overall farm.

Second, the fee simple may be divided in terms of usage rights. For instance, the right to extract minerals such as oil or coal or to cut timber may be sold or leased to another party. In such cases, the owner is divested of the right to exploit these resources in exchange for a one-time payment or a series of royalty or lease payments over time.

Third, the fee simple may be split into time periods, creating both present and future interests held by different persons. Some examples follow.

Life Estates and Future Interests

Students of property law are exposed to the complexities of future interests and life estates. Such interests in real property result from the splitting of a fee simple into various time periods or "estates" by means of a will or trust. Typically, a will may specify that, upon the death of the owner, his or her property will pass to the spouse for that individual's lifetime and thereafter descend to surviving children. The surviving spouse thus receives a *life estate* consisting of the right to beneficial use of the real property for his or her remaining lifetime. Children living at that time are vested with a *future interest* in that they will inherit the property upon the death of the second parent. When that event occurs, the children's future interests automatically become present possessory interests in fee simple. Where more than one child is involved, each then owns an undivided fraction of the total fee simple, which is awkward to sell if cash is needed. Alternatively, the property may be physically partitioned and allocated by mutual agreement, or it may be sold and the proceeds divided among the heirs.

Spouses often hold real property as joint tenants with rights of "survivorship." When either spouse dies the survivor automatically is vested with a fee simple ownership of the property (subject to any existing leases, liens, or other limitations).

The complexities of life tenancies and future interests need not detain us further. It is enough to say that ownership of property may be divided among multiple parties, some with present and some with future interests, some possessory and some contingent on a future event. All of these must be ascertained through a title search when the property is bought or sold.

Leaseholds and Tenancies

Owners of real property may obtain income from their land by renting or leasing it for various purposes. The words "rental" and "lease" are interchangeable, although they respectively suggest terms of less than, or more than, a year in duration. In either case, a written agreement between the landlord on the one hand and tenant or lessee on the other specifies the duration of the arrangement and the rights and duties of each party. In the case of an apartment rental, the landlord normally must provide clean, livable space while the tenant must promise to preserve the premises in good order and to pay rent on a regular schedule. Provision for utilities and heat should be specified in the rental or lease agreement. The owner remains liable for the payment of property taxes and conformity to local zoning and other public regulations. Either party may withdraw upon notice to the other party according to the terms of the agreement. Shorter rental agreements such as a "month-to-month" contract may be verbal rather than written. This leaves the renter with no protection against eviction or rent increase, subject to a month's notice.

Farmland is frequently rented on a year-to-year basis where the owner does not wish to farm the land but wants to keep it available for sale when needed. Rental also helps the tenant farmer who needs extra land but cannot afford to buy it. Longer-term leases are used for mineral extraction, recreational facilities, and forestry where the lessee needs greater security to protect a major investment in equipment and labor.

A less formal, temporary arrangement is the "license." Under a license, the owner may allow someone to occupy or use the land indefinitely by virtue of friendship, family relationship, or other reason. Normally a written document is not used and rental payments may or may not be involved. The distinguishing feature of a license as compared with a formal rental or leasehold is that the occupant may be required to leave at any time by the owner. This situation is sometimes called a "tenancy at will."

Easements

Easements are limited interests in real property held by individuals other than the principal owner, or by the general public. Easements are most easily described in terms of the purposes they commonly serve. Typical kinds of easements include:

1. *Utility easements*   Corridors for utility lines, pipelines, or other purposes may be established permanently across private land through purchase of easements providing rights of access along a defined narrow strip or right of way.

2. *Easements of access*   Building lots lacking frontage on a public way may be accessible by means of an easement granting the right to cross intervening property owned by another person. (Zoning laws, however, may prohibit construction on a lot with inadequate frontage, regardless of easements.)

3. *Recreation easements*   Public access to rivers, coastal shorelines, ponds, or upland areas may require easements of access across intervening private land.

Each of these types of easements involves a formal conveyance of a right of access to some party, for example, a power company, a neighbor, or a public recreation agency. In the absence of such an easement, the desired access could occur only by illegal trespass or by license, which could be revoked at any time.

To obtain legal access on a continuing basis, the party desiring such benefit may offer to purchase an easement from the property owner. As with a leasehold, an easement is expressed in a formal written document that sets forth the terms of the agreement, its duration, the obligations of each party, and provisions for its termination. An easement cannot be revoked by a subsequent buyer of the property. The buyer thus receives title to the land subject to the easement unless the holder of the latter is willing to release it.

The property over which the easement extends is referred to as the "burdened estate," while adjoining land that is served by the easement is the "benefited estate." In the case of a public recreation easement, no specific land is benefited, and the easement is said to extend to the public "in gross."

A different kind of easement of considerable interest to students of land use control is the "scenic easement," otherwise known as an "easement of development rights," or a "conservation easement." This device does not necessarily involve access to the property burdened by such an easement. It does create rights in parties other than the owner to whom the easement runs, to prevent the owner from altering the character of the premises through development, subdivision, cutting of timber, or other means, as provided in the legal instrument creating the easement. This is sometimes referred to as a "negative easement" in that the owner of the land subject to the easement is prevented from doing certain things.

Scenic or conservation easements are commonly used to preserve the natural or open character of particular land while leaving legal title in the original owner. In this manner, a community or private conservation organization that seeks to preserve open land may pay owners to convey a scenic easement that binds them; existing uses such as a residence, farming, or woodlot management may be continued and modest changes or additions to existing buildings may be permitted under the terms of the easement. Basically, such an easement provides a flexible tool for preserving open land by agreement with the owner without transferring ownership of the entire property to a public agency. Usually the property tax valuation of the land is reduced in light of the scenic easement. If the owner is willing to donate a scenic easement to a charitable or public entity, a federal tax deduction may be claimed by the donor.

Covenants

As derived from English usage beginning in the 17th century, "covenants" are commitments or promises contained in a legal agreement (contract of sale or lease) affecting the ownership of real property.

Developers usually include various restrictive covenants in deeds transferring the ownership of residential building lots. By accepting covenants, the lot buyer promises to use the lot in a specified manner, for example, to construct a single-family home, to install and maintain landscaping, to refrain from nuisance-type activities, and in general to use the land in an orderly and considerate manner. Since each lot buyer in a subdivision must agree to an identical set of covenants, each is considered to acquire rights against other lot buyers to enforce the covenants, even after the developer has disappeared from the scene. The lot buyers are then said to be "third-party beneficiaries" of the original agreement between each buyer and the developer. Covenants are said to "run with the land" and are enforceable against subsequent purchasers of the property to which they apply. (The buyer is presumed to have notice of any covenants, easements, or other restrictions that have been properly recorded with the registry of deeds.)

Covenants are a powerful tool of private land use control since they are created by voluntary (but irrevocable) agreement between a buyer and a seller. They may reinforce public zoning and other land use regulations and indeed may deal with subjects beyond the scope of zoning, such as landscaping and architectural design, pets, and the decibel level of stereo systems.

Enforcement of restrictive covenants is justified by the fact that they are contractual in nature and accepted voluntarily. However, once a covenant is in effect, it may be eventually subject to termination by a court on the ground that conditions in the area have so changed that the covenant is rendered meaningless. In this way it differs from an easement, which normally is permanent unless otherwise specified when it is created.

Liens

Liens are basically claims against real property asserted by parties to whom the owner owes money. If property taxes are unpaid, the local or county government will file a tax lien against the property and eventually seize it for sale. A painter, carpenter, or other contractor who is owed money for work done on a premises may file a "mechanic's lien" against the property. Like a tax lien, the mechanic's lien may eventually be "perfected" by a court order requiring the property to be sold to satisfy the debt. Anyone purchasing real property must be careful that unsatisfied liens are cleared by the seller before transfer of the property so that the buyer will not acquire the outstanding debts.

Options

An option is a contract between a landowner and a prospective buyer under which the latter has a right to buy the property at an agreed price within a stated time period. An option allows a potential buyer to prevent the land from being sold to someone else pending decisions regarding such matters as financing and zoning. The cost of an option is a small fraction of the total price, perhaps 10 percent. But it is not refunded if the full price is not paid within the agreed time period. The option price is usually deducted from the sales price.

Options are useful to public and private agencies seeking to preserve open land. If a parcel of land is about to be subdivided or developed, the agency may seek to purchase an option to maintain the status quo for a few weeks or months to see if funding can be obtained to buy the tract. There is, however, no obligation on the part of the owner to sell an option and thus tie up the marketability of the property. If no option can be obtained, a public agency may use its eminent domain power to take the property upon payment of a price determined in court. A private agency or individual, however, has no such power.

Acquisition and Disposition

Real property is "alienable," that is, it may be transferred from one party to another. The usual ways in which real property may be alienated, either voluntarily or involuntarily, are (1) purchase or sale, (2) gift, (3) inheritance, (4) involuntary forfeiture, and (5) eminent domain (condemnation).

The marketability of real property through purchase or sale is a key element of the value of property as an economic asset. The law of property seeks to promote marketability by providing an orderly and secure process by which title may be transferred from one party to another.

Normally the conveyance of ownership of real property is a two-stage process. The first stage involves the execution of a *contract* between the buyer and seller specifying the property in question, the price to be paid by the buyer, and any covenants or commitments to be performed by either party.

The second stage is the *closing*, when the legal deed to the property is transferred to the buyer in exchange for the purchase price or promissory notes (if the seller is financing the buyer). Normally, the buyer borrows a significant part of the purchase price from a bank or other lending institution. To secure its loan, the lending institution requires a *mortgage* or promise by the borrower to repay the lender in regular monthly installments. Failure to do so will result in foreclosure by the lender and sale of the property to recover the outstanding balance of the loan plus interest. Thus the mortgage agreement between the buyer and bank must occur prior to the closing between the buyer and seller. Immediately after the closing, the deed and mortgage instrument are *recorded* at the county Registry of Deeds so that the respective interests of the lender and buyer are protected.

Real property may be given to anyone whom the owner selects. Frequently, portions of property belonging to a parent may be conveyed as a gift to children or other relatives. Real property may be donated to nonprofit organizations for charitable or conservation purposes. It may also be donated to a governmental agency. In the case of a gift to a public agency or a qualified private organization (for example, Massachusetts Audubon Society, The Nature Conservancy, and so on), the value of the gift may be deducted from the donor's taxable income. To be valid, a gift of land must be legally accepted by the recipient. Occasionally, land may be offered to a public entity that is unwilling to accept it due to future maintenance costs and loss of tax revenue. No gift occurs in that case.

Real property, like personal property, may be devised by the owner through a will that is properly signed and witnessed. Where no valid will can be found, property of a decedent is inherited by "next of kin" under state law. If no relatives can be found, property escheats to the state.

The value of inherited property is reduced by death taxes levied by federal, state, and sometimes local governments. A branch of property law involves the establishment of trusts and other devices for conserving the value of the decedent's estate by minimizing taxes.

One form of involuntary forfeiture is "foreclosure" by a lender when a borrower fails to make mortgage payments on time. This is, unfortunately, common during periods of economic recession. Similarly, the county or municipal government may foreclose on property that is subject to unpaid taxes.

A different kind of forfeiture occurs through the process of *adverse possession*. This refers to the occupancy of land by a squatter for a lengthy period of time. If the occupancy is "open and notorious," and without consent of the owner, the occupant may claim legal ownership after a period of years specified by state law. The purpose of adverse possession is to protect *squatter's rights*, where the owner takes no interest in the land and someone else works hard to make productive use of the land. While this is chiefly a doctrine affecting rural land, urban "squatting" in abandoned apartment buildings occurs in older cities.

A *prescriptive easement* is a form of adverse possession asserted by the general public rather than a private occupant. It arises where the public uses a footpath, vehicular right of way, beach, or other private land without permission of the private owner. If continued for the statutory period, the owner may be precluded by statute or common law from preventing the continuation of the public trespass. But the public right is limited to the particular right-of-way or tract itself and does not extend to the rest of the owner's property.

Eminent domain ("condemnation") is the taking of title to private land by a public agency or publicly regulated utility company. This topic is discussed in connection with public acquisition in Chapter 9.

Land Use Conversion

The development of land is a crucial and essentially irreversible decision. Once occupied by buildings and pavement, a parcel of land is unlikely to revert to agriculture or other material uses (except possibly subsurface mining). Economically, land that is ripe for development or is in fact developed is many times more valuable than agricultural or other rural land. While an acre of average cropland on the urban fringe might be worth up to $5,000 or so for farm purposes, the same acre might be worth $100,000 or more if suitable for three or four residential building lots. If the site could be developed with a multistory office building, the same acre might be worth over a million dollars.

In an idealized private land market, the decision as to how land should be utilized, and particularly when it should be developed, is theoretically up to the private fee simple owner. As described in textbooks on urban and economic geography (Palm 1981), the owner is motivated by considerations of "economic rent" or the desire to maximize the economic return from the use of the land, which in turn is determined in part by the location of the land within the metropolitan land market.

Absent public intervention, the private market allocates land to that use which optimizes the "economic rent" that can be realized at the location in question. Before the 1970s, location was chiefly evaluated in terms of accessibility to a downtown central business district (CBD). Today, distance (or driving time) to an interstate highway interchange, regional office park, airport, or recreational amenity such as a seashore or ski resort may strongly influence the timing and objectives of land investment decisions as well. According to a cliché of the real estate business, the three most important determinants of land value are "location, location, and location."

But location can no longer be regarded as a question only of distance to anything. The political or institutional context within which the landowner and other participants in the development process make their respective decisions may outweigh the importance of distance per se. Kaiser and Weiss (1970) identify three sets of factors that underlie the timing and form of development:

1. *Contextual factors* The political and socioeconomic characteristics of the community and region

2. *Property characteristics* The physical and institutional aspects of the site itself

3. *Decision agent characteristics* For example, willingness to take risks or respect for the natural qualities of the land

Among these sets of factors, the public sector looms large, both at the community/regional scale and at the site level. Distance to employment is not irrelevant, but zoning, taxation, development incentives, natural hazards, and environmental regulations may matter even more.

Before turning to the public sector, there is one more topic to be considered in this review of the private sector—namely, the legal geography of property and political boundaries.

Where Is Land?—Legal Boundary Descriptions

Anyone owning or buying real estate must know exactly which land is theirs. Similarly, governmental bodies must know their exact boundaries. A *legal description* is a precise means of defining the boundaries of a parcel of real property or a unit of political jurisdiction and thereby pinpointing its location and size. This subject provides a refreshing dose of precision in contrast to the somewhat vague concepts that pervade discussions of land use policy. While routine use of legal descriptions is the province of the lawyer more than of land use planners and geographers, anyone concerned with the use of land must understand why and how it is delineated legally.

Uses of Legal Descriptions

Legal descriptions of property and political boundaries serve several purposes. First, legal descriptions permit precise delineation of the boundaries and extent of private property. This is crucial to anyone investing in real property who must know exactly which land they own. At many dollars per square foot on the urban fringe and much more in prime building locations, buyers must be assured they are receiving all the land that they bargained for. Similarly, mortgage lenders must be assured that the real property that is security for a loan is exactly the same land that the borrower is buying. Where doubt exists, a survey must be made to delineate the boundaries of the parcel in question.

A second use of legal descriptions is to *avoid disputes* between adjoining property owners regarding their common boundaries. Legal descriptions sometimes refer directly to adjoining parcels by name of the owner to ensure that no overlap exists. Thus, one boundary of a parcel may be described as "the south boundary of property owned by one C.W. Miller." Although Miller may subsequently transfer his land to someone else, it is clear that the boundary of the parcel at the time it was owned by Miller is to serve as the boundary of the adjoining property. However, a dispute may arise as to where Miller's boundary really was.

Certainty as to the location of boundaries also promotes *efficiency* in the use of land. Adjoining property owners may use their entire land area to the parcel boundaries without fear of trespassing on neighboring land.

A fourth use of legal descriptions is to identify the ownership of land for purposes of *property taxation*. Without precise boundary descriptions, some land might be taxed to more than one person and other land might escape taxation altogether.

Types of Legal Descriptions

Three types of legal descriptions are prevalent in the United States: (1) metes and bounds, (2) descriptions based on the Federal Land Survey, and (3) lots numbered on recorded subdivision plats. All three types are used today in various locations and circumstances.

Metes and bounds define the perimeter of a parcel of land through a series of straight-line segments and references to physical features (see Figure 4-3). Typically, the survey directions begin at one corner of the parcel, which is marked at the time of survey by a stone monument, iron pin, or other device. From this starting point, each straight-line segment is defined by a precise compass direction and distance (usually expressed in surveyor's measurement units—chains, rods, and links). Corners or points where the boundary changes direction may be marked by further monuments or pins.

Physical features such as streams, roads, or railroads may be mentioned in a metes and bounds description. Questions may arise concerning changes in stream channel, shorelines, or road alignments.

Two further difficulties with early metes and bounds surveys appear in this description of the western boundary of Massachusetts, prepared in 1787:

Beginning at a monument erected in 1731 by commissioners from Connecticut and New York, distant from the Hudson River twenty miles, and running north 15 degrees, 12' 9" east 15 miles 41 chains and 79 links to a red or black oak tree marked by said commis-

FIGURE 4-3   Excerpt from a "metes and bounds" property survey.

sioners, which said line was run as the magnetic needle pointed in 1787."

Quoted in U.S. Geological Survey 1976, p. 13.

First, the reference to a "red or black oak tree," besides being botanically uncertain, leaves the boundary unmarked with the eventual disappearance of said tree. Second, the use of magnetic compass directions, which was universal at this time, left uncertainty as to the degree of compass error or divergence between magnetic and true north, which varies from one place to another on the earth's surface. Normally a survey using a magnetic compass would note the "deviation" or departure from true north for the area in question.

Metes and bounds legal descriptions thus present many problems when old boundaries are resurveyed. Error was introduced from various sources including inaccuracy of instruments, careless procedures, change of physical conditions, and illegibility of early field notes. Yet property and political boundaries laid out in early times must be followed as faithfully as possible. The modern surveyor is armed with an array of new technology, including geographic position systems (GPS), satellite imagery, and laser beams. Despite all this paraphernalia, where an ancient boundary must be redrawn, the modern surveyors must attempt to follow exactly in the footsteps of their predecessors.

Metes and bounds descriptions are cumbersome and susceptible to mistakes. A small error in direction, "west" instead of "east," for instance, will send the boundary off into the blue, and no area is thereby enclosed. A major source of error is simply the copying by hand or typing of a metes and bounds description. The metes and bounds system was too laborious to serve the needs of settlers of the trans-Appalachian public domain. Accordingly, at the dawn of its existence, the nation quickly devised a new and simpler system: the Federal Land Survey.

The *Federal Land Survey* system was probably the most lasting and influential achievement of the pre-Constitutional Confederation. It also provided the most visible evidence of the "impress of central authority" on land use in the United States west of the original 13 states. The basic principles for the Federal Land Survey were established in the Land Ordinance of 1785 and the survey itself commenced in that year. From its "point of beginning" where the Ohio River crosses the western border of Pennsylvania, the survey eventually extended westward as far as the Aleutian Islands of Alaska and southward to Key West, Florida (U.S. Geological Survey 1976).

The basic geographic unit of the federal survey is the *township*–a near rectangle six miles on each side containing 36 "sections" of one square mile each. Townships are identified with respect to "principal meridians" and "baselines," which are designated for each state in which the survey is used. Townships are located with reference to their positions east or west of a principal meridian and north or south of the designated baseline.

Principal meridians and baselines may continue across several states. The 40th parallel is the baseline for part of Illinois and also for Kansas

A Hypothetical Excerpt from the Federal Survey System

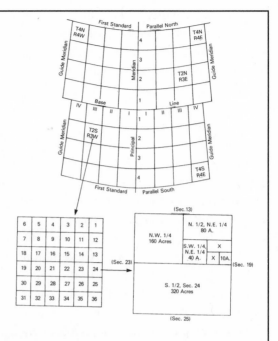

For states or portions of states surveyed under the Federal Survey System, one or more east-west base lines and north-south principal meridians have been designated. Units in the upper diagram represent individual survey townships of 36 square miles each, designated with reference to the applicable base line and principal meridian. At lower left, one township is broken out—in the second tier south of the base line and the third range west of the principal meridian. At lower right, one square mile "section" of this township, "Sec. 24," is further subdivided into parcels designated as fractions or fractions of fractions of section 24.

By way of illustration, let us determine the legal description of Parcel X in the diagram above. First, the fractional portion of section 24 is expressed as:

The north half of the southeast quarter of the northeast quarter of section 24 plus the southwest quarter of the southeast quarter of the northeast quarter of section 24.

Next, the township containing section 24 must be located with reference to the overall survey grid: "Township 2 south, Range 3 west of the principal meridian." The full legal description abbreviated as per custom is:

N. 1/2 of the S.E. 1/4 of the N.E. 1/4 of sec. 24 plus the S.W. 1/4 of the S.E. 1/4 of the N.E. 1/4 of sec. 24 of Twp. 2S, Range 3W of the Principal Meridian in __County, State of __, an area of 30 acres.

and Nebraska, which it separates. Farther west, the same parallel serves as the baseline for Colorado (Boulder's Baseline Street lies on this parallel). In some areas local principal meridians and baselines were established to serve the needs of early mining or other settlements—for example, at Grand Junction, Colorado and the Mormon region bordering Great Salt Lake in Utah.

The rectangular federal survey has been described as "a striking example of geometry triumphant over physical geography" (Pattison 1970, 1). Simply, the curvature of the earth dictates that townships will be trapezoidal not square, since their northern boundaries must be shorter than their southern borders. This problem is resolved by offsetting the north-south boundaries of ranges of townships at periodic intervals north and south of the baseline (see box). Other problems arise from natural obstacles such as large water bodies and mountain ranges.

Despite these complications, the Federal Land Survey proved indispensable to the disposition and management of the federal lands. (See Chapter 11.) Altogether some 700 million acres have been transferred out of the public domain, most of it in areas covered by the federal survey. The survey permits precise legal descriptions of parcels of land to be expressed in terms of township, section, and fractions of sections. The 640-acre section is an ideal unit for land transfer and subdivision into fractional parcels.

Obviously this system is far superior to metes and bounds for describing large tracts of land in sparsely settled areas. The federal survey has been most useful in the settlement of level or moderately hilly lands between the Appalachians and the Rocky Mountains. Anyone flying over the nation's heartland on a clear day witnesses the physical legacy of the federal survey in the infinite pattern of rectangular farms, fields, road systems, and urban development, all conforming to the pattern of townships and sections, baselines, and meridians.

Local variations require departures from the strict use of federal survey directions. Legal descriptions for land bordering rivers, lakes, or tidal waters may refer to that feature as a boundary. Metes and bounds may be used where necessary to describe irregular tracts that do not fall precisely into survey fractions.

Urbanization of land covered by the federal survey is shaped by the preexisting grid system. The older street system of midwest and western cities follows section and half-section boundaries. Development after the

1950s, however, was more oriented to the new interstate highway system, which cut through cities without regard to the survey grid. The monotonous results of grid-plan development yielded to a new look in suburban growth after World War II. As influenced by the Garden City movement, this new look emphasized curving streets, irregular lot shapes, and abundant landscaping and greenery. The spread of the residential subdivision brought with it another system for describing the precise location of parcels of land.

A third system of legal description that is today employed throughout the United States is the *subdivision plat*. A subdivision plat is literally a map of a tract of land that is to be divided into smaller lots for sale to individual buyers (see Figure 9-1). Subdivisions usually anticipate residential development, although land is sometimes subdivided for commercial or industrial parks. Buildings may be constructed by the subdivider (who then serves as developer) prior to sale of the improved lots to the ultimate buyer. Alternatively, land may be subdivided for sale as a vacant lot with the buyer responsible for constructing a suitable building. (See Chapter 9.)

In either event the proposed plat (or plan) of subdivision must be submitted for approval to the local planning authorities in accordance with state law. The subdivider must conform with local subdivision regulations concerning street layout, width, and paving; utility placement; drainage; and other details of project development. Once the plan is approved, it is filed with the county recorder of deeds, like any other instrument affecting land title.

As individual lots within the approved subdivision are sold they may be simply described by lot number, as shown on a subdivision plat recorded on a certain date in a certain book and page at the County Registry of Deeds. The plat on file provides exact survey dimensions of each lot. There is no need for a lengthy metes and bounds or federal survey legal description in the deed for each lot (although the lot boundaries must be precisely described in the original plat). (See further discussion in Chapter 9.)

Recording of Legal Interests

Precise legal descriptions are necessary, but not sufficient, to ensure that land may be efficiently bought, sold, and utilized. Equally important is a public record of land ownership and all claims against each parcel of land. Public knowledge of the precise legal status of title to real property is vital. With vast sums of money at stake, the buyer and mortgage lender must be able to ascertain whether they are receiving "clear title" from the seller. Defects that cloud the title include potential claims under wills of former owners, tax and creditor liens, easements, unexpired options, and other irregularities. Once such defects are identified, the seller is required to eliminate them or adjust the sale price to gain the buyer's consent to accept them.

Such claims are discovered through a *title search*. All deeds, probated wills, subdivision plans, liens, options, and other documents affecting title to real property must be filed with the registry of deeds for the county in which the land is located. Claims based on nonrecorded documents are usually not enforceable, but the buyer is presumed to have notice of all claims on record (caveat emptor).

All recorded documents are listed under the name of the owner then in possession of the premises. Past claims may be located by tracing the chain of title backward starting with the current owner to see what has been recorded under each owner's name concerning the property in question. The seller is expected to provide an abstract of title, which is checked by an attorney for the buyer and mortgage lender. Many states also require a borrower to purchase a title insurance policy to protect the lender against undiscovered claims.

Conclusion

This chapter has briefly summarized the institution of real property in the United States, including the rights and duties of the property owner and the purpose and forms of legal descriptions for specifying property boundaries. Such a background is necessary in a book concerned primarily with public land use control for two reasons. First, the common law of real property is itself a system of land use control. The long-established rights and duties of ownership, the procedures for acquiring and alienating land, and the recording of interests in real property using exact legal descriptions all comprise a de facto system for putting land to use. Before public land use controls were introduced in the late 19th century, private property rights were basically the "only game in town." The abuses fostered by that system in terms of overcrowding, unsanitary conditions, and a variety of harmful externalities on neighboring areas led to the assertion of public powers to constrain the excesses of the private land use system. But public controls remain reactive, negative, and supplementary; the private property owner and investor still retain most of the initiative in land use conversion.

Second, understanding of the legal nature of land is as important to those involved in land planning, acquisition, and management as for a doctor to understand the working of the human body. Land is more frequently understood in terms of its physical parameters: geology, geomorphology, hydrology, climate, and vegetation. But overlaying the physical terrain is a "legal terrain" of diverse interests in land. Public land use control programs must cope with the latter as with the former. While detailed knowledge of ownership of land is not requisite for "broad-brush" zoning, the administration of land use controls at the level of individual parcels and developments requires recognition and understanding of the nuts and bolts of property ownership. This chapter therefore serves as a foundation for the discussion of governmental authority to influence the private use of land, as will be considered in later chapters.

References

Kaiser, E.J., and S.F. Weiss. 1970. "Public Policy and the Residential Development Process." *Journal of the American Institute of Planners* 36(1): 30–37.

McPhee, J. 1989. *The Control of Nature.* New York: Farrar, Straus & Giroux.

Moynahan, C.J. 1962. *Introduction to the Law of Real Property.* St. Paul: West Publishing Co.

Palm, R. 1986. "Coming Home." *Annals of the American Association of Geographers.* 76(4): 469–479.

attison, W. 1970. *Beginnings of the American Rectangular Land Survey System: 1784–1800.* Columbus: Ohio Historical Society.

osser, W.L. 1971. *Handbook of the Law of Torts* 4th ed. St. Paul: West Publishing Co.

Trelease, F.J. 1979. *Cases and Materials on Water Law*. St. Paul: West Publishing Co.

U.S. Geological Survey. 1976. *Boundaries of the United States and the Several States*. Professional Paper No. 909. Washington: U.S. Government Printing Office.

Whittlesey, D.W. 1935. "The Impress of Effective Central Authority on the Landscape." *Annals of the Association of American Geographers* 25(1): 25–97.

CHAPTER 5 / Local Governments in the United States

Introduction

The modern political geography of urban America evolved from the English historical precedents discussed in Chapter 3. In particular, the medieval municipal corporation, as adapted to a variety of geographical settings and cultural preferences, became the basic building block of the American local political landscape. It was earlier described in Chapter 3 as a "legal person that could own land, make and enforce local laws, sue or be sued, and exist indefinitely until terminated by process of law." The same characteristics, with a few embellishments, apply as well to contemporary municipal governments. This chapter examines the geographical and legal nature of these ubiquitous but often disregarded participants in the shaping of the American metropolitan landscape.

Geographic Origins and Diffusion

The evolution of municipal institutions in America, while based in part on precedents transplanted from England, was strongly influenced by the physical and cultural circumstances of colonial settlement. Thus, differences among the colonies in terms of factors such as geomorphology, climate, religion, and economic organization yielded contrasting forms of local governments. Although the original reasons for these variations have long since disappeared, historical differences in form, function, and terminology survive to the present time.

The New England Town

The New England town was the earliest form of local government to appear in the American colonies. It has been justly celebrated as ". . . not only the most original but also the most democratic and, perhaps for that reason , . . [it has displayed] remarkable power of survival" (Wager 1950, 46). Despite its origin as a refuge for religious dissidents, colonial New England was noted for its intolerance of individualism, as portrayed in Arthur Miller's play "The Crucible." Nevertheless, paradoxically, the New England town was to approach the ideal of participatory democracy as closely as any governmental institution devised in this nation. And its continuity may be attested by anyone who ventures to the north country in late March to attend an annual town meeting. The officers, procedures, customs, and even some of the issues debated date back to the 17th century.

Circumstances of early settlement that shaped the evolution of the New England town included (1) a common religious bond–Puritanism; (2) a strong sense of independence and defiance of higher authority (other than God); (3) a harsh climate; (4) an intractable terrain requiring cooperative effort for productive utilization; and (5) fear of Indian attack. These factors jointly influenced the establishment of small, compact settlements often widely separated from each other. "The Puritan concept of community presupposed a clustering of people, a physical grouping that would enhance interaction and social cohesion" (Meinig 1986, 104).

These early settlements were closely knit through ties of family, religion, and common purpose in converting the surrounding land to pasture and cropland. Dwellings were clustered in villages, close to the meeting house, which served both civil and ecclesiastical purposes. Today, in many old New England towns the "first church" and town hall stand side by side. Each town regarded itself as a self-governing institution, beholden to neither the colonial assembly nor the Crown. In some cases, these claims were supported by formal grants or charters; in others, they were simply uncontested. In either case, towns generally went their own ways.

From earliest settlement, the New England town served not only as a unit of political, religious, and social organization, but as a resource management entity as well. The historian Samuel Eliot Morrison (1965,

70) describes the allocation of land and water resources within the typical town as follows:

> A committee was appointed to satisfy Indian claimants, to settle on a village site, and lay out lots. Home lots and the meeting house, which served both as church and town hall, were laid out around a village green, with a surrounding belt of planting lots for growing crops. Salt meadows on the coast, or river meads in the interior, valuable for the wild grass which could be cut and stored for winter forage, were laid out in long strips and usually cultivated in common. The rest of the township for many years remained the property of the community, where anyone could cut firewood and timber, or pasture cattle.

The pattern of land tenure varied considerably from one town to another. Milford, Connecticut allocated several dispersed parcels of irregular size, shape, and quality to each founding family. Connecticut River towns such as Wethersfield and Springfield allocated long, narrow strips extending perpendicular to the river (Figure 5-1). The quantity of land allotted to each family was not necessarily equal—differences in position and wealth were recognized (and the more prominent citizens presumably served on the town council) (Meinig 1986, 104). But there appears to have been an effort, as in the feudal manor of England, to allocate to each household a cross section of the available resources, including arable bottomland, upland pasture, and steep, rocky land for wood and game.

Over time, the original pattern of land allocation was drastically transformed as family holdings were split by conveyance or inheritance or augmented by purchase (either from the town's own reserve lands or from other households). Certain individual proprietors, such as William Pyncheon, the founder of Springfield, Massachusetts, amassed sizable personal holdings through direct grants from the colonial assembly. These lands were profitably conveyed to settlers, like selling lots in western land developments to northeastern urbanites today. In the 18th century, most New England towns settled were founded by individual proprietors or speculators who laid out roads, lots, and sites for churches and schools and then sold farm units to the public.

FIGURE 5-1 Types of colonial New England town centers. *Source:* McManis, 1975. Reproduced by permission of Oxford University Press.

Early New England settlements maintained strict control of their population growth. As an early form of "growth management," towns limited the right of outsiders to settle within their corporate limits (Porter 1922, 31). Unwanted residents were forced to leave the community. When land became scarce, new towns split off from older ones. According to Morrison (1965, 70): "When members of a village community felt crowded for space, they petitioned the colonial assembly for a new township, the ideal size being six square miles." Many New England towns were spawned through splitting large territories into smaller ones (McManis 1975, 62). In this manner, the closely linked institutions of church and town could replicate themselves in each new settlement.

Once it reached a sufficient size to support a minister and the other local needs, towns achieved governmental status upon incorporation by the colonial (or later, state) legislature. From then on, towns theoretically served as governments of, by, and for their inhabitants.

Tidewater Counties

The Tidewater region of coastal Maryland and Virginia fostered an entirely different system of local government administration based on the county. According to the perceptive Alexis de Tocqueville (1832/1969, 81):

> We have seen that in Massachusetts the township is the mainspring of public administration. It is the center of men's interests and of their affections. But this ceases to be so as one travels down to those states in which good education is not universally spread and where, as a result, there are fewer potential administrators and less assurance that the township will be wisely governed. Hence, the farther one goes from New England, the more the county tends to take the place of the township in communal life. The county becomes the great administrative center and the intermediary between the government and the plain citizen.

Many of the factors that contributed to the prevalence of the town in New England were absent farther south. The climate was mild. Soils were level, easily worked, and relatively free of glacial rubble, which figures so prominently in the landscape and character of New England. The lengthy shoreline of Chesapeake Bay, deeply incised by navigable estuaries, afforded convenient maritime routes connecting the region's hinterland with England and other overseas destinations. The native populations of the area were relatively friendly, obviating the need for compact, protective communities.

Moreover, the primary impetus toward settlement of the Tidewater region was economic rather than religious. The function of the town as a religious community did not spread to the south. And economically, towns were unnecessary because cultivation of the tobacco staple was conducted on plantations, widely separated, and largely self-sufficient. In the words of Thomas Jefferson (1782/1944, 227):

> We have no townships. Our country being much intersected with navigable waters, and trade brought generally to our doors, instead of our being obliged to go in quest of it, has probably been one of the causes why we have no towns of any consequence. Williamsburg,

which till the year 1780 was the seat of our government, never contained above 1800 inhabitants; and Norfolk, the most populous town we ever had, contained but 6000. . . .

Maryland and Virginia both adopted laws around 1680 to establish new port and market settlements. These acts authorized trustees appointed in each county to acquire through eminent domain the sites, approximately 100 acres in size, from their plantation owners and to lay out towns thereon. The width of streets and the size of lots were specified in the authorizing act, an extraordinary early example of town planning legislation. However, only one of these towns—Norfolk, Virginia—thrived. In Jefferson's pithy words quoted earlier: ". . . the *laws* have said there shall be towns; but nature has said there shall not, and they remain unworthy of enumeration" (p. 227).

The county thus characterized the Plantation South as the town characterized New England. Evolving from distinct geographical conditions, each institution reflected and in turn helped to shape the culture and land use patterns of the region that it served.

The Prairie Synthesis

In the late 18th and early 19th centuries, the New England town and the Tidewater county would combine in the settlement of the "Northwest Territories" beyond the Ohio River. The clash and eventual merger of the two traditions was most dramatic in Illinois, whose earliest settlers migrated from the southern portions of the Atlantic seaboard via the Ohio River. Illinois' first census in 1818 reported that 75 percent of its population was from Kentucky, Tennessee, Virginia, and Maryland (Billington 1970, 91). The county thus arrived first in Illinois and Indiana.

In 1825 the Erie Canal from "Albany to Buffalo" (as the song goes) opened. The canal shifted the center of migration northward as New Englanders and New Yorkers followed the new route westward. "Now the Great Lakes, not the Ohio River, formed the pathway toward the setting sun. . . . In 1834, 80,000 people followed this route westward" (Billington, 92).

The northeasterners brought their towns with them, which quickly spread across the northern plains in modified form as the middle western township or "civil township." In Illinois, this institution was soon adopted within most but not all of the preexisting counties. Thus, the New England and Southern traditions of local government found common ground in Illinois and its neighboring states.

The middle western township, however, only remotely resembled its ancestor, the New England town. By the time of the opening of the Erie Canal in 1825, the concept of the "pure" New England town had already been modified—some might say debased—in New York, New Jersey, and Pennsylvania (Porter 1922, 3). The township lost its roots in the town meeting as it moved westward and became merely a county administrative unit. Civil townships were eventually established in 16 states outside New England: New York, New Jersey, Pennsylvania, Ohio, Indiana, Michigan, Wisconsin, and Iowa, and in portions of Illinois, Missouri, Kansas, Nebraska, Minnesota, North and South Dakota, and Washington State (Wager 1950, 35). These are essentially relics of pioneer sentiment that sought to transplant the form, if not the substance, of town government to the prairie sod and beyond.

Civil or governmental townships must not be confused with "Congressional" or "survey" townships established under the Federal Land Survey described in Chapter 4. The federal survey township is usually a rectangle six miles square. It is numbered rather than named and has no corporate governmental status as such.

But to confuse the issue further, "civil townships" or other governmental units in states covered by the federal survey were sometimes established according to "survey township" boundaries. For example, several Illinois civil townships coincide with survey townships and are thus 36 square miles in size.

The county has fared better than has the town outside its region of origin. From the Southeast, counties diffused eventually to all 50 states, in one form or another ranging from modern metropolitan governments to the rural counties of American folklore. Of the latter, Wager wrote nostalgically in 1950:

> Across the face of America are county seats, and at the heart of each a courthouse in a courthouse square. These courthouse squares have a peculiar American flavor; they suggest spaciousness and leisure, there are benches where old men gather to reminisce and almost invariably a monument to honor the county's military

heroes. The courthouse, if old, has a certain museum quality; it is cold and austere with a slightly musty smell. The newer ones are brighter and have more of the air of office buildings. But nearly everywhere there is an atmosphere of secretiveness in county offices, a certain reluctance to reveal with frankness the details of public business. Politics is played with more finesse than in more robust days, but the professional spirit has not yet been fully adopted. On the other hand, there is a friendliness and warmth–a certain "down to earth" quality about county government that is as American as pumpkin pie (pp. 4–5).

Central Cities

Towns and counties, as we have seen, originated in the agrarian societies of New England and the Tidewater region. Urban communities accounted for only about 5 percent of the national population in 1790. This was to change rapidly with national independence and the industrial revolution. American cities as "centers of assembly, processing, exchange, and distribution" have collectively evolved in response to changes in technology and communication (Borchert 1991, 219). But each major city also has developed its distinct landscape, traditions, and character, reflecting the diverse influences of demographics, culture, physical site, politics, economy, and law. Three examples, Boston, Chicago, and Los Angeles, are illustrative.

The town of *Boston* grew from 18,320 inhabitants in 1790 to 43,298 in 1820 (Whitehill 1959, 73–74). This rapid expansion was accompanied by urban problems such as fires, water shortages, overcrowding of land, disposal of human and animal wastes, street paving, lighting, and crime. In 1822, Boston adopted a city charter, which replaced the town meeting with a mayor and city council. This conversion of Boston from a town to a city symbolized the advent of the modern urban municipality.

Boston's charter clothed it with the formal attire of urban government but left many questions unresolved, such as how large it should be. Like its counterparts elsewhere:

Boston desired more land for residential and economic development. There was also an interest in increasing the city's size, reflecting not only America's passion for bigness but also Boston's need to present a prestigious statistical position to national and international commercial interests. Furthermore, Boston felt that if it were a large political unit, it would have greater political influence in the state legislature and in Congress.

Wakstein 1972, p. 287.

The results of this quest for bigness in terms of annexation and boundary changes are depicted in Figure 5-2. Two towns, Brookline and Chelsea, were early defectors from Boston. Boston however gained South Boston in 1804 and a number of other towns later in the century. The external water supply developed by Boston in the 1840s, as described in Chapter 6, was the primary reason for adjoining towns to unite with Boston (Teaford 1979, 54–55). Between 1867 and 1874, the towns of Roxbury, Dorchester, Charlestown, and West Roxbury voted to join Boston. These additions increased the population of Boston by 116 percent and its territory by 441 percent (Wakstein, 280).

But with the addition of Hyde Park in 1912, Boston's territorial expansion stopped. The establishment of "metropolitan districts" for the provision of water, sewage collection, and parks in the late 19th century gave the suburbs access to water without the need to yield their independence to Boston. Suburban residents could thereafter enjoy the jobs and amenities of the city while living in self-governing towns, which exacerbated the ethnic, racial, and economic polarity between central city and suburbs. Today the City of Boston accounts for about 14% of its CMSA population and 3% of the land area of its metropolitan area (Table 5-1).

Chicago was originally incorporated in 1833 with a territory of only three-eighths of a square mile on the southwest shore of Lake Michigan (Mayer and Wade 1969, 14). Like Boston, Chicago experienced rapid territorial and population growth during the second half of the 19th century, driven by the grain and timber industries of the upper Midwest (Cronon 1991). Before 1870, the city expanded to about 26 square miles through acts of the state legislature without local referenda. Between 1889 and 1893 several entire townships and villages were added to Chicago despite court battles waged by opponents (Teaford, 44–45)(Figure 5-3).

A severe problem for Chicago and its suburbs was the contamination of Lake Michigan as a drinking water source by the raw sewage they

FIGURE 5-2 Territorial evolution of Boston, Massachusetts, 1634–1946. *Source:* Wakstein, 1972. Reproduced by permission of the American Planning Association.

TABLE 5-1   1990 POPULATION AND LAND AREA: BOSTON, CHICAGO, AND
LOS ANGELES

Population (1000s)	Boston	Chicago	Los Angeles
Central city	574	2,784	3,485
CMSA[a]	4,172	8,066	14,532
% central city	13.7%	34.5%	23.9%
Land Area (sq. mi.)			
Central city	46	222.6	463.7
MSA[b]	1,769	3,720	4,069
% central city	3%	6%	11%

Source: *Statistical Abstract of the U.S.: 1991*, Tables 36 and 40.
[a] As defined for the 1990 census.
[b] As defined for the 1980 census (covers only part of 1990 CMSA for which land areas are not available).

were discharging into it. As in Boston, a regional district was established in the 1890s to solve the problem: the Chicago Sanitary District (now the Metropolitan Water Reclamation District). In 1899, the district completed its Ship and Sanitary Canal to convey Chicago's wastes away from Lake Michigan and toward the Illinois-Mississippi river system.

Chicago reached about 90 percent of its present area of 222 square miles by the start of the 20th century and thereafter annexation virtually ended. In 1990, Chicago accounted for about one-third of its CMSA population and only 6% of its metropolitan land area (see Table 5-1).

Los Angeles provides a western example of municipal accretion, largely occurring during the 20th century. The city was originally incorporated in 1850 with a legal territory of 25 square miles centered on the Spanish "plaza." Prior to 1900, urban development was largely limited to this initial territory. Thereafter, annexation added vast new areas to the city—extending southward to San Pedro Harbor, the port of Los Angeles, westward to the Santa Monica Mountains, and northward into the San Fernando Valley (Figure 5-4).

Once again, the legal enlargement of municipal area was motivated by water issues. The annexation of the San Fernando Valley in 1905 was prompted by a desire to increase the city's assessed tax value so that more bonds could be issued to pay for a 250-mile aqueduct from the Owens Valley in the Sierra Nevada to Los Angeles:

Chicago Annexations

ANNEXATIONS   TO   JUNE   1,   1893

Key		Year
1.	Town of Chicago as organized (platted by Canal Commissioners three years earlier)	1833
2.		1833
3.		1833
4.	Town of Chicago as incorporated	1835
5.	City of Chicago as incorporated	1837
6.	Withdrawn 1843 and reannexed	1851
7.	Withdrawn 1843 and reannexed	1851
8.		1851
9.		1851
10.		1853
11.		1853
12.		1863
13.		1863
14.	Part of Lincoln Park	1869
15.		1860
16.		1869
17.		1887
18.		1889
19.		1889
20.		1889
21.	Part of Town of Cicero	1889
22.	Town of Jefferson	1889
23.	City of Lake View	1889
24.	Town of Lake	1889
25.	Village of Hyde Park	1889
26.	Part of Village of Gano	1890
27.	South Englewood	1890
28.	Village of Washington Heights	1890
29.	Village of West Roseland	1890
30.		1890
31.	Village of Fernwood	1891
32.	Village of Rogers Park	1893
33.	Village of West Ridge	1893

FIGURE 5-3   Territorial evolution of Chicago, Illinois, 1833–1893. *Source:* Mayer and Wade, 1969. Reproduced by permission of The University of Chicago Press.

Periods of Annexation

1859 - 1899	1930 - 1939	
1900 - 1909	1940 - 1944	
1910 - 1919	1945 - 1954	
1920 - 1929	1955 - 1972	

1 San Fernando
2 Beverly Hills
3 Culver City
4 County

Original City
of
Los Angeles
Incorporated
April 4, 1850

National Soldiers Home

FIGURE 5-4   Territorial evolution of Los Angeles, California, 1850–1972.
Source: Reynolds, 1976.

If the assessed valuation of Los Angeles could be rapidly increased, its debt ceiling would be that much higher. And what better way was there to accomplish this than to *add to the city*? Instead of bringing more people to Los Angeles–which was happening any-way–*the city would go to them*. It would just loosen its borders as [William] Mullholland [Chairman of the Los Angeles Department of Water and Power] loosened his silk cravat and wrap itself around the San Fernando Valley. Then it would have a new tax base, a nat-ural underground storage reservoir, and a legitimate use of its sur-plus water in one fell swoop.   Reisner 1986, p. 77 (emphasis is Reisner's).

As with Boston and Chicago, the process of growth eventually ran its course as all remaining territory became incorporated in communities determined to preserve their independence. Some of these, notably Bev-erly Hills and San Fernando, are entirely surrounded by Los Angeles. Others ring its perimeter except where it borders public lands or the Pacific Ocean. Annexations since 1955 have been limited to modest-sized tracts scattered along the city's periphery, as well as some inhold-ings that could not conveniently be incorporated as separate municipal-ities. As of 1976, there were 76 incorporated cities within Los Angeles County in addition to the City of Los Angeles. Conversely, the city itself contained 20 postal community names, such as Hollywood and San Pedro, which once were independent communities (Nelson and Clark 1976, 21 and 28).

The City of Los Angeles now occupies a land area of 463.7 square miles, more than twice the size of Chicago and 10 times the size of Boston. Despite this impressive size, Los Angeles occupies only 11 per-cent of the land area of its metropolitan area. And despite its enormous expansion earlier in this century, Los Angeles resembles other central cities in exercising jurisdiction over the land and resources of only an odd-shaped fragment of the total urbanized region of which it is the heart.

Suburban Proliferation: Hardy American Weed

The evolution of metropolitan America during the "Gilded Age" (1870–1895) was a race between new municipal incorporations on the one hand and the enlargement of existing cities on the other (Teaford

1979). The former process involved the fragmentation of urbanizing regions among hundreds of small municipal units. The latter process attempted to combine small fragments into larger urban communities. As we have seen, the consolidation movement thrived briefly in various cities only to subside as incorporated suburbs opted to remain separate from both the central city and from each other. Municipal fragmentation has since prevailed as the determinant of the political geography of most American metropolitan areas, although small-scale annexation to existing municipalities continues in many regions. In 1990, 48.5 million people, almost one-third of all U.S. urban residents, were scattered among 18,219 municipal units of fewer than 25,000 inhabitants (see Table 5-2).

A major factor behind the proliferation of incorporated places in this country was the adoption of very permissive incorporation and laws by many states beginning in the early 1800s (Teaford, 6–7). This permissiveness was consistent with American traditions of self-government and home rule. It further facilitated the establishment of new "cities" in remote mining areas, ports along the inland river system, and elsewhere that the path of pioneer settlement led (Reps 1965). But as practiced in burgeoning metropolitan areas, permissive incorporation has fostered a spirit of rivalry, and even hostility, which has obstructed efforts to promote regional solutions to shared problems.

Despite the stereotypes of suburbia offered by novelists such as John Cheever, John Updike, and John O'Hara, suburbs differ greatly in size,

TABLE 5-2   U.S. INCORPORATED PLACES BY SIZE, 1990

Size	Number	Population (millions)	% of Total Population of Incorporated Places
1 mill. +	8	20.0	13.0
500,000–1 mill.	15	10.1	6.6
250,00–500,000	41	14.2	9.3
100,000–250,000	131	19.1	12.5
50,000–100,000	309	21.2	13.9
25,000–50,000	567	20.0	13.0
10,000–25,000	1,290	20.3	13.3
< 10,000	16,929	28.2	18.4
Totals	19,290	152.9	100.0

Source: Statistical Abstract of the U.S.: 1994, Table 45.

economic function, and growth characteristics. The historian Sam Bass Warner (1978) has traced the origins of "streetcar suburbs" in the latter 19th century. With the advent of the automobile, suburbs proliferated rapidly until the Great Depression. Harris (1943/1959) found that by World War II, the degree of suburbanization differed from one functional type of central city to another, and that suburbs themselves appeared to be either "bedroom" or "manufacturing." In the mid-1980s, Kenneth T. Jackson (1985, 5) observed that "American suburbs come in every type, shape, and size: rich and poor, industrial and residential, new and old."

Today, we may distinguish five types of suburban jurisdictions that have little in common except for their legal autonomy within a larger metropolitan area. First, many older suburban municipalities such as Evanston, Illinois; Boulder, Colorado; Cambridge, Massachusetts; and White Plains, New York have sizable territories and populations and display a broad range of urban functions and land uses. These would be viewed as *full-fledged cities* in their own right but for their proximity and relation to nearby larger cities. Some, such as Stamford, Connecticut, have experienced spectacular growth and prominence as a haven to major corporations seeking lower-cost commercial space and more amenable surroundings than older central cities. Others, such as Newark, New Jersey, have experienced the opposite phenomenon: disinvestment, declining economic base, pervasive social and ethnic problems, and a crumbling infrastructure.

Second, white collar *bedroom suburbs*, many very affluent such as Grosse Pointe, Michigan; Lake Forest, Illinois; or Lincoln, Massachusetts represent the archetypal suburb caricatured by fiction writers. Such communities often are characterized by large lots, huge homes, manicured lawns, and an absence of manufacturing and multifamily housing (except a few luxury condominiums for "empty nesters"). Municipal autonomy has permitted these municipalities to insulate themselves, legally, fiscally, and often racially, from the central cities.

A third type of suburban municipality is the *industrial* or "blue collar" suburb such as Chelsea, Massachusetts; Elizabeth, New Jersey; or Hamtramck, Michigan. These may have originated as industrial enclaves or as speculative working-class land subdivisions. They are likely to be ethnically and racially diverse in comparison with their affluent neighbors. They are often afflicted by poverty, unemployment brought about by plant closings, and inadequate schools and other public facilities. While sharing many of the social, economic, and environmental ills of the central cities, they may lack the resources and technical sophistication to qualify for federal and state assistance. Nor do they have the population size or notoriety of a Newark to attract state and national attention to their plight.

A fourth type is the *splinter* suburb of minuscule size and sometimes negligible population, which is scattered here and there in many metropolitan areas. According to the Advisory Commission on Intergovernmental Relations (1969, 75):

> The overwhelming majority of metropolitan local governments are relatively small in population and geographic size: ... about half of the nearly 5,000 municipalities in [MSAs] have less than a single square mile of land area, and only one in 5 is as large as 4 square miles. Two-thirds of them have fewer than 5,000 residents; one-third fewer than 1,000.

Historically, splinter municipalities often were incorporated to promote or avoid moral concerns. Local laws differ widely on liquor, gambling, and other vices, as does local enforcement of state laws on matters such as prostitution. Teaford (p. 20) found that the emerging fragmented metropolis of the early 20th century "resembled a moral checkerboard with alternating squares of state law." In Minnesota, for instance, a law allowing municipalities to own and support themselves from municipal liquor stores gave rise to a number of incorporations involving only a city block and a few hundred persons. Avoidance of taxing and zoning policies of neighboring jurisdictions is another frequent motive, shared alike by affluent, exclusive suburbs and industrial enclaves. Burns Harbor, Indiana, for example, was incorporated in 1968 by Bethlehem Steel Corporation. Total assessed valuation of Burns Harbor in 1970 was listed at $39 million despite the presence of a substantial portion of a new quarter-billion-dollar steel plant (Platt 1972, 160).

A fifth type of suburb may be called the *mushroom* variety due to its tendency to erupt practically overnight (and with a seeming lack of permanence or relation to its surroundings). Mushroom suburbs ("mushburbs" for short) may begin as a rural crossroads, a small farm village, or simply as agricultural or wooded land near the advancing metropolitan

fringe. Private investment decisions affecting the area are usually triggered by public sector decisions concerning, for instance, the location of
interstate highway interchanges, new water or sewer service, or commuter mass transit stops (such as outlying stations of the Washington,
D.C. Metro). Given the necessary financing and legal approvals, the site
erupts from its bucolic state into a late-20th century "urban village,"
(Leinberger and Lockwood 1986) or "Edge City" (Garreau 1991) complete with glistening office parks, a super-regional shopping mall with
hundreds of stores, big-name hotels with conference facilities, all set
amid manicured landscaping and parking lots.

A good example of a "mushburb" or Edge City is Schaumburg, Illinois,
which in the late 1950s was a sleepy farm village 20 miles northwest of
Chicago's Loop. Schaumburg erupted in the late 1960s as part of the
general development boom triggered by the construction of several interstate highways and the rapid expansion of O'Hare Airport. By 1970,
Schaumburg already boasted the world's largest indoor shopping mall
(at the time) with a population of only 18,500. Its spatial area and municipal population grew rapidly with annexation and development of surrounding farmlands. Today, Schaumburg is the home of Sears, Inc.,
which moved there during the 1980s from its 110-story Sears Tower in
the Chicago Loop.

Although local political geography differs from one state to another,
Schaumburg clones may be identified in many fast-growing U.S.
metropolitan areas—for example: Tysons Corner, Virginia; King of
Prussia, Pennsylvania; Framingham, Massachusetts; Irvine, California.
Mushburbs pose distinct and intractable issues for public policy, including lack of affordable housing; lack of educational, cultural, and
aesthetic amenities; an absence of civic traditions and sense of community; and a general lack of integration of planning and design among the
various developments that comprise them (Muller 1975; Leinberger and
Lockwood 1986).

The conventional pessimism of urbanists toward what is here termed
the "mushroom suburb" is in part challenged and in part reinforced by
Joel Garreau's provocative 1991 book: *Edge City: Life on the New Frontier.* Defined as a newly developed cluster having at least five million
square feet of office space and 600,000 square feet of retail space, among
other criteria, Garreau identifies more than 200 "Edge Cities" scattered
across the United States. These collectively contain two-thirds of all

American office space and are in fact eclipsing conventional urban "downtowns." More office space is found in the Edge Cities of New Jersey than in the Financial District of Manhattan (Garreau, 5). The megamalls that form the cores of Edge Cities have long competed successfully with downtown stores, many of which have moved out to the new centers. South Coast Mall in Orange County, California does more business in a day than all of downtown San Francisco (p. 63).

Edge Cities in Garreau's view are no longer peripheral to traditional central cities: they are "the crucible of America's future [which have] become the place in which the majority of Americans now live, learn, work, shop, play, pray, and die" (p. 8). Like William H. Whyte's (1956) classic investigation of the postwar suburban habitat of "The Organization Man," Garreau weighs the impact of the new Edge Cities on the well-being of their inhabitants. For those in the right age group (30s and 40s) and profession (finance, information, high tech), they appear to work well, despite their conspicuous lack of history or community. Those who do not qualify by reason of age, ethnicity, or skills are left behind (literally and politically) in the older central cities and suburbs.

Edge cities however are not "governments" in a strict sense. They comprise tightly controlled islands of private development amid the general web of municipal, county, and state authority that interlaces metropolitan America. With reference to an archetypal New Jersey Edge City called "287 and 78" (an interstate highway intersection), Garreau finds that it ". . . still has no overall leader, no political boundaries that define the place. It is governed only be a patchwork of zoning boards and planning boards and county boards, and townships boards . . . swirling like gnats–not any elected ruling structure" (p. 46). In short, Edge Cities are not usually cities in a legal sense.

Politically speaking, the typical American metropolitan region thus comprises one or more central cities surrounded by a mosaic of incorporated suburbs of the various types listed above, interspersed (except in New England) with pockets of unincorporated land under county jurisdiction. Figure 5-5 depicts the chaotic municipal geography of Cook County, Illinois. But Cook County is also overlain by an average of 4.8 special districts at any given location, hundreds in all, which contribute to the overall political fragmentation of the county and region (Stetzer 1975). And splattered across the pattern of political jurisdictions is the

FIGURE 5-5   Municipal geography of Cook County, including Chicago (shaded area).

geography of urbanization and development, of which Edge Cities are the latest manifestation.

Local Government Jurisdiction and Powers

We have traced the evolution of the political geography of metropolitan America. The balance of this chapter will turn to the legal characteristics of contemporary "local governments," which for present purposes include:

- Municipalities–incorporated cities, towns, villages, or equivalent units

- Counties

- Special districts and regional authorities

Municipalities

AREAS OF JURISDICTION

Aside from New England, most states still experience new incorporations and annexation of land to existing municipalities. Although state laws on these matters differ somewhat, the following principles have generally governed the spatial evolution of municipal units:

1. Municipalities are always *mutually exclusive* in their geographic areas. No area of land is incorporated in more than one general-purpose unit of local government. Nor may one municipality "pirate" territory from another incorporated area. Land must be unincorporated to be eligible for annexation.

2. Annexed land must normally be *contiguous*, or physically connected to the annexing municipal territory. In suits challenging proposed annexations (for example, by neighboring municipalities competing for lucrative development sites), courts generally interpret contiguity to mean a substantial common border reflecting a mutuality of interest in the sharing of municipal responsibilities. Contiguity is thus related to the feasibility of extending municipal services to adjoining

land. (There are, however, examples of annexations of areas tangent only at a corner or connected by a narrow strip or "ribbon" of incorporated land.)

3. Annexations must usually be *mutually agreeable* to the annexing municipality and the annexee property owner or developer. Often a majority of property owners or the owners of a majority of the land in question are sufficient to bind dissenting owners whose inclusion is necessary to achieve contiguity.

4. Many states permit "pre-annexation agreements" between owners of land that will be developed and the annexing municipality regarding public services, zoning, and other issues relating to development.

Some municipal boundaries follow obvious physical features such as rivers, lakes, or tidal coastlines, which may shift over time. Streams that serve as political boundaries are bordered by different jurisdictions on the opposite sides, leading to problems of floodplain and watershed management (Platt et al. 1980). Some boundaries follow highways, railroads or other cultural features, and some are straight-line segments established in a land survey. Many boundaries however seem to be entirely arbitrary zigs, zags, and jogs whose explanation lies in obscurity.

The aggregate result in most U.S. metropolitan areas is a political geography of byzantine complexity (see Figure 5-5). Despite their irregularity, the fortuitous location of local political boundaries exerts profound influence over the morphology of urban areas, in terms of land use patterns, property tax rates, land values, and the quality of local public services such as schools, parks, and libraries. Computerized geographic information systems may be used to plot the "legal stratigraphy" of public authority over land.

POWERS

Municipalities, the basic workhorses of local governments, include central cities and the various types of incorporated suburbs listed above (excluding "Edge Cities," which are not governmental entities). Municipalities are traditionally "creatures of the state" and are authorized by state laws and home rule doctrines to exercise a wide variety of legal powers affecting the health and welfare of their citizens. The fundamental rights and powers of municipal corporations have changed little since medieval times: (1) to sue and be sued as a "body politic"; (2) to enter into contracts; (3) to acquire, hold, and dispose of land; (4) to establish ordinances or bylaws; (5) and to possess a seal. To these must be added a modern necessity: (6) to obtain revenue, to borrow, and to spend.

Recitation of these broad powers, however, does not suggest the potential scope of their application. For what purposes may municipalities enter into contracts, buy land, make ordinances, or impose taxes? How much autonomy and immunity from state review may local governments claim? According to Teaford (1979, 5-6):

> In 1868, the eminent legal authority Thomas Cooley observed that "the American legal system is one of complete decentralization, the primary and vital ideal of which is, that local affairs shall be managed by local authorities." During the following four decades Americans seemed dedicated to realizing the ideal as Cooley had stated it. Local self-determination was the rallying cry of Americans, and this meant that each fragment of the metropolis would enjoy the right to govern itself and to decide its destiny. Local government was a sacred element of the American civil religion, and the nation's lawmakers were devout in their adherence to the faith.

But, as with other religions, the hopes of the faithful were sometimes badly served. At the turn of the century, American cities were dominated by bosses and political machines that turned the ancient municipal prerogatives to personal gain. Abuses were (and still are) rampant with respect to municipal contracts, land deals, and patronage in public employment. In the early decades of the 20th century, the corruption of municipal government prompted a reform movement that reasserted tighter control by states over their wayward municipal "children."

Contrary to the myth of local autonomy, municipalities in fact are not sovereign entities. They are incorporated under state law and thereafter are controlled by the state in many respects such as selection of officials, contracts, bonded indebtedness, taxation, and land use control. The history of municipal government in the United States has been a continuing struggle between states and local governments regarding the relative degree of control imposed by the former on the latter (Clark 1985).

One outgrowth of this struggle was the *home rule movement* under which certain states, beginning with Missouri in 1875, adopted state constitutional amendments expanding the scope of municipal autonomy. Under this doctrine, a community could perform functions if they were not forbidden by the state legislature or otherwise in conflict with constitution or statute. The home rule movement reached only about 15 states, however, and has been characterized as ". . . an uncertain privilege, for it depends entirely on the whim of the legislature and may at any time be repealed or modified" (Zink 1939, 121).

Regardless of home rule status, questions arise frequently as to the validity of a municipal action in light of state delegation of authority. Clearly, latitude is needed to go beyond the literal provisions of state law, or municipal governments would be stifled in responding to local needs and circumstances. The fundamental question therefore is: How may a municipality ascertain the limits of its available powers?

The classic response to this question is "Dillon's Rule," which was first expressed in 1911 and remains solid law today:

> . . . a municipal corporation possesses and can exercise the following powers and no others. First, those granted in express words; second, those necessary or fairly implied in or incident to the powers expressly granted; third, those essential to the accomplishment of the declared objects and purposes of the corporation—not simply convenient but indispensable.
>
> Sands and Libonati 1982, sec. 13.04.

Dillon's Rule is a long-settled principle that is cited by courts in resolving challenges to municipal innovation. It is an elastic test, however, and affords much judicial discretion in applying it to actual controversies.

Municipalities are usually limited in the exercise of their allotted powers to their corporate limits. But many states authorize *extraterritorial* powers to develop public water supplies, since many communities do not have adequate water sources within their incorporated areas. Extraterritorial land also may be acquired in some states for nature refuges, parks, sewage treatment plants, and airports. Municipal services are often sold extraterritorially. Chicago supplies water from its Lake Michigan treatment works to suburban communities, at higher rates than its own residents pay.

Counties

A total of 3041 *counties* or equivalent units virtually blanket the nation's land area. Each state is divided into counties or equivalent units (parishes in Louisiana). A few cities are independent of any county, notably Baltimore, Maryland; St. Louis, Missouri; and some 40 cities in Virginia. Denver, Colorado is a combined city/county unit of government. There are also several examples of metropolitan governments involving complete or partial merger of city and county functions: for example, Miami-Dade County, Florida; Indianapolis-Marion County, Indiana; and Nashville-Davidson County, Tennessee.

Many counties display a split personality. For some purposes they are agents of the state, as in the management of the county courthouse, prison, roads, and welfare programs. In another sense, they are units of local government for "unincorporated areas" (areas not yet absorbed into an incorporated municipality). In such areas, they may exercise powers equivalent to municipalities, including land use planning and zoning.

Counties differ from state to state in their functions and importance to land use control. In southern New England, where all land is incorporated, counties in Massachusetts are comparatively impotent, and those in Connecticut and Rhode Island have been abolished as governmental units. In Maryland and Virginia, however, counties serve as the basic units of local government, except in freestanding cities. Elsewhere in the nation, counties generally provide local government services to rural areas and unincorporated urban settlements.

Certain metropolitan counties such as Cook (containing Chicago, Illinois), Nassau and Suffolk (on Long Island, New York), and Los Angeles serve as major regional governments (Advisory Council on Intergovernmental Relations 1974; Duncombe 1977). Los Angeles County, for instance, with about 8 million people has a public works budget of tens of millions of dollars. Municipalities within the county, including the City of Los Angeles and some 76 suburban jurisdictions, retain their local zoning prerogatives. However, the county or its surrogate special districts influence land use within municipalities indirectly through the location, timing, and capacity of regional facilities such as flood control, storm water drainage, sewage treatment, or water supply.

Special Districts

Special districts (other than school districts) comprise a very numerous and diverse potpourri of governmental units established for many purposes. Special districts numbered 28,588 in 1982, an increase of 2626 or nearly 10 percent in just five years (U.S. Bureau of the Census 1986, Table 470). Functions performed by individual special districts range from aviation to zoo administration. In some metropolitan areas, they provide such critical services as mass transportation, water supply, sewage treatment, solid waste disposal, parks and recreation, and air and water pollution control. Most districts, however, are created to provide only a single function. Districts serving different purposes may overlay each other, as well as general-purpose units of government, but districts of the same type are geographically mutually exclusive.

Special districts almost never engage in land use planning and zoning, which remain municipal and county prerogatives. But special districts, especially those operating at a regional scale, clearly influence land usage through the spatial distribution of their services and facilities. The location and capacity of sewer and water lines, for instance, is a crucial factor in land development patterns. Bollens (1957, 30) refers to a large number of special districts as "phantom governments" unknown to the people served by them.

At the other extreme, certain major special districts are very visible and powerful units of regional government with thousands of employees, extensive revenue sources, and bonded indebtedness in billions of dollars. Examples include the Metropolitan Water District of Southern California, the Cook County Forest Preserve District in Illinois, and the Port Authority of New York and New Jersey. Regional entities of this scale are major providers of water, sewage treatment, transportation, parks, and other vital services in many metropolitan areas, or portions of them. Ideally, they bring professionalism and relative freedom from political influence to the management of urban problems.

But in some cases, they can be highly political and ruthless. New

York's Robert Moses, whose biography is entitled *The Power Broker* (Caro 1974), was the exemplary technocrat. Never elected to any office, Moses assembled a network of special authorities and city agencies that reshaped the face of New York City, Long Island, and portions of New York State. During the 1930s, he built parkways and parks, including the immensely popular Jones Beach on the south shore of Long Island. Later he built highways, housing projects, the United Nations complex, and the 1964 World's Fair, overcoming opponents with cunning and occasional cruelty. The memory of Moses still rankles those he overwhelmed legally or politically to push his projects through. The question inevitably arises: Did the ends he achieved justify the means he used?

Revenue and Debt

A primary issue for local governments in 1995 (as well as the state and federal governments) is that of revenue. Local revenue may be obtained from a variety of sources, which local governments constantly seek to augment.

The fundamental revenue source for most municipalities and counties is the *ad valorem property tax*. This is the annual tax imposed on all taxable real property based on a specified percentage of the assessed value of each parcel, including land and buildings. The percentage of tax levied ("tax rate") is uniform throughout a taxing jurisdiction, although tax rates often differ substantially from one governmental unit to another.

Tax rates are usually expressed in terms of "mills per dollar of assessed value" or "dollars per $1,000 of assessed value." The ad valorem tax levy is not applied to tax-exempt property, which includes all publicly owned land and buildings, plus property owned by charitable, religious, educational, or other exempt organizations as defined by state law. Also, allowable increases in property tax rates over the previous year may be constrained by tax limitation referenda in some states such as California and Massachusetts, and of course by political hostility to tax increases everywhere.

Subject to these constraints, computation of the municipal tax rate and individual tax payment ("tax levy") is simple in concept. First, the governmental unit determines its budgetary needs for the next fiscal year. It deducts revenue from nontax sources such as federal and state transfer payments to determine the net amount that must be obtained from property taxes, which yields the amount of revenue needed to be obtained from local taxes. It then divides that figure by the total taxable assessed property value within the jurisdiction to yield the tax rate. Thus, if a small town needs $750,000 from property taxes and has $50 million total assessed property valuation, the computation is:

1. Needed Revenue divided by Total Assessed Value = Tax Rate
   $750,000 / $50,000,000 = 1.5% = ($15 per $1,000 or 15 mills per dollar)

2. Applying the tax rate to an individual owning property assessed at $80,000, the tax payable is: $15 × 80 = $1,200

Certain kinds of local public improvements may benefit particular property owners more than the public at large, for instance, the repaving of sidewalks or replacement of local sewers. Such improvements may be financed through *special assessments* instead of the general ad valorem tax. A special assessment is a tax imposed on property benefited by a local public improvement. It may be one lump sum or payable over several years.

Large-scale public projects such as new bridges, police and fire stations, public garages, schools, and parks require a sizable outlay of funds at one time. The normal mechanism to assemble such funds is the *general obligation bond*. General obligation bonds issued by any governmental unit are repaid out of the ad valorem tax revenue and other monetary resources of that unit over time. If that proves insufficient, such bonds are backed by the "full faith and credit" of the issuer, who must raise taxes, sell property, or otherwise raise the funds to repay the bondholders.

Bonds are sold to investors through national and international bond markets. The rate of interest payable over the term of the bond is a function of the creditworthiness of the issuing governmental unit, as well as the term of the bond and the general economic climate. Some states impose constitutional limits to the amount of bonded indebtedness that a municipality or county may incur in relation to its total assessed value. Such limits, however, do not usually apply to special districts. Thus, states such as Illinois, with strict debt ceilings, are awash in special districts created to circumvent debt limits on general-purpose local governments.

Certain public facilities such as swimming pools, golf courses, and solid waste disposal facilities, however, are expected to pay for themselves over time through the imposition of user fees. Such facilities may be funded through *revenue bonds*, which are exempt from ceilings on general obligation bonds. Revenue bonds are repaid only from fees generated from the facility in question and are not backed by the issuer's "full faith and credit."

Fees for permits and services comprise a growing source of local government revenue. In Massachusetts, for instance, when a referendum (Proposition 2-1/2) limited ad valorem tax revenue in many communities, fees for sewer, water, sanitary landfill, and other services were raised to offset the shortfall.

Finally, *intergovernmental transfers* comprise a significant proportion of revenue to municipalities, counties, and some special districts. During the 1970s, the federal government consolidated many of its individual grant programs to local governments under the new programs of "general revenue sharing" and Community Development Block Grants. In the mid-1990s, the Republican-dominated Congress also plans to replace many federal grant programs with lump sum transfers to states. State governments also transfer massive sums of money (mostly from sales and income taxes) to local governments. Such allocations are usually earmarked for specific purposes such as schools, welfare, health services, housing, and conservation areas.

Beyond these traditional revenue sources, certain municipal governments are authorized by state law to tax personal and corporate income and even to impose a local sales tax. Taxes on hotel rooms, meals, liquor, and cigarettes yield additional revenue in some cities. As state and federal aid to local governments declines in the 1990s, the latter may be expected to redouble their efforts to devise new sources of revenue.

Conclusion

Once the proud legal expression of the autonomous medieval city, the municipal corporation in America is now an ironic metaphor for governmental inadequacy in the face of external economic, political, and environmental forces. It is a victim of its own success, having been replicated in such vast numbers that each individual municipality retains only a fragmentary role in the management of the overall metropolitan area.

The specific roles of local government with respect to land use control will be the subject of Chapters 7–9. Meanwhile, the last word on the geography of metropolitan America may be granted to political scientist Robert Wood (1961, 1) referring to the New York Region, which even 30 years ago had assumed its present chaotic form:

> On the eastern seaboard of the United States, where the state of New York wedges itself between New Jersey and Connecticut, explorers of political affairs can observe one of the great unnatural wonders of the world: this is a governmental arrangement perhaps more complicated than any other that mankind has yet contrived or allowed to happen. A vigorous metropolitan area, the economic capital of the nation, governs itself by means of 1467 distinct political entities (at latest count), each having its own power to raise and spend the public treasure, and each operating in a jurisdiction determined more by chance than by design. The whole 22-county area that we know as the New York Metropolitan Region provides beds for about 15 million people and gainful employment for about 7 million of them. Its growth, which is rapid, takes place almost entirely in its outer, less crowded parts, and this means that the Region is becoming more alike in the density of its population and jobs, more alike in community problems. But the responsibility to maintain law and order, educate the young, dig the sewers, and plan the future environment remains gloriously or ridiculously fragmented.

References

Advisory Commission on Intergovernmental Relations. 1969. *Urban America and the Federal System*. Washington, D.C.: ACIR.

——. 1974. *The Challenge of Local Government Reorganization*. Washington, D.C.: ACIR.

Billington, R.A. 1970. "The Frontier in Illinois History." In *An Illinois Reader*. Clyde C. Walton, ed. Dekalb, IL: Northern Illinois University Press.

Bollens, J.C. 1957. *Special District Governments in the United States*. Berkeley: University of California Press.

Borchert, J.R. 1991. "Futures of American Cities." In J.F. Hart, ed. *Our Changing Cities*. Baltimore: Johns Hopkins University Press.

Caro, R. 1974. *The Power Broker*. New York: Alfred A. Knopf.

Clark, G.L. 1985. *Judges and the Cities*. Chicago: University of Chicago Press.

Cronon, William. 1991. *Nature's Metropolis: Chicago and the Great West*. New York: W.W. Norton.

de Tocqueville, A. 1832/1969. *Democracy in America* J.P. Mayer, ed.; George Lawrence, trans. Garden City: Doubleday Anchor.

Duncombe, H.S. 1977. *Modern County Government*. Washington, D.C.: National Association of Counties.

Garreau, J. 1991. *Edge City: Life on the New Frontier*. New York: Doubleday Anchor Books.

Harris, C.D. 1943/1959. "Suburbs." In *Readings in Urban Geography*. H.M. Mayer and C.F. Kohn, eds. Chicago: University of Chicago Press.

Jackson, K.T. 1985. *Crabgrass Frontier: The Suburbanization of the United States*. New York: Oxford University Press.

Jefferson, T. 1782/1944. "Notes on Virginia." In *The Life and Selected Writings of Thomas Jefferson*. A. Koch and W. Peder, eds. New York: Random House Modern Library.

Leinberger, C.B., and C. Lockwood. 1986. "How Business Is Reshaping America." *The Atlantic* 258(4): 43–52.

Mayer, H.M., and R.C. Wade. 1969. *Chicago: Growth of a Metropolis*. Chicago: University of Chicago Press.

McManis, D.R. 1975. *Colonial New England: A Historical Geography*. New York: Oxford University Press.

Meinig, D.W. 1986. *The Shaping of America: Vol. 1–Atlantic America, 1492–1800*. New Haven: Yale University Press.

Morrison, S.E. 1965. *The Oxford History of the American People*. New York: Oxford University Press.

Muller, P.O. 1975. *The Outer City: Geographical Consequences of the Urbanization of the Suburbs*. Resource Paper No. 75-2. Washington, D.C.: Association of American Geographers.

Nelson, H.J., and W.A.V. Clark. 1976. *Los Angeles: The Metropolitan Experience*. Cambridge: Ballinger.

Platt, R.H. 1972. *The Open Space Decision Process*. Paper no. 142. Chicago: University of Chicago Geography Research Series.

Platt, R.H., et al. 1980. *Intergovernmental Management of Floodplains*. Monograph no. 30. Boulder: University of Colorado Natural Hazards Center.

Porter, K.H. 1922. *County and Township Government in the U.S.* New York: The MacMillan Co.

Reisner, M. 1986. *Cadillac Desert: The American West and Its Disappearing Water.* New York: Penguin Books.

Reps, J.W. 1965. *The Making of Urban American: A History of City Planning.* Princeton: Princeton University Press.

———. 1972. *Tidewater Towns: City Planning in Colonial Virginia and Maryland.* Charlottesville: University of Virginia Press.

Reynolds, D.R. 1976. "Progress Toward Achieving Efficient and Responsive Spatial-Political Systems in Urban America." In *Urban Policymaking and Metropolitan Dynamics.* J.S. Adams, ed. Cambridge: Ballinger.

Stetzer, D.F. 1975. *Special Districts in Cook County: Toward a Geography of Local Government.* Research Paper no. 169. Chicago: University of Chicago Department of Geography.

Teaford, J.C. 1979. *City and Suburb: The Political Fragmentation of Metropolitan America 1850–1970.* Baltimore: The Johns Hopkins University Press.

Wager, P.W. 1950. *County Government Across the Nation.* Chapel Hill: University of North Carolina Press.

Wakstein, A.M. 1972. "Boston's Search for a Metropolitan Solution." *Journal of the American Institute of Planners* (Sept.), 285–295.

Warner, S.B., Jr. 1978. *Streetcar Suburbs: The Process of Growth in Boston 1870–1900.* Cambridge: Harvard University Press.

Whitehill, P. 1959. *Boston: A Topographic History.* Cambridge: Harvard University Press.

Whyte, W.H. 1956. *The Organization Man.* New York: Simon and Schuster.

Wood, R. 1961. *1400 Governments.* Cambridge: Harvard University Press.

Zink, H. 1939. *Government of Cities in the United States.* New York: Macmillan.

Part III / *Reinventing Cities:*
Testing the Limits
of Intervention

CHAPTER 6 / Urban Reforms of
the 19th Century

Introduction

The origins and modern concepts of private ownership of land and municipal governments have been examined in the last three chapters. In this part of the book (Chapters 6 through 9) we turn to the history and present status of the struggle between the private and public sectors (owners versus "government") over the issue of their respective roles in shaping and reshaping the physical layout and use of urban land.

The modern industrial city came of age in Europe and North America during the 19th century. The population and geographic extent of many urban places mushroomed at unprecedented rates. With rapid expansion came a paroxysm of threats to life, health, and morality. In the early decades of the century tenements proliferated, sanitation collapsed, crime and disease flourished, and life expectancy declined. Gradually, the horrors of uncontrolled urbanization were recognized, at first by a few perceptive individuals, and ultimately by a broader spectrum of society and its law-making bodies.

Beginning in the 1830s, three fundamental avenues of public and private response to urban deterioration evolved in England and America. Each involved legal and institutional innovation in addition to progress in engineering technology, urban design, and the social sciences. The first of these approaches was *regulation*. Beginning with the British Public Health Act of 1848, perception of squalor, overcrowding, and lack of basic sanitation yielded a series of public police power measures intended to gain some degree of control over the building of cities. These would lay a constitutional foundation for the proliferation of land use and environmental regulations to appear in the 20th century.

The second approach was *redevelopment*, the physical replacement of expansion of urban infrastructure in the form of wider streets, paving and lighting, water systems, mass transportation systems, and urban parks. This anticipated the urban renewal and revitalization efforts of the mid-20th century in Great Britain, the United States, and elsewhere.

Third, there were the advocates of *relocation* of people from existing overcrowded and unhealthy cities to newly built model towns in outlying locations. These new towns were to be carefully planned, both physically and socially, to uplift the spirit as well as to provide an honest living and healthful surroundings. The building of New Lanark, Pullman, and Letchworth Garden City involved new forms of finance and institutions of governance. The experimental communities of the 19th and early 20th centuries inspired much larger-scale new town programs after World War II in Great Britain, France, Israel, the Soviet Union, India, China, Hong Kong, and (with less enthusiasm) the United States.

This chapter first summarizes the statistical growth of cities and then considers in turn each of these three fundamental forms of response during the 19th century to the perils of laissez-faire urbanization.

Urban Growth During the 19th Century

The advent and concentration of manufacturing activities in certain locations led to an astonishing increase in the level of urbanization in Europe and the United States during the 19th century. The growth of cities during that century was precisely documented in a classic study by Adna F. Weber (1899/1963), which an anonymous preface characterized as "the first really sound, comprehensive, and complete contribution to urban studies by an American."

Three aspects of urban growth during the 19th century that emerge from Weber's study are (1) the absolute and proportional increase of *urban population*; (2) the emergence of large numbers of *new urban places*; and (3) the phenomenal expansion of *very large cities* such as London, New York, and Paris. These are interrelated facets of the prevailing movement of people to urban places from the countryside and from other countries.

In England and Wales, the total population of places exceeding 20,000 grew tenfold from 1.5 million to 15.5 million between 1801 and 1891. The urban proportion of the total population rose from 16 percent to 53 percent. Eighty percent of the population growth of England and Wales between 1801 and 1891 was urban (Weber, 43). In France, population of places exceeding 10,000 quadrupled from 2.6 million in 1801 to 9.9 million in 1891, with the urban share of national population rising from 9 percent to 26 percent. The United States, starting with a negligible urban population in 1800, had 8.2 million people living in places exceeding 8000 by 1890, representing 29 percent of its population. (Urban population in the United States would exceed rural population by 1920.)

The shift of energy source from running water to coal, and later to electricity, facilitated the spread of manufacturing towns during the 19th century. This was reflected in the rapid increase in the number of urban places. Cities exceeding 20,000 inhabitants in England and Wales rose from 15 to 185 during the period 1801–1891. In France, places of more than 10,000 rose from 90 in 1801 to 232 in 1891. In the United States, places exceeding 8000 increased from merely 6 in 1800 (Philadelphia, New York, Baltimore, Boston, Charleston, and Salem) to 448 in 1890.

But while urbanization was spreading to smaller towns and cities in outlying locations, the principal cities nevertheless attracted the major share of population growth, largely due to immigration. London expanded by 625 percent to 5 million between 1801 and 1891. Its share of the population of England and Wales accordingly rose from 9.7 percent to 14.5 percent during that period. New York City grew tenfold from 1800 to 1850 and then tripled again in the next four decades, reflecting the arrival of large numbers of immigrants from Ireland and Continental Europe. Boston grew from a modest town of 24,900 in 1800 to a world-class city of 448,500 in 1890 (Weber, 450). Paris quadrupled from 547,000 in 1801 to 2.4 million in 1891, rising from 2 percent to over 6 percent of the nation's population. Berlin grew from 201,000 to 1.6 million between 1819 and 1890.

Second-tier cities also grew rapidly during the nineteenth century. In England and Wales, no cities except London had over 100,000 inhabitants in 1801. By 1851, there were eight cities of that size besides London with a total population of 1.6 million; by 1891, there were 23 such cities with a total of 5 million inhabitants, slightly more than London itself.

The United States was more decentralized. Weber counted 28 "great cities of 1890" totaling 9.7 million people, of which New York accounted for about 28 percent. Thus, a broader distribution of large-city growth is more apparent in 19th century America than in Great Britain, reflecting both the larger geographic size of the former and the westward migration of American settlement. Paris (with 2.5 million out of 4.5 million inhabitants of 12 "great cities" in 1891) dominated France as London did England. In the more decentralized German Empire, however, Berlin accounted for only 1.6 million out of 5.9 million inhabitants of 25 German "great cities" in 1890–comparable to the status of New York in the American system of cities.

Regulation: Public Sanitary Reform

Urban Squalor

The building of dwellings to accommodate the astronomic increase in urban populations in the industrializing nations during the 19th century lagged far behind demand. Overcrowding to inhuman levels was ensured by the prevailing building practices of the times. Unfettered by any public regulations, these practices were guided on the one hand by the need for proximity–housing had to be within walking distance to locations of employment–and, on the other hand, by the builder's greed. Thus, dwellings were minute in size and packed together with space left unbuilt only to the minimum extent necessary to provide physical access to each unit.

A prevalent building pattern in English industrial cities during the first half of the 19th century was the "court system." Dwellings were constructed facing streets with a second row, back to back with the first row, which faced only onto an interior court or alley. Narrow tunnels connected these interior courts with the streets and outside world (Figure 6-1). In the absence of any means for removing sewage and refuse from the premises, the courts, alleys, and streets served as waste receptacles. With sunlight and ventilation blocked out, the stench and health hazards were unimaginable (Figure 6-2).

Numerous eyewitness accounts of conditions in the mid-19th century were provided by socialists and other reformers. Friedrich Engels described Manchester in 1845 as follows:

FIGURE 6-1   Diagram of a tenement courtyard in Nottingham, England, ca. 1840. *Source:* Benevolo, 1967. Reproduced by permission of Routledge & Kegan Paul Ltd.

Here one is in an almost undisguised working-man's quarter, for even the shops and beer-houses hardly take the trouble to exhibit the trifling degree of cleanliness. But all this is nothing in comparison with the courts and lanes which lie behind, to which access can be gained only through covered passages, in which no two human beings can pass at the same time. Of the irregular cramming together of dwellings which defy all rational plan, of the tangle in which they are crowded literally one upon the other, it is impossible to convey an idea. And it is not the buildings surviving from the old times of Manchester which are to blame for this; the confusion has only recently reached its height when every scrap of space left by the old way of building has been filled up and patched over until not a foot of land is left to be further occupied. . . . he who turns [into the maze of passageways and courts] gets into a filth and disgusting grime the equal of which is not to be found. . . . In one of these courts there stands directly at the entrance a privy without a door, so dirty that inhabitants can pass into and out of that court only by passing through foul pools of urine and excrement. Below it on the river there are several tanneries which fill the whole neighborhood with the stench of animal putrefaction.

Quoted in Benevolo 1967, p. 23.

Not only were the dwelling units pitifully small to begin with, but they were hopelessly overcrowded. According to Rosen (1958, 206), Manchester in 1841 "had 1500 cellars where three persons, 738 where four, and 281 where five slept in one bed." Liverpool, Bristol, Leeds, Glasgow, and London all contained sizable districts of similar nature. Liverpool in 1884 was reported to have certain districts with up to 1210 persons per acre (Ashworth 1954, 10). In the United States, high-density tenement

FIGURE 6-2   Broadside protesting inaction of improvement commissioners regarding sewerage, 1832. *Source:* Benevolo, 1967. Reproduced by permission of Routledge & Kegan Paul Ltd.

districts flourished in ports of entry for European immigrants. New York's Lower East Side had a density of 272 persons per acre in 1860, which doubled in the next 30 years as further waves of Irish and Italian immigrants arrived (Weber, 460).

Public Health Implications and Reforms

The pervasive overcrowding and lack of sanitation and basic hygiene, water supply, fresh air, and opportunity or provision for outdoor recreation, combined with long working hours in the factories and mills, inevitably magnified human misery and shortened life expectancy. Tuberculosis or "consumption" was the leading cause of death in urban England during the 19th century. TB was inevitably associated with undernourishment, poor ventilation, and general debilitation (Flinn 1965, 11). TB, however, attracted little social consternation before the 1840s since it was viewed as an inevitable, albeit undesirable, aspect of the working-class existence. Also, statistics on TB were unreliable due to the difficulty of diagnosing the disease and the absence of a central governmental office for collecting statistics on morbidity and mortality. As long as people of influence were unthreatened by tuberculosis and its companion urban killer, typhus, nothing was done about it.

Cholera was another story. This Asian import struck London in 1831–1832, and reappeared in 1848–1849, 1854, and 1867. In terms of numbers of deaths and chronic level of threat, cholera was far less important than tuberculosis or typhus. But its effects were not confined to poor districts. Cholera struck with particular force in the wealthy neighborhoods where plumbing and connection to central (polluted) water supplies facilitated its spread. Together with a growing incidence of crime against property, cholera galvanized consternation of the elite regarding the conditions of urban squalor in their midst:

> Even if he were not his brother's keeper, every man of property was affected by the multiplication of thieves; everyone who valued his life felt it desirable not to have a mass of carriers of virulent diseases too close at hand.
>
> Ashworth, p. 47.

And another pithy account:

Cholera frightened people. It stirred even the moribund, degraded, unreformed municipal corporations into fits of unwonted sanitary activity. It was the clearest warning of the lethal propensities of the swollen towns of the new industrial era.   Flinn 1965, p. 8.

Cholera frightened the elite, but fear per se is a poor basis for public action. Converting fear into rational public response required, not simply emotional rhetoric, but sound scientific investigation and documentation. The period between 1832 and 1860 was to be the "golden age" of sanitary surveys, which led to the modern public health movement (Rosen 1958, 213).

Besides the cholera scare, two other factors helped lay a foundation for sanitary reform. One was the development of the *science of statistics* and its application to the analysis of social problems. The first British census was undertaken in 1801, partly to start a database for the calculation of premiums for government-sponsored life insurance. The field of vital statistics was pioneered by William Farr, a dedicated statistician and officer of the Register-General's Office. His statistical reports "provided the ammunition used in the campaigns against disease in the home, in the factory, and in the community as a whole" (Rosen, 227).

The other factor was the appearance of a *political philosophy* that urged government intervention to remedy social ills that impeded the economy. The necessary framework was provided by the Philosophic Radicals, a small group of intellectuals headed by the energetic and enigmatic Jeremy Bentham (whose earthly remains dressed in his own clothes today reside in a hallway at University College, London). Among other reforms in the fields of law, education, and birth control, the Philosophic Radicals called for a review of the Poor Laws. Their objective was not to make the poor more comfortable, but rather to centralize relief to the poor and to ensure that the system promoted rather than discouraged working for a living [an unexpected forerunner of the "Contract with America" in the 1990s!].

That the appointment of a Royal Poor Law Commission in 1832 would eventually lead to sanitary reform was in large part due to the driving force of a key individual: Edwin Chadwick. Like Robert Owen, Frederick Law Olmsted, and Ebenezer Howard, Chadwick exemplified the 19th century tradition of the inspired amateur. Like Howard, Chadwick would eventually be knighted for distinction in a field in which he had no formal training. Through a close association with Jeremy Bentham (for whom he served as secretary), Chadwick was appointed in 1832 as secretary to the new Poor Law Commission where he remained until 1847. Before 1838, Chadwick's interest in public health was minimal insofar as the commission's attention was largely devoted to factory and Poor Law reform (Flinn, 35). But inevitably his research into the causes of public outlays for "poor rates" (welfare payments) led to the long-ignored physical environment of industrial slums. Assisted by three physicians, Chadwick prepared a commission report in 1838 that linked for the first time the incidence of disease fostered by unsanitary living conditions to the economic costs borne by the nation through the payment of poor rates.

This report marked the beginning of a series of sanitary surveys that applied the new science of statistics to the analysis of patterns of illness and death. Essential to this task was a geographic perspective. With reasonably accurate vital statistics supplied by William Farr, the spatial patterns of disease could be mapped and related to environmental factors such as water supply. For example, there were 2000 deaths from cholera in 1854 in Newcastle-on-Tyne, while in Tynemouth, eight miles away, where new drainage regulations were in force, only four deaths occurred (Ashworth, 61).

The year 1838, then, was an important turning-point in the history of the public health movement. Although its roots stretch back 50 years, the movement was, before 1838, unorganized, leaderless, and in a legislative sense—the only sense that mattered in the long run—aimless. Essential foundations had been laid, preconditions established, but, important as these were, effective action was missing. This is what Chadwick supplied (Rosen, 35).

The seminal document of the sanitary survey literature was the 1842 "Report of the Poor Law Commissioners Concerning the Sanitary Condition of the Labouring Population of Great Britain." Written largely by Chadwick, it was based, on the one hand, on a broad empirical investigation of the incidence and causes of disease in poor districts based on statistical surveys and expert accounts. On the other hand, it reflected Chadwick's personal research in the scientific literature on epidemiology and urban health. It was graphic and candid in its portrayal of the squalor prevailing in Great Britain's industrial towns. In its effort to relate physical deficiencies to human health and quality of life,

Chadwick laid a foundation for future work in urban sociology as well as public health. Like the commission convened by Charles II after the London Fire, it anticipated the modern "blue ribbon commission" as a vehicle to inform decision makers on the details of a serious problem.

Although the report emerged from a review of the public costs of poor rates, the economic implications are in fact subordinated to issues of human suffering. After thus reviewing the social, health, and moral effects of urban slum conditions in the first four chapters, the report turns to: "Pecuniary Burdens Created by Neglect" and "The Effects of Preventive Measures," including actions by public authorities and employers to improve sanitary conditions. Chapter 7, which reviews existing legal authorities relating to sanitation and public safety, is surprisingly reticent about directly proposing any reforms. Evidently, Chadwick did not want to alienate his conservative audience by calling too blatantly for governmental intervention in the private land development process.

The report's final section focuses on technology rather than legal measures to improve sanitary conditions. Public authorities are urged to install "water carriage drainage" and water supply systems to provide for the removal of wastes from the human habitat. Chadwick was also a strong proponent of reviving the medieval custom of "night soil," the application of human wastes to agricultural land.

The 1842 report was thus indirect on the need for stronger building laws to require the use of safer construction methods, to reduce overcrowding through occupancy limits, to make adequate provision for ventilation and isolation of wastes, and to limit the number of dwellings per unit of land. Such limitations on the private sector were still too controversial even to be suggested. But Chadwick performed a unique public service in documenting the nature, extent, causes, and economic implications of urban squalor.

The following year, Parliament established a Royal Commission of the State of Large Towns and Populous Districts (Health of Towns Commission): The role of the Health of Towns Commission was thus to substantiate by more systematic and widespread survey the accuracy of Chadwick's axioms, and to point more precisely to the details of any necessary legislation. In this way the Royal Commission was a logical and reasonable extension of Chadwick's work (Flinn, 67).

Although not appointed as a member of the commission (perhaps to avoid the appearance of bias), Chadwick served as unofficial consultant and actually wrote much of its two reports in 1844 and 1845 (Flinn, 67–68). These included legislative proposals that Chadwick felt obliged to postpone in 1842, such as (Benevolo, 91–93):

- Delegation of responsibility for sanitary regulation to local health authorities, under royal supervision

- Preparation of detailed sanitary surveys within a district before planning a drainage system

- Coordination of sewer construction with road improvements

- Establishment of minimum sanitary requirements for new dwellings

- Requirements for ventilation and cleaning of existing dwellings

- Construction of new public parks in industrial cities

In 1848, faced with a new outbreak of cholera, Parliament finally adopted England's first comprehensive Public Health Act. This law culminated a decade of investigations beginning with the 1838 Poor Law Commission Report. It was squarely based on the 1845 Royal Commission Report which, in turn, drew heavily from the 1842 report, all drafted by Chadwick. Thus a major legislative reform was achieved in response to the perception of environmental threat documented in these and other investigative reports. Like the Act for Rebuilding London after the Fire of 1666, the 1848 Public Health Act demonstrated the capacity of the British legal system to respond (albeit belatedly) to the need for innovation in the face of disaster (Figure 6-3).

The 1848 Act was a fairly tame beginning. It established a General Board of Health and authorized the creation of local district health boards but for only five years, reflecting a reluctance of Parliament to establish a permanent national role in sanitary reform. The powers delegated to the district boards were generally permissive rather than mandatory. However, they were required to prepare "a map exhibiting a system of sewerage for effectually draining their district . . . " Furthermore, new dwellings within established health districts must be equipped with drains and a lavatory, a totally unprecedented public requirement. Other provisions dealt with refuse collection, removal of

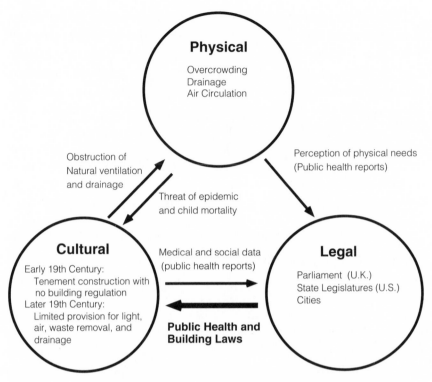

FIGURE 6-3 Model of 19th century public health and sanitary reforms.

harmful wastes, inspection of slaughterhouses and lodging houses, paving and upkeep of roads, establishment of public gardens, water supply, and burial of the dead (Benevolo, 96–97).

It is of course one thing to pass a law and another to bring about the physical changes desired. While the 1848 Act did not overnight make working districts habitable, nor even lower the death rate appreciably, it did serve as the beginning of the modern era of public involvement in the growth of cities:

> The Act of 1848 constituted a tentative and uncertain start to government action in a major field.... Nevertheless, it had put a foot through a door which had hitherto defied all attempt at opening, and although the detailed administrative arrangements it laid down were scrapped within half a dozen years, its principle of state responsibility was not discarded. It was this principle which the [1842] "Sanitary Report" had sought to establish. Flinn, p. 73.

Chadwick's work and the 1848 Act that codified his recommendations influenced subsequent sanitary reform in Great Britain and elsewhere. The British Public Health Act of 1875 and Housing of the Working Classes Act of 1890 were direct legacies of the 1848 Act (Benevolo, 100). The English reforms were watched closely in Europe and influenced parallel efforts in the United States where industrialization and immigration were rapidly overcrowding American coastal cities. By mid-century, sanitary investigations inspired by Chadwick's work were underway in New York, Boston, and other cities, with new public health laws soon to follow. The New York (State) Metropolitan Health Act of 1866 was the first major American law in this field. (The U.S. federal government would play no major role in urban environmental issues until the 1960s.)

The sanitary reforms of the mid-19th century launched not only modern public health but also the field of city planning. Peterson (1983) identifies three results of 19th century sanitary investigations that underlie modern town planning: (1) water-carriage sewerage; (2) sanitary survey planning; and (3) townsite consciousness, as reflected in the urban parks movement. While one may quibble with the exact points of influence, there is no question that sanitary reform gave birth to the urban planning movement of the early 20th century. The conduct of sanitary surveys helped to develop the methodology of general planning investigations through the assembly, display, and interpretation of diverse data, including physical, demographic, and cultural. Also, the surveys elevated the geographic scale of investigation from selected neighborhoods or problem areas to entire cities, and even metropolitan regions.

Sanitary reforms were the logical prerequisite to the consideration of a broader range of urban planning issues such as transportation, housing, economic development, zoning of land, and environmental protection:

> Sanitary legislation would have to develop within the general framework of town-planning legislation, and that, once one problem had been isolated for consideration—that of sanitation—all others would necessarily follow.
>
> Benevolo, p. 93.

Ultimately, building and public health legislation, primitive though it was, laid a constitutional foundation for the acceptance of broader land use zoning and environmental regulations in the 20th century.

Redevelopment: A Century of Municipal Improvements

Advent of Public Responsibility

The rapid growth in urban population during the 19th century yielded both intensification and outward sprawl of cities. Existing built-up areas, which were originally tailored to medieval or colonial levels of population, became increasingly overcrowded, leading to the dangerous conditions discussed in the preceding section. Cities also expanded spatially to encroach on adjacent rural lands as horse-drawn and, later, electric streetcars and subways placed a new suburban hinterland within reach of middle-class office workers (Warner 1978). Some of this expansion occurred within the political limits of the central city, either as already established (as with New York City's growth northward on Manhattan Island), or as enlarged politically (e.g., annexations to Boston and Chicago in the 1870s). Increasingly, however, peripheral development occurred outside the political limits of the central city in independent suburbs, thus marking the inception of the modern metropolitan region (Jackson 1985).

Concomitant to the demographic and geographic growth of 19th century cities was the emergence of government as an active participant in the process of urban development. London, which had possessed a municipal charter of self-government since 1193, nevertheless by 1800 still lacked the ability or the will to provide basic urban services such as water supply, drainage, paving, and street lighting to most of its inhabitants. For those not fortunate enough to live in one of the privately planned estate developments, the haphazard activities of the improvement commissions and a few widely ignored municipal regulations represented the extent of public interest in their welfare. Paris, which, unlike London, had not burned in recent history, remained medieval in its physical appearance and state of infrastructure.

The impress of public authority on European cities in 1800 was largely of royal origin. London's Hyde Park was a former royal hunting ground that was opened to public recreational use around 1640 (Rasmussen 1967, 92). In Paris, the Bois de Boulogne and Bois de Vincennes were former royal parks. The Champs Elysees originated in 1670 at the direction of Louis XIV's minister Colbert. The Place de la Concorde was laid out in the mid-18th century by Louis XV. Berlin's Tiergarten was another former royal hunting ground. The great Unter den Linden Boulevard, the

"Champs Elysees of Berlin," was laid out by Frederick William in the mid-17th century.

Demand for more plebeian parks was for a time satisfied by privately operated "pleasure gardens" that offered a broad array of amusements, food and drink, and recreation in lush horticultural settings. Foremost among these were the Vauxhall Gardens and Renelagh House Gardens in London: "By the mid-18th century London had several dozen pleasure gardens of all sizes, social gradations, and architectural ambitions, but Vauxhall and Renelagh reined supreme" (Girouard 1985, 192). Counterparts appeared in most European cities, and later in America. But as private enterprises, these mostly succumbed eventually to rising property values. The best-known remaining example of a pleasure garden is the Tivoli in Copenhagen. Today, private amusement parks and "theme parks" modeled on the original Disneyland offer a contemporary version of the pleasure garden, although at vastly greater expense.

In America, urbanization had scarcely begun in 1800, let alone the emergence of urban institutions. Bridenbaugh (1964) documents the struggle of incipient urban communities to cope with chronic problems of water supply, fires, epidemics, and crime. Boston and New York, for instance, passed municipal laws during the 17th and 18th centuries requiring suitable construction and periodic inspection of chimneys. In the absence of a public fire department, each Boston householder was required to possess a bucket, ladder, and long-handled swab for extinguishing rooftop fires. Lacking a municipal water supply, the standard method for halting the spread of fires in colonial America, as in 17th century London, was to pull down or blow up houses in the path of the conflagration (Bridenbaugh, ch. 7).

Necessary public facilities in colonial American towns were usually provided through private initiative, often with the benefit of a monopoly granted under a license from the colonial legislature or municipal authorities. Thus the Mill Dam constructed in Boston in the 1630s at the present site of Government Center was constructed by private citizens who leased sites for tidal-powered mills (Whitehill 1968, 5). The first bridge across the Charles River between Cambridge and Boston was constructed privately by entrepreneurs in 1768 (whose claim to a monopoly over river crossings was later rejected in a landmark court decision) (Kutler 1971). Boston's first public water supply was established at Jamaica Pond by a private company in 1796.

The rapid demographic and spatial expansion of both European and American cities in the early 19th century rendered such ad hoc and profit-oriented solutions outmoded as responses to many urban needs. While some services such as urban transportation, mills, and wharves continued to be provided through enfranchised private entrepreneurs, the urgent need to develop larger-scale facilities for common benefit, such as water and sewer systems, parks, highways, and firefighting capabilities, demanded that urban governments retool themselves, legally and technologically, to meet modern challenges.

Transition in London: The Nash Improvements

To the delight of Anglophiles and the agony of traffic engineers, London historically has refused to be a planned city. From the Fire of London to the Nazi blitz, proposals for a sweeping redesign of the metropolis have failed to win popular support. Aside from the neoclassical geometry of the West End squares and their imitators, the city as a whole has grown and evolved organically with a minimum of preconceived planning. The celebrated exception to this history of incrementalism was the work of John Nash:

> Once, and only once, has a great plan for London, affecting the development of the capital as a whole, been projected and carried to completion. This was the plan which constituted the "metropolitan improvements" of the Regency . . . carried out under the presiding genius of John Nash.   Summerson 1962, p. 177.

John Nash, born in 1752, was a prominent architect, society habitué, and close friend of the Prince Regent (who ruled in place of his insane father George III from 1811 until the latter's death in 1820, and then in his own right as George IV until 1830). Nash was to be the leading architectural influence of "Regency London" whose works included the famous Cumberland Terrace and Buckingham Palace. But it was his role as city planner in the conception and execution of Regent Street and Regent's Park that concerns us here.

The impetus to these projects was the reversion to the Crown in 1811 of a sizable tract of rural land at the (then) northern edge of London known as Marylebone Park. The English practice of leasing estates for long terms made the expiration of a leasehold a propitious time for converting land to more profitable uses. The newly installed Prince Regent therefore regarded the reversion of this land as an opportunity to create an aristocratic new suburb for himself and his friends, and also to enrich the royal household.

A major obstacle to this concept was the isolation of Marylebone Park from the City, the Court at St. James, and from the clubs on Pall Mall where gentlemen spent much of their time. In 1809, a preliminary plan for the property prepared by the Royal Surveyor General had envisioned the establishment of a new north–south street to connect the Park to the city. Nash elaborated on this concept and proposed the construction of an elegant street rivaling Napoleon's Rue de Rivoli in Paris extending between the future Regent's Park and the Prince Regent's doorstep at Carleton House. For the park itself, he proposed to convert the site into a vast picturesque landscape, punctuated by opulent villas and rows of aristocratic townhouses set in terraces or circular patterns (Figure 6-4).

Nash also proposed the creation of Trafalgar Square, the redesign of several streets in its vicinity, and the construction of Regent's Canal to serve as a navigation artery and water source for the lake and fountains of Regent's Park (Summerson, 177). Altogether, it was for London a program of unprecedented magnitude, aside from the grandiose proposals to rebuild the city after the 1666 fire. And unlike those, it was accomplished.

The importance of this vast undertaking as a transition between royal and public initiative is apparent in the contrast between the ends and the means involved. The Prince Regent made no secret of his wish to eclipse Napoleon as an imperial city builder and to enhance royal income (Summerson, 177). But he lacked the financial resources to accomplish the work, particularly the building of Regent Street. An appropriation from Parliament was required: "In order to obtain this, there must have been some social aim in view, and the building of the new street was granted in 1813 as a means of improving the sanitation of the unhealthy quarters" (Rasmussen, 274).

The alignment of the new street in fact involved an early exercise in "scientific" city planning. The route traversed the western edge of the shabby and cheap districts of Soho, directly adjacent to the more opulent Mayfair neighborhood. Thus Nash, the *planner*, fulfilled the parliamentary purpose of eliminating some rundown housing while acquiring the right-of-way as cheaply as possible. The choice of alignment

FIGURE 6-4 London improvement designed by John Nash, 1812–1835. Regent Street connects Regents Park at top to central London at bottom. *Source:* Benevolo, 1967. Reproduced by permission of Routledge & Kegan Paul Ltd.

simultaneously ensured that the new street would be assimilated to the fashionable West End district, thereby enhancing the value of frontage on both sides of Regent Street for business and residence. In Nash's own words, the new street would provide: ". . . a boundary and complete separation between the streets and squares occupied by the nobility and gentry, and the narrow streets and meaner houses occupied by mechanics and the trading part of the community" (quoted in Davis 1966, 66). (This idea was similar in concept to the U.S. urban renewal programs of the 1950s and 1960s.)

Mindful of the need to satisfy the vanity of his royal patron and potential investors, Nash as *architect* designed elegant neoclassic facades for his Regent's Park terraces and Regent Street frontage. Park Crescent, where the street meets the park, is a fine surviving example of "pure Nash"—a curving, colonnaded exterior of creamy stucco. This stylish facade, reminiscent of Wood's Royal Crescent at Bath, at once provides a satisfying backdrop to the greenery of the park and merges an entire row of townhouses into a continuous, majestic unity.

Finally, Nash as *landscape architect* achieved brilliance in the design of Regent's Park itself. Between 1796 and 1802, Nash had been a partner with the landscape architect Humphry Repton, whose influence on the design of Regent's Park is striking:

> It was from Repton that Nash obtained the idea of "appropriation," so that each villa commanded a pleasant prospect whilst not in view from any other villa, the management of the water (except the formal canal) was Reptonian, with its extremities concealed by bridges and by planting; the planting itself, in its blending of wood and lawn, or the contrast between villa and background, owed much to Repton; whilst even the idea of the canal traffic enlivening the scene is akin to Repton's use of cattle to give interest and scale in a park. . . ."
>
> Chadwick 1966, p. 31.

At first, there was nothing "public" about the plans and execution of Regent's Park. In concept it was simply a grandiose version of the West End squares laid out by landed aristocrats for their peers. The public was not admitted to Regent's Park until 1838, and even then there was little provided for the enjoyment of the horseless working class (Chadwick,

32). But over time, Regent's Park evolved from a "garden suburb" for the aristocracy to a public pleasure ground bordered by expensive town-houses. Today, Regent's Park is one of London's largest and most heavily used parks and contains, among other amenities, the London Zoo and vast flower gardens.

Nash was associated with two other park projects in central London, both designed to be public from the outset. One was St. James Park, a Crown property since the reign of Henry VIII, which Nash redesigned in 1828, again with Reptonian flourishes. Chadwick (p. 34) considers St. James Park to be the first English public park, although technically not in public ownership.

Trafalgar Square was, by contrast, public from the outset in both ownership and use (Figure 6-5). As London's equivalent of New York's Times Square, Trafalgar Square has always been the place for crowds to gather to protest governmental policies, to celebrate victories, or to welcome the New Year. This may not have been the intention of Nash, and certainly not of his royal patron. But in 1830, the latter died and the Square opened, symbolizing the passing of royal pretense and the advent of planning for "the people."

Haussmann's Transformation of Paris

The Nash "regency program" in London was but an appetizer to the banquet of urban and metropolitan improvements in Paris undertaken by Emperor Napoleon III and his alter ego, Baron Georges-Eugene Haussmann. The rebuilding of Paris between 1853 and 1870, with work continuing until the outbreak of war in 1914, touched every inhabitant of Paris and its suburbs. It ingeniously blended the aesthetic with the functional. It pioneered new methods of finance and public administration. It converted Paris from an overcrowded, unhealthy medieval town into the fabled "City of Light."

The onset of comprehensive redevelopment of Paris coincided with the election of Louis-Napoleon as president of the Second French Republic after the Revolution of 1848. Returning from exile in England, this nephew of Napoleon Bonaparte immediately undertook to revive and continue the program of public works initiated in Paris by his uncle and carried on spasmodically under the Bourbon Restoration. Perhaps influenced by the recent cutting of Regent Street and laying out of

FIGURE 6-5   John Nash's Trafalgar Square, London, established in 1830.

Regent's Park in London, Louis-Napoleon turned his attention first to the streets and parks of Paris. Following the coup d'état of 1851 and his assumption of the title of emperor, he selected Haussmann, then a rising lawyer and provincial administrator, to serve as Prefect of the Seine in 1853:

> This was a very special post not only because the Seine was the richest and most densely populated Department in France, and Paris the hub of national political life, but also because on grounds of public policy, the Prefect of the Seine acted both as head of the Department and as municipal head of the city of Paris itself, two posts of immense influence and powers.   Chapman 1953, p. 179.

Haussmann's powers were civil and municipal in nature, not delegated directly by the newly installed emperor. While the latter certainly provided much of the stimulus to the redevelopment of Paris, the actual program was a joint undertaking of the state, city, and private sector, utilizing essentially modern forms of legal procedures, financing, and contracting. Regal in scale and inspiration, the rebuilding of Paris was civic and bourgeois in execution.

Napoleon III's motives for undertaking the program are subject to debate. The conventional wisdom ascribes the cutting of the great boulevards and the star-shaped "places" (most notably the Place de l'Etoile) to military considerations, namely the need to protect the government against the socialist rabble who flourished in the labyrinthine streets of Old Paris (Peets 1927). Certainly the revolutions of 1830 and 1848 may have influenced thinking, but great boulevards are two-way streets, as the Germans demonstrated in 1871 and 1940. A more humanitarian view is suggested by Smith (1907, 369), who attributes to him an understanding of the "sociological and hygienic condition of modern civilization [which] . . . forced upon him the sympathetic duty of making a suitable home for [his] people." Chapman (1953, 182) suggests three motives: (1) military considerations; (2) economic revitalization; and (3) "to make Paris into a capital city worthy of France, a capital provided with the light, beauty, and cleanliness essential to human dignity in cities."

Even before Haussmann arrived on the scene, his future patron was already engaged in planning new avenues and redesigning Paris's great western park, the Bois de Boulogne. The latter was a former royal hunting ground that the City of Paris took over from the Crown in 1848 on the understanding that the City would improve it as a public park: "The Emperor himself was vastly interested in the scheme, which he saw as a future rival to Hyde Park and the other royal parks of London which he had known earlier as a refugee in England" (Chadwick, 153).

With the appointment of Haussmann in 1852, the urban rebuilding program began in earnest. Haussmann's first act was to order the preparation of an accurate survey of the city, using temporary timber towers to provide clear sight lines over the tops of buildings. The first phase of new avenue construction was approved in an 1855 law appropriating 60 million francs. This phase involved the construction of new principal north–south and east–west routes to reestablish the ancient Roman road crossing at the city's heart (Smith 1907, 372).

The great boulevards laid out under this and subsequent phases of work are the most familiar and cherished elements of post-Haussmann Paris (Figures 6-6 and 6-7). Clearly inspired by neoclassical and baroque precedents, notably Louis XIV's Palace of Versailles, the Haussmann boulevards were widely acclaimed and set the style for ambitious cities around the world. For example, an ecstatic American architectural critic wrote in 1907:

The Avenue Napoleon, now de l'Opera, is a perfect modern French street; not too long, spacious, well-built and furnishing axial vista to a fine symmetrical monument. This is the culmination of the classic scheme of axial symmetry, conceived in the Hellenic period, more perfectly suggested in the Roman, carried a little farther in the Renaissance, fully understood by the Bourbon designers in France and brought to an ideal and complete realization by Haussmann in the Avenue de l'Opera.

Smith, p. 496.

To a greater extent than Nash's Regent Street in London, Haussmann's avenues and boulevards extended from point A to point B through whatever lay in their path. Not simply a widening of existing streets, these projects involved the acquisition, demolition, and replacement of the adjoining frontage on both sides of the new street. The result, as visible today along the Boulevards Sebastopol, de Saint-Michel, de l'Opera, among others, is a broad, tree-lined avenue separated into through-traffic lanes, local-service access lanes, and ample pedestrian sidewalks. The avenues are bordered by substantially uniform facades of

FIGURE 6-6   Bird's-eye view of two Haussmann boulevards, Paris, ca. 1870s.
Source: Benevolo, 1967. Reproduced by permission of Routledge & Kegan Paul Ltd.

FIGURE 6-7   A street scene along a Haussmann Paris boulevard.

stylish, balconied, Second-Empire buildings. Unlike West End London, where residential quarters were isolated from commerce, the new frontage buildings in Paris have always been multipurpose. The ground floor is devoted to shops, cafes, banks, and restaurants. The next three or four principal floors contain elegant apartments for the upper middle class. Above them, the attics beneath the mansard roofs contain artists' studios and garret rooms for the poor (Saalman 1971, 26–27).

The frontage bordering the new avenues experienced a phenomenal increase in value, as Haussmann expected. It was his hope that the city would retain ownership of the frontage and lease or sell it on the open market to capture the increase in value and thereby defray part of the cost of building the streets. This creative use of excess condemnation, however, was opposed by the financial community and was finally prohibited by the Council of State in 1858, which ordered that frontage lots, once cleared, should be returned to their previous owners (Benevolo, 135–136). This promoted a lively speculation in land expected to be acquired for new streets. Construction of the new frontage buildings proceeded under private auspices but with uniformity of style ensured by a combination of public building restrictions and the dictates of the fashion of the time. In this respect, the rebuilding of Paris resembled the laying out of Back Bay in Boston, which was occurring simultaneously.

The architectural critic Siegfried Giedion (1962) disliked the "great length" of Haussmann's boulevards, which he suggested were overly dominated by traffic concerns. But he praised the architectural treatment of the facades:

Haussmann showed his sagacity in refusing to allow any tricks to be played with facades. Simply and without discussion, he spread a uniform facade over the whole of Paris. It featured high French windows, with accents provided by lines of cast-iron balconies like those used in the Rue de Rivoli under Napoleon I. He employed, unobtrusively, Renaissance shapes of a pleasantly neutral nature. A last touch of the unity which marked baroque architecture can still be felt. The neutral facades and the general uniformity make Haussmann's enormous work of rebuilding better than any other executed in or after the fifties of the nineteenth century.

Giedion, p. 672.

Another legacy of the Napoleon III-Haussmann collaboration was a new system of parks and open spaces. The smallest of these were carved out of the existing medieval clutter at the junctions of major streets. These have since provided oases of foliage, gardens, statuary, playgrounds, and benches for the elderly and homeless. (These small squares were perhaps intended to replicate the atmosphere of the West End squares of London, which themselves were inspired by Paris's Place Royale.) Three larger "parcs-interieures" and the gardens of the Champs Elysees provided a middle scale of parks within the city. The regional parks of the Bois de Boulogne in the west and Bois de Vincennes in the east were elaborately redesigned to serve the well-to-do and the working-class populations of Paris on holidays. This three-tiered hierarchy of public open spaces qualifies Haussmann to be honored as "the creator of the first real urban park system" (Chadwick, 152).

Other Haussmann-era legacies to Paris included the former markets of Les Halles, the Opera, the completion of the Place de l'Etoile, several churches and theaters, major additions to the Louvre and the Sorbonne, and various hospitals and other institutions (Chapman, 185). Haussmann also tried unsuccessfully to develop regional cemeteries outside the city to prevent further contamination of local water supplies (Chapman and Chapman 1957, 126–130).

These projects visibly transformed the face of Paris but, aside from the new parks, did little for the city's health. Industrialization arrived in France a few decades later than in England, and by mid-century a coalition of physicians and social philosophers demanded sanitary reforms along the lines of the Chadwick proposals in England (Rosen, 252). Haussmann persuaded the emperor of the need to create a regional water supply system for Paris to replace its reliance on local wells, cisterns, and the foul Seine. Like Robert Moses, New York's legendary "power broker" of a later generation (Caro 1974), Haussmann was adroit at skirting the law to achieve his purpose: "He quietly went ahead with his plans for new aqueducts, his surveys, and the buying of sites, so that when finally permission was obtained he could immediately begin operations" (Chapman, 186). By 1870, when both the emperor and his chief engineer had been removed from office, work was underway on two aqueducts to bring fresh water to Paris from the Aisne and Loire river basins, far from the city.

The other fundamental contribution to public health of the Hauss-mann era was the Paris sewer system, a network of underground canals varying in width from four to 18 feet and totaling some 600 miles in length. Principal interceptor sewers and galleries were laid beneath the new avenues as those arteries were constructed, a significant departure from earlier practice of regarding new streets simply in terms of traffic capacity and as decorative amenities. The canals conducted street drainage and raw sewage to an underground reservoir beneath the Place de la Concorde, from which it flowed to the Seine a few miles down-stream from the city (Chapman, 187). Haussmann took special pride in the sewer system, which was not anticipated in the emperor's program (Chapman and Chapman, 104).

In terms of public works both seen and unseen, Paris was substantially transformed during the two decades of the Second Empire. And despite rancor over Haussmann's high-handed financial schemes, work contin-ued on many of his projects under subsequent governments until World War I.

As important as the physical results of this program, however, were its political and institutional implications. On a much vaster scale than Regency London, the French Second Empire involved the devolution of the authority of the sovereign to the service of the people: The royal or imperial whim was replaced in practical terms by the public interest, or at least the interests of the elite and the bourgeoisie, if not the working classes (Saalman 1971, 23).

In retrospect, the transformation of Paris under Napoleon III and Haussmann was an epic contribution to the evolution of modern cities. In form, it was inherently conservative and imitative. Precedents for baroque city plans were readily available—Wren's unused proposal for rebuilding London; the reconstruction of Lisbon after the 1755 earth-quake by Pombal; Peter the Great's capital at St. Petersburg; L'Enfant's 1792 Plan for Washington, D.C.; and the 1822 plan for Karlsruhe, the capital of Baden—all anticipated to some degree the outward appearance of post-Haussmann Paris.

But in other respects, the rebuilding of Paris was a unique, path-breaking experience that bridged the gap between the cities of the 18th and 20th centuries. Its legacies to modernizing cities elsewhere may be summarized under five headings: (1) aesthetic style; (2) functionalism; (3) metropolitanism; (4) finance; and (5) administration.

AESTHETICS

The architecture and plan of Second-Empire Paris were widely cele-brated as the ideal translation of classical and Renaissance principles into "modern" city planning (Smith, 406). The broad boulevards termi-nating in monumental focal points, the small and large parks, the statu-ary and fountains, the atmosphere of wealth and power—all set the model for aspiring cities around the world. Paris was imitated in late 19th century redevelopment in Vienna, Berlin, Barcelona, London, Rome, Budapest, and many other European national and regional capi-tals. In the United States, Haussmann's Paris was enshrined in the City Beautiful Movement, whose apotheosis was the 1893 Chicago World's Fair. Daniel Burnham, principal architect of the fair, also drew on Hauss-mann precedents profusely in his 1902 Plan for the Washington, D.C. park system and his 1909 Plan for Chicago. (See Chapter 7.)

The ornate "beaux arts" style has fallen into subsequent disfavor. The architectural critic Siegfried Giedion deplored the setback inflicted on American architecture, particularly the Chicago School, by imitators of Haussmann. The geographer Peter Hall (1988, 176) ridicules the early 20th century craze for City Beautiful plans and public buildings ". . . in the great commercial cities of middle and western America, where civic leaders built to overcome collective inferiority complexes and boost business."

FUNCTIONALISM

While the appearance of Haussmann's Paris was thus an important, if not totally admired, legacy, a more lasting contribution may be identified in his integration of urban infrastructure into the process of redevelop-ment. Thus the City Beautiful was also the "city functional." The impres-sive new avenues were pathways, not only for surface traffic, but also for sewers, as mains, water conduits, and, in the near future, metro tunnels and stations. All of the elements of the "metabolism of cities" were addressed somewhere in Haussmann's plans: housing, communications, food, water, gas, sewerage, commerce, education, culture, recreation, hospitals, cemeteries. Haussmann may be viewed as a founder of mod-ern comprehensive city planning.

METROPOLITANISM

In two respects, Haussmann contributed to recognition of the metropol-itan region as the appropriate geographic unit for management of the urban environment. The first was his successful advocacy of the legal expansion of the city to incorporate surrounding "faubourgs" or suburbs that had flourished outside the old city walls and therefore outside its taxing jurisdiction. In 1859, 11 communes containing some 400,000 inhabitants (many living in industrial tenements) were legally annexed to Paris, yielding its present area of legal jurisdiction. The annexed areas then had to contribute to the Paris tax revenues but in turn received costly public improvements (Chapman and Chapman, 135–138).

Similar enlargements of municipal territories occurred in London in 1888, in New York in 1898, in Berlin in 1923, and in Boston and Chicago as noted earlier. In the 20th century, however, annexations to central cities tapered off as metropolitan systems for providing water and other services to both central cities and suburbs became widespread. The Paris regional water system, reaching beyond the city limits as necessary to obtain and discharge water, was the other primary Haussmann contribution to metropolitanism.

FINANCE

A fourth Haussmann legacy was his development of modern fiscal approaches to urban redevelopment. About two-thirds of the total cost of improvements under his direction during the period 1853–1870 was derived from national and municipal grants and the sale of public lands and materials. (The municipal contribution was facilitated by the significant rise in tax revenues attributable to the improvements themselves.) The remaining one-third was financed through borrowing from private banks and other lenders. This "deficit financing," so familiar today, was novel and controversial in Haussmann's time. His optimistic expectations were proven accurate, however, and the loans were repaid (Chapman and Chapman, 236–237).

ADMINISTRATION

Finally, the Haussmann era marked an administrative revolution: the advent of the modern technocrat. With objectives established by higher authority—emperor, state council, or city—it was Haussmann's role to carry out the will of his superiors. According to Benevolo (p. 134):

> Precisely because he did have the Emperor's support, Haussmann was always able to avoid having to justify his actions politically and could present them as technical and administrative measures

deriving from objective necessities. . . . Haussmann set the pattern for the town-planner as a specialist worker who declines all responsibility for initial choice, and therefore in practice for the town-planner who is at the service of the new ruling class.

The transformation of Paris under Haussmann's direction was unparalleled in 19th century urban history; aside from wars or natural calamities, Haussmann's closest 20th century counterpart has been New York's Robert Moses (Caro 1974). Although Haussmann's program was high handed, expensive, elitist, and unpopular at the time with many Parisians, it created one of the world's most elegant, beloved, and (in the absence of war damage) enduring monuments of late-baroque city planning. Post-Haussmann Paris was a unique blend of the human and the majestic. On the one hand, its alleys, garrets, cafes, and universities nurtured literary and artistic exuberance—the Paris of Renoir, Monet, Gertrude Stein, Fitzgerald, and Hemingway. On the other hand, it served as exemplar of the baroque world capital with its boulevards, parks, museums, and visions of grandeur. And beneath it all lay the sinews of a modern metropolis.

Water Supply for New York and Boston

American urban communities in 1800 were few in number, small in size, and coastal in location. The colonial period had bestowed on each of these settlements the incipient infrastructure of a preindustrial settlement: streets (mostly crooked and unpaved), docks, a town meeting hall, some common open spaces, firefighting implements, a constabulary and jail, and a primitive water supply. As population growth began to soar in the early decades of the 19th century, the inadequacy of the latter was perceived to be the chief liability and limitation on urban health and prosperity.

The water problem for New York and Boston was especially acute. Situated respectively on an island (Manhattan) and a peninsula (Shawmut), the cities were bordered by tidal, brackish water with no available fresh water streams. Both therefore depended on wells or rainwater cisterns for their water needs. By 1830, New York had grown to 200,000 inhabitants and Boston to more than 58,000. In that year, Thomas Crapper (!) invented the flush toilet and thenceforth water consumption per capita would rise rapidly as waterborne sewerage gradually replaced on-site privies and night soil collection (Weidner 1974, 55).

Although they lacked the ability to foresee the future rise in demand for water, the citizens of New York and Boston were already dissatisfied with their existing supplies in 1800. The water table aquifers on which they depended were easily contaminated with wastes from privies. Wells close to the shore could become brackish due to saltwater intrusion. And with limited surface recharge of local groundwater, the reliable yield of springs and wells was insufficient. Rainwater cisterns added little to the general supply.

During the early decades of the 19th century, the provision of urban water supply was regarded as a private rather than a public function (Blake 1956, ch. 4). New York, Boston, Baltimore, and several small towns relied initially on enfranchised private companies in preference to assuming the burden directly. An exception was Philadelphia, where recurrent outbreaks of yellow fever at the turn of the 19th century prompted a more aggressive municipal response. In 1801, Philadelphia constructed at public expense a pumping plant on the Schuylkill River powered by two steam engines. This project was designed and promoted by the noted engineer Benjamin Latrobe. It marked both a technological and an institutional breakthrough, namely in the use of the steam engine to pump water, and the use of public taxation to establish a municipal water supply (Blake, 33).

Meanwhile in 1796, the Jamaica Pond Aqueduct Company was chartered to supply water to Boston. The company laid hollow-log pipelines four miles to Boston from Jamaica Pond in Roxbury, then an independent town. This early example of an extraterritorial water supply however was inadequate for firefighting or to meet the needs of the growing Boston population (Nesson 1983, 1–2).

In New York, the Manhattan Water Company was chartered in 1799 with an exclusive franchise to supply the city with water. It constructed a reservoir in lower Manhattan to supply a few hundred households from local groundwater:

> But this water proved both scarce and bad; the company, neglecting the ostensible purpose of its organization, soon turned its attention

almost exclusively to banking affairs and thus lost the confidence of the community, and it was not long before the new works were voted a failure.

Booth 1860, p. 666.

In 1811, a plan for the future expansion of New York was prepared by a special commission established by the state legislature. The "Commissioners' Plan" projected future streets marching miles into the countryside of upper Manhattan as far as "155th Street." The plan was an accurate, if monotonous, forecast of the spatial growth of the city. The opening of the Erie Canal in 1825, which connected the Hudson River with the Great Lakes, established the city's economic preeminence in the nation and doubled its population to 200,000 in the decade 1820–1830. Local water sources were hopelessly inadequate to serve this rapid rate of growth in terms of quantity, quality, and pressure. Various schemes were debated fruitlessly.

Finally, catastrophes in the form of fires (1828 and 1835) and cholera (1832) forced an end to the dithering. Colonel DeWitt Clinton, Jr. was retained by the city to assess the water crisis and propose a solution. His report predicted that Manhattan would reach a population of 1 million by 1890 (he was late by 12 years). His proposal was simple in concept and vast in magnitude, namely, to tap the Croton River 40 miles north of the city to obtain a reliable supply of 20 million gallons per day of pure upland water. (Clinton assumed a low per capita demand, not foreseeing the impact of the flush toilet.) The elevation of a Croton River reservoir at 200 feet above sea level would permit the water to flow by gravity through an aqueduct to be constructed with enough "head" to serve the needs of taller buildings and firefighting in the city (Weidner 1974, 28–31).

The Croton River project required the construction of storage and conveyance facilities unprecedented since the Roman Empire. With the total cost estimated at several million dollars, the project was too large and too important for private enterprise. Accordingly, the City of New York, under authority from the state legislature, undertook to plan and execute the Croton River project directly. A water commission was quickly appointed, financing was approved by the city's voters in 1835, and construction began in 1837.

The project involved five major structural elements: (1) a masonry dam 50 feet high and 270 feet long impounding a reservoir with a surface area of 440 acres and storage capacity of 600 million gallons; (2) a 40-mile covered masonry aqueduct with a cross section of 7-by-8 feet; (3) a 1450-foot-long "high ridge" to convey the aqueduct across the Harlem River into Manhattan; (4) a 35-acre receiving reservoir located within the future site of Central Park; and (5) a 4-acre, masonry-walled distributing reservoir located on the present site of the New York Public Library at Fifth Avenue and 42nd Street. The first Croton River water arrived in Manhattan on July 4, 1842, an event celebrated with church bells, cannon, and a 5-mile-long parade (Weidner, 45–46). The event was both a technological and an institutional threshold: the City of New York had arrived of age.

Six years later, Boston would hold a similar celebration. In 1845 John Jervis, who directed the Croton River project and was "America's foremost water supply engineer" (Nesson 1983, 4), was hired to study Boston's water dilemma. He recommended adoption of an earlier plan to create a water supply at Long Pond (later Lake Cochituate) in Natick, a distance of 17 miles from Boston. The Massachusetts legislature in 1846 authorized the Long Pond project to be constructed by the City of Boston and provided state backing of municipal bonds to finance it (Nesson, 9). The project was completed in two years and the westward march of Boston's quest for water was underway.

By 1860, Boston was using the entire safe yield of Lake Cochituate. With legislative backing, the city developed a new reservoir in Chestnut Hill and six smaller reservoirs in the Sudbury River watershed to augment the Lake Cochituate supply. Thus by 1878, Boston had tripled its supply to about 63 million gallons per day.

In 1898, Greater New York was formed through the consolidation of Manhattan, the Bronx, Queens, Brooklyn, and Staten Island into a single city of 3.5 million inhabitants. Despite enlargement of the Croton River system with a new aqueduct completed in 1891 and a new, much larger dam in 1906, the city required new sources of water. Between 1907 and 1929 it developed a series of reservoirs and a new aqueduct to draw water from the Catskill Mountains, 100 miles north of the city. The Catskill Aqueduct crossed the Hudson River by means of an "inverted siphon" 3000 feet long and 1100 feet below the surface of the river (Weidner, 161). This feat was repeated in the 1940s when the city reached out to the head waters of the Delaware River in central New York State. The Delaware River Aqueduct consisted of the world's longest continuous aqueduct tunnel of 105 miles (Weidner, 300). By the 1960s, the combined systems were supplying New York City with over 1 billion gallons per day, of which 41 percent was derived from the Catskill system, 36 percent from the Delaware River, and 18 percent from the Croton River.

Meanwhile, Boston was pursuing a similar course of action but under a different governmental framework. Whereas New York City itself established and continues today to operate its water supply system even in upstate New York, Boston's system in 1895 was sold to a newly created regional authority, the Metropolitan Water District. The District was charged by state legislation to develop new water supplies to serve Boston and its immediate suburbs. In 1908 the District completed Wachusett Reservoir, in central Massachusetts, connected by an 18-mile aqueduct to the Sudbury-Cochituate system. The 400-billion-gallon Quabbin Reservoir, 75 miles west of Boston, was constructed in the 1930s, completing the present metropolitan Boston water system, which serves 2.5 million people in the city and 43 suburbs (Platt 1995).

Thus, the water supply systems of both New York and Boston during the 19th century evolved from dependence on primitive, privately constructed local sources to large-scale, regional systems constructed and operated by governmental agencies. The transition reflects both the advance of modern technology (for example, the ability to construct underground aqueducts with high-pressure siphons) as well as the evolution of municipal and regional institutions capable of serving the public interest. As in Paris, the emergence of these institutions was characterized by the development of new forms of finance, the application of modern concepts of eminent domain (land taking), and the administrative skills of technical experts.

The New York/Boston model of interbasin diversion from distant, upland sources influenced many other American cities as well. Of course, long-distance diversions were not always required: Great Lakes cities found an ample source at their doorstep. (Chicago, however, had to dig a diversion channel to avoid polluting its water source with sewage discharges.) Western cities such as Los Angeles, San Francisco, Denver, and Phoenix have aggressively pursued scarce water wherever it could be found, developing whatever technical and institutional measures were necessary to procure it. In some cases, such as the Owens Valley project of Los Angeles, the legal means were shady and the technical execution flawed, as demonstrated in the collapse of the St. Francis Dam in 1905 (Reisner 1986). But the basic premise behind these western water wars was the same as that which motivated the Croton and Cochituate projects: Employ modern technology and political power to obtain water from wherever it may be found to ensure an unlimited supply of cheap water to the urban populace.

Urban Parks in America: The Olmsted Legacy

Imagine New York without Central Park, Philadelphia without Fairmont Park, San Francisco without Golden Gate Park, Boston without its "Emerald Necklace," and Chicago without its lakefront parks. How impoverished would be the urban habitat of America's older cities without their distinctive and spacious parks—their "green lungs" as the Victorians called them. The existence of the great city parks is perhaps taken for granted today by the residents of those cities. But, like urban water supply systems, parks did not simply happen to fall into place. They were established through deliberate public action, often amid controversy. Their creation during the second half of the 19th and early 20th centuries required vision, money, political power, artistic genius, legal innovation, manpower, and technology. The great urban parks were the embodiment of the maturing city as an instrument for social betterment. They have long been its most visible, accessible, and often most abused artifacts.

The advent of the American parks movement may be traced to 1853, the year that New York's Central Park was authorized by the New York State Legislature. Central Park represented several firsts: (1) the first deliberately planned urban park in the United States (Chadwick 1966, 190); (2) the first park project of Frederick Law Olmsted; (3) the first accomplishment of landscape architecture as a profession in the United States (Fabos et al. 1968); and (4) perhaps the first use of land-value increment taxation to finance a portion of the costs of a public improvement.

In just two decades of migration from the political turbulence in Europe between 1840 and 1860, Manhattan gained about a half-million new inhabitants. In 1845, Dr. John C. Griscom published: "A Brief View of the Sanitary Condition of the City," which, like Chadwick's studies in England, documented the abysmal conditions of overcrowding and incidence of disease in the city's tenement districts (Rosen 1958, 236). One implication of the growing crisis had already been addressed in the development of the new Croton River water supply, which reached the city (but certainly not all of its households) in 1842. But another need identified in Griscom's report, as in most sanitary reform literature of the time, was for public parks and open spaces where the working class could devote their few hours of leisure time to outdoor recreation and exercise.

In 1853, New York possessed only a handful of small parks, totaling about 117 acres (Olmsted and Kimball 1928/1973, 20). These were supplemented by some private "pleasure gardens" modeled on Vauxhall Gardens in London, but by 1850 these were disappearing as their site value for building rose. The only other open spaces available were cemeteries (Olmsted and Kimball, 21–22).

The proposal to establish a large central park in New York actually arose, not from the sanitary reformers, but from the city's literary and artistic community. During the middle decades of the century, cultivated Americans were aroused by the beauties of nature and wilderness as depicted by artists such as John James Audubon, Thomas Cole, and Frederick Church, writers such as George Perkins Marsh and Henry David Thoreau, and poets such as William Cullen Bryant and Henry Wadsworth Longfellow. In 1844, Bryant, as editor of the New York *Evening Post* wrote that "If the public authorities, who expend so much of our money in laying out the city, would do what is in their power, they might give our vast population an extensive pleasure ground for shade and recreation" (Olmsted and Kimball, 22). Bryant's appeal was reinforced by landscape architect Andrew Jackson Downing, whose journal "The Horticulturist" urged that New York should emulate England in the creation of large public parks.

But lacking a legacy of royal lands as in London, New York had to purchase land for a park from private owners. To obtain a sizable tract of land at a reasonable cost, it was necessary to look beyond the limits of the existing built-up city–about 34th Street in 1850–to the still rural precincts of upper Manhattan. At that time the proposed site of Central Park was a messy landscape of squatters, goats, mud, and rubbish, a 30-minute walk from the existing city. Its advocates, however, correctly anticipated that all of Manhattan would soon be urbanized and thus the park would be central indeed.

In 1853 the New York State Legislature authorized the city to establish Central Park. It was originally to comprise a rectangle of 770 acres, of which 150 acres was occupied by two Croton reservoirs completed in 1842 and 1858. The park was later expanded to 110th Street on the north, bringing its total area to 843 acres, about a half-mile by 2.5 miles.

The conversion of this huge and squalid tract of land into one of the world's great urban parks was the masterpiece of Frederick Law Olmsted. Olmsted possessed no particular training for the field that he would dominate. Born in 1822, he studied agricultural science and engineering at Yale and then devoted himself to farming, travel, and writing. He moved from his farm on Staten Island directly to the post of superintendent of the new Central Park project in 1857 (Sutton 1971, 7). In collaboration with Calvert Vaux, he prepared the winning plan in a design competition for the park. In 1858, he was appointed Architect in Chief to execute his own plan.

Olmsted and Vaux's "Greensward plan" for Central Park (Figure 6-8) was influenced by the English picturesque landscape tradition of Nash's Regent's Park and Paxton's Birkenhead Park in Liverpool (Chadwick 1966, 71–72). The essence of this tradition was deliberate informality, contrast between open meadow, groves of woods and water, and attention to the park's borders with the surrounding city. While as carefully planned and engineered as a formal baroque park such as Versailles, the picturesque style sought to create the illusion of an artificial "countryside." Olmsted wrote in 1872 that his purpose in designing Central Park was "to supply to the hundreds of thousands of tired workers, who have no opportunity to spend their summers in the country, a specimen of God's handiwork that shall be to them, inexpensively, what a month or two in the White Mountains or the Adirondacks is, at great cost, to those in easier circumstances" (Olmsted and Kimball, 46).

A distinctive feature of Central Park, later widely imitated, was the separation of different forms of circulation. Pedestrians were removed from the path of equestrians and carriages, and internal pleasure routes were isolated from crossroads for through traffic. Where routes serving different purposes met, Olmsted provided under- or overpasses to eliminate stopping points and to enhance the illusion of open countryside.

The building of Central Park was the largest public work yet undertaken in the City of New York, involving thousands of jobs and millions of dollars. Tammany Hall and the "Tweed Ring" hampered Olmsted in the execution of his plans during the 25 years of his official connection

FIGURE 6-8   Excerpt from "Greensward Plan" for New York's Central Park by
Olmsted and Vaux, 1858. *Source:* Fabos et al., 1968.

with Central Park. He actually resigned from the project five times (Sutton, 9). (The politics of Central Park were described by Frederick Law Olmsted, Jr. and Theodora Kimball.) Central Park has continued to spark civic controversy ever since, as with the "Tavern on the Green" battle during Robert Moses' term as Parks Commissioner in the 1960s (Caro 1974).

Despite its political travails, Central Park was a spectacular financial success. The total cost of acquiring its site of 843 acres from private owners was $7.4 million. This amount was reduced by $1.8 million charged to owners of frontage property on the theory of betterment of their property values. Thus, the net cost to the city of acquiring the land was about $5.6 million. The cost of improvements to the site was about $8.9 million, yielding a total cost to the city of $14.5 million (Olmsted and Kimball, 54 and 95). The project was self-funding through increases in property tax collections on surrounding land. In the 1870s, the annual increase in such taxes was estimated to exceed the annual interest on the park project costs by over $4 million (Olmsted and Kimball, 95). Today, condominiums with a view of Central Park cost upwards of $1 million apiece, with city tax revenues accordingly enriched.

From its inception, Central Park was also a functional success. In 1871, usership of the park amounted to some 30,000 visitors per day and over 10 million per year (Olmsted and Kimball, 95), or about 10 visits per capita for the entire population of Manhattan. The park was designed by Olmsted and Vaux to encourage active use in many ways, such as horseback riding, boating, carriage driving, skating, cycling, and strolling. Deliberate informality in the picturesque tradition dominates most of the park plan, with the exception of the formal baroque-style mall. Open meadows, rocky outcrops, wooded areas, and water surfaces encourage spontaneity and the sense of freedom which the "gilded age" associated with a rural landscape.

Olmsted was not reticent in extolling the success of Central Park. In 1880 he wrote:

. . . to enjoy the use of the park, within a few years after it became available, the dinner hour of thousands of families permanently changed, the number of private carriages kept in the city was increased tenfold, the number of saddle horses a hundredfold, the business of livery stables more than doubled, the investment of many millions of private capital in public conveyances made profitable.

It is often said, How could New York have got on without the park? Twelve million visits are made to it every year. The poor and the rich come together in it in larger numbers than anywhere else, and enjoy what they find in it in more complete sympathy than they enjoy anything else together. The movement to and from it is enormous. If there were no park, with what different results in habitat and fashions, customs and manners, would the time spent in it be occupied.

And the Park of Brooklyn [Prospect Park] . . . is sure, as the city grows, to be a matter of the most important moulding consequence—more than the great bridge [Brooklyn Bridge], more so than any single affair with which the local government has had to do in the entire history of the city."

Quoted in Sutton, 255.

The use of the term "moulding" [sic] is perhaps deliberately intended to suggest two meanings. First, Central Park and its counterparts in other cities were designed to "mould" the physical form and structure of the surrounding city. Parks were conceived to be oases of open space and bucolic scenery around which the city would grow. Second, parks were intended to "mould" the moral character of the populace. Olmsted frequently pontificated on the benefit of open space and outdoor recreation on the physical and mental health of the city dweller. These views became articles of faith in 20th century urban and regional planning.

Most of Olmsted's major urban parks have been undergoing renovation in recent years, with much debate between those who favor restoring Olmsted's original designs and plantings versus those who seek to adapt these spaces to more contemporary uses and pastimes. A new project proposed for Brooklyn's Prospect Park goes one step further, namely to replace Olmsted and Vaux's plantings, which have not fared well, with flora indigenous to the site before the park was established. The objective is to achieve sustainability and lower maintenance costs (*The New York Times* 1995, pp. 1 and 44).

But Olmsted's most important contribution to modern city planning was the recognition of parks and open space as integral elements of the urban system:

> The success and popularity of Central Park started a trend, and city administrators throughout the country woke up to the advantages of open spaces. The land they were willing to purchase and sacrifice for this purpose, however, was usually some site undesirable for commercial or residential buildings, and in no way integral to the established patterns of city life, for example: the Fens in Boston; the mountain in Montreal; the swamps in Buffalo; the marshlands in Chicago. In general, the officials adopted simplistic notions of a park, separating it in their minds from the activities of the city. *Olmsted's effort was to integrate the two.*
>
> Sutton, pp. 10–11; emphasis added.

The "Emerald Necklace" plan for the Boston park system, formulated in the 1880s, was a logical progression from the concept of Central Park (Figure 6-9). The Emerald Necklace comprised a series of major and minor open spaces, some existing and some proposed, to roughly encircle central Boston on its landward side. One anchor for the necklace was the old Boston Common and the Public Garden (laid out in 1839). The other terminus of the necklace would be the proposed Franklin Park. These were to be connected by a series of parkways and greenways bordering local streams. The achievement of these links was to be incorporated within the ongoing development of new land created by draining the Back Bay marshes in the 1860s. Commonwealth Avenue, a broad parkway, formed the main axis of the fashionable new Back Bay district and simultaneously served as a link in the Emerald Necklace.

The next link was less obvious. Olmsted urged that a remaining stretch of marsh bordering the humble Muddy River, a tributary to the Charles River, be set aside as open space with some modification, rather than be filled. Viewed in isolation, the Muddy River Fens were befouled with rubbish and sewage and generally unpromising as urban park space. But Olmsted enumerated multiple benefits to be achieved in rehabilitating the swamp: (1) abatement of a "complicated nuisance"; (2) "reconciliation of convenient means of general public communication through the adjoining districts of the city; (3) "dressing and embellishment of the

FIGURE 6-9   Olmsted's "Emerald Necklace" plan for the Boston Park System, ca. 1885. *Source:* Fabos et al., 1968.

banks"; and (4) an element of a "general scheme of sylvan improvement for the city" (quoted in Sutton, 227). Olmsted's "Fenway" is today sadly degraded by an elevated highway and lack of maintenance. It is chiefly known for its namesake, Fenway Park, the home of the Red Sox, and for several cultural and educational institutions in its vicinity.

The two paradigms of Olmsted's legacy were thus reflected in Central Park and the Emerald Necklace. The former involved the use of open space as the "working man's White Mountains" and the latter, the use of a series of connected open spaces to interrupt the spread of urbanization. Olmsted enjoyed a wealth of opportunities to apply these two paradigms to various cities of North America. In contrast to Haussmann, who dealt with all planning issues of a single city, Olmsted dealt with a particular issue, open space planning, in more than a dozen major cities. Olmsted is most celebrated for his achievements under the first paradigm, the creation of the great urban parks. But this legacy produced few sequels in 20th century America as the nation boarded its streetcars, electric commuter trains, and automobiles and turned its back on cities. The process of low-density suburbanization would ultimately promote interest in open space as a means of urban containment and separation— the second paradigm (Platt, Rowntree, and Muick, eds. 1994).

Olmsted's contribution to the evolution of urban and regional planning, as distinct from park design, was furthered in his Chicago activities. In 1869, he and Vaux designed a prototypical garden suburb at Riverside on the Des Plaines River, a few miles west of Chicago (Jackson 1985, 79–81). Riverside's curvilinear streets, common greenways, and spacious residential lots impressed Ebenezer Howard, who visited there in 1876 and incorporated these characteristics into his influential garden city proposal. (See next section.)

Olmsted returned to Chicago in 1890 as landscape architect to the Columbian Exposition of 1893. He planned the lakefront site for the Fair, which later became Jackson Park, to accommodate the great pavilions and exhibition halls amid open courts, lagoons, reflecting pools, and statuary. Alongside this beaux arts "White City" was a touch of pure Olmsted, a wooded island "to contrast with the artificial grandeur and sumptuousness of the other parts of the scenery" (Sutton, 194).

Behind the grandiose stage set of the White City, the Fair was celebrated for its unprecedented level of functional organization and planning. Transportation, food, lighting, water supply, waste disposal, and mechanical energy were all incorporated into its design. To highlight its function as a showcase for electricity, President Cleveland activated its lighting and fountains by pushing a button in Washington, D.C. Thus, while the Exposition looked backward to Haussmann, Versailles, and antiquity for its architectural inspiration, it looked forward to the 20th century in its application of technology to the design of a new community, albeit a temporary one. The contrast between the planned environment and what lay beyond its borders was widely noted according to Mayer and Wade (1969, 193):

> The [Exposition] was an artificial city that conflicted with the actual city in almost every important element. Where the American metropolis was chaotic and disorganized, the Exposition was planned and orderly; while the real city was private and commercial, the ideal was public and monumental; where Chicago was sooty and gray, the White City was clean and sparkling.

Olmsted as landscape architect was of course not responsible for the functional arrangements of the fair. But he may be credited for having successfully assimilated the demands of technology and aesthetics in his site design. This was in effect a land use plan incorporating both the built and the unbuilt elements of a "city." The application of this integrative approach to actual cities and their surrounding regions, most notably in the 1909 plan of Chicago, would be the work of Daniel H. Burnham, a Chicago architect and Director of Works for the fair. In effect, the torch of national preeminence in the art of planning cities passed from Olmsted to Burnham at the 1893 Exposition.

Burnham, whose contributions are considered in the next chapter, commemorated Olmsted's entire career in a tribute to:

> The genius of him who stands first in the heart and confidence of American artists. . . . He who has been our best adviser and our common mentor. In the highest sense he is the planner of the Exposition. No word of his has fallen to ground since first he joined us. . . . An artist, he paints with lakes and wooded slopes; with lawns and banks and forest-covered hills; with mountain-sides and ocean views. [We honor him] not for his deeds of later years alone, but for what his brain has wrought and his pen has taught for half a century.
>
> Quoted in Chadwick 1966, p. 196.

Relocation: The Ideal Communities Movement

This chapter has so far considered two avenues of public response to urban deterioration during the 19th century: *public health regulation* and *municipal redevelopment*. These two approaches went hand in hand, the first yielding building and sanitary codes to be applied by local public authorities and the second fostering the development of new streets and residential districts, water systems, sewers, and parks and other infrastructure. The regulatory and the redevelopment approaches addressed the ills of existing cities directly, with gradual, uneven, but generally positive results. The principal European and American cities of 1900, despite their much greater size, were arguably safer, healthier, and more habitable than they had been earlier in the century.

In contrast to these efforts to regulate and rebuild existing cities, a handful of influential idealists proposed a completely different approach, namely *relocation* of workers to new, planned industrial villages in rural settings. Such communities, it was argued, would promote health, happiness, productivity, and morality through the influence of a salubrious environment. Several individuals in Europe and America put their beliefs into practice and created model villages to inspire wider imitation. Although they did not succeed in the latter goal, the experimental communities and the theories of socioeconomic organization that prompted them have deeply influenced 20th century planning ideology.

The remainder of this chapter considers the experience of three pre-eminent 19th century ideal community proponents. To list them is to indicate that this was no tightly circumscribed school or movement, but rather a diverse collection of individualists motivated by quite different goals and assumptions. Those considered here are the Welsh-born utopian Robert Owen, the Chicago sleeping-car magnate George Pullman, and the stenographer/progressive Ebenezer Howard. These and their like-minded contemporaries had little in common except for a repugnance for large cities, an impatience with conventional reforms, and a faith in environmental determinism.

An important heritage that influenced the ideal industrial communities was the spiritual utopia movement that proliferated in the United States and elsewhere beginning in the late 18th century. The movement included a few long-lasting and economically viable communities such as the Shaker villages of New England and New York, the Oneida settlement in New York, the Amana colonies in Iowa, and the Mormons in Illinois and, later, Utah. They also included a variety of more ephemeral utopian experiments, whose religious or philosophical objectives perhaps overshadowed economic and functional practicality, as with Brook Farm in Massachusetts or the 30 Fourierist "phalanxes" established in the United States between 1843 and 1858 (Hayden 1976, 149). Concepts for spiritual utopias floated in the wind of mid-19th century America like cottonwood seeds. According to Ralph Waldo Emerson in 1840: "Not a reading man but has a draft of a new community in his waistcoat pocket" (quoted in Hayden, 9).

Utopian settlements established for religious or philosophical purposes were by definition limited to adherents to those beliefs, while industrial model towns were intended for a broader cross section of the working class. Also, the spiritual communities valued total isolation from mainstream society, while the industrial communities required access to main transportation routes (obviously a sleeping-car factory had to be connected to mainline railroads).

Religious communes, however, undoubtedly influenced the concept and form of industrial model towns and garden cities. Fundamental elements of both types of communities included: (1) centralized control over the use of land and structural development (usually through ownership of the site by sect or corporation); (2) proximity of work and residence; (3) population limits with overflow to be accommodated in new settlements in the vicinity; (4) a rural setting with much open space within and surrounding the community; and (5) facilities and programs for social, cultural, and moral betterment.

Owen: From Practice to Theory

Robert Owen (1771–1858) and Ebenezer Howard (1850–1928), respectively, opened and closed the 19th century symmetrically. Owen moved from practical experience gained in a preexisting community–New Lanark, Scotland–to articulate a general theory of cooperative socioeconomic organization. Howard first formulated his concept of the "garden city" and then successfully applied it in the establishment of new communities at Letchworth and Welwyn. Both proselytized public opinion but with quite different styles and results. Howard's "peaceful path to reform" promised a humanitarian experiment involving "no direct attack upon vested interests" (Osborn 1965, 131). He was rewarded with a knighthood in 1927. Owen's advocacy of labor organization earned him the adulation of subsequent socialists but no knighthood.

The laboratory for Owen's far-ranging theories was New Lanark, a village founded in 1783 as a site for cotton-spinning mills on a rapids of the Clyde River in south central Scotland (Figure 6-10). Owen, on marrying the daughter of one of the founders in 1800, assumed the position of manager of the mills, which then employed over 1100 workers, two-thirds of them children. Owen devoted the next 14 years and much of his personal profits to the improvement of New Lanark, both physically and institutionally. Living conditions first attracted his attention:

> The great bulk of their houses . . . consisted of one single room, and before the door of that room was, as often as not, a dung-heap. One of Owen's first acts was to build another story to each of these houses, thus giving the family two rooms, and to remove the dung-heaps to a less unhealthy and unsightly position.   Cole 1953, p. 54.

Owen also had the streets cleaned and paved and reorganized the provision of food and coal to the inhabitants.

Owen's chief contribution to New Lanark was in the area of education. He espoused the view, remarkable at the time, that children should be in school rather than in the mills—at least until the age of 10. His Institute

FIGURE 6-10   View of Robert Owen's New Lanark, ca. 1818. *Source:* Allen, 1986. Reproduced by permission of New Lanark Conservation Trust.

for the Formation of Character opened in 1816 (by which time he had bought the mills with several fellow investors including Jeremy Bentham). The institute provided child care and instruction beginning when a child could walk. It was designed to provide a balance of classroom teaching, exercise, and training in music and the arts and the "useful arts" (Benevolo, 40).

No more humble than Haussmann or Olmsted, Owen referred to New Lanark as "the most important experiment for the happiness of the human race that has yet been instituted at any time in any part of the world" (Allen 1986, 3). But the scope of his increasingly utopian schemes was rapidly expanding beyond the possibilities for practical implementation in the "experimental cell" of New Lanark (Ashworth, 119). In response to a national inquiry into the problem of unemployment and public unrest after the close of the Napoleonic Wars, Owen articulated his vision for "villages of cooperation." The advent of mechanization, Owen argued in his 1817 "Report to the Committee for the Relief of the Manufacturing Poor," displaced workers from their former jobs, who now were crowding the cities and depending on meager poor-law relief.

Owen proposed the creation of a network of communal, agricultural villages to accommodate this surplus population. His loosely described land use plan foreshadowed Howard's "green belt" concept and even Frank Lloyd Wright's "Broadacre City" of the 1930s. He envisioned village units of about 1000 inhabitants, set in a predominantly agricultural landscape. The populace would chiefly be occupied in farming activities, although some "manufactories" would also be provided. Like a feudal manor, each village would be largely self-sufficient in food (Cole, 110).

The design of the village nucleus, or "parallelogram" as he called it, was described more precisely. Owen specified the size, use, and arrangement of buildings for communal living, dining, education, and relaxation. Supportive facilities included churches, stables, slaughterhouses, breweries, corn mills, and so on. Missing from this list were courts of law and prisons, which Owen deemed superfluous in a community designed to optimize human happiness and freedom from need.

The villages-of-cooperation concept was restated in Owen's 1820 Report to the County of Lanark:

This Report was very much more than a proposal for dealing with the problem of unemployment in a single Scottish county, or even

with the Poor Law as a whole; it is, in fact, the most reasonable and complete statement of Owen's socialism, much clearer and more defined than the wild words of 1817.
Cole, pp. 134–135.

Even rational words, however, were insufficient to Owen at this time. According to his son, Robert Dale Owen (1874, 211), his father's "one ruling desire was for a vast theater on which to try his plans of social reform." He became convinced that such a theater could be found, not in Britain, but in the hinterland of America. The site of his second practical experiment in social organization was New Harmony, Indiana, on the Wabash River. In 1825, he purchased a communal village already established there by followers of the utopian George Rapp, together with 20,000 acres of alluvial farmland and forest. He and his son moved there to establish a village of cooperation.

The enterprise was a failure. Unlike New Lanark, New Harmony lacked an existing economic base to undergird its social principles. Furthermore, Owen attempted to carry these principles much further than at New Lanark, to make every adult settler an equal partner in the ownership, operation, and economic yield of the land and manufacturing assets of the village: "Liberty, equality, and fraternity, in downright earnest!" (Owen, 254). This goal, to which Owen pledged his personal wealth, was defeated by the unsuitability of the people who had been attracted to settle there: ". . . a heterogeneous collection of radicals, enthusiastic devotees to principle, honest latitudinarians, and lazy theorists, with a sprinkling of unprincipled sharpers thrown in" (Owen, 254). In 1827, Owen declared the project a failure and returned to England, having lost four-fifths of his own fortune.

This was Owen's last attempt to found or restructure a social community himself; subsequent experiments of this kind were conducted by his Owenite disciples (with similarly disastrous results). Owen devoted the remainder of his life to the cause of trade unionism and the advocacy of worker cooperatives.

Pullman: The Perils of Paternalism

George M. Pullman (1831–1897), one of America's most prominent unionbusters, was an incongruous successor to Robert Owen in the field of ideal town building. Like the early Owen of New Lanark, Pullman was a capitalist entrepreneur who recognized that a worker is likely to be more productive if he or she is well housed, well fed, healthy, and entertained. But whereas Owen departed from the profit motive to explore the possibilities of pure socialism at New Harmony, Pullman remained a stalwart industrialist. Ironically, despite the apparent success of his town in terms of bricks and mortar, Pullman's experiment in socioeconomic engineering was ultimately defeated by his obstinate capitalism as surely as Owen's obstinate socialism proved *his* undoing at New Harmony. Pullman, Illinois is probably better known for the great labor strike that occurred there in 1894 than for its physical amenities. Perhaps the underlying similarity of both men was their inability to compromise.

George Pullman invented the railroad sleeping car that bore his name in 1864 and thereafter dominated the construction and operation of such cars on railroads throughout the United States. To establish a new works for his burgeoning Pullman Palace Car Company, Pullman in 1880 purchased 4000 acres of prairie and boggy wetland adjoining Lake Calumet, 20 miles south of downtown Chicago. This site was certainly not selected as a rural utopia, but for the sound reasons of cheap land and accessibility to mainline railroads. There was, however, nowhere for a work force to live without a long train ride. Making a virtue of necessity, Pullman undertook to build a brand new town as a model of enlightened corporate planning and good employer–employee relations (Figure 6-11).

There were few precedents to draw on: Since New Lanark, only a handful of industrial model towns had actually been constructed in Europe and America (Ashworth, 126). The best known were Titus Salt's woolen-mill town Saltaire in England, completed in 1871, and the Massachusetts towns of Lowell and Holyoke, which produced textiles and paper, respectively. But with the help of a New York architect, Pullman essentially designed his town himself.

The basic elements of the town were the car works, the residential district, a commercial and cultural arcade, a covered market, parks, a hotel, a theater, and an interdenominational church. All were built and owned by Pullman through a holding company. Details of the town are provided by Buder (1967). In physical terms, it was progressive, humane, and "ideal." Housing of diverse size and rental cost was provided to accommodate both laborers and managers. Even the lowest-cost units con-

FIGURE 6-II   Map of Pullman, Illinois from *Harper's Monthly,* 1885. *Source:* Buder, 1967. Reproduced by permission of Oxford University Press.

sisted of brick row houses lining paved streets at densities of 8 to 10 per acre, far less crowded than usual at the time. (Even Saltaire had 32 houses per acre.) Human wastes were collected and conveyed by pipeline to agricultural land south of the town that produced commodities for sale in the local market. Consistent with Owen, and later Howard, alcoholic beverages were banned from sale in the town, but schools, a fine library, a theater, and other morally uplifting amenities were provided at Pullman's expense.

The town attracted immediate public attention:

> From 1880 to 1893, the town was intensely surveilled. Hundreds of thousands saw this most modern and novel of communities and an overwhelming majority left impressed. . . . Here was an American utopia that people wanted to succeed.
>
> Buder, pp. 92–93.

The town was touted at the company's exhibit at the 1893 World's Fair as a place ". . . where all that is ugly, and discordant and demoralizing, is eliminated, and all that inspires to self-respect, to thrift and to cleanliness of thought is generously protected" (Buder, 148).

Unfortunately, similar protection was not extended to the right to form a labor union or to object to company policies on wages, hours, and costs of rent, water, and food in the company town. The paternalism that benefited the 8000 inhabitants in prosperous years became their scourge when recession forced wage cuts and layoffs in 1894. The hand that fed them could also starve them. The resulting strike lasted three months and provoked the first use of federal troops in U.S. labor history. George Pullman died three years after the strike, vilified by those whom he thought he was helping. The town, severed by legal action from the company in 1904, gradually deteriorated into obscurity until gentrification set in during the 1960s. Pullman's worker row houses are now solid investments for Chicago yuppies.

Howard: From Theory to Practice

It was perhaps inevitable that an Ebenezer Howard should appear at the close of the 19th century. England and America were rife with utopian and progressive indignation concerning the state of large cities. Someone had to synthesize the many strands of thought, word, and deed into a practical program. This was Howard's contribution. In his own words: "I have taken a leaf out of the books of each type of reformer and bound them together by a thread of practicability" (Osborn 1945/1965, 131).

In effect, Howard blended Owen's New Lanark cooperative socialism with Pullman's bricks-and-mortar paternalism (although neither are discussed in his book). He incorporated impressions of landscape design experienced during his visit to Olmsted's Riverside, Illinois. He was influenced by Henry George's theory of a single tax on land rent to recoup undeserved profits of land ownership for the public welfare. He was enthralled with Edward Bellamy's 1889 tract "Looking Backward," which envisioned American society recast on Owenite principles with centralized planning, cooperative enterprise, and equality of income (Fishman 1977, 33). He obtained the idea of a town core and green belt from James Buckingham's utopian plan for Victoria (Osborn, 126). His admiration for small agrarian villages was derived from Peter Kropotkin (Fishman, 36).

There was in fact very little that was original in Howard's garden city proposal. But the assimilation of these and other intellectual "leaves" yielded his seminal tract: *To-morrow: A Peaceful Path to Real Reform* (published in 1898 and reissued in 1902 as *Garden Cities of To-morrow*). According to Lewis Mumford in his preface to the 1965 edition of Howard's book (Osborn, 29), "*Garden Cities* . . . has done more than any other single book to guide the modern town-planning movement and to alter its objectives."

Howard was the last of the great 19th century amateurs in urban reform. By trade, he was a court stenographer and inventor, implying an ability to record faithfully the statements of others and to assemble components into a workable machine. Both skills, his admirers have noted, served him well in formulating his garden city theory, first in assimilating the ideas of the time, and second, in visualizing a community as a system or "machine." F.J. Osborn (1945/1965, 21), Howard's chief disciple, described him as ". . . not a political theorist, not a dreamer, but an inventor." Another biographer, Dugald MacFadyen (1933/1970, 11), identifies a trait of "Americanism" in Howard's personality:

> The special inheritance of the Puritan as we see it philosophically in Emerson, practically in Ford, is a real conviction that mind triumphs over matter, that a clear idea tends to actualize itself by the inherent force that is in it. The mind of old England works from the concrete to the abstract—the New Englander works from the ideal to the real.

While Howard was scarcely a New Englander, the analogy is apt: in contrast to Owen, he effectively moved from theory to the practical.

The garden city idea was represented by Howard's famous magnet metaphor (Figure 6-12) wherein town and country are opposed. The former affords economic opportunity and culture at the expense of health, high prices, and crowding, while the latter provides a healthy environment but also boredom, poverty, and "lack of society." Howard's remedy was represented by a third magnet, "town-country," which incorporated the advantages and minimized the negative features of the other two.

FIGURE 6-12   Howard's "Three Magnets" diagram. *Source:* Osborn, ed., 1945/
1965. Reproduced by permission of the M.I.T. Press.

This was Howard's fundamental synthesis, which appealed strongly to
the Hegelian spirit of the time.

Howard's magnet metaphor had additional significance. He rejected
compulsion by a central authority as a means of accomplishing resettlement of population to the new garden cities. He viewed migration as a
voluntary, individual decision. Thus, his proposed garden city(ies) would
offer inducements–social, environmental, and economic–that would
draw working class people away from the miserable conditions of the
large cities and would intercept rural migrants headed toward the same
cities. In Howard's diagram, "'The People' are poised like iron filings
between the magnets" (Fishman, 39).

The physical plan of the garden city reflected Howard's "central idea
that the size of towns is a proper subject of conscious control" (Osborn,
10). His recommended population size was about 32,000 people, sufficient to attract industry and sustained cultural and social activities but
small enough to retain a healthy and uncrowded environment. Such a
community was to be situated on a tract of about 6000 acres, of which

GARDEN CITY AND RURAL BELT

FIGURE 6-13   Howard's diagram of Garden City and its "Rural Belt." *Source:* Osborn, ed., 1945/1965. Reproduced by permission of the M.I.T. Press.

the town itself would occupy a central core of 1000 acres. The remainder would be devoted to a circumferential green belt of agriculture and other rural activities (Figure 6-13). Garden cities were to be located within convenient rail distance of a central metropolis (for example, London) but should develop a local economic base to discourage long-distance commuting to work.

Internally, the garden city would provide a spectrum of housing opportunities to attract families of different socioeconomic levels (as in Pullman). Dwellings were to be situated along broad sylvan boulevards or local interior streets. The center of the town would be devoted to a community park surrounded by a "crystal palace" or enclosed shopping arcade together with public and cultural facilities including "town hall, principal concert and lecture hall, theater, library, museum, picture-gallery, and hospital" (Osborn, 53). Privately tended gardens and common open spaces would interlace with the village core and residential areas (the Olmsted factor). An outlying industrial district would accommodate smokeless, "nonsweat" industry (Figure 6-14).

Crucial to the importance of Howard's proposal was its means of accomplishment. The entire site of the garden city, including its agricultural green belt, was to be acquired, planned, and managed in perpetuity by a limited-dividend charitable corporation or trust. This entity would raise capital from philanthropically inclined private investors in exchange for a modest, fixed rate of return. The trust would derive all of its revenue from rents on land utilized for residence, business, industry, and agriculture. Any revenue accruing to the trust over and above the dividend to investors and operating costs would be returned to the community for beneficial purposes (the Henry George factor). As owner of the land, the trust would strictly control land use and development according to a community master plan.

Limitation of population size would be achieved by limiting the supply of dwelling units and by establishing additional garden cities at a suitable distance. Howard envisioned that the prototype community would lead to a cluster of such towns, separated by their green belts, which in

FIGURE 6-14   Howard's diagram of Garden City "Ward and Centre."
Source: Osborn, ed., 1945/1965. Reproduced by permission of the M.I.T. Press.

time would comprise a formidable "magnet" drawing the working-class populace out of the cities.

Howard and his supporters actually built two garden cities: Letchworth, starting in 1903, and Welwyn in 1920. Of the two, Letchworth is the more faithful to Howard's principles and the more widely acclaimed. The author visited Letchworth in the 1980s and found it thriving. Its 1981 population was 31,560. Its residential district is graced by "cottage picturesque" architecture set amid gardens, parks, and grassy commons. The town plan of 1903 by Barry Parker and Raymond Unwin smoothed the rigid symmetry of Howard's diagrams in favor of a more organic, informal design. It includes prototypical suburban cul-de-sacs, as well as a network of footpaths. The commercial core lacks the central park and crystal palace of Howard's imagination but instead provides retail spaces ranging from a Victorian arcade (reminiscent of Pullman), to a linear shopping street, narrowed into a pedestrian and bus mall, to a contemporary shopping center. Letchworth remains surrounded by an agricultural green belt, albeit comprising only about 2000 acres now.

Land use control over the total area of Letchworth is still rigid today. Permits for land use conversions must be approved by both the Letchworth corporate authority and by the North Hertfordshire District Council under the national Town and Country Planning Act. In 1963, the original Letchworth corporation, First Garden City, Ltd., was replaced by a public corporation created by an Act of Parliament at the request of the town inhabitants. The new corporation performs the same role as its predecessor as trustee for the local public welfare. In 1982, it turned over 273,000 pounds from excess land rents to some 60 social and cultural organizations in Letchworth to support their activities. Howard's dream is alive and well in Letchworth.

Howard's hope that garden cities would proliferate once their potential was demonstrated was dashed by depression, war, and the rise of the public sector. However, the garden city thesis, as promoted by F.J. Osborn and the Town and Country Planning Association, substantially influenced the postwar New Towns and Greenbelt programs. The British New Towns and their counterparts in France, India, the Soviet Union, Hong Kong, and elsewhere scarcely resemble Letchworth in scale or form of organization. They are predominantly high-rise, publicly constructed communities with populations far exceeding 32,000. Yet the elements of unified ownership and control of land, mixture of functions, and their goal of metropolitan decongestion are all faint images of Howard's third magnet.

Conclusion

This chapter has surveyed three approaches to the problems of rapid urbanization during the 19th century: (1) *regulation* of building and sanitary conditions; (2) *redevelopment* and expansion of urban infrastructure; and (3) *relocation* of factory workers to planned model communities in nonurban settings. The first two approaches involved primarily governmental actions. The third approach involved private initiatives taken by well-meaning individuals of widely differing backgrounds and motivations. All three, however, required the development of new legal measures, authorities, and doctrines to modify the existing abusive practices of urban development.

Each of these three approaches in turn served as a precedent for more expansive intervention into the private land market by government during the 20th century. *Regulation* would lead directly to the zoning movement that began just after World War I and continues to the present time. Regulation also proliferated in the various public programs of environmental management concerned with clean air and water, wetlands, toxic wastes, pesticides, and many other issues. *Redevelopment* emerged after World War II as the focus of the public urban renewal programs and its various offshoots. *Relocation* has been the self-selected strategy of millions of central city residents who have moved to suburban areas or back to the hills and byways of rural America. While not overtly a governmental policy, many laws and programs (such as the Interstate Highway System and federal tax benefits for home ownership) have contributed to the impetus to abandon older central cities. These topics will be covered in later chapters.

References

Allen, N. 1986. *David Dale, Robert Owen and the Story of New Lanark*. Edinburgh: Moubray House Press.

Ashworth, W. 1954. *The Genesis of Modern British Town Planning*. London: Routledge & Kegan Paul.

Benevolo, L. 1967. *The Origins of Modern Town Planning*. J. Landry, trans. Cambridge: The M.I.T. Press.

Blake, N.M. 1956. *Water for the Cities*. Syracuse: Syracuse University Press.

Booth, M.L. 1860. *History of the City of New York*. New York: W.R.C. Clark and Meeker.

Bridenbaugh, C. 1964. *Cities in the Wilderness*. New York: Capricorn Books.

Buder, S. 1967. *Pullman: An Experiment in Industrial Order and Community Planning 1880–1930*. New York: Oxford University Press.

Caro, R.A. 1974. *The Power Broker*. New York: Alfred Knopf.

Chadwick, G.F. 1966. *The Park and the Town: Public Landscape in the 19th and 20th Centuries*. New York: Praeger.

Chapman, B. 1953. "Baron Haussmann and the Planning of Paris." *The Town Planning Review*. 24: 177-192.

Chapman, J.M., and B. Chapman. 1957. *The Life and Times of Baron Haussmann: Paris in the Second Empire*. London: Weidenfeld and Nicolson.

Cole, M. 1953. *Robert Owen of New Lanark*. London: The Batchworth Press.

Davis, T. 1966. *John Nash: The Prince Regent's Architect*. London: Country Life.

Fabos, J.Gy., G.T. Milde, and V.M. Weinmayr. 1968. *F. L. Olmsted, Sr.: Founder of Landscape Architecture in America*. Amherst, MA: University of Massachusetts Press.

Fishman, R. 1977. *Urban Utopias in the Twentieth Century*. New York: Basic Books.

Flinn, M.W., ed. 1965. *Edwin Chadwick's Report on the Sanitary Condition of the Labouring Population of Great Britain*. Edinburgh: Edinburgh University Press.

Giedion, S. 1962. *Space, Time and Architecture*. Cambridge: Harvard University Press.

Girouard, M. 1985. *Cities and People*. New Haven: Yale University Press.

Hall, P. 1988. *Cities of Tomorrow*. London: Basil Blackwell.

Hayden, D. 1976. *Seven American Utopias: The Architecture of Communitarian Socialism, 1790–1975*. Cambridge: The M.I.T. Press.

Jackson, K.T. 1985. *Crabgrass Frontier: The Suburbanization of the United States*. New York: Oxford University Press.

Kutler, S.I. 1971. *Privilege and Creative Destruction: The Charles River Bridge Case*. New York: Norton.

Mayer, H.M., and R.C. Wade. 1969. *Chicago: Growth of a Metropolis*. Chicago: University of Chicago Press.

MacFadyen, D. 1933/1970. *Sir Ebenezer Howard and the Town Planning Movement*. Cambridge: The M.I.T. Press.

Nesson, F.L. 1983. *Great Waters: A History of Boston's Water Supply*. Hanover, N.H.: University Press of New England.

Olmsted, F.L., Jr. and T. Kimball. 1928/1973. *Forty Years of Landscape Architecture: Central Park*. Cambridge: The M.I.T. Press.

Osborn, F.J., ed. 1945/1965. *Ebenezer Howard's Garden Cities of To-morrow*. Cambridge: The M.I.T. Press.

Owen, R.D. 1874. *Threading My Way*. London: Turner & Co.

Peets, E. 1927. "Famous Town Planners: Haussmann." *The Town Planning Review* 12: 181–190.

Peterson, J.A. 1983. "The Impact of Sanitary Reform Upon American Urban Planning 1840–1890." In *Introduction to Planning History in the United States*. D.A. Krueckeberg, ed. New Brunswick: Rutgers Center for Urban Policy Research.

Platt, R.H. 1995. "The 2020 Water Supply Study for Metropolitan Boston: Demise of Diversion." *Journal of the American Planning Association* (Spring) 61(2): 185–199.

Platt, R.H., R.A. Rowntree, and P.C. Muick, eds. 1994. *The Ecological City: Preserving and Restoring Urban Biodiversity*. Amherst: University of Massachusetts Press.

Rasmussen, S.E. 1967. *London: The Unique City*. Cambridge: The M.I.T. Press.

Reisner, M. 1986. *Cadillac Desert*. New York: Penguin Books.

Rosen, G. 1958. *A History of Public Health*. New York: MD Publications, Inc.

Saalman, H. 1971. *Haussmann: Paris Transformed*. New York: George Braziller.

Smith, E.R. 1907. "Baron Haussmann and the Topographical Transformation of Paris under Napoleon III." *The Architectural Record*, 21–38.

Summerson, J. 1962. *Georgian London*. Baltimore: Penguin Books.

Sutton, S.B., ed. 1971. *Civilizing American Cities: A Selection of Frederick Law Olmsted's Writings on City Landscape*. Cambridge: The M.I.T. Press.

The New York Times. 1995. "Urban Backyard to be Revitalized" (April 9, 1995).

Warner, S.B. 1978. *Streetcar Suburbs*. Cambridge: Harvard University Press.

Weber, A.F. 1899/1963. *The Growth of Cities in the Nineteenth Century: A Study in Statistics*. Ithaca: Cornell University Press.

Weidner, C.H. 1974. *Water for a City*. New Brunswick: Rutgers University Press.

Whitehill, W.M. 1968. *Boston: A Topographic History* 2nd ed. Cambridge: Harvard University Press.

CHAPTER 7

/ Land Use Zoning:
Origins and Practice

Introduction

Local municipal governments since the 1920s have been the front line of public response to private land use initiatives. And the most prevalent instrument wielded by local governments in performing that function is the two-edged blunt sword of land use zoning. Although it originated in Germany in the late 19th century, zoning is a quintessentially American institution with the blend of idealism and greed which that implies (Toll 1969). It is especially associated with the decade of 1916–1926, marking, respectively, the years of its inception in the New York City Zoning Ordinance and of its constitutional approval by the U.S. Supreme Court. That decision, *Village of Euclid v. Ambler Realty Co.* 272 U.S. 365 (1926), lent the nickname "Euclidean zoning" to the institution that dominated local land use control until the 1970s and survives in thousands of communities today.

In the words of the late planning lawyer Richard F. Babcock (1966, 3): "Zoning reached puberty in company with the Stutz Bearcat and the speakeasy. F. Scott Fitzgerald and the Lindy Hop were products of the same generation." In a more statistical vein, the arrival of zoning coincided roughly with the 1920 census, which reported that urban Americans outnumbered rural inhabitants for the first time.

Zoning is certainly not the only land use regulatory measure available to local governments. They also possess important powers to regulate land subdivision; to enforce building code requirements; to regulate the use of floodplains, wetlands, or seismic risk areas; to designate historical districts; to control signs; and to perform a variety of other functions under state enabling legislation and/or home rule authority. Furthermore, like other levels of government, local governments may acquire property for public purposes, either through negotiated sale or through eminent domain (condemnation). They may also utilize tax incentives and other devices to encourage desired land use patterns. (See Figure 7-1 and discussion below.)

But land use zoning is the most widespread local land use control

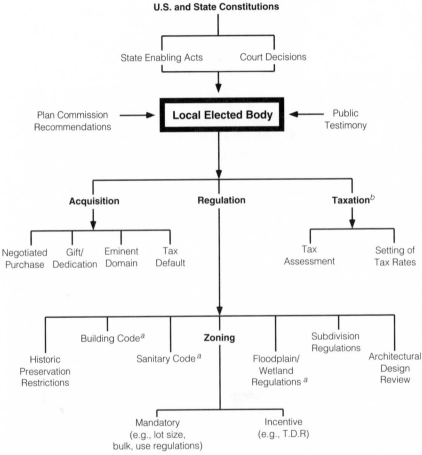

U.S. and State Constitutions

State Enabling Acts   Court Decisions

Plan Commission Recommendations → **Local Elected Body** ← Public Testimony

Acquisition   **Regulation**   **Taxation**[b]

Negotiated Purchase   Gift/ Dedication   Eminent Domain   Tax Default   Tax Assessment   Setting of Tax Rates

Historic Preservation Restrictions   Building Code[a]   Sanitary Code[a]   **Zoning**   Floodplain/ Wetland Regulations[a]   Subdivision Regulations   Architectural Design Review

Mandatory (e.g., lot size, bulk, use regulations)   Incentive (e.g., T.D.R)

[a]In many states, certain regulations are adopted by the state and enforced by local governments.

[b]Setting of tax rates and assessment of real property are local functions that may influence land use patterns, in addition to federal and state tax policies.

FIGURE 7-1   Diagram of municipal land use control inputs and outputs.

tool, in use in every major U.S. city (except a long-time holdout: Houston, Texas) as well as many thousand smaller communities and counties. It is the broadest of land use control techniques, applying to virtually any private use of land and many public uses within zoned jurisdictions. And it certainly has been the most contentious of land use institutions, generating passionate advocacy during the 1920s and '30s, equally vehement denunciation and proposals for reform during the 1960s and '70s, and weary resignation in the 1980s and '90s.

Precursors to Zoning

Three strands of long-term response to urban deterioration in the 19th century—regulation, redevelopment, and relocation—were traced in Chapter 6. Each of these approaches fostered corresponding lines of action on a much larger scale in response to urban and metropolitan growth during the 20th century. In the United States, the three approaches have respectively yielded (1) land use and environmental regulations; (2) urban redevelopment and revitalization; and (3) suburbanization, as encouraged by federal home ownership incentives and the interstate highway system. The advent of zoning in 1916 may be viewed as a further enlargement of the public regulation approach that originated in the British Public Health Act of 1848, the New York Metropolitan Health Act of 1866, and their counterparts elsewhere.

In the critical period of 1900 to 1916 leading up to the advent of zoning, several immediate precursors may be identified: (1) the City Beautiful Movement; (2) the Garden City Movement; (3) public legislation regulating nuisances and building heights under the "police power"; (4) the advent and proliferation of the skyscraper and related technology; and (5) the Progressive Movement. Collectively, these laid a foundation for public receptivity to limited governmental intervention in the private land market, as reflected in the rapid spread of zoning and its eventual approval by the U.S. Supreme Court.

The City Beautiful Movement

The 20th century opened with the commissioning of the nation's first city and regional plan, which was prepared for Washington, D.C. in commemoration of that city's centennial as the federal seat of government. A special blue ribbon panel, subsequently known as the McMillan Commission after its Senate sponsor James McMillan, was appointed in 1900 to report on "the development and improvement of the entire park system of the District of Columbia" (U.S. Congress 1902, 7). Reflecting the continuing influence of the 1893 Chicago World's Fair, the panel consisted of four principals of that enterprise: architects Daniel H. Burnham and Charles F. McKim, landscape architect Frederick Law Olmsted, Jr. (who had assumed his ailing father's practice), and sculptor Augustus Saint-Gaudens.

The basic plan for streets, parks, and public buildings of the future Washington, D.C. was originally laid out by Pierre L'Enfant, a French military engineer, in 1792 (who was inspired in part by Louis XIV's palace and grounds at Versailles, an ironic motif for the future capital of the "Free World"). The growth of the city during the 19th century was faithful in general outline to the L'Enfant Plan, but much clutter and encroachment on public spaces had occurred.

The McMillan Commission visited several European capitals and were particularly inspired by Haussmann's Paris (itself another legacy of Versailles). The Commission's report (U.S. Congress 1902) proposed a monumental redevelopment program, which Frederick Gutheim (1976, 38) describes as "an inspiring set piece of the City Beautiful Movement that was to sweep the nation." The Mall, as the city's major axis, was proposed to be redesigned, replanted, and extended to include the future reflecting pool and Lincoln Memorial. It was to be cleared of encroachments and embellished with new public buildings, fountains, gardens, and statuary (Figure 7-2). Most of the Commission's Mall improvements were subsequently carried out, including the replacement of an encroaching rail terminal by the gleaming Beaux-Arts Union Station northwest of the Capitol designed by Burnham in 1903 (today also the site of a three-level shopping concourse).

In contrast with the monumental scale and design of the city's core, the commission was influenced by F.L. Olmsted, Jr. to recommend a more functional system of parks and open spaces along the Potomac and Anacostia rivers and Rock Creek, and the laying out of scenic routes such as the Mount Vernon Parkway. Thus the work and concepts of Olmsted, Sr., who died in 1903, were perpetuated by his son.

The McMillan Commission plan, following his prominent role in the

FIGURE 7-2 The 1901 McMillan Commission Plan for the Mall in Washington, D.C. *Source:* Gutheim, 1976, figure 16.

1893 Columbian Exposition in Chicago, established Daniel H. Burnham as the high priest of City Beautiful architecture and city planning. The District of Columbia plan was rapidly followed by Burnham's plans for Cleveland (1903), San Francisco (1905), and Manila (1905) (Wilson 1990). So successful was Burnham's architectural practice that he donated his services in preparing these city plans (Hines 1979, 217).

But his own home city of Chicago most intrigued and challenged Burnham. His 1909 *Plan of Chicago* (Burnham and Bennett 1909) prepared in collaboration with Edward Bennett for the Commercial Club of Chicago, was his masterpiece. It was in 1907 in the course of preparing that plan that Burnham uttered his famous adage: "Make no little plans; they have no magic to stir men's blood and probably will not be realized" (Wrigley 1983, 71).

The *Plan of Chicago* was a major conceptual leap beyond the earlier City Beautiful plans. In fact, its most City Beautiful element–a baroque civic center at the confluence of radiating boulevards flanked by Haussmann-style building facades–was never built: It evidently did not "stir men's blood" (Figure 7-3). The functional elements of the plan however would reshape the face of the city over succeeding decades. The Plan itself, surely one of the most magnificent documents in the history of city planning, addressed a variety of public needs including parks and forest preserves, streets and boulevards, bridges, and rail and port facilities. It also included a chapter on legal aspects of achieving its proposals. As popularized in a manual and textbook, the Plan influenced a generation of Chicago taxpayers to support, among other projects, the completion of the city's lakefront park system; the double-decking of Wacker Drive, and a traffic bridge across the rail yards south of the Loop; the consolidation of rail terminals; and, at a regional scale, the establishment of the Cook County Forest Preserve system (Figure 7-4).

Aside from the formal and elegant Grant Park–the city's "front yard"–most of the Chicago plan improvements were practical in nature, serving the objectives of economic efficiency, convenience, and public well-being. The *Plan of Chicago* thus marked a major step away from the earlier City Beautiful plans dominated by pompous aesthetics. But like its predecessors, the Chicago Plan largely disregarded needs other than public improvements, such as housing and neighborhood planning. Goodman (1968, 22) notes as a serious defect in all City Beautiful plans:

FIGURE 7-3 Burnham and Bennett's 1909 Plan of Chicago: proposed downtown and harbor improvements (implemented in part). *Source:*
Mayer and Wade, 1969. Reproduced by permission of The University of Chicago Press.

FIGURE 7-4 Burnham and Bennett's 1909 Plan of Chicago: proposed parks and forest preserves. Reproduced from the original plan. (Compare with contemporary open spaces plan for Chicago area shown in Figure 9-7.)

... the lack of legitimation of any public control over the private actions that were decisive in setting the quality of the urban environment. The early planners merely avoided the issue when they made "planning" coterminous with parks, boulevards, and civic centers.

Even more acerbic is the appraisal of the City Beautiful style in America by the distinguished urban philosopher Lewis Mumford (1955, 147): "Our imperial architecture is an architecture of compensation: It provides grandiloquent stones for people who have been deprived of bread and sunlight."

The Garden City Movement

As discussed in Chapter 6, a very different vision of the planned community was provided by Ebenezer Howard's book *Garden Cities of Tomorrow* and the founding of Letchworth in 1903. American admirers of his theories established the Garden Cities Association of America (GCAA) in 1906, which attracted the ". . . same kinds of civic and political leaders who had supported Howard's ideas in England" (Schaffer 1982, 32). This organization proposed to house 375,000 families in a series of garden communities to be constructed in several eastern states, but without result. F.L. Olmsted, Jr.'s 1912 design for Forest Hills, New York, sponsored by the Russell Sage Foundation, however, reflected Howard's garden city principles (a reciprocal tribute to Howard's admiration for Olmsted, Sr.'s design for Riverside, Illinois).

The GCAA was dissolved in 1921 and replaced two years later by the much more influential Regional Planning Association of America (RPAA), of which the young Lewis Mumford was a charter member. This group successfully promoted several garden city-style projects, most notably Radburn, New Jersey in 1927 (Parsons 1994). Howard's influence was thus more prominent in American planning circles by the time of the U.S. Supreme Court *Euclid* decision that upheld zoning in 1926 than when zoning first appeared in 1916.

But while the *process* of garden city establishment was relatively unfamiliar before the 1920s, the *form* of the garden city—particularly its emphasis on the sylvan, low-density residential neighborhood and the segregation of homes and commerce—accorded perfectly with the image of turn-of-the-century American suburbia. Lacking the control provided by a unified land ownership trust of the Letchworth type, it was natural for the new suburbanites to seek a legal means of perpetuating the bucolic environment that they had fled the cities to attain. Zoning was therefore welcomed as a means to achieve this objective.

Nuisance and Height Regulations

In 1915, a year before New York's first zoning ordinance, the U.S. Supreme Court upheld an unusual ordinance adopted by the City of Los Angeles that prohibited the operation of brick kilns within a specified three-square-mile district in an area recently annexed to the city. The measure was challenged by the owner of a clay pit and brick kiln that predated both the ordinance and the annexation of the site by the city. The Court upheld the regulation against the charge that it substantially reduced the value of the property and did not apply to similar businesses elsewhere in Los Angeles (*Hadacheck v. Sebastian*, 239 U.S. 394). This decision has been criticized by legal scholars for its harsh and arbitrary impact on a preexisting business (Williams 1975, sec. 116.03). But whatever its value as a constitutional precedent, the case reflects the surprisingly permissive state of public nuisance law on the eve of the appearance of zoning.

Hadacheck was consistent with a line of Supreme Court decisions extending back to the 1870s that upheld state and local regulation of particular uses of private property without compensation. These cases contrasted with the prevailing ethos of laissez faire and social Darwinism, which opposed even minimal public intervention in the business economy, as reflected in the Court's disapproval of a New York statute regulating child labor in *Lochner v. New York* (198 U.S. 45, 1905) (Toll 1969, 16-18).

Where a private use of land or economic activity threatened the public interest, as opposed to the interest of individual workers, the Court was remarkably progressive. As early as 1872, a New Orleans ordinance that vested a monopoly in livestock slaughtering in one enterprise and banned all competitors without compensation was upheld by the U.S. Supreme Court with the resounding declaration that:

Unwholesome trades, slaughter-houses, operations offensive to the senses, the deposit of powder, the application of steam power to propel cars, the building with combustible materials, and the burial of the dead, may all . . . be interdicted by law, in the midst of dense masses of population, on the general and rational principle that every person ought to use his property as not to injure his neighbors; and that *private interests must be made subservient to the general interests of the community. This is called the police power.*

> . . . Slaughterhouse Cases, 16 Wall 36, 1872; emphasis added.

In 1887, the Court upheld a Kansas law that prohibited the manufacture and sale of alcoholic beverages and closed existing breweries (*Mugler v. Kansas*, 123 U.S. 663), stating:

A prohibition simply upon the use of property for purposes that are declared by valid legislation to be injurious to the health, morals, or safety of the community, cannot, in any just sense be deemed a taking or an appropriation of property for the public benefit [in violation of the Fifth Amendment to the U.S. Constitution]. Such legislation does not disturb the owner in the control or use of his property for lawful purposes nor restrict his right to dispose of it. . . . (123 U.S., at 667-8).

In a more tenuous case, the Court upheld a ban on the production and sale of oleomargarine in *Powell v. Pennsylvania* 127 U.S. 678 (1888). And it supported a state ban on the use of fish nets in certain waters in *Lawton v. Steele* 152 U.S. 133 (1894) declaring:

The extent and limits of what is known as the police power have been a fruitful subject of discussion in the appellate courts of nearly every state in the Union. It is universally conceded to include everything essential to the public safety, health, and morals, and to justify the destruction or abatement . . . of whatever may be regarded as a public nuisance. . . . A large discretion is vested in the legislature to determine, not only what the interests of the public require, but what measures are necessary for the protection of such interests (152 U.S., at 135).

A key element of the developing doctrine of the police power at the turn of the century was the recognition of the need for prospective regulation of private activity rather than simply after-the-fact mitigation. As stated by Ernst Freund in his seminal 1904 treatise *The Police Power:*

> The common law of nuisance deals with nearly all the more serious and flagrant violations of the interests which the police power protects, but it deals with evils only after they have come into existence, and it leaves the determination of what is evil very largely to the particular circumstance of each case. The police power endeavors to prevent evil by checking the tendency toward it and it seeks to place a margin of safety between that which is permitted and that which is sure to lead to injury or loss. This can be accomplished to some extent by establishing positive standards and limitations which must be observed, although to step beyond them would not necessarily create a nuisance at common law.

The proposition that the police power might address conditions that would not necessarily constitute a traditional common law nuisance opened the door wide to the introduction of public regulation of the use of land and the dimensions of buildings. Furthermore, there was growing precedent for the establishment of different regulations for different geographical districts of a community, that is, incipient zoning. *Hadacheck,* for instance, involved restriction on land use applicable to a particular area of Los Angeles.

The leading prezoning decision on building dimensions that utilized a districting approach was the 1909 Supreme Court opinion in *Welch v. Swasey* 214 U.S. 91. *Welch* involved a Massachusetts law that imposed a limit of 125 feet for new buildings in designated commercial districts of Boston and either 80 or 100 feet in residential districts. The Court upheld the measure, assuming that the legislature had good reasons for making such a distinction. (It suggested that women and children are more likely to be at risk from fire in residential areas and thus buildings should be smaller.)

Welch and thousands of subsequent decisions applied a judicial *presumption* that a legislative act is valid in the absence of overwhelming proof that it is arbitrary or capricious. While justified in the interest of judicial efficiency, deference given by courts to legislative determinations even of tiny suburban enclaves has often insulated questionable zoning practices from searching judicial review. (See Chapter 8.)

These decisions reflect the degree of judicial tolerance of police power measures at the eve of comprehensive zoning. Supreme Court opinions, it must be remembered, are only the tip of the iceberg of what is happening in the society at large. For each disputed measure reviewed by the highest court, dozens were resolved in lower courts and hundreds went unchallenged. Height limitations, for instance, were quite widespread by the time of the *Welch* decision. As early as 1889 a height limit was imposed in Washington, D.C. to enhance views of the Washington Monument and the Capitol. (Due to that measure, Washington remains strikingly horizontal today in contrast to the vertical profiles of other American central cities.) By 1913, 22 U.S. cities had some form of height controls, of which four (including Boston and Washington) applied such limits on the basis of districts (Delafons 1969, 20).

Skyscrapers and Related Technology

The proliferation of prezoning height limitations reflects the evolution of legal institutions in response to perceived changes in technology and the urban environment. In this case, the physical change involved the unprecedented concentration of workers and economic activities in high-rise office buildings of virtually unlimited height and bulk. Two technological innovations underlay this architectural revolution: the elevator and steel frame construction. The former was invented by Elisha Graves Otis and introduced to the world at the 1853 New York Crystal Palace Exposition (Toll 1969, 47). The latter involved the support of a tall building by a steel skeleton in place of weight-bearing walls. Burnham and Root's 16-story Monadnock Building, completed in Chicago in 1891, was the tallest and last product of the era of weight-bearing-wall construction. The steel frame was inaugurated in the 10-story Home Insurance Company Building in Chicago (1885) and the 11-story Tower Building in New York (1888). According to Toll (p. 51): "Until the steel frame appeared, seemingly immutable structural principles curbed the economic appetite. The steel frame, in effect, repealed this restraint and the law offered no substitute. Quite literally the sky became the limit."

The skyscraper thrived particularly in Manhattan. In 1905, Burnham's

Flatiron Building reached 20 stories and 300 feet. In 1907, the Singer Building on Lower Broadway reached 612 feet. In 1919, the Metropolitan Life Insurance Building rose to 700 feet, only to be topped by the Woolworth Building in 1913, at nearly 800 feet. By that year there were over 50 buildings in Manhattan above 20 stories and nine above 30 stories (Delafons, 21).

The Singer, Metropolitan, and Woolworth towers were exemplars of the skyscraper style—ornate, slender, tapering to a pyramid or cupola—they fairly represented the mood of exuberance and prosperity of prewar America. But at street level, these and their bulkier neighbors cut off light and air from business districts and flooded the sidewalks with office workers. Furthermore, fire equipment could reach only 100 feet above ground (Toll, 153). The tragic Triangle Shirtwaist Company fire on March 25, 1911, which gutted a 10-story building and killed 146 young women, prompted investigation into the need to control the size and design of commercial structures (Toll, 26). Soon thereafter, the loss of 1503 lives in the sinking of the *Titanic* on April 15, 1912, due to reckless operation and an insufficient number of lifeboats, further aroused the public to the perils of laissez faire in the face of technological change and corporate arrogance.

The Progressive Movement

The Progressive Movement that swept the nation in the first decade of this century essentially embraced most of the "precursors" just mentioned. The essence of the movement in the words of historian Richard Hofstadter (1955, 5) was

> . . . that broader impulse toward criticism and change that was everywhere so conspicuous after 1900, . . . While Progressivism would have been impossible without the impetus given by certain social grievances, it was not nearly so much the movement of any social class, or coalition of classes, against a particular class or group as it was a rather widespread and remarkably good-natured effort of the great part of society to achieve some not-very-clearly-specified self-reformation. Its general theme was the effort to restore a type of economic individualism and political democracy

that was widely believed to have existed earlier in America and to have been destroyed by the great corporation and the corrupt political machine; and with that restoration to bring back a kind of morality and civic purity that was also believed to have been lost.

With respect to cities, progressives were greatly concerned with the two interrelated evils of overcrowding and political corruption. Both of these conditions were products of the continuing surge of immigration to eastern seaboard cities from Europe. The highest-ever annual level of immigration to the United States was recorded in 1907 when 1.3 million foreigners arrived. In 1910, 13.3 million foreign-born persons were living in the United States, comprising one-seventh of the nation's total population (Hofstadter, 176). These destitute and largely non-English-speaking refugees readily supported the big city political machines, which offered them jobs and food in exchange for votes.

Reform proposals were first articulated through a deluge of muckraking writings. Jacob Riis's *How the Other Half Lives* (1890/1972) documented through prose and photography the deplorable state of New York's tenement districts. In 1904 another crusading journalist, Lincoln Steffens, scrutinized big city bossism and corruption in *The Shame of the Cities* (1904/1957). The moral implications of urban overcrowding were lamented by the Reverend Josiah Strong in his 1898 tract *The Twentieth Century City*. Upton Sinclair in *The Jungle* (1906) exposed the abuses of the meatpacking industry. These and other classics of muckraking literature stimulated an outpouring of more than 2000 articles on social conditions in American magazines and newspapers between 1903 and 1912 (Ciucci et al. 1979, 188).

Apart from the issue of corruption in city governments, the most politicized urban concern of progressives was "congestion." Like "environmental deterioration" in the 1970s, "congestion" was used by reformers in the century's first decade to cover a variety of ills: disease-ridden tenements, mobbed streets in office districts, loss of light and air, and inadequate open space for recreation. Congestion was the rubric under which progressive ideology was translated into practical city planning measures, including zoning.

One of the first progressives to advocate planning to achieve social reform was Frederick C. Howe, whose 1905 book, *The City: The Hope of*

Democracy, urged the adoption of German city planning practices. Howe's book strongly influenced Benjamin C. Marsh, a young social activist and political organizer. In 1907, at the age of 28, Marsh was appointed executive secretary to the newly formed Committee on Congestion of Population (CCP) in New York City. Like James Chadwick, who launched the British sanitary reform movement in his capacity as secretary to prestigious committees whose reports he wrote, Marsh made good use of his position. In 1908, he organized an exhibition on the evils of congestion, which was displayed at the American Museum of Natural History. In the following year, after travels in Europe, Marsh privately published a short book, *An Introduction to City Planning*, which opened with the heading: "A City Without a Plan is like a Ship Without a Rudder." Like Howe, Marsh advocated adoption by American cities of German planning techniques including public control over street location and design, advance acquisition of land prior to development, taxation of increased value of land (to discourage speculation), and the districting or zoning of urban land to regulate building height and volume. In contrast to Burnham's *Plan of Chicago*, published later the same year, which largely addressed public improvements, Marsh emphasized the need for public regulation of private land development.

Marsh then organized on behalf of CCP the First National Conference on City Planning and Congestion to elaborate and publicize the themes of his book. This event, which is often considered the birthplace of the modern planning movement in the United States, was held in Washington, D.C. on May 21–22, 1909. According to Kantor (1983, 69-70):

> The forty-three conferees met in an air of excitement and hope. Many of the nation's leaders in urban affairs attended, including Frederick Howe, Jane Addams, ... John Nolen, [and] Frederick Law Olmsted, Jr. ... Representatives of municipal art, social work, architectural, civil engineering, and conservationist groups also attended. The meeting vividly reflected the many interest groups concerned with city planning at the time.

The conference papers, which summarized the state of the art of city planning in the United States and abroad, were subsequently published as a senate document (U.S. Congress 1910). The major theme of the conference, the evils of congestion, was articulated in the opening address by Henry Morgenthau:

> There is an evil which is gnawing at the vitals of the country, to remedy which we have come together—an evil that breeds physical disease, moral depravity, discontent, and socialism—and all these must be cured and eradicated or else our great body politic will be weakened. This community can only hold its preeminence if the masses that compose it are given a chance to be healthy, moral, and self-respecting.
>
> U.S. Congress 1910, p. 230.

The conference marked a major watershed in American planning history as reflected in the remarks by landscape architect Robert Anderson Pope indicting the City Beautiful Movement as impractical and elitist (Daniel Burnham was not present):

> . . . We have assumed without question that the first duty of city planning is to beautify. We have made the aesthetic an objective of itself. In most of our cities the movement has characterized itself by the expenditure of huge sums for extensive park systems, with broad boulevards and bridle paths, for far-outlying reservations; inaccessible improvements designed to protect the needs of future generations, now, however, made available to but a small portion of the community—the wealthy and leisure classes, who of all society needs these advantages the least.
>
> Again, we have rushed to plan showy civic centers of gigantic cost, in design the expression of, at best, only a small group of individuals, . . . brought about by civic vanity, and bears the character of external adornment, when pressing hardby we see the almost unbelievable congestion with its hideous brood of evil, filth, disease, degeneracy, pauperism, and crime. What external adornment can make truly beautiful such a city?
>
> U.S. Congress 1910, p. 75.

In place of the City Beautiful, Pope argued that "city planning is of primary importance as a social and economic factor" (ibid., 76). Instead of "showy civic centers," Pope advocated: (1) decentralizing and more

equitable distribution of land values; (2) widening of streets and establishment of radial and belt thoroughfares; and (3) the adoption of land
use zoning as practiced in Germany to regulate: "... building heights,
depth of blocks, number of houses per acre, and land speculation with all
its attendant evils" (ibid., 77). Pope reflected a belief among urban
reformers at this time that city planning was essential to national and
ethnic survival:

> The average recruit in the German army is much taller, stronger,
> and heavier than the British soldier, spends less time in hospital,
> and has a lower death rate. . . . The modern tendency toward con-
> gestion in cities and the increase of unhealthful living conditions
> have been so ably combated in Germany that no real impairment of
> her manhood can be detected. . . . While it is admitted that many
> causes have contributed to this result, city planning is known to be
> a very important factor.
>
> Ibid., p. 77.

In 1910, a second conference was held (with "Congestion" significantly dropped from its title, reflecting the dwindling influence of Marsh
and the CCP). Subsequent national conferences on city planning provided an annual forum for the development of the planning profession.
Thenceforth, fewer social workers and civic reformers attended, and the
conference was more concerned with ". . . data, statistics, techniques,
management, standards, efficiency, and evaluation" (Kantor, 71).

Meanwhile, Marsh continued to lobby for anticongestion policies in
New York. In 1910, he persuaded the city to establish an official Commission on Congestion of Population and was duly appointed its secretary. The commission's 1911 report recited the litany of reformist views
on congestion and city planning, including Marsh's own pet notion of a
progressive tax on land value increments, which caused the commission's Chair, Henry Morgenthau, to resign (Marsh 1953, 29).

Social progressives such as Marsh, Howe, and Jane Addams thus
joined in common cause with practitioners of city design such as Frederick Law Olmsted, Jr., John Nolen, and Charles Mulford Robinson to prepare a fertile soil for the advent of zoning. The actual planting of the seed,
however, was motivated by an impulse quite distinct from either slum
eradication or urban design, namely, hostility to neighborhood change.

The proximate cause of the zoning was the hostility of influential merchants along the New York's Fifth Avenue toward encroachment by garment factories and offices, who themselves had recently displaced the mansions of the city's elite (Toll 1969). Since the unwanted activities generally occupied taller buildings, the merchants urged adoption of controls on building size by district, to protect existing commercial property values. Thus began the long tradition of using zoning to reflect what is now called the "NIMBY syndrome" ("Not in My Backyard"). Pursuant to the reports of two city commissions established at the behest of the Fifth Avenue merchants, a zoning enabling act was adopted by the New York State Legislature, which led to the adoption of the nation's first zoning ordinance in New York City in 1916.

Euclidean Zoning

Conventional "garden variety" land use zoning is often referred to as "Euclidean zoning" because it was originally approved by the U.S. Supreme Court in the landmark decision in *Village of Euclid v. Ambler Realty Co.* (272 U.S. 365) in 1926. It refers to the use of the public regulatory power ("police power") to specify how private land may be developed and used. As with any exercise of the police power, no compensation is paid to the owner. Private parties affected adversely by zoning however may challenge particular applications of zoning administratively, and ultimately in court. Upon review, courts must determine whether the challenged use of zoning is "constitutional," as considered in the following chapter (Chapter 8).

Unconventional "non-Euclidean" zoning includes various approaches to guide land use more flexibly and creatively than conventional zoning allows. Since land use regulation is largely a creature of state and local law, not a federal function, there is scope for states and local governments to experiment with alternative approaches within the overall constraints of the U.S. Constitution. Also, zoning is but one of an array of techniques and approaches available to local governments and counties to influence land use within their jurisdictions. (See Figure 7-1 and Chapters 8 and 9.)

Euclidean zoning nevertheless has proven durable as a land use control institution, perhaps because it is familiar—"the devil known is better than the devil unknown." Although it has been modified somewhat in most states over the years, in basic procedures and terminology it has remained remarkably unchanged from its origins in the decade 1916–1926. The following summarizes the elements of that fundamental institution, which still operates in thousands of localities and counties today.

Authority to Adopt Zoning

Authority to plan and zone land use is delegated to municipalities and counties by state legislatures through "enabling acts." State zoning acts do not require local communities to adopt zoning, but if they do (and most have), they must follow the requirements of the state law. These requirements are largely procedural rather than substantive—they address *how* zoning must be adopted and administered, with little attention to *what* local zoning regulations may require. Limitations on substantive content have been applied primarily by courts rather than by state legislatures.

While state zoning acts differ somewhat due to amendments over the years, most originated from a common source. The Standard Zoning Enabling Act (SZEA) was developed in 1926 by an Advisory Committee on Zoning established within the U.S. Department of Commerce by then Secretary of Commerce, Herbert Hoover. The SZEA was furnished to all state legislatures and municipalities and was widely adopted in place of earlier acts that had been haphazardly developed during the previous decade (Bassett 1936, 28–29). A parallel State Planning Enabling Act was similarly promulgated in 1927.

It is axiomatic that an exercise of the public regulatory power must serve to protect the public health, safety, and welfare. The relationship of zoning to these goals was articulated in the SZEA and most state enabling acts as follows:

> Such regulations shall be made in accordance with a comprehensive plan and designed to lessen congestion in the streets; to secure safety from fire, panic, and other dangers; to promote health and the general welfare; to provide adequate light and air; to prevent the overcrowding of land; to avoid undue concentration of population; to facilitate the adequate provision of transportation, water,

sewerage, schools, parks, and other public requirements. Such regulations shall be made with reasonable consideration, among other things, to the character of the district and its peculiar suitability for particular uses, and with a view to conserving the value of buildings and encouraging the most appropriate use of land throughout such municipality.

Bassett, p. 51–52.

This statement reflects the welter of concerns that underlay the advent of zoning, including congestion in housing and streets, fire, loss of open space, and neighborhood change. Much of the statement is rhetorical: Zoning cannot ipso facto "facilitate the adequate provision of transportation, water, sewerage, schools, and parks." It is arguable that public spending and locational decisions regarding these services influence the way land may be zoned rather than vice versa.

Two institutional fixtures of American zoning practice that originated in the model acts are the *planning board* or commission and the *zoning board of appeals*. The former serves as the sounding board for assimilating expert advice and community opinion in order to formulate recommendations to the local elected body regarding the adoption and modification of zoning. The latter comprises a quasi-judicial panel that is authorized to grant exceptions from the strict rules of the zoning ordinance to individual property owners in appropriate cases.

What Zoning Regulates

Euclidean zoning regulates (1) the use of private land; (2) the density of structural development per unit of land; and (3) the dimensions or "bulk" of buildings. Initially, each of these variables was addressed by a separate set of districts: The Euclid ordinance involved use, height, and area zones. This proved to be cumbersome, and zoning practice soon resorted to the division of a community into a single system of zones designated by use, with bulk and lot-size requirements specified accordingly.

The principal classes of land use for zoning purposes are residential, commercial, and industrial. These are normally divided into subclasses such as single-family residence, one- or two-family residence, rural residence, neighborhood business, highway business, and so forth. Each type of zone involves specific rules on use, building size, and lot size.

Land use regulations specify for each class of zone which activities are

(1) permitted "as of right"; (2) prohibited; and in more recent ordinances, (3) permitted conditionally if a special permit is obtained. Originally, zoning was *cumulative* in its structure, resembling a pyramidal hierarchy of land use districts (Figure 7-5). At the apex of the pyramid was
the exalted single-family residence zone in which all other uses were
prohibited. Next was the multiple-family zone, which allowed either
single- or multifamily dwellings. Commercial zones allowed both businesses and residential uses. Industrial zones were essentially unrestricted, except perhaps designated nuisance-type activities. Thus, despite its instigation by Fifth Avenue merchants, zoning soon emerged as
a tool to protect the residential areas from business, but not vice versa
(Toll 1969).

Cumulative zoning has been replaced in most communities by *noncumulative zoning* in which each class and subclass of zone is mutually
exclusive as to use. Thus, homes cannot be built in commercial districts,
just as businesses are barred from residential zones. Noncumulative zoning requires equal attention to all parts of the community, not just its
prime residential areas. This imposes a much more complex burden on

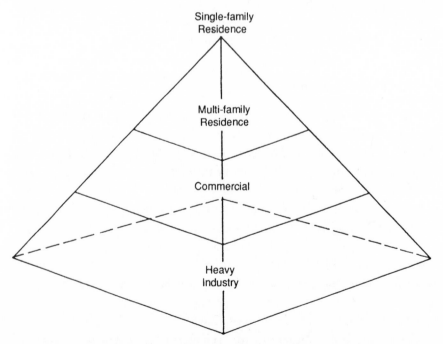

FIGURE 7-5   Diagram of hierarchy of Euclidean zoning classifications.

the planning commission, its staff, and consultants to try to envision the most appropriate use of each section of land in the community. The result has been a proliferation of classes of zones, each with its specific rules regarding use, bulk, and area. The Town of Amherst, Massachusetts, for instance, with a permanent population of 27,000 has 19 classes of land use districts (Table 7-1).

Population density in residential areas is regulated through establishment of minimum lot sizes for dwellings or groups of dwellings. Lots for single-family homes typically range from 12,000 to 80,000 square feet (about one-quarter to two acres). Lot size roughly correlates with size and cost of the home, with less expensive dwellings normally built on land zoned for smaller sized lots. (In the 1990s, however, small tract

TABLE 7-1   Table of Zoning Districts

Section 2.0		Zoning Districts
The Town is hereby divided into the following classes of zoning districts:		
2.10	Residence District:	
	R-LD	Low Density Residence
	R-O	Outlying Residence
	R-N	Neighborhood Residence
	R-G	General Residence
	CR	Campus Residence
	R-F	Fraternity Residence
	PURD	Planned Unit Residential Development
2.02	Business Districts:	
	B-G	General Business
	B-L	Limited Business
	B-VC	Village Center Business
	OP	Office Park
	COM	Commercial
2.03	Industrial Districts:	
	LI	Light Industrial
	PRP	Professional and Research Park
2.04	Educational Districts:	
	ED	Educational
2.05	Conservation Districts:	
	FPC	Flood-Prone Conservancy
	WP	Watershed Protection
	ARP	Aquifer Recharge Protection
	WD	Wetlands District

Source: Town of Amherst, Massachusetts, zoning bylaws, 1987.

homes originally costing $20,000–30,000 in the 1960s may cost more than five times as much.) Developers usually prefer smaller lots that allow more homes per total project area and reduce the costs per unit of streets and other infrastructure provided by the developer.

Density in commercial or office districts is regulated by establishing *floor area ratios* (FARs). An FAR specifies the maximum enclosed floor area within a structure as a multiple of the site area. Thus an FAR of 10 allows a 10-story structure to cover an entire building site, or a 20-story building on half the site. (FARs are frequently raised in central city locations when a developer provides "amenities" such as a public plaza, off-street parking, or residential units.)

Beyond the traditional trio of use, density, and bulk regulations, zoning has encompassed other land planning concerns. Modern zoning ordinances typically address: minimum off-street parking requirements in multifamily and nonresidential areas; rules regarding billboards and other forms of outdoor advertising signs; extraction of sand, gravel, and other minerals; secondary or accessory uses such as professional offices within homes and "mother-in-law" apartments; and special overlay districts for shorelines, floodplains, and wetlands. An overlay district imposes additional regulations beyond the basic Euclidean requirements for the applicable zone. Alternatively, special restrictions for sensitive lands such as wetlands may be expressed in a separate ordinance apart from the local zoning law. (See Chapter 9.)

Zoning Map and Text

The essence of zoning is that it "zones" the community into areas with different land use rules. Drawing boundaries between different kinds of land use zones is thus legally significant, equivalent to the written content of regulations. A zoning ordinance therefore consists of two legally adopted elements: the *zoning map* and the *zoning text*. The first defines where specific regulations apply, and the second gives the content of those regulations.

The actual legal zoning map of a municipality or county is located in the office of the building inspector or other enforcement officer. The zoning map must be at a scale large enough to be able to identify individual parcels: Tax assessment maps are often used as the base for the master zoning map. Smaller-scale copies of the zoning map may be purchased from the appropriate municipal office, but where important decisions are involved, referral to the master zoning map is necessary (Figure 7-6).

The delineation of zone boundaries is the responsibility of the local elected body. Boundaries are typically recommended by the planning

FIGURE 7-6   Excerpt from the Town of Amherst, Massachusetts zoning map, 1987.

commission, based on the advice of the planning staff or consultants and testimony from the public at a public hearing.

Zoning primarily operates prospectively. Preexisting uses that do not conform to zoning may continue as *legal nonconforming uses*. Zoning applies to substantial rebuilding of existing structures but has little influence otherwise in older communities. Also, zoning applies most forcefully to privately owned land. Land owned by the federal government is exempt from local zoning; state land may or may not be exempt depending on state law. A municipality technically must obey its own zoning in the use of local public land, but it can readily amend the zoning to meet its needs. Nevertheless, zoning maps normally cover the entire municipal jurisdiction, developed and vacant, private and public. Special classes of zones may be utilized for land that is outside the normal land market–for example, institutional, conservancy, or open space.

Zoning is an exercise in the art of rational line drawing: locating of zone boundaries can be highly contentious. Where streets serve as boundaries, property on opposite sides of the street is assigned to different zones with perhaps very different economic implications (such as shopping versus residential). Also, boundaries may split larger parcels of land into two or more zones.

Once a given parcel is located on the master zoning map, one refers to the zoning text to determine what restrictions apply to the class of zone to which that parcel is assigned. Each zone is designated on the map by a designator code. The designator code is located in the table of use regulations (Table 7-2) to determine the allowed, prohibited, or conditionally allowed uses applicable to the zone containing the site. The code is then located in the table of dimensional regulations to determine the lot size, FAR, or other dimensional limitations that apply to the proposed use if allowed (Table 7-3). Parking, signage, and other regulations may be specific to zones or may be community-wide. These are covered in subsequent sections of the zoning text.

Flexibility

Euclidean zoning, in theory, attempts to predetermine the use of all vacant private land according to a comprehensive plan. This of course is a quixotic venture that continually encounters the windmills of reality. One of the claims made on behalf of zoning from its inception was that

TABLE 7-2 Excerpt from Town of Amherst Zoning Bylaw: Table of Use Regulations (Y = allowed; N = not allowed; SP = allowed by special permit)

Bylaw Number	Land-Use Classification	Standards & Conditions	Zoning District R-O				R-F	B-G	B-L		OP	LI	PRP	FPC
			R-LD	R-N	R-G	CR			B-VC	COM				
Section 3.31	Extensive Uses													
3.310	Forestry and the harvesting of forest products.		Y	Y	Y	Y	Y	Y	Y	Y	Y	Y	Y	Y
3.311	Orchard, market garden, nursery, or other use of land for commercial agricultural production.		Y	Y	Y	Y	Y	Y	Y	Y	Y	Y	Y	Y
3.312	Commercial greenhouse; salesroom or stand for the sale of nursery, garden, or other agriculture produce (including articles of home manufacture from such produce).	The majority of the produce and products sold shall be produced by the owner of the land or made from the products so produced. The farm shall be a minimum of five acres in size.	Y	Y	N	N	N	N	Y	N	Y	SP	SP	SP
3.313	Commercial poultry or livestock farm, or the raising of pets for gainful purposes.		Y	N	N	N	N	N	N	N	N	SP	SP	SP
3.314	Reservation, wildlife preserve, or other conservation use.		Y	Y	Y	Y	Y	Y	Y	Y	Y	N	Y	Y
3.315	Country club, organized camp, sporting grounds, or other predominantly outdoor recreational use.	Not to be conducted as a gainful business.	SP	SP	SP	SP	SP	SP	SP	SP	SP	N	SP	SP

TABLE 7-3   Amherst Table of Dimensional Regulatons

Zoning District	Basic Minimum Lot Area (sq ft)	Cluster Minimum Lot Area (sq ft)	Additional Lot Area per Family (sq ft)	Basic Minimum Lot Frontage (ft)	Cluster Lot Frontage (ft)	Minimum Front Setback (feet)	Minimum Side & Rear Yards (ft)	Cluster Minimum Side & Rear Yards (ft)	Maximum Building Coverage (%)	Maximum Lot Coverage (%)	Maximum Floors	Maximum Height (feet)
R-LD	80,000	25,000	10,000	200	100	40	20	15	10	15	2 1/2	35
R-O	30,000	15,000	10,000	150	100	40	25	15	15	25	2 1/2	35
R-N	20,000	10,000	6,000	120	80	30	15	15	20	30	3	35
R-G	12,000	6,000	2,500	100	50	25	10	10	25	40	3	40
CR	12,000		2,500	100		25	10		25	70	3	40
R-F	40,000			150		40	20		20	45	3	40
B-G	12,000		2,500	100		20			70	95	3	50
B-L or COM	20,000		4,000	125		20	25		35	70/85	3	35
B-VC	20,000		4,000	125		20	25		20	50	3	35
OP	40,000			100		40			20	70	2 1/2	35
LI						20			25	65	3	50
PRP	30,000			100		30			25	70	3	35
FPC	80,000			200		40	20		10	15	1	20
ED	See Section 3.213											

it would provide stability and predictability for the benefit of property owners and investors. While it has done this to some extent, there is a contradictory trend in the evolution of zoning–toward greater flexibility to cope with the unexpected and the unfair. From its earliest days, zoning involved two means of addressing those concerns, namely, amendments and variances. Later these were joined by special permits or conditional use permits, floating zones, cluster zoning, planned unit developments (PUDs), and transfer of development rights (TDRs), among other devices.

Amendments are formal changes to the zoning ordinance that are adopted, like the original ordinance, by the local elected body in response to advice of the planning board and public testimony. Amendments may alter either the text of the zoning ordinance, the zoning map, or both. A map amendment involves a change of boundaries and possibly the redesignation of certain areas to a different class of zone. If a new zone class is created through a text amendment, it is usual (but not absolutely necessary) to rezone some land on the map to that class. If no land is immediately rezoned for that purpose, the new class is said to be a "floating zone," which may come down to earth in a later map amendment. Floating zones may be used to implement planned unit developments (Dawson 1982, 41–42).

Amendments of either text or map are intended to remedy areawide needs or problems and should normally involve more than one parcel of land. Amendments that benefit only one property owner are subject to challenge (usually by neighbors) as unconstitutional "spot zoning." However, rezoning of a single parcel is sometimes upheld. The Connecticut Supreme Court in *Bartram v. Zoning Commission of Bridgeport* 68 A.2d 308, 1949, sustained a zoning change of one parcel from residential to business, making the following distinction:

Action by a zoning authority which gives to a single lot or small area privileges which are not extended to other land in the vicinity is in general against sound public policy and obnoxious to the law. It can be justified only when it is done in furtherance of a general plan properly adopted for and designed to serve the best interests of the community as a whole (68 A.2d, at 310).

The Court in *Bartram* held that the zoning commission had an adequate planning basis to justify the zone change in terms of providing convenience shopping to a residential neighborhood. Many cases hold the opposite, however, in challenges to amendments that favor only one parcel of land.

By contrast, *variances* almost always involve a single parcel. A variance is an administrative exception granted by the zoning board of appeals to relieve a "hardship" to property owners who cannot make reasonable use of their land if the applicable zoning regulations are strictly enforced. The burden of proof is on the property owner to demonstrate such hardship. The variance is essentially a constitutional safety valve to remedy cases in which zoning unreasonably restricts the use of a particular parcel.

Since variances invite favoritism, courts usually view them sternly as compared with amendments. No presumption of validity operates in favor of a variance. According to the Pennsylvania Supreme Court in *Devereaux Foundation Inc. Zoning Case*, 41 A.2d 744, 1945:

> The strict letter of the ordinance may be departed from only where there are practical difficulties or unnecessary hardships in the way of carrying it out; and in such manner that the spirit of the ordinance may be observed, the public health, safety and general welfare secured and substantial justice done. No other considerations should enter into the decision (41 A.2d, at 745).

The Massachusetts Zoning Act limits the availability of variances to circumstances involving:

> ... the soil conditions, shape, or topography of such land or structures and especially affecting such land or structures but not affecting generally the zoning district in which it is located ... and desirable relief may be granted without substantial detriment to the public good and without nullifying ... the intent or purpose of such ordinance .... (Mass. G.L.A. Ch. 40A, sec. 10).

This act allows local towns and cities to abolish "use variances" within their jurisdictions. Variances to permit property to be used for a different purpose than specified in the zoning rules are considered to be more pernicious than "dimensional variances," which merely adjust the rules to accommodate owners of odd-shaped lots.

Either type of variance may be denied by a board of appeals or invalidated by a court if the alleged hardship is viewed as "self-created." Property owners who buy a parcel and then seek a variance from the zoning in force at the time of purchase are viewed as creating their own hardship. Similarly, if they sell off part of a parcel, they cannot later claim that the remainder deserves a minimum-area variance.

Special permits entered zoning practice after World War II to provide municipalities with greater discretion in dealing with development proposals than amendments or variances could afford (Babcock, 7). The special permit (sometimes called a conditional use permit or special exception) is essentially a "maybe." Rather than list a particular use as either allowed or prohibited in specific zones (for instance, a branch bank or convenience store in a residential zone), it is listed "SP" in the Table of Use Regulations. This means that the use may be permitted in that zone if approved by the Board of Appeals. As with a variance, a public hearing is held with notice to neighboring property owners. In the absence of strenuous objection or countervailing planning reasons, the special permit is likely to be granted. Unlike a variance, the applicant need not allege a hardship.

Some communities use special permits for virtually all development, allowing each proposal to be reviewed in light of existing circumstances. This process resembles the system in Great Britain and many other countries where development approval must be obtained for any new construction. Special permits, however, should not be confused with *building permits*, which are required in most American communities for new construction or alterations of existing structures. If a proposed improvement conforms with applicable zoning and building codes, a building permit is routinely issued. If a zoning problem exists, an amendment, variance, or special permit must be obtained to remedy the problem before a building permit can be issued.

Cluster zoning and planned unit developments (PUDs) are products of the public concern about urban sprawl and loss of open space, which emerged in the 1960s. Both techniques involve a relaxation of minimum lot size requirements in exchange for the preservation of a portion of the project site as natural or recreational open space. A PUD also involves the possibility of mixed land uses and house types. In effect, it throws out the existing zoning rules for a major development and substitutes a set of special rules negotiated between the municipality and the developer. The goal is to achieve a higher quality of development with diversity of uses and retention of open land. (See Figure 7-7.) While a number of excellent PUDs have been constructed, the technique is applicable primarily to large developments. Small-scale developers cannot afford the front-end legal and design costs of a PUD and opt instead to follow the path of least resistance under the prevailing zoning rules.

Many states and cities incorporate various types of density bonus incentives into their zoning laws. Massachusetts, for instance, since 1975 has authorized municipalities to issue special permits allowing "increases in the permissible density of population or intensity of a particular use in a proposed development" in cases where the developer undertakes to provide ". . . open space, housing for persons of low or moderate income, traffic or pedestrian improvements, installation of solar energy systems, protection for solar access, or other amenities" [*Mass. General Laws Annotated* (MGLA), Chap. 40A, sec. 9]. Transfer of development rights (TDR) is another non-Euclidean technique to provide greater control over open space and landmark sites, as discussed in Chapter 9.

Nonconforming Uses

As mentioned above, uses already in existence upon the adoption of zoning or rezoning may continue as legal nonconforming uses. (In zoning jargon, they are "grandfathered.") According to Bassett (1936, 105): ". . . buildings erected according to law, even if out of place, should be allowed to stand indefinitely . . . . Zoning seeks to stabilize and protect and not to destroy."

But such uses, while tolerated, are second-class citizens compared with activities that conform to zoning. Segregation of uses was an article of faith in traditional Euclidean zoning, and nonconforming uses have therefore long been regarded as a necessary evil to be phased out if and when possible.

State laws modeled on the U.S. Department of Commerce Standard Zoning Enabling Act have placed limits on nonconforming uses. They may not be enlarged physically or converted to a new use as a matter of right. Typically, a variance must be sought to expand or change a nonconforming use, with the burden of proving hardship on the owner as with any variance. It is therefore difficult to change the use of nonconforming commercial space—say, a drug store to a dry cleaner—even

FIGURE 7-7   Plan for a clustered "Planned Unit Development" (PUD) including diverse types of residential units, schools, recreation, open
space, and a commercial site.

though there may be a natural market for the services of the latter. This
frustrates entrepreneurship and may cause a marginal use to continue in
a building that is increasingly dilapidated for lack of maintenance.

Another limitation is that nonconforming uses that are discontinued
may be deemed to be abandoned after a given period of time, usually two
years, and may not thereafter be revived. Nonconforming structures that
are substantially destroyed by fire, flood, or other calamity may have to
be replaced in conformity with zoning use and dimensional regulations.

Efforts to phase out nonconforming uses through "amortization" (loss
of legal protection after a specified period of years) have been attempted
in several cities (Delafons 1969, 63–64), but without notable success.
The only exception has been the elimination of billboards in certain
states and communities.

Clearly, the rezoning of a community should endeavor to avoid
placing existing structures into nonconforming status. This is difficult in
an older community with great diversity of land use and structural type.
The rigidity of Euclidean zoning regarding segregation of uses is incompatible with such heterogeneous but often thriving neighborhoods. A revival of the cumulative approach to zoning would resolve some of these

difficulties where some areas could be essentially unrestricted. Alternatively, certain areas may be deliberately zoned for multiple uses, as in cases of older cities that zone their downtown business districts to encourage residential dwellings above streetfront commercial space.

References

Babcock, R.F. 1966. *The Zoning Game*. Madison: University of Wisconsin Press.

Bassett, E.M. 1936. *Zoning*. New York: Russell Sage Foundation.

Burnham, D.H., and E.H. Bennett. 1909. *Plan of Chicago*. Chicago: The Commercial Club.

Ciucci, G. et al. 1979. *The American City: From the Civil War to the New Deal*. Cambridge: The M.I.T. Press.

Dawson, A.D. 1982. *Land Use Planning and the Law*. Hadley, MA: the author.

Delafons, J. 1969. *Land Use Controls in the United States* 2nd ed. Cambridge: The M.I.T. Press.

Freund, E. 1904. *The Police Power: Public Policy and Constitutional Law*. Chicago: Callaghan.

Goodman, W.I. 1968. *Principles and Practice of Urban Planning*. Chicago: International City Managers Association.

Gutheim, F. 1976. *The Federal City: Plans and Realities*. Washington, D.C.: Smithsonian Institution Press.

Hines, T.S. 1979. *Burnham of Chicago: Architect and Planner*. Chicago: University of Chicago Press.

Hofstadter, R. 1955. *The Age of Reform*. New York: Knopf.

Howe, F.C. 1905. *The City: The Hope of Democracy*. New York: Charles Scribner's.

Kantor, H.A. 1983. "Benjamin C. Marsh and the Fight Over Population." In *The American Planner: Biographies and Recollections*. D.A. Krueckeberg, ed. New York: Methuen.

Marsh, B.C. 1909. *An Introduction to City Planning*. New York: Benjamin C. Marsh.

——. 1953. *Lobbyist for the People*. Washington, D.C.: Public Affairs Press.

Mumford, L. 1955. *Sticks and Stones: A Study of American Architecture and Civilization*. New York: Dover.

Parsons, K.C. 1994. "Collaborative Genius: The Regional Planning Association of America." *Journal of the American Planning Association* 60(4): 462–482.

Riis, J.A. 1890/1972. *How the Other Half Lives.* Williamstown, MA: Corner House Publishers.

Schaffer, D. 1982. *Garden Cities for America: The Radburn Experience.* Philadelphia: Temple University Press.

Sinclair, U. 1906/1985. *The Jungle.* New York: Penguin Books.

Steffens, L. 1904/1957. *The Shame of the Cities.* New York: Hill and Wang.

Strong, J. 1898. *The Twentieth Century City.* New York: Baker and Taylor.

Toll, S. 1969. *Zoned American.* New York: Grossman Publishers.

U.S. Congress. 1902. *The Improvement of The Park System of the District of Columbia.* Senate Report no. 166. (57th Congress, 1st Session). Washington, D.C.: U.S. Government Printing Office.

——. 1910. *City Planning.* Senate Doc. no. 422 (61st Congress, 2nd Session). Washington, D.C.: U.S. Government Printing Office.

Williams, N. 1975. *American Planning Law: Land Use and the Police Power.* Chicago: Callaghan.

Wilson, W.H. 1990. *The City Beautiful Movement.* Baltimore: The Johns Hopkins University Press.

Wrigley, R.L., Jr. 1983. "The Plan of Chicago." In *Introduction to Planning History in the United States.* D.A. Krueckeberg, ed. New Brunswick: Rutgers Center for Urban Policy Research.

CHAPTER 8 / Constitutional and Policy Issues of Urban Planning

Introduction

Every man holds his property subject to the general right of the community to regulate its use to whatever degree the public welfare may require it.

Theodore Roosevelt, Speech at Osawatomie, August 31, 1910.

The general rule at least is, that while property may be regulated to a certain extent, if regulation goes too far, it will be recognized as a taking.

Oliver Wendell Holmes in *Pennsylvania Coal Co. v. Mahon* 1922.

For most of this century, land use regulation has provoked controversy. Zoning and related police power measures affect the use and value of property belonging to millions of households and businesses in thousands of communities. They are administered at the grassroots level by tens of thousands of volunteer board members, many of whom have little professional knowledge of planning or law, but have deep roots in their communities. Land use regulations therefore often reflect personal instincts or loyalties, rather than abstract planning theory. Zoning in particular remains defiantly localistic and parochial, despite efforts to broaden its geographic area of concern.

Zoning has been called upon to serve diverse and sometimes conflicting objectives, such as environmental protection and economic development, often failing to serve any of them well. However, zoning is but one tool, and a weak one at that, amid an increasingly complex array of local,

251

state, and federal programs and policies affecting land use. This chapter examines key constitutional and policy issues arising from the practice of zoning and other noncompensatory land use controls over the past 70 years.

The Basic Constitutional Provisions

The framers of the U.S. Constitution in 1787 could scarcely have foreseen that the United States would eventually be a "nation of cities," in the phrase of historian Sam Bass Warner (1966). But reflecting the writings of John Locke, William Blackstone, and other English political theorists, they were acutely concerned with the protection of private property ownership against unreasonable governmental action. But it was also recognized that government should provide for the "general welfare," as expressed in both the Preamble and in Article I, section 8. This implies the existence of what has become known as the "police power" (Freund 1904) that is the basis for land use zoning and other noncompensatory public limitations on private freedom.

Private property rights as such were not directly mentioned in the original Constitution but were addressed by the Fifth Amendment in the Bill of Rights, added in 1791:

> No person shall be . . . deprived of life, liberty, or property, without due process of law; nor shall private property be taken for public use without just compensation.

This concern was addressed again in the 14th Amendment, added in 1868:

> No State shall . . . deprive any person of life, liberty, or property, without due process of law; nor deny to any person within its jurisdiction the equal protection of the laws.

These pithy phrases thus express the concepts of "due process," "equal protection," and the "takings" clause. (The Bill of Rights is presumed to be incorporated into the 14th Amendment by implication, and thus the "takings clause" applies to the states and local governments, as well as to

Congress.) Each of these, as applied by courts, defines to some degree the scope of the public power to regulate land use under the police power.

The requirements of due process and equal protection each represent major branches of constitutional law beyond the scope of this discussion. The term "due process" has evolved with two broad and distinct meanings: procedural and substantive. Procedural due process "centers not so much on what is done but on how it has been done, stressing general fairness in governmental procedures" (Dawson 1982, 26). As applied to land use regulation, this concept requires compliance with procedural requirements established in the applicable statutes concerning notice to all concerned, public hearings, and deadlines for public action. Violation of such procedural requirements is a ground for invalidation of the action, upon challenge by an affected party.

Substantive due process is closely related to the taking issue, to be discussed in detail below. This concept concerns the *purpose* of the government action, while the taking issue considers its *economic impact.*

In weighing the purpose of challenged regulations, courts generally apply a twofold test. First, do the regulatory objectives serve to protect the "public health, safety, and welfare"? In a rephrasing of this test, the Supreme Court in *Agins v. Tiburon* 106 S.Ct. 2138, 1980 stated that land use regulation does not affect a taking if it "substantially advance[s] legitimate state interests" (as cited in *Dolan v. City of Tigard* 114 S.Ct. 2309, 1994, at p. 2316).

Second, does the regulation reasonably promote the achievement of a valid objective? For instance, a regulation that requires all houses in a community to be painted the same color would probably flunk the first test, because there is no public interest to be served by such a requirement (except possibly in a historic district). A regulation that limits building height to two stories as a means of alleviating traffic congestion might be held invalid under the second test, because traffic volume is not necessarily related to building heights.

Courts, however, seldom invalidate police power measures under substantive due process unless "fundamental constitutional rights" such as racial discrimination are involved. It is normally presumed by courts that the action of a state or local legislative body is valid unless the plaintiff proves that the action is "arbitrary, capricious, or unreasonable." (Hamann 1986, 9-10). Nine times out of ten, courts will hold a challenged zoning ordinance to be reasonable—not necessarily demonstrating "wisdom or sound policy in all respects" but at least arguable: "If the validity of the legislative classification for zoning purposes be fairly debatable, the legislative judgment must be allowed to control" (*Village of Euclid v. Ambler Realty Co.* 272 U.S. 365, 1926, at 375). The challenging property owner thus bears a heavy burden of proof to overturn the presumed validity of a legislative action. The measurement must be proven to be "arbitrary and capricious" and not merely "fairly debatable." As discussed below, recent U.S. Supreme Court decisions have lightened this burden on the challenging property somewhat when it appears that a regulation has effectively destroyed all value of the property in question (the *Lucas* case) or allows public access to private property without compensation (*Nollan* and *Dolan*).

The equal protection clause poses the issue of equity or fairness of treatment of citizens. The Constitution is not construed to forbid all discrimination among property owners for that would nullify land use zoning altogether. It does require, however, that rules be uniform within zoning districts and that the boundaries between districts be drawn objectively. Equal protection requires that "similarly situated property owners must be treated similarly." The determination of similarity or dissimilarity for zoning purposes must be based on objective planning criteria so as not to be deemed arbitrary or capricious.

Reasonableness

In actual litigation, the various constitutional grounds tend to become blurred. The plaintiff typically alleges that all possible constitutional guarantees have been violated—for example:

> The amended complaint alleges that the ordinance . . . [and a later amendment] work an undue hardship as to use, destroy the greater part of its value, are discriminatory as a denial of the equal protection of the law, and amount to a taking of private property without just compensation contrary to due process and, as such, are invalid and void. (*Vernon Park Realty Inc. v. City of Mount Vernon* 121 N.E.2d 517, 1954, at 519).

Such a shotgun approach invites a nonanalytical, all-purpose response by the courts. Rather than examining each allegation in detail, the court applies a single litmus test: Is the measure "reasonable"? The court in *Mount Vernon* simplified the plaintiff's allegations as follows: "While the common council has the unquestioned right to enact zoning laws respecting the use of property . . . it may not be exerted arbitrarily or *unreasonably."* (121 N.E.2d, at 522; emphasis added)

"Reasonableness" is thus often used as a surrogate for "constitutionality." Although it may beg the question, reasonableness has provided a convenient rubric for courts to resolve zoning challenges. The inquiry takes the following form: Is the ordinance reasonably related to a valid purpose of the police power and does it reserve for the owner some reasonable way to use the property (although not necessarily the most profitable one)? In *Mount Vernon*, the city had zoned the plaintiff's property, which adjoined the railroad station, for a residence or a parking lot. The owner, who wanted to build for a commercial use, convinced the court that parking lots should be provided by public acquisition, not zoning:

"The owner . . . has met the burden of proof . . . that the property . . . has no possibilities for [reasonable use as zoned]." The court accordingly held the zoning as applied to the plaintiff's property to be ". . . so unreasonable and arbitrary as to constitute an invasion of property rights, contrary to constitutional due process and, as such, [is] invalid, illegal, and void. . . ." (121 N.E.2d, at 521).

But even though the plaintiff bears the burden of proving that a zoning measure is unreasonable and arbitrary, the municipality must still present some valid reasons for its action. The court will not usually second-guess the wisdom of a land use plan, but a total absence of planning strongly suggests arbitrary and capricious use of the regulatory power. In short, the "reasonableness" (read constitutionality) of a land use regulation is a function of its basis in *planning*.

The Role of Planning

It is axiomatic that land use zoning is subordinate to planning (Babcock 1966, 120). This doctrine dates back to the pioneers of zoning—Marsh, Nolen, Robinson, and the 1909 City Planning Conference. The argument that zoning is legitimized by planning was articulated by planning attorney Alfred Bettman:

Zoning is based upon a thorough and comprehensive study of developments of modern American cities, with full consideration of economic factors of municipal growth, as well as the social factors. . . .

. . . The zone plan is one consistent whole, with parts adjusted to each other, carefully worked out on the basis of actual facts and tendencies, including actual economic factors, so as to secure development of all the territory within the city in such a way as to promote the public health, safety, convenience, order, and general welfare.

Brief in *Village of Euclid v. Ambler Realty Co.*, reprinted in Comey, 1946, p. 174.

The role of planning was codified in state laws that followed the standard zoning and planning enabling acts (which Bettmann helped to draft). State zoning acts often provide that zoning should be ". . . in accordance with a comprehensive plan." Planning enabling acts adopted by many states specify the powers and duties of local planning commissions–for example:

. . . to make and adopt a master plan for the physical development of the municipality. . . . Such a plan, with the accompanying maps, plates, charts, and descriptive matter, shall show the commission's recommendations for the development of said territory. . . .

In the preparation of such plan the commission shall make careful and comprehensive surveys and studies of present conditions and future growth of the municipality and with due regard to its relations to neighboring territory.

Mass. *General Laws Annotated* MGLA, ch. 41, Sec. 81.

The relationship of planning and zoning from 1905 to 1935 is depicted graphically in Figure 8-1. A modest number of "comprehensive plans" such as those prepared for Chicago and San Francisco by Daniel Burnham appeared earliest. Ongoing city planning commissions first emerged about 1912 and increased rapidly until the Depression. Zoning ordinances followed a parallel rapid rate of growth after 1920. But comprehensive plans, with which zoning is supposedly "in accord," lagged far behind during the 1920s. Whatever the planning commissions were doing, it apparently was not the preparation of comprehensive plans.

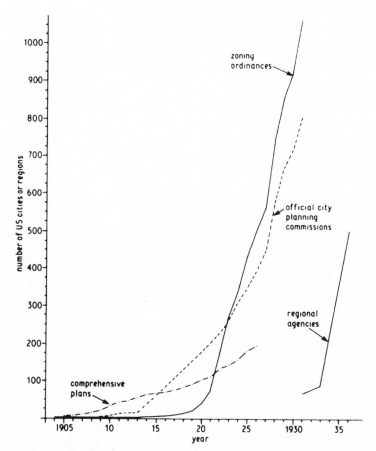

FIGURE 8-I   Cumulative number of municipalities with planning and zoning, and of regional planning agencies. *Source:* Kreuckeberg, 1983, fig. 1.6. Reproduced by permission of Methuen.

After nearly four decades of national experience with zoning, Haar (1955a, 1157) reported: "For the most part, however, zoning has preceded planning in the communities which now provide for the latter activity, and indeed, nearly one-half the cities with comprehensive zoning ordinances have not adopted master plans at all." Clearly, judicial acceptance of zoning laws was not dependent on the existence of a master plan. Haar found that the statutory (and constitutional) requirement that zoning be "in accordance with a comprehensive plan" often is construed to mean that zoning be ". . . logically related to something broader than and beyond itself" (Haar 1955a, 1167). The meaning of "comprehensive plan" therefore differs from one court and jurisdiction to another:

> The analysis of the "comprehensive plan" requirement in terms of itself is a common judicial phenomenon. The reasoning seems to be that a comprehensive ordinance, one which blankets the entire area and is internally consistent, is automatically "in accordance with a comprehensive plan." The plan is the ordinance and the ordinance the plan, . . .
>
> Haar 1955a, p. 1167.

Until the late 1950s, the comprehensive or master plan was a technical document, heavily oriented toward physical land use patterns and public infrastructure. Although it did not necessarily serve as the "comprehensive plan" for zoning purposes, it did guide other local land-related functions such as the provision of streets, parks, schools, water and sewer services, and other infrastructure. Beginning in the early 1960s, the master plan—and indeed zoning itself—was viewed with increasing skepticism and indignation by reputable critics such as William H. Whyte, Richard Babcock, John Reps, and Norman Williams. Much of the impact of this criticism affected the form and process of planning, which gradually became more open and issue-oriented as Haar (1955b) had urged. It is, however, difficult to discern any immediate improvement in the use of zoning in response to these changes in planning. Except where jolted in new directions by court orders or new state and federal legislation, the piecemeal practice of zoning in some 10,000 communities has chugged along as before. According to Delafons (1969, 24): "The lack of any substantial relationship between the legal machinery and a clear concept of city planning is the firmest impression left by the origin and later course of land use control in America."

The Taking Issue

The most enduring issue confronting zoning and other land use regulations is the "taking issue"—to what extent can regulations reduce the value of private property without compensation to the owner? The taking issue, it should be noted, is not confined to municipal zoning but applies to any land use regulation by any level of government.

The taking issue arises from the final clause of the Fifth Amendment to the U.S. Constitution (and its counterparts in most state constitutions): ". . . nor shall private property be taken for public use without just compensation." Where private property is deliberately taken for a public use or purpose, as for streets, parks, or schools, the public authority clearly must pay the private owner "just compensation." This means fair market value as established by a jury. Such an action involves the public power of "eminent domain" (also referred to as "condemnation"). Eminent domain is legal as long as the correct procedures are followed, the public purpose is legitimate, and compensation to the private owner is "just."

But where land use regulation is concerned, the public neither seeks legal ownership of the property nor pays any compensation to the owner. Instead, the use of the property is restricted in the interest of the public health, safety, and welfare. Zoning thus encounters a paradox. On the one hand, one of its long-standing purposes, dating back to the New York Fifth Avenue merchants, is to protect and enhance property values, a somewhat strained but long-accepted interpretation of the "general welfare." On the other hand, zoning necessarily reduces some property values by limiting the range of choice and manner in which the property may be developed and utilized. Should such reduction in the value of some property for the benefit of others be compensable? In other words, is such a reduction in value a taking for public benefit within the scope of the Fifth Amendment?

At the time of zoning's genesis, the police power as applied to the abatement of nuisances was enjoying a high degree of judicial favor, as recounted in the preceding chapter. *Welch v. Swasey* (1909) and *Hadacheck v. Sebastian* (1915) lent confidence to those such as planning lawyer Edward M. Bassett who defended the constitutionality of zoning as a noncompensatory exercise of the police power, even in the face of substantial property value reduction.

But this optimism was to be dampened by the 1922 Supreme Court decision in *Pennsylvania Coal Co. v. Mahon* (260 U.S. 393). This case did not involve zoning per se, which had not yet come before the High Court. It did involve the police power in the form of a Pennsylvania statute that limited the right of coal producers to undermine developed areas if surface subsidence would result. The plaintiff coal company, which had purchased the mineral rights to all the coal under the defendant's land, claimed that the statute "took" their property right in the coal without compensation. Mahon however invoked the Pennsylvania statute as a bulwark against having his house undermined, although a preceding owner had sold the underlying mineral rights to the coal company. The Supreme Court, in a landmark opinion by Justice Oliver Wendell Holmes, agreed with the coal company. Holmes conceded that some reduction in property values due to necessary public regulations is acceptable:

> Government hardly could go on if, to some extent, values incident to property could not be diminished without paying for every such change in the general law. As long recognized, some values are enjoyed under an implied limitation, and must yield to the police power (260 U.S., at 413).

But Holmes went on to break new ground with the following statement that has been cited by thousands of irate property owners ever since and which underlies the taking issue debate in the 1990s:

> The general rule at least is, that while property may be regulated to a certain extent, if regulation goes too far, it will be recognized as a taking (260 U.S. at 415).

Justice Louis Brandeis in dissent urged that the police power may properly protect against threats to life and property without payment of compensation. While Holmes viewed the issue as a "case of a *single private house*" (260 U.S., at 413; emphasis added), Brandeis took a broader geographical perspective; he regarded land subsidence as a matter of *public safety* affecting many property owners and public facilities through the danger of surface collapse:

> Restriction imposed to protect the public health, safety, or morals from dangers threatened is not a taking. The restriction here in question is merely the prohibition of a noxious use. The property so restricted remains in the possession of its owner. The state does not

appropriate it or make any use of it. *The state merely prevents the owner from making a use which interferes with paramount rights of the public* (260 U.S., at 417; emphasis added).

The contrasting perspectives of Holmes and Brandeis define respectively the "conservative" position on the one hand and the "progressive" or "liberal" position on the other, concerning the role of law in defining the balance between private property and the public interest. The former position views the role of law as protecting rather than diminishing private property values. The latter views law as an instrument for the protection of the public welfare to which property ownership is subordinate. These also reflect differing *geographical* perceptions as to the relevant spatial context to be considered in weighing public regulations: the specific property whose use is being regulated or the wider area subject to possible externalities from the use of that land.

In the view of Bosselman, Callies, and Banta (1973, 134), Holmes in the *Pennsylvania Coal* opinion: "rewrote the Constitution" and interpreted the Fifth Amendment to imply that the difference between regulation and taking is a "difference of *degree not kind*" (emphasis original). But Holmes' test has withstood the test of time, challenging courts ever since to determine whether a regulation "goes too far." (As discussed below, the Supreme Court in 1987, the *Keystone* case, upheld a state law similar to the one rejected in *Pennsylvania Coal*, yet the majority chose to distinguish rather than overrule the hallowed Holmes opinion.)

Four years after *Pennsylvania Coal*, the constitutionality of land use zoning was presented to the U.S. Supreme Court. By the mid-1920s, zoning had spread like dandelion seeds across the United States, and property owners sought a test case to cast a constitutional death blow to zoning everywhere. The case that ultimately became the landmark decision in American land use law involved the zoning ordinance of Euclid, Ohio, a newly developing suburb of Cleveland. The circumstances involved in *Village of Euclid v. Ambler Realty Co.* (272 U.S. 365, 1926) have prompted an English commentator to write: "a severer test for zoning could hardly have been devised. The merits of the case were certainly dubious and the damage to private property values was impressive" (Delafons 1969, 26).

The site in question consisted of 68 acres of vacant land bordered by rail lines on the north and a major avenue on the south. It was divided by

Euclid's zoning ordinance into two principal zones and a buffer strip between them. The northern portion was zoned for industry and (cumulatively) anything else. The problem for the owner arose from the residential classification of the southern portion of the tract. It was agreed that the value of the latter would be $10,000 per acre for industry but only $3,500 for residential use.

The Federal District Court for Northern Ohio (the trial court) in no uncertain terms held Euclid's zoning ordinance to be unconstitutional (*Ambler Realty Co. v. Village of Euclid*, 297 F. 307, 1924). The judge of course quoted the recent Holmes opinion in *Pennsylvania Coal*. But he went on to declare a scathing indictment of zoning based on substantive due process and equal protection grounds:

> The plain truth is that the true object of the ordinance in question is to place all the property in an undeveloped area of 16 square miles in a straitjacket. The purpose to be accomplished is really to regulate the mode of living of persons who may hereafter inhabit it. In the last analysis, the result to be accomplished is to classify the population and segregate them according to their income or situation in life.

If this opinion had been upheld by the U.S. Supreme Court, the face of metropolitan America might look rather different today. However it was reversed.

The full story of the dramatic rescue of zoning before the Supreme Court is recounted by Seymour Toll in *Zoned American* (1969). After a full hearing, it appeared that Village of Euclid would lose and an unusual rehearing was requested and granted. To bolster the municipal position in the rehearing, Alfred Bettman, a Cincinnati planning lawyer, was retained by the National Conference on City Planning and other pro-zoning organizations to submit a brief as "amici curiae" ("friends of the court"). Bettman's brief, one of the seminal documents in the history of zoning, sidestepped the facts of the *Euclid* case in favor of broadly addressing the theory and constitutionality of zoning, including the issue of compensation. (The brief is reprinted in its entirety in Comey 1946, 157–193.)

Bettman argued that reduction of value per se cannot be the test of constitutionality since that "begs the question." Any police power measure, including many already approved by the Supreme Court as in

Hadacheck v. Sebastian, had involved measurable and perhaps severe economic impact to affected property owners. If the purpose is appropriate and necessary, Bettman maintained, loss of value is constitutionally tolerable.

Regarding the necessity of zoning, Bettman compared (but did not equate) it with the familiar governmental function of abating public nuisances. This was an easier task in relation to the height, bulk, and density provisions of zoning, since decisions such as *Welch v. Swasey* had already approved building regulations on a districting basis (Bassett 1936, 46). Regulation of use was a more difficult proposition since the separation of homes and commerce could not be viewed as abating a nuisance in the common law sense.

Bettman argued that modern urban development was producing unprecedented problems of congestion and inefficiency. He argued that orderliness of land usage pursuant to a master plan is a proper use of the police power. In effect, he urged in Holmes' terms that zoning did not go "too far" and did not amount to a compensable taking.

In a 6 to 3 decision (both Holmes and Brandeis voted with the majority), the Court upheld zoning. Its opinion reflected the tutorial on city growth provided in Bettman's brief and oral argument:

Building zone laws are of modern origin. They began in this country about twenty-five years ago. Until recent years, urban life was comparatively simple; but with the great increase and concentration of population, problems have developed, ... which require ... additional restrictions in respect of the use and occupation of private lands in urban communities. Regulations, the wisdom, necessity and validity of which as applied to existing conditions, are so apparent that they are now uniformly sustained, under the complex conditions of our day. ...

And the law of nuisances, ... may be consulted, not for the purpose of controlling, but for the helpful aid of its analogies in the process of ascertaining the scope of the [police] power. Thus the question whether the power exists to forbid the erection of a building of a particular kind or for a particular use ... is to be determined, not by an abstract consideration of the building or other thing considered apart, but by considering it in connection with the circumstances and the locality.

A nuisance may be merely the right thing in the wrong place–
like a pig in the parlor instead of the barnyard (272 U.S., at 370).

The *theory* of land use zoning was thus held to be constitutional. But
the Supreme Court left open the possibility that individual *applications*
of zoning might be rejected if a property owner proved that a restriction
was arbitrary or unreasonable as applied to his or her property. While
most cases of individual hardship have been remedied through the variance procedure, landowner challenges to local regulations based on the
taking issue have persisted to the present time. The Supreme Court itself
has left the resolution of these issues largely to the state courts, providing
only the sketchy guidance of Holmes' *Pennsylvania Coal* test as a basis
for decision.

In 1987, the U.S. Supreme Court revisited the taking issue in three
important decisions. In *Keystone Bituminous Coal Assn. v. DeBenedic-
tis*, 107 S.Ct 1232, a 5 to 4 decision, it upheld a Pennsylvania state law
resembling the one invalidated in the 1922 *Pennsylvania Coal* decision.
The *Keystone* opinion distinguished the earlier decision (rather than
directly overruling it) in holding the new Pennsylvania Subsidence Act
to serve public purposes not mentioned in the earlier version. But the
impact of a change in judicial perception and cultural values is admitted:
"The Subsidence Act is a prime example that 'circumstances may so
change in time . . . as to clothe with such a [public] interest what at other
times . . . would be a matter of purely private concern'" (107 S.Ct., at
1243). Thus, the public interest argument of Brandeis' dissent would be
embraced by the Court after 65 years, but without impugning the Holy
Writ of Holmes' balancing test, which is alive and well in the 1990s.

With a switch of one vote (Justice White), the *Keystone* majority
became a minority in the other two 1987 property rights cases. *First English Evangelical Lutheran Church v. County of Los Angeles* 107 S.Ct.
2378 involved a county moratorium on rebuilding of a camp for handicapped children in a canyon after a flash flood swept through the area. A
5 to 4 majority sustained a theory of "inverse condemnation," which
allows an owner to recover monetary damages for loss of value during
the time a restriction is in effect, if the restriction is subsequently held to
be invalid. The Court did not decide whether the Los Angeles County
moratorium was in fact a taking and remanded the question to the state

court, which held that it was not. Even if it were, the obvious hazards of the site would make it unlikely that much value had been "taken" by the ordinance (Epstein 1987, 27). Epstein argued however that no matter how trivial the compensable loss, interim damages should have been paid in *First English*, which he predicted would become "a permanent fixture in every land use battle in the United States" (p. 31).

The third 1987 case, *Nollan v. California Coastal Commission* 107 S.Ct. 3141, involved a restriction on a rebuilding permit for an ocean-front home that required the owners to allow the public an easement to walk along the dry sand (private) portion of the beach in front of their home. This was consistent with similar restrictions placed on new and rebuilt shorefront homes by the Commission to promote public access along beaches. The Commission also argued that the easement was needed to offset the loss of "visual access" to the ocean caused by enlargement of the plaintiff's home. With the same 5 to 4 alignment as *First English*, the majority opinion by Justice Scalia held that the access easement lacked an "essential nexus" with the goal of maintaining visibility of the ocean from public streets:

> The Commission may well be right that [the public interest will be served by a continuous strip of publicly accessible beach along the coast] but that does not establish that the Nollans (and other coastal residents) alone can be compelled to contribute to its realization. Rather, California is free to advance its "comprehensive program," if it wishes, by using its power of eminent domain for this "public purpose" . . . but if it wants an easement across the Nollans' property, it must pay for it (107 S.Ct., at 3150).

The case thus reflected a long-standing doctrine that the police power may properly be used to prevent public harm but not to confer public benefits without compensation (Sax 1964, 49–50). But in dissent, Justice Blackmun argued that the majority hold "a narrow conception of rationality . . . [that] has long been discredited as a judicial arrogation of legislative authority. 'To make scientific precision a criterion of constitutional power would be to subject the State to an intolerable supervision hostile to the basic principles of our Government.'"

Two additional Supreme Court opinions have further buttressed the view of property owner interests that the "taking issue" should be a substantial deterrent to public land use regulation. The first of these, *Lucas v. South Carolina Coastal Council* 112 S.Ct. 2886, 1992, involved a challenge by the owner of two lots on the oceanfront of South Carolina against the denial of building permits by the defendant. The latter was guided by the 1988 South Carolina Beachfront Management Act, adopted after Lucas acquired his lots, that prohibited new building seaward of an erosion setback baseline. Due to recent fluctuations of the shoreline, the baseline ran entirely landward of Lucas' lots. Although homes had been built on adjoining lots before the law went into effect, the Coastal Council denied approval for any construction on the Lucas lots. Lucas did not challenge the validity of the Beachfront Management Act per se, but claimed that its application to his lots destroyed all of their value (Platt 1992).

The trial court agreed and ordered the state to pay Lucas $1.2 million as compensation. The South Carolina Supreme Court (404 S.E.2d 895, 1991) in a 3 to 2 vote reversed the trial court, holding the permit denial to be a valid application of the police power consistent with the U.S. Supreme Court *Keystone* opinion. The Supreme Court accepted Lucas' appeal from the state decision; the resulting national attention attracted numerous "amicus curiae" briefs by interested parties on both sides of the issue. Its potential importance was reflected in an editorial in the *Boston Globe* (March 5, 1992):

> The case has far-reaching implications for the enforcement of regulations concerning everything from billboards to wetlands, as well as the coastline. Environmentalists fear that if the court decides in Lucas' favor, virtually every environmental restriction placed on the use of property will be considered a taking, thus making environmental protection too expensive.

The Supreme Court reversed the state ruling in a 6 to 3 decision, holding that where a regulation "denies all economically beneficial or productive use of land" (112 S.Ct., at 2893), it is a "categorical" compensable taking, equivalent to a physical invasion of the property by governmental action. Justice Scalia in his majority opinion argued that the need to compensate for "total takings" could not be avoided by merely reciting harms that the regulation would prevent. But in an awkward distinction, he wrote that compensation would however not be required for total takings where a regulation merely reflected a state's "background principles of nuisance and property law" (idem, at 2901) (apparently meaning that Lucas could have been prevented from building on his lots due to state public or private nuisance doctrines).

Justice Blackmun in dissent wrote: "Today the Court launches a missile to kill a mouse." Citing *Keystone* among other cases, Blackmun argued:

> These cases rest on the principle that the State has full power to prohibit an owner's use of property if it is harmful to the public. Since no individual has a right to use his property so as to create a nuisance or otherwise harm others, the State has not 'taken' anything of value when it asserts its power to enjoin the nuisance-like activity . . . It would make no sense under this theory to suggest that an owner has a constitutionally protected right to harm others, if only he makes the proper showing of economic loss (112 S.Ct., at 2912).

It is Holmes and Brandeis all over again. Both Scalia for the majority and Blackmun in dissent agree that government can restrain private owners from causing external harm in their use of land. They differ as to what comprises "harm" and who should make that determination, the legislature or the courts. Moreover, they differ as to whether the state has a higher obligation to compensate if the case involves a "total taking" rather than a partial loss of value. (The case was remanded to the state court, which found that no such common law nuisance was involved and agreed that it was a temporary taking for the time that the restriction remained in effect. The state ended up paying Lucas and then selling the properties—with building permits.)

The legal significance of the *Lucas* case has been far outweighed by its political impact. Pro- and antiregulation factions have vied with each other to interpret the decision favorably to their positions. For example, one property rights advocate has paraphrased the decision as follows: "The U.S. Supreme Court said [in *Lucas*] that it will require close scrutiny of land use regulations that devalue private property" (Stoddard 1995, 30). An environmental writer, on the other hand, views *Lucas* as "A decision full of sound and fury signifying nothing" (Sugameli 1993).

On June 24, 1994, the Supreme Court announced a 5 to 4 decision in another much-awaited property rights case: *Dolan v. City of Tigard* 114 S.Ct. 2309. Like *Nollan*, this case involved the imposition of a disputed condition ("exaction") upon the plaintiff property owner in order to be granted a permit to enlarge an existing structure (a hardware store in this case). The conditions were that the owner dedicate to the city a portion of her property lying in the 100-year floodplain, plus an additional strip to be used as part of a public bikeway system. The U.S. Supreme Court, elaborating on its *Nollan* ruling, reversed the Oregon Supreme Court in another 5 to 4 decision and held these conditions to be invalid takings.

The majority opinion in *Dolan* by Chief Justice Rehnquist required the defendant city to demonstrate "rough proportionality" between the burden on the property owner and the benefit to the public: "No precise mathematical calculation is required, but the city must make some sort of individualized determination that the required dedication is related both in nature and extent to the impact of the proposed development" (114 S.Ct., at 2329-2320). The majority felt that this test (never before enunciated) was not met by the city and the mandatory dedication of the bikeway at least was therefore invalid.

As with *Lucas*, the political importance of the decision far transcended its narrow legal significance. As Justice Stevens dryly observed in dissent: "The mountain of briefs that the case has generated . . . makes it obvious that the pecuniary value of [the owner's] victory is far less important than the rule of law that this case has been used to establish. It is unquestionably an important case" (idem, at 2322).

Stevens argued that this "rough proportionality" test places the burden of proof on the city, reversing the long-standing presumption of validity extended by courts to the regulatory actions of local governments. "Rough proportionality," he stated, also is difficult to satisfy in relation to such statistically uncertain phenomena as flooding and traffic congestion. In language calculated to raise the spirits of planners and floodplain managers, Stevens declared:

> In our changing world one thing is certain: uncertainty will characterize predictions about the impact of new urban developments on the risks of floods, earthquakes, traffic congestion, or environmental harms. When there is doubt concerning the magnitude of those

impacts, the public interest in averting them must outweigh the private interest of the commercial entrepreneur (idem, at 2329).

With a shift of one justice, this could have been the majority view and thus the "law of the land."

The New York Times reported the decision with the headline: "High Court Limits the Public Power on Private Land . . . Opinion by Rehnquist Curbs Environmental and Other Land Use Measures" (June 25, 1994). But this apocalyptic view, shared by some other media and the property rights movement, is exaggerated. The majority opinion by Rehnquist, but for its outcome, is rife with favorable commentary on city planning, floodplain management, greenways, bike paths, and other elements of planning. For example:

Undoubtedly, the prevention of flooding along Fanno Creek and the reduction of traffic congestion in the Central Business District qualify as the type of legitimate public purposes we have upheld . . . It seems equally obvious that a nexus exists between preventing flooding along Fanno Creek (114 S.Ct., at 2318).

But as with *Lucas*, the importance of the *Dolan* case may not lie so much in its narrow legal significance, but in what it is thought to represent, namely a broadening of property owner rights in relation to public land use regulations. This perception, whether or not strictly justified by the decisions themselves, may become a self-fulfilling expectation if political bodies, administrative agencies, and lower courts are persuaded that the pendulum is swinging in the direction of private rather than public interests.

Metropolitan Needs and Exclusionary Zoning

Land use regulation, especially zoning, is challenged not only by property owners but also by urban professionals who view it as excessively parochial as administered by local governments. This tendency has appeared in at least three forms, each of which has been widely criticized in professional literature:

- *Exclusionary zoning*—the use of zoning to deter construction of homes or siting of mobile homes for moderate-income families or members of racial or other minorities.

- *Fiscal zoning*—the use of zoning to minimize local property taxes by encouraging revenue-generating activities such as shopping centers and industrial parks while discouraging revenue-demanding uses such as lower-cost homes for families with children (regardless of race).

- *NIMBY*—the use of zoning and other legal means to resist the location of unwanted uses, facilities, or activities within the municipality (such as regional incinerators or toxic waste disposal sites, prisons, mental health facilities, oil refineries, public housing). The acronym stands for "not in my backyard."

These forms of parochialism in local zoning arise from somewhat different motivations such as racial or ethnic snobbery, economic self-interest, environmental concerns, neighborhood aesthetics, or a sense of security and peace of mind. These motives are not mutually exclusive and they frequently overlap. More socially acceptable concerns such as environment and aesthetics sometimes serve as the "sheep's clothing" for the "wolf" of racial or economic motives (Bosselman 1973).

Localism in zoning is not necessarily a bad thing. The local government is most familiar with the circumstances of particular land use decisions and has a valid interest in protecting the public health, safety, and welfare of its inhabitants. It is arguably the best qualified level of government to plan and regulate the use of private land within its borders. But in the hands of the multifarious municipalities, many of them minuscule in territory and population, localism in zoning can and does obstruct broader regional or national objectives. The essence of the issue is *which public* is implied in constitutional protection of the "general welfare"—the strictly local public, or the larger publics of the region, state, nation, or globe? (see Clark 1984; 1985).

Richard F. Babcock (1966) was one of the first to criticize the conventional wisdom that zoning is necessarily constitutional if it is "in accordance with" a local comprehensive or master plan. Babcock asserted that such accordance is a necessary but not sufficient condition of constitutionality:

> The local plan . . . is imperative as a device to bring some consistency and impartiality in local administrative decisions among residents of the same municipality.
>
> It is an error, however, to dignify the municipal plan with more authority than this limited function. But to measure the validity of zoning by the degree to which it is consistent with a municipal plan does just that. The municipal plan may be just as arbitrary and irresponsible as the municipal zoning ordinance if that plan reflects no more than the municipality's arbitrary desires. If the plan ignores the responsibility of the municipality to its municipal neighbors and to landowners and taxpayers who happen to reside outside the municipal boundaries, and if that irresponsibility results in added burdens to other public agencies and to outsiders . . . then a zoning ordinance bottomed on such a plan should be as vulnerable to attack as a zoning ordinance based on no municipal plan.
>
> Babcock 1966, p. 123.

The "Metropolitan Factor"

The possibility of conflict between municipal and larger regional objectives in zoning policy was recognized as early as the *Euclid* decision. By the 1920s, suburbanization and metropolitan expansion had been in progress for decades—since the advent of horse-drawn streetcars and electric railways. Euclid, Ohio itself was a suburb of Cleveland. Bettman's brief somewhat disingenuously extolled zoning as a tool for bringing order to the "modern American city" while ignoring that a "city" such as Euclid comprised only a fragment of its metropolitan region. The Court's opinion however included a portentous remark on this issue:

> It is not meant . . . to exclude the possibility of cases where the general public interest would so far outweigh the interest of the municipality that the municipality would not be allowed to stand in the way (272 U.S., at 390).

Bettman himself addressed the "metropolitan issue" a year after *Euclid:*

> The last word has not as yet been uttered on this question of the relationship of the metropolitan factor to the validity of specific zone plans. . . . Insofar as the fact of the location of a municipality within a metropolitan urban area has a bearing upon these factors of development trends, land values, and appropriateness of use, such fact has a relation to the social validity and, consequently, in the last analysis, to the constitutional validity of the zone plan.
>
> Quoted in Comey, p. 55

The 1928 Department of Commerce Standard City Planning Enabling Act, which Bettman helped to write, included in the coverage of a municipal master plan: ". . . any areas outside of its boundaries which, in the planning commission's judgment, bear relation to the planning of such municipality." Also, the purpose of such plan was stated to be "the harmonious development of the municipality *and its environs* (emphasis added) (quoted in Beuscher et al. 1976, 272–3).

Many state planning acts today permit municipalities to exercise limited planning and regulatory control over unincorporated land within a specified distance (for instance, two miles outside their corporate boundaries). But this merely reflects the expectation that such land will eventually be annexed to that municipality. It is scarcely a mandate to consider external implications of local zoning policies, particularly to other municipalities and their inhabitants.

The Cresskill Decisions

Surprisingly few cases addressed the regional context of zoning before the 1960s. Two early landmark decisions involved the obscure New Jersey Borough of Cresskill. *Duffcon Concrete Products, Inc. v. Borough of Cresskill* 64 A.2d 347, 1949, upheld Cresskill's ban on industry in light of available sites in nearby jurisdictions. The court's opinion included what has been called "probably the best judicial statement on regional planning" (Haar 1963, 204):

> What may be the most appropriate use of any particular property depends not only on all the conditions, physical, economic and

social, prevailing within the municipality and its needs, present and reasonably prospective, but also on the nature of the entire region in which the municipality is located and the use to which the land in that region has been or may be put most advantageously (64 A.2d, at 349-50).

The principle was restated in *Borough of Cresskill v. Borough of Dumont* 104 A.2d 441, 1954, in which three neighboring boroughs challenged Dumont's rezoning for a small shopping center a single parcel that coincidentally abutted the boundaries of all three plaintiff jurisdictions. In response to Dumont's assertion that "the responsibility of a municipality for zoning halts at the municipal boundary lines," the court stated:

Such a view might prevail where there are large undeveloped areas at the borders of two contiguous towns, but it cannot be tolerated where, as here, the area is built up and one cannot tell when one is passing from one borough to another. Knickerbocker Road and Massachusetts Avenue are not Chinese Walls separating Dumont from the adjoining boroughs. At the very least Dumont owes a duty to hear any residents and taxpayers of adjoining municipalities who may be adversely affected by proposed zoning changes ... To do less would be to make a fetish out of invisible municipal boundary lines and a mockery of the principles of zoning (104 A.2d, at 445-6).

But both Cresskill cases were exclusionary, rather than inclusionary. One holds that a municipality may, and the other that it must, *exclude* land uses that conflict with the interests of adjoining areas. That was step one toward recognition of a metropolitan dimension to zoning. Step two, beginning in New Jersey and Pennsylvania in the 1960s, would assert that a municipality must also zone to *include* those land uses necessary to meet regional deficiencies.

Opening the Suburbs

The exclusion of apartments from single-family neighborhoods was approved by the U.S. Supreme Court in a widely cited dictum in *Euclid:*

... the development of detached house sections is greatly retarded by the coming of apartment houses ... very often the apartment house is a mere parasite, constructed in order to take advantage of the open spaces and attractive surroundings. Moreover, the coming of one apartment house is followed by others, ... until, finally, the residential character of the neighborhood and its desirability as a place of detached residences are utterly destroyed. Under these circumstances, apartment houses, which in a different environment would be ... highly desirable, come very near to being nuisances (272 U.S., at 394–5).

If "municipality" is substituted for "neighborhood," this would appear to legitimize zoning that excludes apartments and other multifamily housing from entire communities. This issue probably did not occur to the Court, nor did the plaintiff in *Euclid* seek to build apartments. The Court was merely airing its views on the bulky, non-setback apartment buildings that were invading single-family neighborhoods in the 1920s (Williams 1975, Vol. 6, Plates 6 and 7).

Beginning in the 1930s, the federal government actually reinforced the practice of segregation in the location, design, and occupancy of new residential construction. Kenneth T. Jackson (1985, ch. 11) attributes the origins of socioeconomic "redlining" of neighborhoods and communities to the appraisal practices of the Home Owners Loan Corporation (HOLC) established by Congress in 1933. HOLC's mission was to provide federal mortgage assistance at low interest rates to forestall owner default on home loans during the Depression.

To promote the reliability of lending practices, HOLC conducted surveys of residential neighborhoods. These studies codified prevailing real estate assumptions regarding the effects of race, religion, and wealth on residential property values. Detailed "residential security maps" prepared by HOLC for many cities and suburbs throughout the nation influenced the lending practices of financial institutions and thus became self-fulfilling prophecies. Furthermore, the home loan guarantee programs of the Federal Housing Administration (FHA) beginning in 1934, and the Veterans Administration (VA) after 1944, reflected for many years the racial and economic assumptions regarding neighborhood quality and housing type fostered by the HOLC. The post-war white middle-class, single-family suburb was the result (Jackson, 206–209).

Municipal exclusion of apartments was to remain virtually unchallenged until the Pennsylvania Supreme Court addressed the issue in 1970. In *Appeal of Girsh* 263 A.2d 395, the plaintiff, who sought to construct "two nine-story luxury apartments, each containing 280 units," challenged the local zoning ordinance, which designated no land within the township for apartments. In upholding the plaintiff, the court quoted extensively from its own prior decision that invalidated a 4-acre minimum lot requirement in *National Land and Investment Co. v. Easttown Twp. Board of Adjustment* 215 A.2d 597, 1965:

> The question posed is whether or not the township can stand in the way of the natural forces which send our growing population into hitherto undeveloped areas in search of a comfortable place to live. We have concluded not. A zoning ordinance whose primary purpose is to prevent the entrance of newcomers in order to avoid future burdens, economic and otherwise, upon the administration of public services and facilities cannot be held valid. . . .
>
> Zoning is a tool in the hands of governmental bodies which enables them to more effectively meet the demands of evolving and growing communities. It must not and cannot be used by those officials as an instrument by which they may shirk their responsibilities. Zoning is a means by which a governmental body can plan for the future. . . . Zoning provisions may not be used . . . to avoid the increased responsibilities and economic burdens which time and natural growth invariably bring (263 A.2d, at 397).

Girsh, National Land, and another 1970 Pennsylvania decision, *Appeal of Kit-Mar Builders* 269 A.2d 765 (invalidating a 2–3 acre minimum lot size) reflected a recognition by the Pennsylvania court that the geographical functions and morphology of suburbs were changing. No longer simply bedrooms for central city executives, suburbs were increasingly attracting new jobs, thereby creating a demand for a wider range of housing opportunities. According to these cases, suburbs that welcome new commercial investment may not use zoning to avoid the burden of accommodating new residents and building types. The concept of a "fair share" of regional housing needs was thereby introduced into Pennsylvania zoning law. A portentous footnote to the *Girsh* opinion stated:

... as long as we allow zoning to be done community by community, it is intolerable to allow one municipality (or many municipalities) to close its doors at the expense of surrounding communities and the central city (263 A.2d, at 399).

Girsh fired a warning shot across the bow of exclusionary-minded communities in Pennsylvania and, while not directly applicable to other states, it bolstered similar challenges elsewhere through its constitutional rationale. But *Girsh* was vague as to what a municipality must do to avoid exclusionary challenges, and it did not involve lower-cost housing. Indeed the luxury apartments proposed by Girsh were perhaps more akin to the "parasitic" apartments invading single-family districts of the *Euclid* era than to subsidized housing of the late 1960s. Also, the Pennsylvania cases including *Girsh* did not specify which geographic types of communities were "denying the future"—developing suburbs, central cities with remaining vacant land, rural townships? How were each of these to be judged as to the adequacy of their zoning?

The onerous task of applying a *Girsh* -type rationale to the specific circumstances of regional housing markets was assumed by the New Jersey Supreme Court in its landmark 1975 unanimous decision in *Southern Burlington County NAACP v. Township of Mount Laurel* 336 A.2d 713 (*"Mount Laurel I"*). As early as 1962, Justice Hall, who wrote this opinion, had signaled the judicial revolution to come in a famous dissent in *Vickers v. Township Committee of Gloucester Township* 181 A.2d 129. In objection to the majority's upholding of a total ban on mobile homes by a large rural township, Hall had declared:

> The import of the holding gives almost boundless freedom to developing municipalities to erect exclusionary walls on their boundaries, according to local whim or selfish desire, and to use the zoning power for aims beyond its legitimate purposes (181 A.2d, at 140).

The conversion of his viewpoint from dissent in *Vickers* to majority opinion in *Mount Laurel* was influenced by research at Rutgers University (Williams and Norman 1974) that documented the practice of exclusionary zoning in four northeastern New Jersey counties. Of 474,000 acres of vacant buildable land in those counties, 99.5 percent was zoned for single-family use and no land was available for mobile homes. Minimum lots of an acre or more were required for 77 percent of suitable land. Only 0.5 percent of the four counties was zoned for multifamily dwellings. Although Mount Laurel is not within the counties included in that study, the Williams and Norman findings clearly influenced the court's perception in the case that arose there.

Mount Laurel, New Jersey is a flat, sprawling, 22-square-mile township of mixed developed and agricultural land uses within commuting distance of Camden and Philadelphia. Between 1960 and 1970, its population more than doubled to 11,221. Most of the vacant land remaining at the time of the lawsuit was zoned for industry. In the court's opinion:

> The record thoroughly substantiates the findings of the trial court that over the years Mount Laurel "has acted affirmatively to control development and to attract a selective type of growth" . . . and that "through its zoning ordinances has exhibited economic discrimination in that the poor have been deprived of adequate housing, and has used federal, state, county, and local finances and resources solely for the betterment of middle- and upper-income persons."
>
> There cannot be the slightest doubt that the reason for this course of conduct has been to keep down local taxes on *property* . . . and that the policy was carried out without regard for non-fiscal considerations with respect to *people*, either within or without its boundaries (336 A.2d, at 723; emphasis is Justice Hall's).

The opinion explicitly raises for perhaps the first time the constitutional issue as to "whose general welfare must be served or not violated in the field of land use regulation" (336 A.2d, at 726). The court answered its own question by declaring that the constitutionality of zoning requires that in the case of "developing municipalities" (that is, growing suburban jurisdictions with available vacant land):

> Every such municipality must, by its land use regulations, presumptively make realistically possible an appropriate variety and choice of housing . . . at least to the extent of the municipality's fair share of the *present and prospective regional need therefor* (336 A.2d, at 724; emphasis added).

Thus it was no longer constitutional in New Jersey for communities in the "developing" category to use zoning to serve only their own parochial objectives. They were now required to accommodate a "fair share" of the regional demand for lower-cost housing. The court ordered Mount Laurel and other developing municipalities to revise their zoning accordingly.

The constitutional reverberations of *Mount Laurel* thundered across the land. Although a state court decision, it was widely regarded as a national precedent. An appeal to the U.S. Supreme Court was dismissed for "want of jurisdiction" (98 S.Ct. 18, 1976) since the Hall opinion was deliberately based on state law, not federal constitutional grounds (although both involve the same principles). *Mount Laurel* thus avoided possible reversal by the U.S. Supreme Court.

The reaction in New Jersey was a deluge of lawsuits against other municipalities based on *Mount Laurel* grounds as well as political hostility to the court's intervention in local affairs (Babcock and Siemon 1985, ch. 11). The Hall opinion had not provided detailed guidance as to the meaning of key concepts—for example, "region," "developing municipality," and "fair share." Nor was it clear whether a municipality must do more than merely rezone land for lower-cost housing and wait to see if a developer comes along. In a lengthy 1977 opinion in *Oakwood at Madison v. Twp. of Madison* 371 A.2d 1192, the New Jersey court advised trial courts to examine the substance of challenged zoning ordinances and to look for bona fide efforts to meet *Mount Laurel* obligations. It declined to specify a particular numerical approach:

> We do not regard it as mandatory for developing municipalities whose ordinances are challenged as exclusionary to devise specific formulae for estimating their precise fair share of the lower income housing needs of a specifically demarcated region . . . firstly, numerical housing goals are not realistically translatable into specific substantive changes in a zoning ordinance . . . Secondly, the breadth of approach by the experts to the factors of the appropriate region and to the criteria for allocation of regional housing goals to municipal "sub-regions" is so great and the pertinent economic and sociological [and geographical, ed.] considerations so diverse as to preclude judicial dictation or acceptance of any one solution as authoritative (371 A.2d, at 1200).

The court, however, could not long avoid the task of bringing order to the legal and planning chaos resulting from *Mount Laurel I*. In 1983, it responded in a 270-page unanimous decision in *Southern Burlington County NAACP v. Township of Mount Laurel* 456 A.2d 390 ("Mount Laurel II"). It began by stating that the court was ". . . more firmly committed to the original *Mount Laurel* doctrine than ever" but recognized a "need to put some steel into that doctrine." In a level of detail more characteristic of a legislature or the federal courts, the New Jersey court articulated a series of policies and standards for the resolution of the myriad *Mount Laurel* cases then clogging the state's lower courts. Among these were the following:

1. Every municipality must provide lower cost housing opportunities for its resident poor.

2. The concept of "developing municipality" was replaced by "growth areas" designated in the State Development Guide Plan (SDGP).

3. Municipalities must demonstrate that they are providing specific numbers of lower-cost housing units to meet their fair share of immediate and prospective regional needs. "Numberless" determinations based on provision for "some" lower-cost units will be insufficient

4. A special panel of judges was to be designated to hear *Mount Laurel* cases.

5. Municipalities must do more than merely rezone land for lower-cost housing. Affirmative action may be required such as subsidies, tax incentives, density bonuses, and mandatory set-asides of lower-cost units in new developments.

Two years later, the New Jersey Legislature enacted a state Fair Housing Act (*N.J. Laws* 1985, ch. 222) which codified the *Mount Laurel II* approach with some modification. The Act established a Council on Affordable Housing, which is empowered to determine housing regions and calculate regional housing needs and municipal fair-share allocations. The Act also provides a mediation and review process to resolve *Mount Laurel* litigation, a procedure for "substantive certification" of municipal zoning ordinances, authority for "regional contribution agreements" among municipalities, amendment of the state zoning law to require a housing element, and a program of financial assistance to help municipalities meet their fair-share allocations (Rose 1987, 448–449).

In another mammoth opinion, *Hills Development Co. v. Somerset County* 510 A.2d 621, 1986 (*"Mount Laurel III"*), the New Jersey Supreme Court held the Fair Housing Act to be constitutional despite objections that it diluted the impact of the court's earlier decision. Rose (1987) welcomed the assumption of responsibility for housing policy by the state legislature in place of the court's, which he considers ill-suited and inappropriate forums to resolve technical housing issues. On the other hand, he believes that the legislature was too "servile" to the "fair-share" concept established by the court which: ". . . has converted a generally acceptable principle of justice and equity to a commandment that requires the creation of a government megastructure and an army of government officials to do battle with the partisans of real estate development in the statistical warfare provoked by that concept (Rose, 473).

Overall, Rose appraises the Act, as follows:

Although it is significantly less than a perfect program to provide housing for all the low- and moderate-income persons in the state, the law nevertheless establishes several principles and creates a number of programs and procedures that put the state of New Jersey in the forefront of creative housing policy in the United States.

Rose, p. 458.

Babcock and Siemon (1985, 233), in contrast to Rose, praise the New Jersey court for its activism in Mount Laurel: "We believe New Jersey should be applauded for this daring step. Without such experiments our federal system would lose much of its resistance and its capacity to survive. It is hard to imagine Congress or the U.S. Supreme Court daring to venture into such socially and politically treacherous waters."

By late 1988 the New Jersey experiment was making slow progress, according to *The New York Times* (Nov. 13, 1988, Sec. 4, p. 5):

. . . Progress toward the goals of the Mount Laurel decisions which required the states' 567 communities to provide zoning for low and moderate income housing, has been slow and hampered by lawsuits, experts say. Only about 30 percent of the cities and towns have submitted affordable housing plans . . .

The last word on the New Jersey approach to the problem of exclusionary zoning has certainly not been uttered. It will require many years and certainly more litigation before the results of this judicial/legislative revolution may be fairly evaluated. It is clear, however, that the *Mount Laurel* experience is consistent with the model set forth in Chapter 2, and that legal innovation in land use control arises from the changing perception of those in authority that the existing legal rules are yielding undesirable consequences in the real world. *Mount Laurel* demonstrates the power of empirical research of a strongly geographical flavor to influence public decision making. The case also exemplifies the role of states as laboratories for legal innovation that may subsequently diffuse to other jurisdictions.

Urban Housing for the Poor

While housing activists labored to open the suburbs to affordable housing, existing stocks of older housing in the central cities continued to decline. During the 1950s and 1960s, efforts to save or replace urban housing followed two general approaches: public housing and urban renewal. Both involved a partnership of federal funding and technical guidance with local administration. Both approaches were to be challenged as ineffective and counterproductive.

Direct federal assistance to local public housing programs began with the Public Works Emergency Housing Corporation in 1933 (Feiss 1985, 176). In 1938, Congress established the Slum Clearance Program for replacement of tenements with publicly owned housing projects. By 1970 this program, as modified in various later housing acts, had resulted in the construction of about 870,000 units of low-rent public housing. If fully occupied, these could accommodate about 3 million people or 1.5 percent of the nation's population—compared with 25 million people (13 percent of the population) who were below the federally established poverty level in 1970 (Downs 1973, 48).

Although "shamefully small in relation to the nation's housing needs" (Fried 1971, 73), the actual picture was even worse. Many public housing units were uninhabitable by the mid-1960s due to inappropriate design, isolated location, occupancy policies, and lack of upkeep. Most were in large high-rise projects that lacked convenient access to jobs, decent schools, social services, and physical security for their inhabitants. Rife with crime and drug problems, much of the public housing built with federal assistance has been abandoned. The infamous Pruitt-Igoe Project in St. Louis, for example, consisted of 43 eleven-story buildings. By 1970, 26 of these were boarded up, and in 1972 all were demolished by the city's housing authority (Newman 1972; 1995).

Aside from poor design, a fundamental objection of civil rights advocates to federal public housing policy was the practice of locating most projects (except elderly housing) in black ghetto areas, thus reinforcing patterns of racial segregation since most occupants were nonwhite. In a suit filed by the NAACP, the federal district court in Chicago held that this practice violated the Fourteenth Amendment and ordered new public housing to be scattered in small clusters throughout the city, including white neighborhoods (*Gautreaux v. Chicago Housing Authority* 296 F. Supp. 907, 1969, and 304 F. Supp. 736, 1970). The subsequent history of this case, which yielded some 20 further opinions including one by the U.S. Supreme Court, has been vividly recounted by Babcock and Siemon (1985, ch. 9).

Little public housing has been built in the United States since the 1960s. As of 1988, the nation had only about one million occupied units of family public housing and 375,000 units of elderly public housing. In the same year, 6.7 million households were below the poverty level, including 31.7 million adults and children (of whom 11 million were nonwhite). (U.S. Bureau of the Census 1991, Tables 750, 751, and 1295). Federal public housing policy since the early 1970s has emphasized housing allowances to eligible households rather than construction of additional public units. The record of federal involvement in housing for the poor, however, has generally been shameful in comparison with the many forms of federal subsidy to the habitability of middle- and upper-class suburbs.

The federal Urban Renewal Program was also widely discredited. Under the Housing Acts of 1949 and 1954, urban renewal funded local authorities to plan, acquire, clear, and redevelop designated areas of "urban blight." With the approval of the U.S. Supreme Court in *Berman v. Parker* in 1954 (see Chapter 9), the program cleared thousands of acres of inner-city tenements and displaced tens of thousands of low-income households and small businesses. Aside from areas rebuilt with public facilities such as schools and parks, most urban renewal land was sold at a subsidized price to private redevelopers to be reused according to the urban renewal plan. This resulted in the construction of new office buildings, hotels, shopping malls, and medium- to high-cost dwelling units in place of the former tenements. Some sites were never redeveloped, leaving pockets of litter-strewn vacant land in many inner-city neighborhoods to the present time.

Urban renewal was attacked from several standpoints. Housing advocates complained that poor people displaced by the projects could not afford the new units built on the same sites and were given little help in finding alternative housing. More than 400,000 lower-income units were demolished by urban renewal during its first 18 years, while new housing constructed on those sites included only 10 percent of that number of units for low- and moderate-income households (Fried 1971, 86). Also, there was no compensation by urban renewal authorities to displaced tenants and small businesses (Berry, Parsons, and Platt 1968). In response to these criticisms, the Federal Uniform Relocation Assistance Act of 1970 authorized grants and relocation assistance to households and businesses displaced by federally funded projects.

Another criticism was that federal subsidies were enriching private redevelopers by clearing sites in favorable locations that were not necessarily blighted (Abrams 1965). Others criticized the disruption of ethnically diverse urban neighborhoods and their replacement by sterile, unsafe high-rise developments (Jacobs 1961; Gans 1962; Newman 1972).

Other forms of discrimination, however, preceded urban housing on the civil rights agenda. The Civil Rights Act of 1964, inspired by the Freedom Riders and the 1963 March on Washington, D.C. led by Dr. Martin Luther King, Jr., prohibited racial discrimination in voting, public accommodations, public education, and employment but did not reach the issue of housing. In 1965, Congress created the Department of Housing and Urban Development (HUD) as recommended by President Johnson's Task Force on Metropolitan and Urban Problems to serve as an umbrella for federal housing programs (Weaver 1985). In 1966, the Demonstration Cities and Metropolitan Development Act of 1966 launched the "Model Cities" program, which sought to upgrade community facilities, housing, jobs, and social programs in some 150 cities. "Model Cities" was viewed by its proponents as an alternative to urban renewal and a comprehensive approach to making inner-city neighbor-hoods more habitable.

For middle-class black families, however, the prospect of remaining in the inner city, even if better lighted, policed, and rehabilitated, was unac-ceptable. Efforts to open up exclusive white suburbs to minority house-holds led to adoption of the Fair Housing Act (Title VIII of the Civil Rights Act of 1968), which prohibited racial discrimination by lenders, realtors, and other parties to real estate transactions. Within three years, this Act covered 80 percent of the nation's housing supply (Weaver 1985, 466). It also provided a legal basis for challenging exclusionary zoning barriers in the federal courts (for example, *Metropolitan Housing Development Co. v. Village of Arlington Heights* 469 F. Supp. 836, 1979).

In the same year, Congress in the Housing and Urban Development Act of 1968 (P.L. 90-448) reaffirmed the goal of the 1949 housing act to provide: "a decent home and a suitable living environment for every American family." It called for the construction or rehabilitation by 1978 of 26 million dwelling units, including 6 million for low- and moderate-income households (President's Commission on Urban Housing 1968). The Act established new federal subsidies for "lower-income" rental and ownership housing, revised the public housing and urban renewal pro-grams, and launched new programs in urban mass transportation, "new communities," flood insurance, and interstate land sales. This center-piece (and finale) of President Johnson's War on Poverty marked the greatest expansion of federal involvement in urban development since the New Deal. The vast concrete headquarters of HUD and the Depart-ment of Transportation, which occupy adjacent sites of former urban renewal land in the southwest quadrant of Washington, D.C., are monu-ments to this brief but exuberant era of domestic concern (sadly over-shadowed by the other war, in Vietnam).

To enact programs is one thing, to achieve results is another. Robert Weaver (1985), the first Secretary of HUD, writes that federal housing policy has been stymied by its stop–go nature. Programs were piled on top of other programs—public housing, urban renewal, housing subsi-dies, rent supplements, model cities, new communities, and, in the 1970s, housing vouchers. Strategies to "gild the ghetto" conflicted with efforts to open the suburbs, and programs to house lower-income families com-peted for resources with housing for the very poor, who ended up as "the homeless" of the 1990s.

Aesthetics and Historic Preservation

Land use law has long struggled with the limits of achieving aesthetic objectives without compensation. The concept of aesthetics as "beauty" is virtually impossible to define in terms of legislative criteria sufficient to provide objective guidance to zoning officials. In the words of one court:

> [A] primary objection to aesthetic zoning is founded upon its subjective nature, for what may be attractive to one may be an abomination to another.... Therefore many courts have long been unwilling to act as super art critics by ruling on the reasonableness of ordinances which are essentially based on subjective aesthetic considerations, and they have held all such ordinances invalid (*Naegele Outdoor Advertising Co. v. Village of Minnetonka* 162 N.W.2d 206, 1962, at 212).

The early period of zoning was marked by a paradox concerning aesthetics. On the one hand, the basic terms of Euclidean zoning—segregation of uses, minimum lot size, setbacks, and so forth—are inherently aesthetic in nature. They embody the aesthetic of the turn-of-the-century garden suburb: single-family detached homes with spacious, landscaped front yards set back evenly from the street with nonresidential activities banished from the area.

Yet the proponents of Euclidean zoning steadfastly denied that zoning was intended to serve aesthetic purposes. In his *Euclid* brief, Bettman refuted the plaintiff's contention that zoning was motivated by "aesthetic considerations and the promotion of beauty." Bettman urged that the Court view zoning as promoting the "good order of cities" which is ". . . quite different from the artistic or the beautiful":

> The essential object of promoting what might be called orderliness in the layout of cities is not the satisfaction of taste or aesthetic desires, but rather the promotion of those beneficial effects upon health and morals which come from living in orderly and decent surroundings.
>
> Quoted in Comey, p. 172.

The 1926 Standard Zoning Enabling Act made no reference to aesthetics or beauty in its section on purposes. The justification for zoning has subsequently been expressed in terms of "public health, safety, and welfare" as reflected in reduction of congestion, orderly location of land uses, and avoidance of fire, flood, and other public perils.

Billboards

Early decisions involving regulations of billboards and other signs struggled to find a nonaesthetic basis for such laws. In 1919, the Illinois Supreme Court upheld such an ordinance, citing evidence that:

> ... nuisances were permitted to exist in the rear of surface billboards, and physicians testified that deposits found behind billboards breed disease germs which may be carried and scattered in the dust by the wind and by flies and other insects. It was shown that dissolute and immoral practices were carried on under the cover and shield furnished by these billboards (*Thomas Cusack Co. v. City of Chicago* 108 N.E. 340).

This decision may be contrasted in rationale with a 1975 opinion of the Massachusetts Supreme Judicial Court, which upheld a total ban on off-premises billboards in the Town of Brookline, stating:

> We live in a changing world where the law must respond to the demands of a modern society. [*Euclid* quote omitted]. What was deemed unreasonable in the past may now be reasonable due to changing community values. Among these changes is the growing notion that towns and cities can and should be aesthetically pleasing; that a visually satisfying environment tends to contribute to the well-being of its inhabitants (*John Donnelly and Sons, Inc. v. Outdoor Advertising Board* 339 N.E.2d 709, at 717).

Although *Donnelly* applies only to Massachusetts, the acceptance of aesthetics as a purpose of zoning is widely shared in other jurisdictions, at least with respect to billboards. According to Williams (1975, Sec. 11.02): "In no other area of planning law [than aesthetics] has the change in judicial attitudes been so complete." The evolution of this change is frequently divided into three stages: (1) early period–aesthetics impermissible as a basis for zoning; (2) middle period–aesthetics allowable if other valid grounds are present; and (3) modern period–aesthetics acceptable per se without the need for additional grounds.

A major turning point in the recognition of aesthetics in planning law was the 1954 U.S. Supreme Court decision in *Berman v. Parker* (75 S.Ct. 98). The opinion by Justice William O. Douglas, an ardent conservationist, declared:

> The concept of the public welfare is broad and inclusive . . . The values it represents are spiritual as well as physical, aesthetic as well as monetary. It is within the power of the legislature to determine that the community should be beautiful as well as healthy, spacious as well as clean, well-balanced as well as carefully patrolled . . . If those who govern the District of Columbia decide that the Nation's Capital should be beautiful as well as sanitary, there is nothing in the Fifth Amendment that stands in the way (75 S.Ct., at 102–103).

Strictly speaking, Douglas's sweeping statement did not apply to zoning. *Berman*, which arose from a challenge to the constitutionality of the federal urban renewal program, involved the eminent domain power, not the police power or zoning. The plaintiff's store was being condemned and razed by the District as part of a widespread program to eliminate "blighted areas" to make way for modern and expensive new homes and businesses. (The project was located in the southwest quadrant of Washington where the Department of Housing and Urban Development now sits on land cleared by urban renewal). Where government pays for land, much broader latitude exists as to public purpose than when the land is restricted under the police power. Thus, Douglas' statement really applies to the eminent domain function of government, not zoning.

Nevertheless, Douglas' statement has been widely quoted in zoning cases involving aesthetics, including the 1975 *Donnelly* case cited above. Douglas in fact quoted the statement himself in a zoning case that upheld community limitations on the occupancy of dwelling units by more than two unrelated adults (*Village of Belle Terre v. Borass* 94 S.Ct. 1536, 1974).

But the importance of the Douglas dictum should not be overstated. A zoning measure that forbids building on scenic land in the interest of maintaining a "beautiful community" would almost certainly be held invalid. The taking clause of the Fifth Amendment certainly "stands in the way" not withstanding Douglas' sweeping disclaimer.

In practice, aesthetic zoning has not generally attempted to legislate "beauty" or attractiveness in the general urbanizing landscape. As stated earlier, such values may be implicit to Euclidean zoning but seldom are stated explicitly due to the difficulty of drafting suitable legal criteria. Instead, aesthetic zoning has largely addressed two special cases of land use regulation, namely advertising signs and historic landmark preservation. Each of these involve marginal restraints on property that is otherwise economically productive. Even in these special areas of regulation, aesthetic zoning measures may be held invalid on other grounds.

Billboard regulations are authorized in all 50 states and are widely in effect. Restraints and even total bans of billboards have been upheld in many states. There appears to be widespread consensus that billboards and other types of outdoor advertising are per se unattractive, distracting, and exploitive of the captive audience represented by motorists on public thoroughfares. As a class of aesthetic nuisance, billboards have been categorically disfavored though by no means eliminated in many states.

But several issues arise when local governments begin to regulate billboards and other signs. Considerations include the size and characteristics of the sign, whether it is on-site or off-site (advertises the business on whose premises the sign is located), lighted or unlighted, freestanding or supported by a building, commercial or noncommercial. Signs may occasionally assume the status of landmarks, such as the "Citgo" sign that looms over the left field wall at Boston's Fenway Park. Other signs may be obstructions to traffic, pornographic, excessively distracting, or otherwise nuisance-like. Thus, communities do not usually prohibit all signs. But discrimination among different types of signs may generate constitutional difficulty.

In 1981, the U.S. Supreme Court addressed the problem of potential conflict between sign regulation and the First Amendment protection of freedom of speech. The court endorsed the general principle that signs may be regulated in the public interest, but it invalidated an ordinance that banned noncommercial advertising throughout the city while allowing on-site commercial signs, viewing this as impermissible discrimination against noncommercial (for example, political) signs (*Metromedia Inc. v. City of San Diego* 101 S.Ct. 2882).

Historic and Architectural Controls

Historical preservation districts are another instance of aesthetic zoning that has received widespread but often qualified judicial support. The concept of the historical district originated with the designation of the Vieux Carré District in New Orleans through an amendment to the Louisiana Constitution in 1921. Other early districts were established in Charleston, South Carolina; San Antonio, Texas; and Nantucket, Massachusetts. The distinctive architecture and renowned atmosphere of these prototype districts facilitated judicial approval of regulations to control construction, demolition, and renovation. For instance, in 1941, the Louisiana Supreme Court upheld the "Vieux Carré" restrictions in *City of New Orleans v. Impastato* 3 S.2d 559 and *City of New Orleans v. Pergament* 5 S.2d 129. The latter opinion stated:

> There is nothing arbitrary or discriminating in forbidding the proprietor of a modern building, as well as the proprietor of one of the ancient landmarks, in the Vieux Carré to display an unusually large sign upon his premises. The purpose of the ordinance is not only to preserve the old buildings themselves, but to preserve the antiquity of the whole French and Spanish quarter, tout ensemble, so to speak, by defending this relic against iconoclasm or vandalism. Preventing or prohibiting eyesores in such a locality is within the police power. . . .

Historic district regulations typically go beyond traditional zoning controls in requiring approval from a local review board for any alteration or demolition. Even an affirmative duty to maintain the exterior appearance of the premises may be imposed (*Maher v. City of New Orleans* 37 F. Supp. 653).

But given the stringency of these types of regulations, the applicability to particular property owners may be harsh. Many historical districts are less homogeneous or distinctive than the Vieux Carré. Issues arise concerning the status of nonhistoric structures within a designated district, accessory structures (such as solar panels and satellite dishes), mixture of architectural styles, approval of new construction within a district, the need for owner consent, 11th-hour designations to obstruct a redevelopment plan, and the status of religious property in a district (Duerksen 1985, 1503). As with other zoning, objective standards must be provided by the local or state legislative body to guide the local review body in its permitting process.

The validity of an historic landmark designation was upheld by the U.S. Supreme Court in *Penn Central Transportation Co. v. City of New York* 98 S.Ct. 2646, 1978. The Court broadly endorsed the principle of historic preservation: "States and cities may enact land use restrictions or controls to enhance the quality of life by preserving the character and desirable aesthetic features of a city" (98 S.Ct., at 266). The opinion then upheld the designation of Grand Central Station as an historical landmark and the prohibition by the city of either demolition or the construction of a modern office tower in the air rights column above the station. The Court noted that the station provided some economic return to the owner, albeit not optimal, and that the ordinance permitted the owner to transfer its unusable development rights to other parcels of real estate in the vicinity. (See Chapter 9.) This TDR feature and the special nature of Grand Central Station as a quasi-public facility perhaps limit the applicability of the *Penn Central* decision to more mundane historic structures. Public acquisition may still be required in the case of structures that have little economic use and lack a market for transferable development rights.

Nationally, more than 1000 local historic preservation laws were in effect as of the mid-1980s (Duerksen 1985). This branch of aesthetics zoning, like billboard control, is thriving. By 1995, New York City has designated 1021 individual structures and 66 historic districts (*New York Times*, April 9, 1995, p. E-3).

Architectural controls in a nonhistorical context pose a more difficult problem. How can a community regulate the appearance of new structures in relation to an existing potpourri of styles? Many communities have established architectural review boards to certify that a new structure will be compatible with the surrounding area. The problem is to define "compatibility" or "suitability" of a design in the absence of a clearcut historical or otherwise homogeneous style. Response to this problem is approached in two ways, namely, by attempting to write objective standards to guide the architectural board and by designating certain types of experts to be represented on the board. The Ohio Court of Appeals relied on the presence of both these safeguards in *Reid v. Architectural Review Board of City of Cleveland Heights* (192 N.E.2d 74, 1963). It upheld the board's disapproval of a modernistic "flat-roofed complex of 20 modules" in a "well-regulated and carefully groomed community." Some communities have even sought to regulate against "excessive similarity" of building styles.

The regulation of the appearance of new structures is a somewhat elitist exercise practiced chiefly in affluent communities where new homes may be constructed independently. Most residential construction today occurs in subdivisions where either new homes are built by the developer or are constructed by lot buyers in accordance with deed restrictions. Such private land use regulations to which the buyer voluntarily agrees are more potent vehicles for aesthetic control within a subdivision than public zoning and architectural review, although the results may be monotonous.

Permissiveness in aesthetic regulation is not necessarily an unmixed blessing. According to Costonis (1982, 367): "Aesthetics has been transformed from an idea into an ideology that is being employed by preservationists, environmentalists, and developers alike to rationalize pursuits that are at best tenuously related to visual beauty." The notion of aesthetics, Costonis notes, is inherently vague and expansive. Judicial approval of the objectives of aesthetic regulations in the context of signs and historic preservation should not necessarily be extended to any public action nominally taken in the spirit of aesthetic protection.

References

Abrams, C. 1965. *The City Is the Frontier*. New York: Harper and Row.

Babcock, R.F. 1966. *The Zoning Game*. Madison: University of Wisconsin Press.

———, and C.L. Siemon. 1985. *The Zoning Game Revisited*. Boston: Oelgeschlager, Gunn and Hain.

Bassett, E.M. 1936. *Zoning*. New York: Russell Sage Foundation.

Berry, B.J.L., S.J. Parsons, and R.H. Platt. 1968. *The Impact of Urban Renewal on Small Business*. Chicago: University of Chicago Center for Urban Studies.

Beuscher, J.H., R.R. Wright, and M. Gitelman. 1976. *Land Use: Cases and Materials*. St. Paul: West Publishing Co.

Bosselman, F.P. 1973. "Can the Town of Ramapo Pass a Law to Bind the Rights of the Whole World?" *Florida State University Law Review*. Vol. I (Spring): 234–259.

Bosselman, F.P., D. Callies, and J. Banta. 1973. *The Taking Issue*. Washington, D.C.: U.S. Government Printing Office.

Clark, G. 1984. "A Theory of Local Autonomy." *Annals of the Association of American Geographers* 74(2): 195–208.

———. 1985. *Judges and the Cities*. Chicago: University of Chicago Press.

Comey, A.C., ed. 1946. *City and Regional Planning Papers of Alfred Bettman*. Cambridge: Harvard University Press.

Costonis, J.J. 1982. "Law and Aesthetics: A Critique and a Reformulation of the Dilemmas." *Michigan Law Review* 80: 361–461.

Dawson, A. 1982. *Land Use Planning and the Law*. Hadley, MA: the author.

Delafons, J. 1969. *Land Use Controls in the United States* 2nd ed. Cambridge: M.I.T. Press.

Downs, A. 1973. *Opening Up the Suburbs: An Urban Strategy for America*. New Haven: Yale University Press.

Duerksen, C.J. 1985. "Administering Historic Drafting and Ordinances." In *1985 Zoning and Planning Handbook*. J. B. Gailen, ed. New York: Clark Boardman.

Epstein, R.A. 1987. "Takings." *The 1987 Supreme Court Review*. Chicago: University of Chicago Press.

Feiss, C. 1985. "The Foundations of Federal Planning Assistance." *Journal of the American Planning Association* 51 (2): 175–184.

Fried, J.P. 1971. *Housing Crisis U.S.A.* New York: Praeger.

Freund, E. 1904. *The Police Power: Public Policy and Constitutional Law*. Chicago: Callaghan.

Gans, H. 1962. *The Urban Villagers*. New York: Free Press of Glencoe.

Haar, C.M. 1955a. "The Master Plan: An Impermanent Constitution." *Harvard Law Review* 68: 353-377.

———. 1955b. "In Accordance with a Comprehensive Plan." *Harvard Law Review* 68: 1154–1175.

———. 1963. "The Social Control of Urban Space." In *Cities and Space: The Future Use of Urban Land*. L. Wingo, Jr., ed. Baltimore: Johns Hopkins Press.

Hamann, R.G., 1986. *Constitutional Issues in Local Coastal Resource Protection*. Report no. 85. Gainesville: Florida Sea Grant College.

Jacobs, J. 1961. *The Death and Life of Great American Cities*. New York: Random House.

Jackson, K.L. 1985. *Crabgrass Frontier: The Suburbanization of the United States*. New York: Oxford University Press.

Krueckeberg, D.A., ed. 1983. *The American Planner: Biographies and Recollections*. New York: Methuen.

Newman, O. 1972. *Defensible Space: Crime Prevention Through Urban Design*. New York: MacMillan.

———. 1995. "Defensible Space: A New Physical Planning Tool for Urban Revitalization." *Journal of the American Planning Association* 61(2): 149–155.

Platt, R.H. 1992. "An Eroding Base." *The Environmental Forum* 9(6): 10–15.

Rose, J. 1987. "New Jersey Enacts a Fair Housing Law." In *1987 Zoning and Planning Law*. N. J. Gordon, ed. New York: Clark Boardman.

Sax, J.L. 1964. "Takings and the Police Power." *Yale Law Journal* 74(1): 36–76.

Stoddard, G. 1995. "Coastal Policy Implications of Right to Rebuild Questions." *Shore and Beach* (Jan.): 25–35.

Sugameli, G.P. 1993. "Taking Issues in Light of Lucas v. South Carolina Coastal Council: A Decision Full of Sound and Fury Signifying Nothing." *Virginia Environmental Law Review* 12(3): 439–504.

U.S. Bureau of the Census. 1991. *Statistical Abstract of the U.S.: 1991*. Washington: U.S. Government Printing Office.

Warner, S.B. 1966. *Planning for a Nation of Cities*. Cambridge: MIT Press.

Weaver, R.C. 1985. "The First Twenty Years of HUD." *Journal of the American Planning Association* 51(4): 463–474.

Williams, N., Jr. 1975. *American Planning Use: Land Use and the Police Power*. Chicago: Callaghan.

Williams, N., Jr. and T. Norman. 1974. "Exclusionary Land Use Controls: The Case of North-Eastern New Jersey." In *Land Use Controls: Present Problems and Future Reform*. D. Listokin, ed. New Brunswick: Rutgers University Center for Urban Policy Research.

CHAPTER 9 / Beyond Zoning: Urban Land
Use Control by Other Means

Introduction

Euclidean land use zoning remains pervasive in the United States in the 1990s. Virtually all cities, towns, and villages that are authorized under state laws to zone do so. Some municipalities were created explicitly to gain the right to zone land. (See case study of Sanibel, Florida in Babcock and Siemon 1985, ch. 6.) Most of the nation's metropolitan counties and many rural counties also zone land in unincorporated areas within their borders. Yet this nearly ubiquitous and venerable institution continues to provoke disappointment, frustration, and sometimes outrage among practitioners and scholars of land use planning.

Since at least the early 1960s, zoning has been faulted for tolerating, and even fostering, wasteful and unsightly patterns of land use. In 1964, John Reps called for a "requiem for zoning":

> Zoning is seriously ill and its physicians—the planners—are mainly to blame. We have unnecessarily prolonged the existence of a land use control device conceived in another era when the true and frightening complexity of urban life was barely appreciated. We have, through heroic efforts and with massive doses of legislative remedies, managed to preserve what was once a lusty infant not only past the retirement age but well into senility. What is called for is legal euthanasia, a respectful requiem, and a search for a new legislative substitute sturdy enough to survive in the modern urban world.
>
> Excerpted in Listokin 1974, p. 29.

Zoning has particularly been criticized for procedural inadequacies: lax enforcement, favoritism, lack of consistency with planning, and excessive rigidity in some cases and undue flexibility in others. According to Babcock (1960, 154):

> The running, ugly sore of zoning is the total failure of this system of law to develop a code of administrative ethics. Stripped of all planning jargon, zoning administration is exposed as a process under which multitudes of isolated social and political units engage in highly emotional altercations over the use of land, most of which are settled by crude tribal adaptations of medieval trial by fire, and a few of which are concluded by confessed ad hoc injunctions of bewildered courts.

Some of the administrative chaos described by Babcock has been remedied through open meeting laws, conflict of interest penalties, and more aggressive coverage of zoning proceedings by the media. But the fragmented geographical scale, reliance on lay members of the public with diverse vested interests, and the uncertain planning basis for many zoning decisions continue to undermine the credibility and efficacy of zoning as a mainstay of municipal land use control. The painful experience of the New Jersey Supreme Court in attempting to remedy a statewide shortage of affordable housing through zoning reform by 567 communities pursuant to the *Mount Laurel* litigation is illustrative. Proposals to abolish local zoning continue to appear, albeit quixotically (Krasnowiecki 1980; Delogu 1986).

To a certain degree, the widespread dissatisfaction with the performance of zoning is misplaced. As Reps suggested, zoning was designed for the development process and political geography of an earlier, simpler era. Its geographic focus on the local municipality is both too small and too large to correspond with the actual scales of contemporary urbanization. The latter occurs, on the one hand, at a metropolitan or regional scale within which individual municipalities "control" only a small piece of the total affected land area. On the other hand, development is the result of countless piecemeal actions affecting only tiny fragments of a given municipal territory. Thus, the scale of the zoning process corresponds poorly with both the macro- and the microdimensions of the land-development process. Furthermore, the Euclidean zoning practice of designating the use and density of all buildable land within the community, sometimes years before many sites are ripe for development, gives rise to premature constitutional challenges, demands for individual relief through ad hoc adjustments, and disputes over non-conforming uses.

The many shortcomings of municipal-level Euclidean zoning—procedural, constitutional, and practical—have fostered various expedients to better adapt public control of land use to the macro- and microscales of the development process. Within the municipality , measures to supplement zoning include subdivision regulations, growth management, density transfer, and regulation of sensitive lands such as floodplains, wetlands, and coastlines. Above the municipal level, state, regional, or metropolitan plans guide municipalities in land use zoning and the development of physical infrastructure such as highways, parks, sewer and water services, and transportation. Since local governments have not been required to surrender their zoning prerogatives to state or regional planning agencies, such bodies usually operate in an advisory capacity, with variable results.

Subdivision Regulation and Exactions

In 1983, 67.1 percent of U.S. housing units were single-family homes. This figure had declined from 77.3 percent in 1960, reflecting the expansion of multifamily rental and ownership units during the intervening period. Nevertheless, 62.3 percent of new residential units in 1983 were single-family homes on separate lots—an astonishing contrast to the rest of the world, where new housing is predominantly in high-rise apartments. (U.S. Bureau of the Census 1986, tables 1308 and 1296.)

Single-family homes by definition are freestanding structures situated on a separate parcel or lot that satisfies the minimum lot size required by the local zoning law. Most such homes are built on lots resulting from the subdivision of a larger parcel of land into a number of legal building lots, each intended to be owned separately as a homesite. Houses may be constructed on each lot by the subdivider (also known as the "developer") who then sells the home and lot as a package. Or the lots may be sold to speculative builders or housing consumers who erect homes on them individually. In either case, since the 1920s it has been customary to require the subdivider to install certain on-site facilities to serve the needs of the future home occupants—for example, streets, drains, and utility connections. Under state laws modeled on the 1927 Standard Planning Enabling Act, the layout of a proposed subdivision and its infrastructure plan must be reviewed and approved by the local municipality before any lots may be sold and/or construction of houses may begin (Figure 9-1).

Subdivision regulation is thus a fundamental legal tool for municipal guidance of land development. It applies not only to single-family projects, but also to the development of condominiums (which are subdivisions of a volume of space) and to nonresidential subdivisions such as industrial parks. It does not apply to rental apartments or commercial projects where no division of legal ownership is proposed. (The latter may, however, be subject to an equivalent process of site plan review in some states and municipalities.)

Subdivision regulation supplements but does not replace zoning. The use of land, minimum lot size, and bulk of structures to be built in the subdivision all must conform with applicable zoning (as modified by variances in appropriate cases). Subdivision approval requires that in addition to satisfying all zoning provisions, the proposed development will also meet performance standards for the layout and design of new subdivisions. These standards are set forth in published subdivision regulations adopted by the local planning board or equivalent body.

The community exerts considerable leverage through its subdivision approval function. A subdivision plan must be approved before it may legally be recorded. If it cannot be recorded, the lots shown on it cannot be sold individually, since they do not legally exist. Furthermore, lending institutions will not extend credit to purchase or improve land in an unapproved subdivision. Developers are eager to gain approval for their plans, which is prerequisite to starting work on the infrastructure and marketing the lots. The municipality, therefore, may negotiate a variety of concessions from the developer as a condition to subdivision approval.

Since new streets within a subdivision are normally donated ("dedicated") by the developer to the municipality or county for future maintenance, the recipient government is concerned to ensure that those streets are sufficiently wide, properly paved, and aligned to avoid future maintenance or safety problems. New rights of way must be mapped on the

FIGURE 9-1   Excerpt from a Final Subdivision Plan submitted to the Town of
Amherst, Massachusetts, 1987.

proposed subdivision plan and detailed engineering specifications must
conform with the local requirements for street design (which are sometimes extravagant).

Storm drainage is another subdivision review concern. Conversion of
natural land surfaces to impermeable pavement and house sites reduces
infiltration of precipitation into groundwater. Surface runoff is thereby
increased, with possible flooding imposed on land at lower elevation,
either within or outside the subdivision boundaries. Subdividers may be
required to install drains, retention basins, pumps, or other devices necessary to prevent both on-site and off-site drainage problems.

The subdivision plan must provide for the connection of each house
lot to available public services and utilities, including water, sewerage,
gas, electricity, telephone, and even cable television. Overhead wires are
normally prohibited in new subdivisions. If public water and/or sewer
service is not available to the subdivision, each lot must be large enough
to accommodate an on-site septic system and/or a well. Where the

physical character of the site precludes such on-site facilities, subdivision approval or individual building permits may be denied. State laws usually require percolation tests to be conducted by qualified contractors to determine the septic absorption capability of each lot where public sewerage is not available.

When a subdivision plan is formally approved by the appropriate local body (e.g., a planning board in Massachusetts), it is filed with the county Registry of Deeds and becomes legally effective. However, much of the work to be performed by the developer remains undone at that time. Normally, the installation of streets, drains, and other infrastructure is phased over time in relation to the sale of lots. Some of the work promised by the developer will not be completed for months or even years after approval of the plan. Thus it is necessary for the community to be able to ensure that the work will be performed as promised in the subdivision plan.

A community may protect itself against default by the developer in two ways. One is to require the latter to provide a surety bond to the municipality for an amount of money sufficient to cover the costs of completing the necessary work if the developer should become bankrupt or otherwise fail to satisfy its contractual obligations. The other way is to impose restrictive covenants on each lot that must be released by the community before a lot may be sold. If infrastructure serving a lot or group of lots has not been constructed, the municipality will refuse to release its covenant and the developer cannot sell those parcels.

Private Deed Restrictions

Besides the *public* controls of zoning and subdivision requirements, a private subdivision is internally regulated through extensive use of *private* deed restrictions in the form of covenants and easements. As discussed in Chapter 3, these forms of private land use control originated in 17th century England where aristocratic property owners sought to control the use of land in the hands of subsequent buyers or tenants indefinitely. Anyone buying real estate in a subdivision must agree to comply with the private restrictions.

Deed restrictions are useful to control many aspects of a private subdivision. Since they arise by voluntary contract between the developer and the lot purchaser, they involve no public regulatory function and thus do not present problems of "reasonableness" or the "taking issue." Deed restrictions may therefore be more restrictive than the public police power. They may, for instance, regulate the external appearance of a dwelling, the kind of landscaping, or the parking of commercial vehicles in driveways. Minor alterations of a premises that would not involve zoning approval may be prohibited by deed restrictions. Condominium-type subdivisions are often especially tightly controlled through private restrictions.

Enforcement of private deed restrictions may take several forms. They may of course be enforced through legal action by the developer/seller against direct purchasers who violate the contractual restrictions. Other property owners, who are subject to similar restrictions, may enforce such provisions against recalcitrant neighbors. Homeowners or condominium associations established to own and maintain common facilities after the developer departs from the scene are also legally vested with power to enforce deed restrictions. Courts will enforce restrictions upon suit by any of the foregoing parties unless it finds the purpose of the restriction to be unenforceable (a racial restrictive covenant) or it finds that conditions in the area have rendered the restriction moot (a limitation to single-family homes in a high-density urban district).

Some communities include specific amenities in their subdivision requirements. These may include sidewalks, bike paths, natural buffers between the subdivision and adjoining public roads, and retention of large trees and natural drainage ways. The actual aesthetic appearance of a subdivision is the joint result of public zoning and subdivision regulations, deed restrictions imposed by the developer on the lot buyers, and the individual decisions of the latter regarding planting and landscaping. Depending on the market to which the development is directed, amenity requirements through private deed restrictions may be far more detailed and strict than requirements that the public may constitutionally impose.

Subdivision Exactions and Impact Fees

Residential subdivisions often generate costs to the host municipality that exceed the tax revenue produced by the development. New demands are placed on the community's schools, its water and sewage treatment facilities, its police and fire departments, and its parks and recreation areas. A number of states, led by California, have authorized municipalities to require, as a condition of subdivision plan approval, that the developer "dedicate" (donate) land within the subdivision for necessary park and school sites, in addition to the usual street requirements. If the subdivision is very small or has no land suitable for school or park sites, the developer is required to pay a "fee in lieu" of dedication equal to the value of the land that would otherwise be required. These are "subdivision exactions" (Smith 1987).

Subdivision exactions may not be arbitrary: They must be set according to a local standard applicable to all new subdivisions. The critical constitutional issue, however, is how much land or fees in lieu of land the community may reasonably require. In 1971, the California Supreme Court rejected a developer's claim that exactions must be limited to meeting needs attributable to the subdivision, not reflecting the larger community interest:

> We see no persuasive reason in the face of these urgent needs caused by present and anticipated future population growth on the one hand, and the disappearance of open land on the other to hold that a statute requiring the dedication of land by a subdivider may be justified only upon the ground that the particular subdivider upon whom an exaction has been imposed will, solely by the development of his subdivision, increase the need for recreational facilities to such an extent that additional land for such facilities will be required (*Associated Home Builders v. City of Walnut Creek* 484 P.2d 606, at 611, 1971).

The court upheld the community requirement of 2.5 acres per 1000 new residents or a fee equal to the value thereof. The use of such land or fees to remedy community-wide deficiencies, not simply the needs of each new subdivision, was approved in this and many subsequent cases in other states.

A further refinement of subdivision exactions has been to impose "impact fees" on all new development, not simply subdivisions or residential property. Again, the leading state has been California, where Proposition 13 has limited municipal tax revenue in the face of rapid population growth during the 1970s and 1980s. An impact fee is basically a charge levied when a building permit is applied for. Such fees are not limited to subdivisions but may be levied upon offices, shopping centers, or virtually any type of construction. The revenue generated from such fees is devoted to a broad range of municipal purposes including roads, sewer and water facilities, police and fire stations, and even libraries. San Francisco, Boston, and a few other cities have imposed "linkage fees" on new commercial construction to contribute to the cost of affordable housing for the workers to be hired by the building occupants (Juergensmeyer and Blake 1984).

In 1984, the California Supreme Court upheld an impact fee (referred to as a "facilities benefit assessment") imposed by the City of San Diego on all new development in designated vacant and developing areas of the city:

> San Diego's general plan is the instrument through which the City seeks to manage an explosive growth with land use controls, development of new and urbanizing communities over a period of years and the financing of public facilities through assessment of benefited property. We recognize the ordinance for what it is—imposing a present lien on undeveloped property to pay in the future an apportioned share of the costs of public facilities required to accommodate the needs of future residents of the properties upon their development (*J. W. Jones Companies v. City of San Diego* 203 Cal. Rptr. 580, at 587).

The diffusion of subdivision exactions and impact fees around the United States has been uneven. A survey conducted in 1985, which produced 220 responses from 1000 sample communities, reported that 65.9 percent of those responding have some form of traditional on-site subdivision exactions. Off-site exactions (money to be spent elsewhere in the community on the specified purpose) were imposed by 57.8 percent of respondents, while 45.4 percent utilize impact fees. But impact fees were reported by 81.8 percent of the California respondents, by 45.5 percent of those in other western states, 27.8 percent by southern respondents, 13.3 percent by those in the Mid-Atlantic states, and zero in New England (Bauman and Ethier 1987, 57–59).

Thus the focus of subdivision regulation with the *physical* layout of new subdivisions has shifted in recent years to a concern with the *fiscal* impact of new development. Off-site subdivision exactions and impact fees have only an indirect relationship to the habitability of the new subdivision. Such fees supplement local property tax revenues (which new subdivision residents also pay) to fund basic public services within growing communities.

Land use control thereby merges into budget control. Developers seldom challenge impact fees and similar charges since it is cheaper to pay them than to incur much greater costs of delay. The fees are passed along to the ultimate home buyer with the inevitable effect of further increasing housing costs. Like large lot size requirements, high subdivision and impact fees thus serve as de facto exclusionary devices, discouraging the less wealthy from attempting to reside in the community. How far may communities expand the use of impact fees to "privatize" public costs of general government services? According to one experienced planning-law practitioner, the limit may be in sight:

> It is time for local governments to realize that the exaction "party" is over. The end is near, not because of the courts, but because of a changing economy. In the post-World War II era, an abundance of cheap land, and extraordinary demand for housing, and the consequent suburban sprawl brought about an inflow of housing into previously undeveloped or underdeveloped suburbs that required the construction of substantial amounts of physical infrastructure. The combination of low cost land, high housing demand, and demonstrable public need made subdivision exactions tolerable. Now, however, as the newer suburbs compete for glamorous developments, age overtakes the older suburbs, urban neighborhoods deteriorate and regentrify, and commerce abandons the central city for landscaped office parks, and the leverage of local government over development will decrease. Rehabilitation and redevelopment of urban and older suburban areas is unlikely to take place if it is burdened with exactions that represent a disguised and non-uniform system of taxation. In sum, it is time to work toward a consensus between the public and private sectors on which public facility costs a private developer can reasonably be expected to bear.
>
> Smith 1987, p. 30.

The housing recession of the early 1990s and the continued growth of Edge Cities in competition with traditional downtowns have borne out

Smith's prediction: the use of impact fees appears to have diminished since the building boom of the 1980s.

Local control over the subdivision of land has thus expanded since the 1920s from a concern with the layout and paving of streets to a broad range of exactions and fees for both on-site and off-site facilities and services. Traditional subdivision review was primarily a means for regulating the internal planning and habitability of the development and providing for its orderly integration into the physical framework of the community. It still serves this purpose in the majority of states and communities. But impact fees and "linkage" assessments have augmented these public purposes to include reallocation of fiscal burdens from the existing taxpayers to newcomers. This function has little to do with the habitability of the development in question, or with land planning in the community at large. If anything, it may aggravate the tendency to use zoning and other planning tools as a means of optimizing revenue and minimizing public costs. Such goals, which have characterized "fiscal zoning" for many years, are likely to conflict with the explicit purpose of local land use control: to ensure efficient, equitable, and balanced use of available land in the community.

Growth Management

The twin booms of the postwar period, producing quantities of babies and houses, transformed the settlement geography of the United States. Demographic change involved both absolute population growth at various scales and a massive geographic redistribution of households. This redistribution involved both intra- and interregional migration. The former was chiefly characterized by the "white flight" from central cities to suburbs, while the latter took the form of long-distance moves from the "frost belt" of the Northeast and Middle-West census regions to the South and West (Palm 1981, ch. 9).

Population classified as "metropolitan" by the Bureau of the Census grew between 1960 and 1990 from 118 million to 197.7 million, with the metropolitan proportion of the U.S. population rising from 65.9 percent to nearly 80 percent (see Table 1-3a). But within metropolitan areas, central cities as a class gained only 15.2 percent (many of them experienced net losses), while the balance of the metropolitan area ("suburbs") grew by 71.1 percent. Meanwhile, over the same period, the Northeast and Midwest regions (as designated by the U.S. Bureau of the Census) grew by only about 13.9 percent and 15.6 percent, respectively, while the South and West gained 30.5 percent and 88.5 percent, respectively (Table 9-1). By 1990, the latter two regions outnumbered the earlier settled Northeast and Midwest by some 27 million people.

The brunt of metropolitan growth, especially in the newly developing sunbelt states, has fallen most heavily on smaller to medium-sized urban places. Population of cities exceeding 1 million remained relatively unchanged in total population between 1960 and 1980 (although the ethnic composition of that population changed substantially with replacement of whites by nonwhites). The addition of two cities to this class between 1980 and 1990 accounted for an apparent growth of 14.7 percent. Cities of 250,000 to 1 million as a class gained 10.4 percent (reflecting both losses and gains of cities shifting between classes). Urban places of smaller size increased their aggregate populations by about two-thirds for cities between 50,000 and 250,000, with somewhat lower growth rates for cities smaller than 50,000 (Table 9-2).

Smaller and mostly newer suburban communities were frequently ill-prepared for the changes that this rapid population growth in the 25,000–250,000 range signified. Immediate impacts included traffic congestion, demands for new schools and other public services, loss of open space and visual amenities—in general an erosion of their cherished "small-town atmosphere." Although most had some form of basic zoning and subdivision regulations, they generally lacked experience in dealing with "big city" developers. Towns under 25,000 very likely had no professional planning staff and depended on their volunteer boards, occasionally assisted by an outside consultant, to cope with the onslaught. It was among these smaller but fast-growing suburban jurisdictions, especially in the sunbelt states, that the idea of "growth management" became chic during the 1970s and early 1980s.

Growth management has been around as long as Euclidean zoning, which, at least in theory, "manages" new urban growth through limits on land use, bulk, and density. Subdivision regulation also manages growth by imposing design performance standards and exactions on new subdivisions. But by 1970, there was a growing consensus in many faster-growing communities that neither zoning nor subdivision regulation could address (1) the timing or pace at which growth was permitted to

TABLE 9-1   U.S. Population and Growth Rates by Region, 1960–1990 (in millions)

Region	1960	1970	1980	1990	1960–1990 % Change
Northeast	44.6	49.0	49.1	50.8	13.9%
Midwest	51.6	56.5	58.8	59.7	15.6
South	54.9	62.8	75.3	85.4	30.5
West	28.0	34.3	43.1	52.8	88.5
U.S. Total	179.3	203.3	226.5	248.7	38.7

Source: Statistical Abstract of the U.S.: 1991, Table 23.

TABLE 9-2   U.S. Urban Growth by Size of Municipalities, 1960–1990 (in millions)

Size	1960	1970	1980	1990	1960–1990 % Change
1 mill. +	17.5	18.9	17.5	20.0	14.7%
250K–1 mill.	21.9	23.5	22.7	24.3	10.4
100K–250K	11.4	13.9	16.6	19.1	64.6
50K–100K	12.5	16.2	17.6	21.2	69.6
25K–50K	12.7	15.7	18.4	20.0	41.7
10K–25K	15.1	17.6	19.8	20.3	34.4
< 10K	24.9	26.4	28.0	28.2	13.2
Total Urban	115.9	131.9	140.3	152.9	31.9

Source: Statistical Abstract of the U.S.: 1994, Table 45.

occur or (2) the ultimate character of the community when fully developed. "Urban sprawl," a phrase popularized by sociologist William H. Whyte (1958; 1968), produces wasteful patterns of land use that encroached on farmland, floodplains, natural areas, and other open space.

Growth management evolved during the early 1970s in a variety of forms reflecting the lack of any dominant technique or approach. Communities as diverse as Boulder, Colorado; Petaluma, California; Ramapo Township, New York; and Boca Raton, Florida pursued their homegrown strategies with varying success.

A study of 18 local or county programs by Godschalk et al. (1978) disclosed a diversity of both goals and means. The former included such respectable objectives as preserving prime farm land, providing a balanced housing supply, relating new development to public services, and

reducing natural hazard vulnerability. More suspect goals included minimizing tax burdens and preserving a "small-town environment." Means
used by various communities surveyed included capital improvement
programs, annual permit limits, dwelling unit caps, downzoning (to lower
densities), site plan review, fair-share housing plans, and open space
acquisition. Most communities were relying on a combination of existing
and new techniques:

> Many of the tools have been invented or adapted by individual
> local governments. Existing approaches are modified in light of
> experience, changing conditions, or legal challenges. Typical sys-
> tems consist of scattered parts of policies, amendments to develop-
> ment ordinances, and items in capital programs and budgets. Often
> the first time a system is completely described and analyzed in writ-
> ing is by the attorneys who attack and defend it in court.
>
> Godschalk et al. 1978, p. i.

To the extent that it involves the use of the public police power,
growth management faces the same constitutional hurdles as traditional zoning: due process, equal protection, and the taking issue.
Courts have weighed various growth management schemes in light of
these principles.

The Ramapo Plan

The first major growth management case was decided in 1972 by the
New York Court of Appeals (State Supreme Court) in *Golden v. Township of Ramapo* 285 N.E.2d 291. The case involved phasing the tempo of
new development in relation to the construction of capital improvements. The defendant town exercised jurisdiction over 60 square miles of
unincorporated land, located some 30 miles north of New York City. In
response to a doubling of its population in less than a decade, Ramapo in
the mid-1960s undertook to prepare a master plan for its future growth
(Godschalk et al., ch. 7). This was not unusual: Hundreds of communities prepared such plans during the 1960s with the help of "Section 701"
federal planning grants.

But Ramapo's plan had teeth. It included a capital improvements program to provide the entire town with public services within 18 years. A

zoning amendment in 1969 provided that all proposals for residential construction (except individual homes) would be evaluated in terms of the availability of sewers, parks, firehouses, roads, and storm drainage. Points were assigned according to each requirement that was satisfied, and sites lacking at least 15 out of a possible 26 points were not approved (Dawson 1981, 150). In lieu of outright denial of a building permit, however, the town issued a "rain check" in the form of a special permit to become effective in the year when services were scheduled to be provided. The rain check could be sold to other parties to realize some immediate cash return, and property taxes would be reduced during the interim. (Alternatively, the developer could gain points by installing services privately.)

Upon review, the New York Court of Appeals acknowledged that "there is something inherently suspect in a scheme which, apart from its professed purposes, effects a restriction upon the free mobility of a people until sometime in the future when project facilities are available to meet increased demands" (285 N.E.2d, at 300). But it recognized the social and environmental ills associated with rapid growth that gave rise to the plan. The court, in a leap of faith, construed that "phased growth is well within the ambit of existing enabling legislation." It found that a "temporary" delay related to a carefully considered plan for capital improvements and involving no absolute growth cap was reasonable in a constitutional sense:

> We may assume that the present amendments are the product of foresighted planning calculated to promote the welfare of the township. The Town has imposed temporary restrictions upon land use in residential areas while committing itself to a program of development. It has utilized its comprehensive plan to implement its timing controls and has coupled with restrictions provisions for low and moderate income housing on a large scale. Considered as a whole it represents both in its inception and implementation a reasonable attempt to provide for the sequential, orderly development of land. . . . (285 N.E.2d, at 303).

The Ramapo plan added "a third dimension to land use regulation: a temporal aspect to the traditional ones of use and location," and the decision was hailed (perhaps with a touch of hyperbole) as ". . . the most significant land use regulation case other than *Euclid*" (Callies and Freilich 1986, 834). However, according to another planning lawyer: "The wolf of exclusionary zoning hides under the environmental sheepskin worn by the stop-growth movement" (Bosselman 1973, 249). Either way, the approach followed by Ramapo has had few imitators.

The Petaluma Plan

The next landmark in judicial review of growth management arose in Petaluma, California, a Victorian-era chicken-farming town 35 miles north of San Francisco. A surge of new building in 1970–1971 alarmed the community into conducting a major planning exercise. The resulting "Petaluma plan" was a complex set of documents, policies, and programs. Unlike Ramapo, Petaluma established a target population for itself considerably below what existing rates of building would indicate—55,000 instead of 77,000. Policies and measures designed to achieve this reduction included an annual limit on building permits, a moratorium on annexation or extension of services into adjacent areas, and deliberate limitation of sewer and water capacity to the needs of 55,000 people (Figure 9-2). The most controversial feature was the limit of building permits to an average of 500 a year (2000 had been issued in 1970–1971). A point system was introduced by which this quota would be allocated, but no Ramapo-type rain checks were provided.

Upon constitutional challenge and appeal by a building trade association, the Federal District Court and the Federal Court of Appeals reached opposite conclusions on the validity of the Petaluma Plan (*Construction Industry Assn. of Sonoma County v. City of Petaluma* 375 F.Supp. 574, 1974 and 522 F.2d 897, 1975, respectively). The two opinions reflected differing geographical perceptions of the implications of the plan.

The District Court held the Petaluma Plan to be invalid on the ground that it inhibited the constitutional right to travel. This conclusion was based on a scholarly discussion of the regional housing market of the Bay Area, including the concepts of "growth poles" and "trickle down" of housing opportunities as new dwellings are added on the periphery. The court concluded that the Petaluma Plan, if widely imitated, would retard new housing construction and thereby restrict housing availability throughout the region.

FIGURE 9-2   Map of "Planning Referral Area," Petaluma, California, 1987.
Source: City of Petaluma, 1987.

The Court of Appeals (9th Circuit) saw the issue very differently. It ignored theories of urban geography and planning and even objected to the "oversized" brief submitted by the plaintiffs. In contrast to the regional perspective of the lower court, the appellate court viewed the issue strictly within the geographic compass of Petaluma. The Court of

Appeals cited recent decisions of its own and of the U.S. Supreme Court upholding municipal zoning prerogatives where a deliberate intent to exclude was not proven. It found that the plan earmarked 8–12 percent of permits for low- and moderate-income housing (assuming a builder turned up), which it felt obviated any exclusionary motive.

Plan or no plan, the growth of Petaluma lagged even behind its planned level. By 1987, the city's population had reached only about 40,000. Petaluma has continued to refine its plan, however, which in 1987 received the Outstanding Planning Award of the California Chapter of the American Planning Association (City of Petaluma 1987). The following list of chapter topics reflects its broad scope: (1) "Community Character"; (2) "Land Use and Growth Management"; (3) "The Petaluma River"; (4) "Open Space, Conservation, and Energy"; (5) "Parks, Recreation, Schools, and Child Care"; (6) "Local Economy"; (7) "Housing"; (8) "Transportation"; and (9) "Community Health and Safety."

The Livermore Moratorium

The District Court in *Petaluma* warned of a potential diffusion of growth-limitation plans to other developing communities. The voters of Livermore, California in fact had already voted in 1972 to impose a moratorium on any further residential construction pending upgrading of school, sewer, and water services. This differed from Petaluma's plan in utilizing a total ban rather than an annual allotment, and it lacked the timetable for completion of services provided by Ramapo. It was legally a borderline case.

The California Supreme Court in *Associated Home Builders v. City of Livermore* 557 P.2d 473, 1975 declined to view the moratorium as inherently exclusionary or unduly vague. But it also avoided the simplistic approach of the appeals court in *Petaluma* that a local town may act as a world unto itself. Instead, the *Livermore* opinion articulated a new constitutional test:

> . . . whether the ordinance reasonably relates to the welfare of those whom it significantly affects. If the impact is limited to the city boundaries, the inquiry may be limited accordingly; if, as alleged here, the ordinance may strongly influence the supply and

distribution of housing for an entire metropolitan region, judicial inquiry must consider the welfare of that region (557 P.2d, at 487).

The court specified three steps by which a trial court might apply this test: First, it must "forecast the probable effect and duration of the restriction." Second, it must "identify the competing interests affected by the restriction." The third step is to determine "whether the ordinance, in light of its probable impact, represents a reasonable accommodation of the competing interests" (557 P.2d, at 488). The California Supreme Court then returned the case to the trial court to apply this test.

Livermore thus mandated the weighing of geographical evidence on regional housing, economic, and demographic trends as a basis for resolving the constitutionality of growth management plans. Like the lower court in *Petaluma*, the California Supreme Court was groping for a rationale for judging the reasonableness of such plans in terms of their real-world impacts.

A fervent dissent by Justice Mosk viewed the moratorium as deliberately exclusionary. Unlike the majority, which passed the buck to the trial court, Mosk applied his own geographical perception to the issue:

Limitations on growth may be justified in resort communities, beach and lake and mountain sites, and other rural and recreational areas; such restrictions are generally designed to preserve nature's environment for the benefits of all mankind. As Thomas Jefferson wrote, the earth belongs to the living, but in usufruct.

But there is a vast qualitative difference when a suburban community invokes an elitist concept to construct a mythical moat around its perimeter, not for the benefit of mankind but to exclude all but its fortunate current residents (557 F.2d, at 493).

The complex growth-management plans considered so far provoked mixed judicial reactions but were ultimately upheld. More simplistic or blatantly exclusionary measures adopted elsewhere have been emphatically rejected as unconstitutional. A 1979 Florida decision held to be arbitrary and invalid a charter amendment by the City of Boca Raton that attempted to establish an absolute limit of 40,000 dwelling units in the city (*Boca Raton v. Boca Villas Corp.* 371 So.2d 254). In Colorado, an attempt by the City of Boulder to withhold water and sewer service from a proposed development outside its corporate limits but adjacent to areas already served was rejected in *Robinson v. City of Boulder* 547 P.2d 228, 1976. The court held that the city had assumed the status of a public utility as sole provider of water and sewage treatment in the area and could not therefore deny service on the basis of a growth-limitation plan.

Few cases involving growth management have appeared since the 1970s. Partly this is due to the building recession of recent years, but another reason may be that growth management has become a widely accepted practice which, like subdivision approval, generates few constitutional challenges.

Evidence that growth management was alive and well in the 1980s, especially in the sunbelt states, was provided in a survey of 24 county and local programs by Bollens and Godschalk (1987). Their study examined the use of computerized land information systems as a basis for administering growth-management programs:

> Jurisdictions that control growth should maintain supplies of available land large enough to allow for a competitive land market. Policies that assure such a land supply can only be formulated if local government and the private sector have up-to-date information on the locations, amounts, and prices of available land supply. . . . The most important advantage of a monitoring system could be its assistance in the design of growth management policies that will balance land supply and demand without contribution to price inflation in fast-growing areas.   Bollens and Godschalk 1987, p. 316.

A further advantage of such geographic information systems is to bolster the constitutionality of growth management against charges of undue discretion and arbitrariness. Also, such systems may facilitate the identification and alleviation of adverse regional effects of local growth management that concerned the California Supreme Court in *Livermore*.

Transfer of Development Rights

Transfer of development rights (TDR) was widely touted by planners during the 1970s as a means of achieving better regulation of growth while avoiding the problem of the taking issue (Costonis 1974; Wood-bury 1975). TDR conceptually involves severing the "right to develop" from a site that the public wishes to have preserved in low-density or open space condition and transferring that right to another site where higher than normal density would be tolerable. Land uses proposed for protection through TDR include agricultural land, wetlands, coastal or riverine flood hazard areas, historical sites, churches, and other privately owned landmarks. Receiving sites for TDRs may include areas where density above the levels allowed in the applicable zoning could be accommodated without doing violence to planning concerns such as overcrowding of population, fire hazards, traffic congestion, or overtaxing of sewer and water services.

TDRs normally require official sanction through amendment of local zoning or other development-control law. This would provide that the local government would award a zoning bonus in the form of increased height or more dwellings per acre to a developer in the receiving area or "growth zone" upon payment by that party to the owner of a site to be preserved. The amount of the payment would be set by mutual agreement as with any real estate transaction. The seller of the development right would record a permanent restriction on the future development, subdivision, or alteration (in the case of historic preservation) of their site. The buyer of the right would then be issued a density bonus usable at the receiving site.

The owner of the preserved site retains existing use rights while receiving compensation for the developmental value foregone. The public ensures the preservation of the site without paying for it. And the buyer of the development right gains legal approval for a more profitable project (Figure 9-3).

Several pitfalls have hampered the utility of TDRs, however. One is the need for a market for TDRs. Smart developers usually can gain extra density through administrative adjustments (such as variances) and thus have little incentive to buy TDRs unless the zoning process is relatively inflexible and incorruptible. The neighbors of a receiving site may object that the granting of higher density unfairly harms their property values and is "spot zoning." Alternatively, they may demand to be similarly rezoned, thereby eliminating the incentive for further purchases of TDRs. In the case of wetlands and floodplains, it seems illogical to recognize a "development right" in land that is inherently unsafe to develop.

Preservation Zone

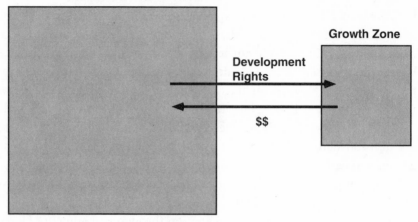

FIGURE 9-3   Diagram of transfer of development rights.

Finally, it is not clear to what extent the uncertain possibility of selling a TDR is adequate to safeguard a restrictive zoning measure against a taking issue challenge.

While not deciding the last question, the U.S. Supreme Court has at least commented favorably on TDRs in *Penn Central Transportation Co. v. City of New York* 98 S.Ct. 2646, 1978. The case arose from disapproval by New York's Landmarks Preservation Commission of the plaintiff's proposal to build a 55-story office tower above its Grand Central Terminal in midtown Manhattan. Although technically the terminal would survive, the aesthetic effect of surmounting it with a tall modern building would have been profound, and civic leaders, including Jacqueline Kennedy Onassis, mounted a defense of both the landmark and the law that protected it.

The law provided, among other features, that development rights not usable on the preserved landmark site could be transferred to nearby sites under the same ownership. Penn Central owned eight structures in the vicinity, but, instead of exercising the TDR option, it challenged the landmarks law as a taking. The High Court upheld the law on the ground that historic preservation is a valid public purpose and that Penn Central was not denied all economic use of the site, which generates revenue from concessionaires. It thus held the restriction not to be a taking regardless of the TDR option, but bolstered its conclusion with the following observation:

> To the extent appellants have been denied the right to build above the terminal, it is not literally accurate to say that they have been denied all use of even those preexisting air rights. Their ability to use these rights has not been abrogated; they are made transferable to at least eight parcels in the vicinity of the terminal, one or two of which have been found suitable for the construction of new office buildings. . . . While these rights may well not have constituted "just compensation" if a "taking" had occurred, the rights nevertheless undoubtedly mitigate whatever financial burdens the law has imposed on appellants and, for that reason, are to be taken into account in considering the impact of regulation (98 S.Ct., at 2666).

Two years earlier and four blocks east, the New York Court of Appeals took a dimmer view of TDRs as a form of compensation. *Fred F. French Investing Co. v. City of New York* 50 N.E.2d 381, 1976 involved a law that prohibited building on two privately owned parks in Tudor City, a fashionable older apartment complex near the United Nations. The owner was permitted to sell the development rights anywhere in central Manhattan but had not done so. The court viewed the restriction as a taking because it forced the owner to "provide a benefit to the public without recoupment." It held the TDR option to be inadequate recompense:

> . . . Development rights, disembodied abstractions of man's ingenuity, float in a limbo until restored to reality by reattachment to tangible real property. Put another way, it is a tolerable abstraction to consider development rights apart from the solid land from which as a matter of zoning law they derive. But severed, the development rights are a double abstraction until they are actually attached to a receiving parcel yet to be identified, acquired, and subject to the contingent future approvals of administrative agencies, . . . By compelling the owner to enter an unpredictable real estate market to find a suitable receiving lot for the rights, . . . the amendment renders uncertain and thus severely impairs the value of the development rights before they were severed (350 N.E.2d, at 388).

According to Dawson (1982, 70): "Probably the court was influenced by the fatal words 'public park' since the use of private property as parkland effectively denies the owner any income at all."

An easier situation involves a voluntary agreement to transfer development rights among adjacent parcels of land to which the only objectors may be neighboring property owners. In *Dupont Circle Citizens Association v. District of Columbia Zoning Commission* 355 A.2d 550, 1976, the development rights from a historic mansion and garden were proposed to be transferred to an adjoining site to permit extra height for a new office building. The court held that the preservation of historic structures is a valid regulatory objective that may be achieved by transferring development rights from one parcel to another, provided the aggregate density is within prescribed limits for the combined land area.

Outside cities, various schemes for preserving open land through TDRs have been proposed but few have borne fruit. Perhaps the nation's most successful program has occurred in Montgomery County, Maryland on the outskirts of Washington, D.C. where several hundred parcels of farmland have been protected through TDRs. Faced with intense development pressure on the one-third of its land area that remained in agriculture, the county in 1980 established an "agricultural reserve" of some 73,000 acres. It downzoned this area from one dwelling per five acres to one per 25 acres. Landowners were allowed to sell one development right for each five acres to developers in the other two-thirds of the county. (In Maryland, counties exercise planning and zoning powers throughout their territories.) To ensure a ready market for development rights, the county established a publicly funded TDR "bank." Its function was to buy and sell rights when private demand languished and thus maintain the confidence of agricultural owners (Tustian 1984, ch. 11).

Floodplain and Wetland Regulation

For decades, Euclidean zoning took little notice of physical variation in the land. Just as the rectangular townships of the Federal Land Survey marched relentlessly across prairie, desert, and mountain, the geometry of suburbia, imposed by zoning until the 1970s, ignored natural impediments to building. Those limitations included such geographically spe-

cific natural hazards as seismic faults, unstable slopes, coastal and riverine floodplains, and wetlands. As a result of this blindness to physical
hazards, much postwar urban development was located "in harm's way"
and resulting losses have been costly.

Since the 1950s, many researchers have documented the double jeop-
ardy of such ill-considered building practices: (1) the risk to life and
property and (2) the damage to natural values and functions of floodplains and wetlands (Hoyt and Langbein 1955; White 1964; 1975; and
Schneider and Goddard 1974). Geographer Gilbert F. White and his
associates (1958) in particular found that flood control projects often
lead to increased flood losses by encouraging encroachment in the "protected" floodplain, which may then be inundated by a flood exceeding
the project's design capacity.

Such disclosures prompted a reversal of public policies that had long
tolerated encroachment on floodplains in reliance upon structural flood
control projects. Consistent with the model in Chapter 2, new approaches to the management of floodplains resulted from better recognition of the impacts of human activities on the natural environment
and vice versa. The federal and state dimensions of this new approach
are considered in Chapters 10 and 12. This section examines the evolution of a judicial basis for regulation of floodplains and wetlands at the
local level.

Physical Characteristics

Floodplains are natural overflow areas adjoining surface waters, including streams, rivers, lakes, estuaries, bays, and the open ocean (Figure
9-4). Riverine floodplains are formed where a watercourse over time has
weathered away bordering uplands and deposited sediment on the resulting level surface adjoining its normal channel. The floodplain is
narrow or nonexistent in steep and less erodible terrain, and tends to be
broader in more erodible lowlands. The latter are characterized by deposits of fertile alluvial soils ideal for agriculture. But in regions such as
Appalachia, floodplains may be the only level land available for urban
development and communications linkages such as highways, railroads,
power lines, and airports. Agriculture is reasonably compatible with occasional flooding, especially that which occurs in the early spring in

FIGURE 9-4   Diagram of a riverine floodplain in cross section. Line A–B is the
width of the flooded area before encroachment; line C–D is the
width of flooded area after encroachment.

northern climes, the "spring freshet." But urban development, unless
suitably designed and/or fortified by protective measures, is inherently at
risk in times of flood.

Where the onset of flooding is very swift ("flash flooding"), threat to
human life is of paramount concern. The Rapid City, South Dakota flash
flood of 1972 took 238 lives as well as destroyed the city's business district (White 1975, ch. V). The 1976 Big Thompson Canyon flash flood in
Colorado killed 143 while scouring most structures out of that narrow
Rocky Mountain canyon (Gruntfest 1987).

Floodplains are not uniformly risk-prone. Levels of hazard are distinguished in terms of estimated frequency of inundation for specific elevations of land within the overall floodplain. Thus, low ground close to the
river may be flooded nearly every year, while slightly higher ground farther from the channel may be flooded on the average only every 50 to
100 years. (The close-in areas of course are flooded more deeply during
those events.) The "100-year floodplain," which has a probability of 1
percent of being flooded in any given year, is the geographic area regulated in most public floodplain management programs in the United
States. Within this regulatory floodplain, different levels of control over
building are applied to the high-risk "floodway" and the less hazardous
"floodway fringe" (see Figure 9-4).

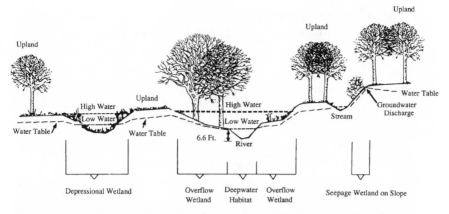

FIGURE 9-5   Cross section of various types of freshwater wetlands. *Source:* U.S. Fish and Wildlife Service.

Wetlands are natural depressions where the groundwater table is normally at or just below the land surface. (Where the water table is normally above the surface, a pond is formed.) The wetness of wetlands and their special biological characteristics provide nutrients to support a rich diversity of flora and fauna. The ecology of wetlands varies according to their location, soil chemistry, hydrology, elevation, and size (Figure 9-5). Coastal wetlands include salt marshes, mudflats, and other estuarine wetlands subject to tidal influence and some degree of salinity. Inland or freshwater wetlands are of many types including the familiar cattail swamp, riparian habitat along stream banks, isolated bogs, prairie potholes, and bottomland hardwoods of the lower Mississippi Valley (Tiner 1984; Kusler 1983). Wetlands of all types are estimated to cover slightly more than 3 percent of the continental U.S. land area—about 70 million acres (U.S. Council on Environmental Quality 1981).

Depending on their location and ecological type, wetlands provide a number of "values" or functions in their natural state:

They serve as food producers, spawning sites, and sanctuaries for many forms of fish and bird life. They produce timber, peat moss, and crops such as wild rice and cranberries. They serve as storage areas for storm and flood waters, reduce erosion, provide for groundwater retention, and at times purify polluted waters.

U.S. Council on Environmental Quality 1978.

Wetlands and floodplains frequently coincide geographically and, as just stated, wetlands help to alleviate downstream flooding in watersheds and damage to landward property in coastal areas. But the management of floodplains and wetlands pursue somewhat different goals. In floodplains, the public seeks to reduce hazards to life and property from flooding, while in wetlands, the public seeks to preserve the site in its natural condition or to restore it to that condition. While a properly designed building can be tolerated in floodway fringe areas, any construction in wetlands is usually harmful to its natural functions.

Public programs for managing floodplains and wetlands have evolved independently at the federal and state levels. The federal government addresses flooding primarily through the National Flood Insurance Program administered by the Federal Emergency Management Agency. Federal wetlands regulations are based on Section 404 of the Clean Water Act and are jointly administered by the U.S. Army Corps of Engineers and the U.S. Environmental Protection Agency. (The goals and methods of these programs and their state analogues differ substantially and are discussed in Chapters 10 and 12.)

At the local level, floodplain and wetland management tend to be more synonymous. Both present similar issues of regulating land alteration and building practices on the basis of imperfect, sometimes crude, scientific data and maps. Until the late 1960s, courts balked at the rare attempts by municipalities to restrain building in either floodplains or wetlands. By the 1970s, however, the pendulum swung in the other direction and courts regularly began to uphold such measures. The judicial "watershed" between these two positions is clearly reflected in the following trilogy of cases, one from New Jersey in 1963 and the other two from Massachusetts and Wisconsin, both in 1972.

The Pre-Environmental Period

Public efforts to regulate floodplains and wetlands were rare before 1960, and so were judicial decisions reviewing them. In the absence of precedents, University of Chicago law professor Allison Dunham (1959) formulated an a priori argument to support floodplain regulations. He urged that such measures are valid to (1) protect unwary individuals from investing or dwelling in hazardous locations, (2) protect riparian landowners from higher flood levels due to ill-considered encroachment on floodplains by their neighbors, and (3) protect the community from the costs of rescue and disaster assistance. This argument was to bear fruit in later cases, notably in *Turnpike Realty* in Massachusetts. But it did not influence the first landmark decision on floodplain/wetland regulation: *Morris County Land Improvement Co. v. Parsippany-Troy Hills Twp.* 192 A.2d 232 (N.J., 1963).

Morris County involved a 66-acre fragment of a 1500-acre freshwater marsh known as the Troy Meadows. The Meadows is located in the headwaters of the Passaic River, a sluggish and polluted stream that drains a heavily developed region of northern New Jersey. About three-quarters of Troy Meadows was owned by a private conservation organization, Wildlife Preserves, Inc. The plaintiff wished to excavate and fill the site to be sold as a building site. Upon complaint by Wildlife, the township rezoned the area as a "Meadows Development Zone." The only permitted uses within this zone were agriculture, horticulture, recreation, and similar open space uses. The plaintiff challenged the rezoning as a taking of its property value in that no remunerative use was allowed. The trial court upheld the ordinance.

On appeal, the New Jersey Supreme Court found that two forms of public benefit were sought by the ordinance: (1) flood control and (2) preservation of the land in its natural state to augment the wildlife refuge. The court thus simultaneously confronted two novel public purposes: flood-loss mitigation and wetland preservation. Having no precedent on either issue, the court reverted to the analysis of Justice Holmes in *Pennsylvania Coal Co. v. Mahon* and concluded that the regulation "went too far."

In the court's defense, the unusual geographic context of this case perhaps explains the result. The site in question was in the headwaters of the drainage system and thus would not be threatened by flooding from upstream. In any event, *Morris County* was to become the leading decision adverse to floodplain and wetland regulation and as such has been widely cited by landowners. The case later proved an embarrassment to the New Jersey court and particularly to Justice Hall (of *Mount Laurel* fame) who wrote the opinion. In 1975, Hall offered the following revealing comment in *A.M.G. Associates v. Springfield Township* 319 A.2d 705:

It is to be emphasized that we deal in this case only with the split lot situation where there is a deprivation of all practical use of the smaller portion thereof. The approach to the taking problem and the result may be different where *vital ecological and environmental considerations of recent cognizance* have brought about rather drastic land use restrictions in furtherance of a policy designed to protect important public interests wide in scope and territory; as for example the coastal wetlands act . . . and various kinds of floodplain use regulation. Cases arising in such a context may properly call for a reexamination of some of the statements made 10 years ago in the largely locally limited *Morris County Land* case . . . (319 A.2d, at 711; emphasis added).

The flexibility of the law to respond to improved perception of human impacts on the physical world has seldom been better stated.

The Post-Environmental Period

For a decade, *Morris County* cast its shadow over floodplain and wetland regulations, and several northeastern states followed its lead. But in 1972, the same year as the Federal Water Quality Amendments and the Coastal Zone Management Act, the Supreme Courts of Massachusetts and Wisconsin provided a fresh perspective. Landmark decisions in those states held such regulations to be valid. These laid a foundation for the subsequent approval of such measures in nearly every jurisdiction that has considered them.

Turnpike Realty Co. v. Town of Dedham 284 N.E.2d 891 (Mass., 1972) turned the tide in the Northeast. The case involved a 61-acre parcel located in a wetland adjoining the Charles River in eastern Massachusetts. Like the Boston Marathon, the Charles flows from the southwestern suburbs to its mouth near downtown Boston. Along the way, it passes through increasingly built-up communities, which it floods from time to time.

The plaintiff's site lay between the Charles and Route 1 in Dedham, a major artery lined with commercial development built partly on filled wetlands (Figure 9-6). The plaintiff wished to continue this trend. The Town of Dedham, however, in 1963 had amended its zoning to establish a "Floodplain District" that prohibited the plaintiff's site from being filled.

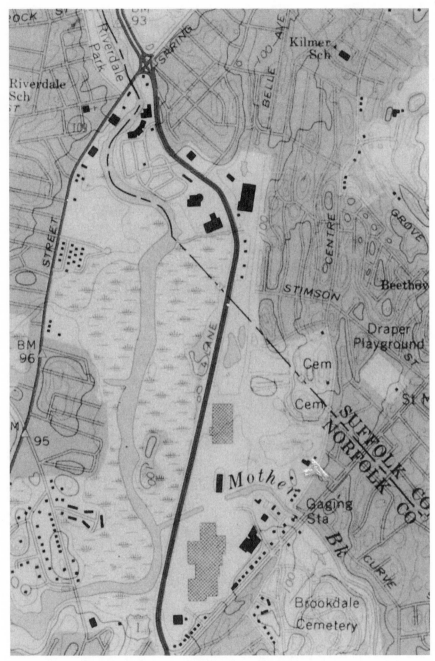

FIGURE 9-6   Site of the *Turnpike Realty Co. v. Town of Dedham* case between
Charles River and Route 1 (heavy dark line).

Dedham was more careful than the New Jersey township in *Morris County* to articulate the purposes of the regulations. They included (1) protection of the groundwater table; (2) protection of public health and safety against floods; (3) avoidance of community costs due to unwise construction in wetlands and floodplains; and (4) conservation of "natural conditions, wildlife, and open spaces for the education, recreation and general welfare of the public." (284 N.E.2d, at 894). The last, of course, raised the specter of "public benefit" that had tainted the *Morris County* ordinance. The Massachusetts court, however, accepted the first three purposes as valid. It ruled that the questionable fourth goal would not justify the measure on its own, but was not fatal since "the by-law is fully supported by other valid considerations of public welfare." Furthermore, the court declared that "the validity of this by-law does not hinge on the motives of its supporters" (284 N.E.2d, at 895).

The court addressed the flood hazard issue carefully. Although the plaintiff claimed that the site was only flooded due to improper operation of a floodgate, the court found the site to be a part of the natural floodplain of the Charles River. It cited testimony as to recent severe flooding of the site. It distinguished *Morris County* as not applicable to a site in a "lower reach" of a stream as was the case in *Turnpike Realty*. Relying on the Dunham (1959) rationale stated above, it upheld the measure, declaring: "The general necessity of floodplain zoning to reduce the damage to life and property caused by flooding is unquestionable" (284 N.E.2d, at 899).

Turnpike Realty thus based its decision on flood hazards rather than wetlands issues, although the site was definitely also a wetland. It left in question the issue of whether a wetland regulation per se could be upheld in the absence of flood risk. That issue was faced in the Wisconsin decision: *Just v. Marinette County* 201 N.W.2d 761, 1972.

Mr. and Mrs. Just owned 36 acres bordering Lake Noquebay, one of thousands of "glacial potholes" strewn across Wisconsin and Minnesota. Like most of that region, their land was a boggy wetland, whose only economic use was to be filled for summer cottages. Marinette County, however, had adopted a shoreland zoning ordinance pursuant to state law that required a permit to be obtained for filling of wetlands within 300 feet of navigable waters. The Just property was covered by this requirement, but they stubbornly proceeded to fill without getting a permit and carried their defiance as far as the Wisconsin Supreme Court, which denied their claim and upheld the county ordinance and state shoreland zoning law.

The *Just* decision rested, not on flood hazards, but on water quality. Wisconsin is a "public trust" jurisdiction in which the state "owns" navigable waters and land beneath them in trust for the people. The court viewed the purpose of the shoreland zoning ordinance as protecting ". . . navigable waters and the public rights therein from the degradation and deterioration which results from uncontrolled use and development of shorelands" (201 N.W.2d, at 765). This is reasonable in light of the problem of septic seepage from shoreline cottages contaminating lakes of this type.

The court could thus easily have upheld the ordinance as simply giving the county the right to review plans for new fill. The Justs would probably have received a permit if they had applied for it. But in the spirit of Aldo Leopold, Wisconsin's environmental philosopher, the court went far beyond such a simple resolution of the case. It chose to view the issue as "a conflict between the public interest in stopping the despoliation of natural resources, which our citizens until recently have taken as inevitable and for granted, and an owner's asserted right to use his property as he wishes" (201 N.W.2d, 767). Shifting into high gear, the court declared:

> It seems to us that filling a swamp not otherwise commercially usable is not in and of itself an existing use, which is prevented, but rather is the preparation for some future use which is not indigenous to a swamp. . . .
>
> The shoreland zoning ordinance preserves nature, the environment, and natural resources as they were created and to which the people have a present right. The ordinance does not create or improve the public condition but only preserves nature from the despoilage [sic] and harm resulting from the unrestricted activities of humans (201 N.W.2d, at 770–1).

This environmental "Magna Carta" was beyond the call of duty or demands of this modest case. To other courts around the country, it was probably seen as beyond the Constitution as well. But *Just* remains "the law" in Wisconsin, and its rhetorical flourishes continue to thrill students and practitioners of natural resource management.

The trilogy of cases discussed in this section delimit the range of possible judicial response to floodplain and wetland regulations. *Morris County* reflected the cautious pre-environmental approach, with Holmes looking over the shoulder. *Turnpike Realty* broke new ground through careful judicial craftmanship. *Just* was a glimpse of utopia. All three cases are cited frequently, although challenges to local floodplain and wetland regulations declined in the 1980s. The constitutionality of such measures is now well accepted.

[The foregoing was written in 1990. By 1995, the growing strength of the property rights movement, as reflected in the *Lucas* and *Dolan* decisions discussed in the previous chapter may have weakened judicial acceptance of wetlands regulation based on strictly natural resource protection grounds, especially where they allow no developmental use. (See *Lopes v. Peabody*, Mass. Land Court, Case No. 139663, 1995.) But the 1991 Illinois case discussed below, although predating *Lucas* and *Dolan*, suggests that state courts will uphold very severe limits on development in floodplains where the hazard is well documented.]

Severe flooding struck the Chicago metropolitan area in 1986 and again in 1987, transforming local urban streams into dangerous torrents that damaged thousands of homes and businesses. Presidential disaster declarations were declared in both years and the state established a Governor's flood control task force to study the causes and recommend legal changes. The Illinois Legislature acted on the commission's report to enact a floodplain management law that prohibited all new residential construction in the 100-year floodway in the Chicago metropolitan area.

The state denied renewal of building permits previously issued, before the new law was adopted, to the owner of two lots entirely in the 100-year floodplain of Butterfield Creek in the southwest suburbs. The Illinois Supreme Court upheld the state law, despite its severe impact on the plaintiff (a "total taking"?), in the following language:

> We agree with defendant that the General Assembly has the authority to prohibit all new residential construction in the 100-year floodway. It is reasonable for the General Assembly to rely on the extensive research contained in the Governor's flood control task force report which documented the demographic and land use changes which have contributed to the increased flooding in the 100-year floodway. It is reasonable for the General Assembly to

accept the recommendation of the task force that a central part in the response to the severe flooding which may occur in a 100-year flood event is the prohibition of all new residential construction in the floodway. It is also reasonable for the General Assembly to rely on the scientific study contained in the report which emphasized the importance of maintaining existing natural storage areas in the watershed to reduce flood damage (*Beverly Bank v. Illinois Department of Transportation* 579 N.E.2d 815, Ill. 1991, at 822).

Thus the cycle of (1) disaster, (2) study and recommendations, (3) adoption of new laws regarding land use leading to (4) safer development practices was completed. The tradition of learning from disaster that began with Charles II and the Act for Rebuilding London of 1667 (Chapter 3) thus continues to operate in the American legal system of land use control.

Public Acquisition

Reasons for Public Acquisition

Certain public objectives regarding the use of land cannot adequately be met through regulation of private land. Public land ownership is required to provide sites for schools, parks, fire and police stations, airports, sewerage and water treatment plants, as well as corridors for streets and highways. Where actual public use is involved, the Fifth Amendment requires payment of "just compensation" to the owner. Police power regulations such as zoning may be used to protect the "public health, safety, and welfare" but not to provide outright public use. As in *Nollan v. California Coastal Commission* and *Dolan v. City of Tigard*, discussed in Chapter 8, an attempt to impose public access through regulation is likely to be struck down as a "taking" without compensation.

Beyond sites for public facilities, public ownership may be desired to maintain tight and long-term control over certain types of land by removing them from the uncertainties of the private market. Thus, areas such as wetlands, coastal barriers, wild lands, or sites of scenic, historic, or cultural importance may best be protected through public ownership. Although some of those areas may arguably be protected through the regulatory power (provided public access is not involved), public acquisition provides greater security against subsequent political change and eliminates worry about the taking issue.

Each level of government—municipal, county, state, and federal—may acquire and own land. Public entities differ, however, in their objectives, fiscal resources, and management policies regarding land. Some local governments diligently pursue long-term open space acquisition programs. Others acquire little or no land for "amenity" reasons but instead may acquire land for resale or lease to promote economic development. Public lands may in some cases be sold as well as acquired, which can lead to favoritism and abuse. The "public trust doctrine" however limits the marketability of public lands in many states such as Wisconsin, Illinois, and Massachusetts (Archer et al. 1994).

Means of Land Acquisition

The usual means of acquiring public ownership of real property, as depicted in Figure 7-1, are the following: (1) negotiated purchase, (2) eminent domain, (3) gift or dedication, and (4) tax default.

Negotiated purchase is the most common way to acquire land for public use. Once authorized by legislation, a governmental agency may approach a private owner like any other prospective buyer. However, a public buyer must obtain one or more independent appraisals of the value of the property and cannot normally pay more than the appraised value so established. (A slight increase may be allowed to avoid condemnation proceedings.) If the offer is accepted, a deed is exchanged for payment and the land becomes publicly owned. No court action is required, the process is reasonably speedy, and everyone is presumably satisfied. If it is impossible to reach agreement on a price within the limit of appraised value, the effort must either be abandoned or pursued through condemnation.

Eminent domain (also known as "condemnation") is an inherent power of government in the United States. It is the compulsory purchase of land from a private owner in exchange for "just compensation" as established by a jury. It is a constitutional prerogative as long as the purpose and value paid are appropriate. (Condemnation should be distinguished from "confiscation," which is an illegal taking without compensation.)

Eminent domain pursuant to legislation appeared in London as early as John Nash's Regent Street project in the 1820s and was used on a larger scale to cut Haussmann's boulevards through the clutter of central Paris. Condemnation of land was used to establish New York's Central Park in the 1850s, and it was increasingly used by municipalities thereafter. Land condemnation by states and the federal government accompanied the expansion of their respective activities in the 20th century. The New Deal involved a vast increase in public works projects such as highways, parks, dams, and airports, which required eminent domain on a large scale. The use of the power by all levels of government peaked in the 1950s and 1960s in the urban renewal and interstate highway programs.

The widening use of eminent domain in programs funded by the federal government was facilitated by judicial expansion of the meaning of "public use." Early in the 20th century, it was generally believed that the Fifth Amendment required literal use by the public to justify condemnation of private land. In 1936, the use of the power to acquire slum property for clearance and residential redevelopment was upheld by the New York Court of Appeals in *New York City Housing Authority v. Muller* 1 N.E.2d 153.

The concept that "public use" might include a "public purpose" without actual use by the general public was confirmed in the landmark 1954 U.S. Supreme Court decision in *Berman v. Parker* 75 S.Ct. 98. Berman challenged the condemnation of his store by the Urban Renewal Authority of the District of Columbia to be cleared and resold to another private enterprise. He argued that the premises was not "blighted" and the resulting use would benefit another businessman, not the public. Nevertheless, Justice William Douglas in a much-quoted opinion upheld the taking as necessary to the achievement of the urban renewal project that was a legitimate public activity. (See Chapter 8.)

One potential use of eminent domain that is not generally sanctioned in the United States is the taking of more land than is needed for a project to lease or resell later at a higher price. This practice, known as "excess condemnation," has been used in Europe beginning with Haussmann's rebuilding of Paris. But it has been frowned upon by U.S. courts. While, arguably, it is a "public purpose" for government to recoup some of the increment of value that its programs bestow on adjoining land, it has not been viewed as a proper use of eminent domain simply to speculate in the land market.

On the other hand, the New York Court of Appeals in 1963 upheld the taking of a private business for an economic redevelopment project (the World Trade Center) although the site was not functionally related to the project but was taken "solely for the production of incidental revenue . . ." (*Courtesy Sandwich Shop Inc. v. Port of New York Authority* 190 N.E.2d 402). The court held that the taking was only an incidental extension of a site required for public use, and was related to the overall purpose of bolstering the city's economic development.

While the use of eminent domain to speculate in the land market is suspect, the public may engage in "land banking" through negotiated purchase. Land may thereby be acquired either for future public use or for eventual lease or resale. This concept was widely advocated during the 1960s but, like transfer of development rights, has been little utilized.

Eminent domain remains a fundamental power of government in the United States but is used more sparingly than in the past. Legally, the only major issue is usually that of value, which is referred to a jury (with sometimes extravagant results). Eminent domain is a politically unpopular technique used generally as a last resort when negotiation fails. Sometimes, however, eminent domain is mutually agreeable as a means of efficiently clearing title to private land where the owner is willing to sell.

Gifts of land to public entities are an important source of open space and natural areas. Many national, state, and local parks originated in a philanthropic gift. Examples include portions of Acadia, Great Smokies, and Grand Teton National Parks donated to the National Park Service by the Rockefeller family and the Harriman State Park along the Hudson River Palisades opposite New York City. The writer's community of Northampton, Massachusetts is graced with Look Park and Childs Park, both donated to the city decades ago together with endowments toward their upkeep.

Gifts of real property to public or nonprofit organizations are usually recognized in federal tax law as charitable contributions. Donors can take the current appraised value of the donated land as a deduction from their taxable income. This tax subsidy for land donations applies also to gifts of interests less than fee (such as a conservation restriction that severs the development rights). It also applies to gifts to nonprofit charitable organizations such as colleges, churches, eligible conservation organizations, and land trusts.

Tax default is another means of acquiring public land at the local level, although it usually is not needed or wanted for public purposes. If an owner fails to pay property taxes on real property, the site is subject to a court lien and possible sale. Occasionally, a tax-delinquent tract may be retained for public purposes, but the former owner may redeem the property on payment of back taxes and interest within a specified period of time.

Costs of Public Acquisition

Public land acquisition through negotiated purchase or condemnation can be very expensive, especially in the face of metropolitan development. Costs per acre in the northeast may range from about $5,000 for raw farmland not yet ripe for development to more than $100,000 for sites snatched from the bulldozer in prime locations. Clearly, early action on land needed for public purposes may save much tax money. Beyond a certain point, public acquisition becomes prohibitively expensive. Furthermore, the direct cost paid to the seller is only part of the total cost of acquisition. The following are some types of costs of public land acquisition:

1. The *direct cost* (purchase price) is reached through negotiation with the owner or through court determination in eminent domain. "Just compensation" implies full market value as estimated by independent professional appraisers. *Appraised* value is usually established by comparison with recent private sales of similar property in the vicinity. The *assessed* value of a parcel of land listed in local tax records is usually not accepted as evidence of market value since assessments tend to be lower than fair market value (even in states that require "full value" assessment).

2. *Legal and administrative costs* associated with the purchase include the cost of negotiation, appraisal fees, land survey, title search, and preparation of legal documents. Where federal or state funding is sought, preparation of the necessary paperwork is another project expense.

3. *Financing cost* of interest on money borrowed to pay the purchase price. Like private buyers, governments often borrow to pay for large capital outlays. Financial instruments for this purpose include

general obligation bonds (repayable from general tax revenues) and revenue bonds (repayable out of user fees, if any, generated by the facility funded by such bonds). Even where a government can pay the full purchase price up front, there is an implicit loss of future interest on such capital if it were otherwise invested (referred to by economists as "opportunity cost").

4. Since public land is "off the tax roll" and exempt from local property taxation, acquisition involves an implicit *cost of taxes foregone*. This may be a large loss to local governments if the site might have been developed privately as a high-revenue-earning facility such as a shopping center or office park. The cost of tax revenue foregone falls on the local taxing jurisdiction (municipal or county) regardless of what level of government acquires the land. Local governments, therefore, sometimes oppose the acquisition by the state or the federal government of developable land within their jurisdictions. States and the federal government offset lost tax revenue to some extent by making "payments in lieu of taxes" to local governments. Such payments then add to the costs of ownership by the higher unit of government.

5. *Costs of improvement and maintenance* include such facilities as roads, walks, parking, restrooms, sports facilities, playgrounds, nature interpretation centers, and so forth. The installation of these is a major initial cost and their maintenance is an annual expense.

6. Since lawsuits against public land management agencies are increasingly common and costly, *liability insurance* may be needed. Governmental units in the past were protected from suit by the doctrine of "sovereign immunity," but that has withered away in most states. The federal government may be sued under the Federal Tort Claims Act, and when it loses a case it pays out of general revenues; in other words, it is a self-insurer. Many states and local governments also self-insure, but it is increasingly common for such units to purchase liability insurance like private landowners. A related trend is that parks and playgrounds are increasingly designed for safety, at the expense of excitement. Some facilities have been closed due to the high costs of maintaining and insuring them.

Counterbalancing the many costs of public land are the direct and indirect benefits that they provide. Some of these are direct economic returns in the form of user fees. Other, and more important, benefits are not easily quantified–such as recreation, scenic amenity, biodiversity, environmental quality, and urban separation. Resource economists such as Marion Clawson have attempted to assign monetary values to such intangible but valuable functions of recreation land. Secondary economic benefits are also important, including money spent by vacationers for motels, food, and supplies in "gateway communities" near public parks.

Funding for Outdoor Recreation

In 1958, Congress established the Outdoor Recreation Resources Review Commission (ORRRC) in response to a growing perception that postwar urbanization was creating a shortage of outdoor recreation opportunities and facilities. ORRRC's legislative mandate was to:

(a) ... set in motion a nationwide inventory and evaluation of outdoor recreation resources and opportunities, ... [and] (b) ... compile such data and ... determine the amount, kind, quality, and location of such outdoor recreation resources and opportunities as will be required by the year 1976 and the year 2000 and shall recommend what policies should best be adopted ... (P.L. 85-470, Sec. 6).

The 27 working papers and final report published by ORRRC over the next four years reflected the best professional thinking of the time on recreation, open space, and urban planning. ORRRC found that "public areas designated for outdoor recreation include one-eighth of the total land of the country" but "the problem is not one of number of acres but of effective acres–acres of land and water available to the public and usable for specific types of recreation" (ORRRC 1962, 49).

The final report discussed statistically, graphically, and in prose the existing and the anticipated status of outdoor recreation opportunities, with the notable exception of central cities. Today, the report seems remarkably dated in its nonrecognition of minorities, handicapped persons, and the elderly. Its photographs uniformly depict white, middle-class families enjoying themselves in bucolic surroundings.

But few national reports have had faster and more lasting results. Soon after its release, a new Bureau of Outdoor Recreation (BOR) was established by Secretary of the Interior Stewart Udall and later ratified by Congress as recommended in the report. ORRRC's proposal to establish a federal land-acquisition fund was immediately endorsed by President Kennedy and ultimately adopted in the federal Land and Water Conservation Fund Act of 1965 (P.L. 88-588).

This act (known as LAWCON) until the mid-1980s was the primary source of federal matching grants for acquisition and improvement of urban and rural open space by all levels of government It is funded through earmarked revenue from specific sources including a portion of off-shore oil and gas royalties. However, Congress must appropriate money annually for LAWCON and program outlays have accordingly fluctuated over the years, reaching rock bottom in the 1990s.

LAWCON funds, when appropriated, are divided, with 40 percent allocated for federal land acquisition and 60 percent distributed to the states in accordance with a Congressional formula. To receive funds under the program, each state must prepare a Comprehensive Outdoor Recreation Plan (SCORP) acceptable to the Department of the Interior. A SCORP identifies how the federal money will be allocated by the state to remedy its recreational needs.

LAWCON provides 50 percent of eligible costs of acquiring and/or improving open space at the state or local level. Many states have created their own funds to contribute an additional 25 percent of local project costs, leaving only 25 percent to be covered by a local or county government. Even this cost is an obstacle to central cities, where land is costly and budgets are tight. The program has long been more utilized by affluent suburbs than by central cities (Platt 1976, ch. 9).

Intergovernmental Cooperation

Given the fragmented political geography of U.S. metropolitan areas described in Chapter 5, it is clearly impractical for each municipality to act independently to meet all of its needs for public land. Land needed for a highway corridor or to protect riparian habitat along a stream may cross local, county, and even state boundaries. Also, the benefits of public open space usually extend beyond the political jurisdiction(s) in which it is situated. Indeed the local government that has tax jurisdiction over a site may prefer to have it privately developed, while neighboring units with no tax interest prefer to have it preserved. Thus, the spatial distribution of the costs and benefits of public open space may be spatially inconsistent with each other (Platt 1972).

Intergovernmental cooperation is therefore needed to acquire and manage land that lies within or affects multiple political units. Regional plans for land acquisition are prerequisite to such cooperation. Such plans may be prepared by a state planning office, a regional planning agency, a council of governments, or by a private civic organization. The Commercial Club of Chicago, for instance, commissioned Burnham's Chicago Plan of 1909, which included the regional open space plan depicted as Figure 7-3 above. Compare it with Figure 9-7, which shows a more recent open space plan for the Chicago region, prepared by the Northeastern Illinois Planning Commission.

Accomplishing such a plan is not simple. Each tract or cluster of tracts requires an individual strategy, often involving more than one unit or level of government. "Horizontal" agreements are needed between neighboring governments that share jurisdiction over a specific resource area. "Vertical" coordination is essential between local, state, and federal levels regarding the sharing of costs.

Such complex arrangements take time. But the private land market does not stand still waiting for government to assemble funds. To rescue key parcels of open land from the bulldozer, intervention by a private conservation organization may be needed. Such organizations play critical roles in many public acquisition programs.

Private Conservation Organizations

There are many kinds of private organizations in the United States that supplement public land acquisition and management efforts. National organizations include The Nature Conservancy (TNC), the National Audubon Society (NAS), and the Trust for Public Lands (TPL). They and others acquire land through purchase and gift, but of course they do not have a power of eminent domain. TNC and NAS own substantial reserves of natural land that they manage primarily for ecological protection, education, and research. TPL serves largely as a conduit for open

FIGURE 9-7   Northeastern Illinois Regional Greenways Plan: 1995. *Source:*
Northeastern Illinois Planning Commission.

lands that it acquires and then resells to public agencies when possible. TPL sells portions of its holdings for development to defray its operating costs.

Similar functions are performed by a variety of organizations operating at the levels of states, regions, or local communities. The Massachusetts Audubon Society operates a statewide system of sanctuaries, which it augments through aggressive acquisition of threatened sites. Sanctuary management balances natural protection, education, and recreation.

Several hundred community or regional land trusts have appeared across the nation since 1970. These may hold land for preservation or serve as agents for public land-acquisition programs. In the latter capacity, a land trust purchases key parcels of open land scheduled for public ownership and holds them until a public agency can muster the funds to buy them from the trust. Many land trusts have "revolving funds" or lines of credit from banks that enable them to move quickly to protect land, pending action by slower-paced agencies.

Greenways

As long ago as Olmsted's 1880s "Emerald Necklace" plan for the Boston parks system, urban designers have proposed systems of linked open spaces that today are referred to as "greenways" (Platt, Rowntree, and Muick, eds. 1994). Greenways are corridors of largely natural open land or connected systems of larger open spaces and parks that provide environmental, recreational, flood reduction, and other benefits. The *National Geographic* has identified "four E's" served by greenways: "(1) environment, (2) ecology, (3) education, and (4) exercise" (Grove 1990). To these, landscape architect Annaliese Bischoff (1995) adds "expression," referring to the role of greenways as corridors of art, communication, and other forms of cultural expression.

Hundreds of greenways have been established or are under development throughout metropolitan America (Little 1990). Most are oriented to linear physical features such as stream valleys, shorelines, ridgelines, or abandoned rail rights of way. Greenways typically cross political boundaries and thus require extensive intergovernmental coordination. A series of case studies by the National Park Service (1991) examines experience with organizing metropolitan greenway projects in Massachusetts, Colorado, California, Florida, Oklahoma, and Georgia.

References

Archer, J.H., D.L. Connors, K. Lawrence, and S. Columbia. 1994. *The Public Trust Doctrine and the Management of America's Coasts*. Amherst: University of Massachusetts Press.

Babcock, R.F. 1960. "The Chaos of Zoning Administration." *Zoning Digest* 12:1 ff.

—— and C.L. Siemon. 1985. *The Zoning Game Revisited*. Boston: Oelgeschlager, Gunn & Hain.

Bauman, G., and W.H. Ethier. 1987. "Development Exactions and Impact Fees: Survey of American Practices." *Law and Contemporary Problems* 50(1): 51–62.

Bischoff, A. 1995. "Greenways as Vehicles for Expression." *Landscape and Urban Planning*, in press.

Bollens, S.A., and D.R. Godschalk. 1987. "Tracking Land Supply for Growth Management." *Journal of the American Planning Association* 53(3): 315–327.

Bosselman, F.P. 1973. "Can the Town of Ramapo Pass a Law to Bind the Rights of the Whole World?" *Florida State University Law Review* 1(1): 234 ff.

Callies, D.L., and R.H. Freilich. 1986. *Cases and Materials on Land Use*. St. Paul: West Publishing Co.

City of Petaluma. 1987. *Petaluma General Plan: 1987–2005*. Petaluma: The City.

Costonis, J.J. 1974. *Space Adrift: Saving Landmarks Through the Chicago Plan*. Urbana: University of Illinois Press.

Dawson, A.D. 1981. "Management of Residential Growth." *1981 Zoning and Planning Handbook*. Chicago: Clark Boardman.

——. 1982. *Land use Planning and the Law*. Hadley, MA: the author.

Delogu, O.E. 1986. "Local Land Use Controls: An Idea Whose Time Has Passed." In *1986 Zoning and Planning Law Handbook*. F.A. Strom, ed. New York: Clark Boardman.

Dunham, A. 1959. "Flood Control Via the Police Power." *University of Pennsylvania Law Review* 107: 1098–1132.

Godschalk, D.R., D.J. Brower, D.C. Herr, and B.A. Vestal. 1978. *Responsible Growth Management: Cases and Materials*. Chapel Hill, NC: University of North Carolina Center for Urban and Regional Studies.

Grove, N. 1990. "Greenways: Paths to the Future." *National Geographic* (June): 277–294.

Gruntfest, E.C., ed. 1987. *What We Have Learned Since the Big Thompson Flood*. Special Pub. 16. Boulder: University of Colorado Natural Hazards Research Center.

Hoyt, W.G., and W.B. Langbein. 1955. *Floods*. Princeton: Princeton University Press.

Juergensmeyer, J.C., and R.M. Blake. 1984. "Impact Fees: An Answer to Local Governments' Capital Funding Dilemma." In *1984 Zoning and Planning Law Handbook*. J.B. Gailey, ed. New York: Clark Boardman.

Krasnowiecki. J. 1980. "Abolish Zoning." *Syracuse Law Review* 31: 719–731.

Kusler, J.A. 1983. *Our National Wetland Heritage: A Protection Guidebook*. Washington, D.C.: Environmental Law Institute.

Listokin, D., ed. 1974. *Land Use Controls: Present Problems and Future Reform*. New Brunswick, NJ: Rutgers Center for Urban Policy Research.

Little, C.E. 1990. *Greenways for America*. Baltimore: Johns Hopkins University Press.

National Park Service. 1991. *A Casebook in Managing Rivers for Multiple Uses*. Washington, D.C.: National Park Service.

Palm, R. 1981. *The Geography of American Cities*. New York: Oxford University Press.

Platt, R.H. 1972. *The Open Space Decision Process: Spatial Allocation of Costs and Benefits*. Research Paper no. 132. Chicago: University of Chicago Department of Geography.

——. 1976. "The Federal Open Space Programs: Impacts and Imperatives." In *Urban Policymaking and Metropolitan Dynamics: A Comparative Geographical Analysis*. J.S. Adams, ed. Cambridge: Ballinger.

Platt, R.H., R.A. Rowntree, and P.C. Muick, eds. 1994. *The Ecological City: Preserving and Restoring Urban Biodiversity*. Amherst: University of Massachusetts Press.

Reps, J. 1964. "Requiem for Zoning." *Planning–1964*. Chicago: American Society of Planning Officials.

Schneider, W.J., and J.E. Goddard. 1974. *Extent and Development of Urban Flood Plains*. U.S. Geological Survey Circular 601-J. Reston, VA: U.S. Geological Survey.

Smith, R.M. 1987. "From Subdivision Improvement Requirements to Community Benefit Assessments and Linkage Payments: A Brief History of Land Development Exactions." *Law and Contemporary Problems* 50(1): 5–30.

Tiner, R.W., Jr. 1984. *Wetlands of the United States: Current Status and Recent Trends*. Washington, D.C.: U.S. Government Printing Office.

Tustian, R.E. 1984. "TDRs in Practice: A Case Study of Agriculture Preservation in Montgomery County, Maryland." In *1984 Zoning and Planning Law Handbook*. J.B. Gailey, ed. New York: Clark Boardman.

U.S. Bureau of the Census. 1986. *Statistical Abstract of the U.S.: 1986*. Washington, D.C.: U.S. Government Printing Office.

U.S. Council on Environmental Quality. 1981. *Environmental Trends*. Washington, D.C.: U.S. Government Printing Office.

———.1978. *Our Nation's Wetlands*. Washington, D.C.: U.S. Government Printing Office.

White, G.F. 1964. *Choice of Adjustment to Floods*. Research Paper no. 93. Chicago: University of Chicago Department of Geography.

———.1975. *Flood Hazard in the United States: A Research Assessment*. Boulder: University of Colorado Institute of Behavioral Studies.

——— et al. 1958. *Changes in Urban Occupance of Flood Plains in the United States*. Research Paper no. 57. University of Chicago Department of Geography.

Whyte, W.H., Jr. 1958. "Urban Sprawl." In *The Exploding Metropolis* Editors of *Fortune*. Garden City, NY: Doubleday Anchor.

———.1968. *The Last Landscape*. Garden City, NY: Doubleday & Co.

Woodbury, S.R. 1975. "Transfer of Development Rights: A New Tool for Planners." *Journal of American Institute of Planners* 38(1): 3–14.

Part IV / *The Search for Broader Land Use Policies*

CHAPTER 10

State and Regional
Land Use Programs

Introduction

States are the sovereign units of the United States. The federal government gained its existence and authority through the delegation of certain powers by the original 13 states in the Constitution of 1787. Also, municipalities and special districts are creatures of the states, exercising powers expressly or implicitly delegated to them by state law. Thus, having divested some of their powers upward to the federal level and others downward to municipalities, what functions do states retain to exercise on their own?

It is difficult to generalize about state land use programs because they differ widely from one state to another. Although basically similar in their legal status and potential capabilities, states have evolved differently in their land use policies and efforts, as articulated in their respective constitutions, legislation, administrative regulations, executive orders, and court decisions. It is a strength of the federalist system of the United States that states are free, within the bounds of the U.S. Constitution, to develop their individual approaches to land use problems according to their respective physical and fiscal resources, politics, and perceived needs. For example, certain "high amenity" states such as Hawaii, Oregon, Vermont, Maine, and Florida during the 1960s and 1970s launched ambitious state land use management programs, while more "resource dominated" states such as Texas, Ohio, West Virginia, and Colorado did not (DeGrove 1984).

Certain fundamental roles of state government may be identified that are performed with differing levels of zeal and effectiveness in all or most of the 50 states. (These are parallel with equivalent functions of the federal government to be discussed in Chapter 12.)

- Land ownership and management

- Funding of state and local public infrastructure–for example, highways and water and sewer systems

- Regulation and permitting of specified land and water uses–for example, power plant siting, waterway encroachments, landfill siting, and design

- Planning and technical assistance

- Taxation

In many cases, states operate as agents for or partners with the federal government. Many federal programs, such as the Land and Water Conservation Fund and the Coastal Zone Management Program, rely on state initiative to promulgate national policies and goals and to utilize federal funds. But states may also act autonomously to influence the use of land and patterns of metropolitan development within their jurisdictions. Or they may sit back and let the federal and local levels of government exercise their respective powers with little state input.

State Parks

Before 1970, practically the only land management function of most states was the operation of state parks and recreation areas. One of the earliest and largest state facilities was the Adirondack State Forest Preserve established in New York State in 1885. (Nash 1982, 119). During the 1930s, many state parks were added, expanded, and improved with federal assistance. Much of the infrastructure of older state parks–including roads, trails, restrooms, recreation fields–dates back to the Civilian Conservation Corps and other public works programs of that era.

Assisted by the federal Land and Water Conservation Fund, and state-level bond issues, many states have substantially enlarged and improved their park systems since the 1960s. In 1984, the 50 state park systems collectively comprised about 10 million acres. Excluding Alaska from both federal and state totals, state parks have about one-third the acreage of the National Park System but more than twice the level of visitation (in "recreation user-days") (Conservation Foundation 1987, 287). State parks tend to be smaller, more widely distributed, and more accessible to metropolitan populations than national parks. Day trip usage is therefore much higher.

Many states have incorporated new kinds of facilities and administrative concepts into their open space preservation programs. These include historic sites, scenic and wild rivers, trail corridors, and greenways along metropolitan streams. Massachusetts has pioneered the concept of the "heritage park" to combine the functions of urban renewal, cultural preservation, and recreation in several old mill cities such as Lowell, Holyoke, and North Adams. New York in 1971 established an Adirondack State Park Agency to plan and control land use for the 6-million-acre Adirondack Park region surrounding the actual state-owned forest reserve (Figure 10-1). Less-than-fee interests, for example, conservation easements, have been used to protect existing parks from visual encroachment. Also, a number of states have asserted ownership rights over the beds of rivers, lakes, and coastal waters under the doctrine of public trust.

Sometimes, states have served as the cornerstone of cooperative intergovernmental approaches to land preservation. Thorn Creek Woods in the south suburbs of Chicago was saved from development in the early 1970s through public purchase by the State of Illinois, the Will County Forest Preserve District, two incorporated villages, and a new state university. None of these public entities could geographically or fiscally preserve the entire woods on their own. The entire joint acquisition was facilitated by federal grants under the HUD Open Space and New Communities programs, amounting to 70 percent of the total costs. Thorn Creek Woods State Park is today managed by the state under cooperative agreements with the other landholding entities.

"The Quiet Revolution"

Between 1965 and 1975, many states dramatically expanded their land planning and management roles in tandem with the reforms at the federal level. This surge of state activism became known as the "Quiet Revolution" after the title of a report prepared for the new Council on

FIGURE 10-1   Location of the Adirondack State Park (areas in black are owned by the state). *Source:* Commission on the Adirondacks, 1990.

Environmental Quality (Bosselman and Callies 1971). The report's introduction stated the situation as follows:

This country is in the midst of a revolution in the way we regulate the use of our land. It is a peaceful revolution, conducted entirely within the law. It is a quiet revolution, and its supporters include both conservatives and liberals. It is a disorganized revolution, with no central cadre of leaders, but it is a revolution nonetheless.

The "ancient regime" being overthrown is the feudal system under which the entire pattern of land development has been controlled by thousands of individual local governments, each seeking to maximize its tax base and minimize its social problems, and caring less what happens to all the others.

The tools of the revolution are new laws taking a wide variety of forms but each sharing a common theme—the need to provide some degree of state or regional participation in the major decisions that affect the use of our increasingly limited supply of land.

Bosselman and Callies 1971, p. 1.

There was in fact a "cadre of leaders," albeit informal and open-ended in its membership. Parallel with the city planning movement in the early 20th century, the "Quiet Revolution" was motivated by a group of lawyers and planners in several states with a center of gravity in Chicago, the location of the Ross, Hardies law firm that included Richard F. Babcock, Marlin Smith, Fred Bosselman, David Callies, and John Banta among its land use specialists. Closely allied with this group was William K. Reilly, editor of *The Use of Land* (Reilly 1973) and a senior staff member of the federal Council on Environmental Quality, which commissioned the Quiet Revolution report. (Reilly later was appointed Administrator of the U.S. Environmental Protection Agency by President Bush in 1989.)

Stimulus was provided to the "revolution" through the drafting of a Model Land Development Code by the American Law Institute (1975). The Code was developed as a model for new state legislation to update the old Planning and Zoning Enabling Acts of the 1920s. Its most notable innovation was Article 7, which proposed state review and possible override of local zoning decisions concerning (1) areas of particular concern, (2) large-scale developments, and (3) developments of regional benefit. In the first two categories, the role of the state was likely to be more protective (less permissive) than local government. The third category raised the possibility of state veto of local zoning that prohibited a locally unwanted but regionally needed facility (e.g., a power plant, prison, incinerator, or wastewater treatment facility). Early drafts of the Code, beginning in 1968, generated widespread praise from "quiet revolutionaries" and alarm among some local governments.

The Code was not entirely adopted anywhere. A few states (Vermont,

Maine, Oregon, Florida) adopted state land planning laws based in spirit on Article 7. It served also as the inspiration for the state management requirements of the federal Coastal Zone Management Act of 1972.

The momentum of the Quiet Revolution diminished in the late 1970s as development pressures abated, due to high interest rates, and energy issues dominated public attention. But the state programs that it inspired remained in place and in several instances were expanded, even during the conservative 1980s (Popper 1988). Some of these programs are statewide in their application—as in Vermont, Oregon, Florida, and the granddaddy of state planning laws, the Hawaii Land Use Act of 1961.

The relative scarcity of comprehensive state planning laws has fostered the view among proponents of centralization that the Quiet Revolution fizzled out prematurely. The Reagan Administration, however, felt that land use was overregulated and advocated regulation-free "enterprise zones" to assist private investment. Popper (1988) disputed both the "liberal" view that we have too little centralized land management and the "conservative" position that we have too much. He argued that since 1970 the nation has achieved a harmonious new balance of local-versus-centralized planning control. In the process many, if not most, states have gained a crucial role in land use control, not usually on a statewide basis, but selectively. The handful of comprehensive state planning programs are augmented by a multitude of state laws focused on either specific geographic areas or specific land use issues.

Special Area Programs: The Pinelands Case

The original Quiet Revolution report studied several state programs focused on specific geographic areas, for example:

- San Francisco Bay Conservation and Development Commission (CA)

- Adirondack State Park Agency (NY)

- Twin Cities Metropolitan Council (MN)

- Tahoe Regional Planning Agency (CA and NV)

- Hackensack Meadowland Development Commission (NJ)

Each of these programs was alive and apparently well in the mid-1990s. Except for the Twin Cities Metro Council, which does not regulate land use, each has survived political and legal challenges to its land management functions. They each have influenced to some degree the pattern of development in their respective regions.

The New Jersey Pinelands Commission, which appeared in the late 1970s, provides a more recent example of a state program, initiated with some federal nudging, that is achieving a remarkable degree of control over the use of sensitive land with an apparently high level of public acceptance. The Pinelands or "Pine Barrens" is a region of about 1 million acres of sandy, wooded terrain in southern New Jersey, of which about two-thirds is privately owned (Figure 10-2). The region is underlain by a vast aquifer estimated to hold some 17 trillion gallons of fresh water. Cranberry and blueberry cultivation are prominent agricultural activities in portions of the region. The Pinelands Region is sparsely settled. Its special historic and cultural identity was portrayed in John McPhee's *The Pine Barrens* (1968).

Lying between Philadelphia and the coast, the region during the 1970s attracted growing interest from real estate developers. With jurisdiction over the Pinelands divided among seven counties and 55 towns and villages, efforts to protect its natural resources at the local level would have been fruitless. Instead, preservationists, armed with McPhee's book and great persistence, achieved a unique threefold designation of the Pinelands Region as (1) a National Reserve; (2) an International Biosphere Reserve; and (3), most important, a special state planning region administered by the New Jersey Pinelands Commission.

This process began with the designation of the Pinelands as the first National Reserve in Section 502 of the National Parks and Recreation Act of 1978. Within the 1.1 million acres so designated, Congress authorized $26 million for land acquisition and planning by the state and localities, provided the state established a special planning commission for the area. In response, New Jersey's Governor Brendon Byrne, by executive order, established the state-level Pinelands Commission and banned new development in the region until a comprehensive plan and land use regulations were prepared. These powers were confirmed in the New Jersey Pinelands Act of 1979 despite vocal opposition (Babcock and Siemon 1985, ch. 8).

The Pinelands Comprehensive Management Plan as finally approved

FIGURE 10-2 Map of the New Jersey Pinelands Region. *Source:* New Jersey
Pinelands Commission.

by the commission, the governor, and the Secretary of the Interior in 1980–1981 was a landmark in state land management. The 1979 law had designated a state Pinelands Area of 933,000 acres (slightly smaller than the Pinelands National Reserve) and divided that into a central "preservation area" of 368,000 acres and a surrounding "protection area" of 565,000 acres. The commission's plan further divided the Pinelands into nine land use zones based on the physical and human characteristics of each area. The preservation area, also known as the "heart of the pines," is described by the commission as follows:

> Here are the unique forests of pygmy pines and oaks known as the East and West Plains. The ruins of long-deserted towns and factories poke through the underbrush amidst a maze of twisting, barely passable sand roads. The solemn gloom of cedar swamps gives way to the flowery brilliance of inland marshes and bogs.
>
> Pinelands Commission 1989, p. 4.

Within this core area, no new residential development is permitted except that "Pineys"–long-term inhabitants of the area–may construct a new home under certain conditions. The remainder of the Pinelands– the "protection area"–is divided into (1) Forest Areas, (2) Agricultural Protection Areas, (3) Regional Growth Areas, and (4) Rural Development Areas. Additional areas are designated as Pinelands Towns and Villages and for military purposes.

A key feature of the plan is the transfer of development rights (TDR) from the inner restricted areas to peripheral locations where growth is encouraged. This plan allows owners of restricted land to sell "Pineland Development Credits" (PDCs) to developers in designated Regional Growth Areas at a specified ratio. For example, one dwelling unit credit may be sold for each 39 acres of upland owned in the Preservation Area, and two credits for an equivalent area in the Agricultural Production Areas. For wetlands, credits are only one-fifth of the upland levels. It is estimated that as many as 24,000 units of housing could be built in the Growth Areas through transfers of credits from restricted areas of the Pinelands, in addition to 86,000 units otherwise permitted to be built in the Growth Areas. Another 74,000 new units are permitted among the designated Pinelands Towns and Villages.

To facilitate the sale of PDCs, two clearinghouses have been established: the State Pinelands Development Credit Bank and the Burlington County Pinelands Development Credit Exchange. PDCs may also be sold privately between property owners in the appropriate zones. As of September 1989, 21 development projects using PDCs were approved or constructed in Pinelands Growth Areas, with another 29 developments proposed (*The Pinelander* 1989).

One of the drafters of the Pinelands Plan, Richard F. Babcock, reports that despite continuing opposition in certain parts of the region, "the CMP has been by all accounts a great success." As evidence of this success he notes that 96 percent of all development subsequent to the Plan's adoption has been located in areas designated for growth, and as of 1985 no litigation against the Plan had been filed (Babcock and Siemon, 156). Also by that time, 36 municipalities and four counties had amended their local zoning and were certified as conforming with the Plan. Babcock credits the professionalism and responsiveness of the Commission staff for the relatively smooth transition to the new era of land planning and control in the Pinelands.

Special-Issue State Programs

The progress of state-level land use controls noted by Popper (1988) and DeGrove and Stroud (1987) has appeared more widely in state laws focused on specific management issues than in those focused on specific geographic regions. For every Pinelands-type regional management program, there are dozens of state laws that address generic issues or clusters of issues. Principal examples are laws concerning farmland preservation, coastal zone management, wetland and floodplain management, housing, siting of large-scale facilities, and the disposal of solid and hazardous wastes. These of course have a geographic dimension to the extent that all land use laws affect land somewhere. But rather than circumscribing the state program within a specially defined subarea of the state, to the exclusion of other areas with substantially similar problems, issue-focused laws apply wherever such issues arise.

States differ as to the comprehensiveness and administration of their land use laws. As mentioned earlier, a few states have land use statutes that are relatively comprehensive, covering many issues within the review process mandated by a single law and administrative process. Thus Vermont's Act 250 requires review of developments falling within its purview in terms of water supply, soil erosion, highway congestion, schools, governmental services, aesthetics, and historic preservation, among other matters (Healy and Rosenberg 1979, 45). Florida's State and Regional Planning Act of 1984 established a statewide planning framework keyed to a legislatively adopted state comprehensive plan. The plan is "a relatively concise statement of goals and policies for 25 major state issues ranging from problems of the elderly to protection of property rights to transportation issues" (DeGrove and Stroud 1987, 7). Regional and local plans are required to conform to the state plan, as are state functional plans including the State Water Use Plan and the State Land Development Plan.

Far more numerous are state laws that address land use issues selectively rather than comprehensively. All 50 states have statutes of this nature, which are most readily found and compared in the Bureau of National Affairs *Environmental Law Reporter*. Many such laws have been adopted in response to or in imitation of federal legislation, as, for instance, the several states with environmental impact laws modeled on the National Environmental Policy Act (NEPA). Others have been passed in response to a severe state problem and/or at the insistence of a strong governor. For instance, both factors applied to the adoption of New Jersey's Fair Housing and State Planning Act in 1985.

Agricultural Land Protection

One frequent area of state attention since 1960 has been the issue of protecting agricultural land from urbanization. The most widespread response has been to alleviate the burden of state and local taxes that might otherwise force a landowner to sell farmland prematurely. According to Furuseth and Pierce (1982, Table 8), 42 states (and five Canadian Provinces) have adopted some form of preferential assessment or deferred payment of property taxes on productive farmland in locations subject to development pressures. Twenty-eight states have provided some form of relief from state inheritance taxes to avoid forcing farmland to be sold at the death of its owner.

Certain states or counties have established programs for the direct pur-chase of farmland development rights–for example, Massachusetts, Con-necticut, New Jersey, Maryland, and California, as well as Suffolk County, New York and King County, Washington. These programs involve the appropriation of funds to acquire development rights at a negotiated price from interested farm owners. The latter continue to own the land and may, but are not compelled to, continue farming it. It may be sold subject to the agricultural restriction, as with other forms of transfer of development rights. Selection criteria are imposed by the state in terms of land quality, location, and productivity.

Agricultural districts and zoning are additional techniques used in a few states. New York since 1969 has authorized counties to establish, upon petition of farmland owners, "agricultural districts" within which public projects that facilitate development are discouraged and a variety of other farmland protection measures apply. Districts have included as much as one million acres of New York farmland. Maryland also has uti-lized the district approach on a farmer-initiated basis. Building and zon-ing regulations are relaxed on farm-related activities within districts in exchange for a commitment by owners to maintain their land in agricul-ture for at least five years (Furuseth and Pierce, 64). California has employed both agricultural districts and agricultural zoning. Exclusive agricultural zoning has also been extensively used under Oregon's state land use planning program.

Floodplains, Wetlands, and Coastal Areas

Floodplain, wetland, and coastal zone management share considerable geographic overlap, yet are administratively fragmented at both the fed-eral and state levels. Furthermore, states differ greatly in their particular approaches to each of the three areas. Generalizations and comparisons of state programs are difficult.

A recent survey of state regulations for riverine floodplains (L. R. Johnston Associates 1989, Table 11-3) found remarkable diversity among approaches. Twenty-six states reported that they restrict new development in designated floodways, either directly or through local conformity to state standards. Nine states define "floodways" more restrictively than the federal NFIP standards. Twenty states regulate building in the "floodway fringe" (balance of the 100-year floodplain), and 18 impose state-level building construction standards in floodplains. Sixteen states however reported having none of the foregoing measures at the state level, although most provide technical assistance to local floodplain management activities. The same survey disclosed comparable diversity among states with respect to coastal and lakeshore flooding.

State wetland laws date back to the early 1960s and may be very complex within even a single state. Massachusetts, for instance, has a wetland protection law regulating both inland and coastal wetlands through review of development proposals by local conservation commissions. Greater control is provided through separate coastal and inland wetland restriction laws under which Massachusetts may limit all development of designated areas through a recorded restriction. The latter approach has been primarily applied to certain coastal salt marshes and only rarely to freshwater wetlands.

At least 17 states have some form of coastal wetland program, mostly requiring permits to be obtained from the state or local authorities for disturbance of such areas (Mitsch and Gosselink 1986). Some 25 states are reported to have laws that directly or indirectly regulate the alteration of inland wetlands. The relationship between state wetland laws and the federal Section 404 wetlands program is not easy to define. In a few states, formal agreements exist between the state wetlands program and the Army Corps of Engineers for joint application and review procedures. Under certain circumstances, the Corps may defer to the state determination in wetland regulation. But often, developers and landowners must obtain both federal and state permits, necessitating both delay and expense.

Some 29 coastal states and territories participate in the federal Coastal Zone Management Program to be discussed in Chapter 12. To be approved for federal funding, state coastal plans must provide some form of state-level control over significant coastal development decisions. Some states such as California and North Carolina accomplish this through comprehensive state coastal laws. Others piece together a network of specialized statutes, regulations, and executive orders. Some of these involve the flood hazard and wetland programs already mentioned. Other objects of state coastal planning include recreation and public access, pollution abatement, economic development, protection of endangered species and other wildlife habitat, commercial and sport fisheries, and navigability.

To accomplish these objectives, states employ several types of development controls including permit requirements, detailed review of large projects, specialized regulations for critical areas, mitigation of wetland loss, land acquisition, and the promotion of particular types of development. At least 11 states have seized the initiative by adopting their own erosion setback regulations (National Research Council 1990; Platt et al. 1992). North Carolina, a leader among coastal state programs, requires new homes to be set back a distance at least equal to 30 times the average annual erosion rate (AAER) and larger structures 60 times that rate (Owens 1985). The 30-year AAER standard has also been applied by Florida, Michigan, Rhode Island, and New York.

South Carolina has adopted a 40-year AAER standard, which posed a substantial problem for owners of shorefront homes destroyed by Hurricane Hugo in 1989 and was subsequently weakened by amendment (Platt, Beatley, and Miller 1991). The South Carolina Beachfront Management Act of 1988 was the subject of the *Lucas* case discussed in Chapter 8. While its application to the property owner was ultimately held to be a "taking," the act itself was not challenged and remains in effect.

Metropolitan and Regional Planning

Before the 1950s, metropolitan and regional planning was generally a nongovernmental activity. Two leading examples included Daniel Burnham's 1909 "Plan for Chicago" sponsored by the Commercial Club of Chicago and the 1929 plan for Greater New York prepared by the Regional Plan Association.

In the 1930s, the National Resources Planning Board (NRPB) promoted state and regional comprehensive planning:

> During the period of its existence the NRPB was in the forefront of promoting and developing regional planning. Among the difficult problems, never fully resolved then or later, were how to define a "region"—by natural features, such as river systems, or by economic interests; whether to follow or to disregard state boundaries;

whether to have regions for all purposes follow the same boundaries, and other problems. In its own work, the NRPB used "flexible" boundaries, the exact contours depending upon different
activities.

Clawson 1981, p. 167.

Generally, the concept of region as used by the New Deal planning
boards entailed interstate or subnational units. Regional planning commissions were established for groups of states such as New England and
the Pacific Northwest. A principal function of these commissions was to
plan and coordinate the flow of federal funds and activities within the
regions in question. A closely related initiative was the formation of state
planning boards in nearly every state between 1933 and 1936. Some of
these bodies continue to the present while others have been abolished.
The NRPB itself was abolished in 1943 by Congress, which was frustrated by years of the Executive Branch meddling with its prerogatives.

Section 701 Plans

Although planning was sometimes equated with "communism" (Cassella
1983, 20), Congress paradoxically at the height of the McCarthy Era
enacted Section 701 of the Housing Act of 1954, the nation's first comprehensive planning assistance law. Section 701 authorized "planning
grants to state, metropolitan, and other regional planning agencies . . .
to encourage comprehensive planning, including transportation planning, for states, cities, counties, metropolitan areas and urban regions,
and the establishment and development of the organizational units
needed therefor."

During the 27 years of the program's existence, annual federal appro-
priations for local planning assistance increased from $1 million to $100
million; by the time the program ended in 1981, it had allocated more
than $1 billion to local planning (Feiss 1985, 175). The 701 program nur-
tured a generation of plans and planners.

To the extent that it supported local planning, Section 701 reinforced
rather than resisted the dominance of localism in land use control. But it
was supplemented by the Housing Act of 1959 which supported the
preparation of comprehensive plans at the metropolitan, regional, state,
and interstate levels (Brooks 1988, 243). The precedent was thereby
established for federal support of nonfederal planning at various scales

that would later characterize the Coastal Zone Management Program and other federal initiatives of the 1970s.

Regional Clearinghouses

The 1954 Housing Act (Section 204) also established a new procedure for "regional clearinghouse" review of federal spending actions. This required that requests from local governments and other applicants for federal assistance under several dozen funding programs be reviewed by "an areawide agency which is designated to perform metropolitan regional planning for the area . . ." Each state was to designate an "areawide agency" within each metropolitan region. These were of two principal types: regional planning agencies (RPAs) and councils of governments (COGs).

RPAs are established under state law as quasi-governmental entities that may hire staff, enter into contracts, and advise governments within their planning area on a variety of issues–for example, transportation, housing, land use, open space, sewer and water services, education, and elderly services. Local governments appoint representatives to serve on the RPA advisory body. By contrast, COGs are actually assemblies of elected officials (or their representatives) from constituent local and county governments. COGs perform the same planning functions as RPAs but may exert more influence over the actions of local governments due to the direct involvement of elected officials. Neither type of planning organization normally has taxation or land acquisition powers. Their funds are derived from constituent governments and from federal, state, and private support.

The regional clearinghouse function, until its demise in 1981, provided both RPAs and COGs with a modest degree of political leverage. As a clearinghouse, the regional agency would evaluate local requests for federal assistance in terms of compatibility with the agency's regional comprehensive plan. A negative recommendation from the regional agency was not binding on the federal government but could be used to achieve modification or even cancellation of local projects. This function became known as the "A-95 Areawide Review Process," after the federal directive which implemented it.

By 1979, some 39 distinct federal programs were financially supporting and/or requiring regional planning (McDowell 1983, 31). In 1980, regional planning organizations (mostly COGs) served about 99 percent of the counties in the nation with about three-fourths of their collective budgets provided by the federal government. By the late 1980s, budgets for many of these agencies were drastically reduced due to withdrawal of federal funding. Many agencies survive on funding for special-issue studies such as solid and hazardous waste management, water supply, and transportation.

Appalachian Regional Commission

The Appalachian Regional Commission (ARC) was established by the Appalachian Redevelopment Act of 1965, an element of President Lyndon Johnson's War on Poverty. The geographic area defined as the "Appalachian Region" encompasses all of the State of West Virginia and portions of 12 other states extending from New York to Mississippi. (Figure 10-3). This area covers 397 counties, with a total land area of 195,000 square miles. The population of the region in 1986 was 20.6 million people. (For a detailed discussion of the ARC, see Bradshaw 1992.)

Physical conditions and resource management issues that led to the designation of the Appalachian Region include its steep, rugged terrain, poor soil, widespread erosion, flash flood hazards, physical isolation, water pollution, mine surface subsidence, acid mine drainage, and unstable mining waste tips. Social problems as of 1960 included the following:

- One-third of families below poverty level
- Average per capita income one-third below national level
- Unemployment 40 percent above national level
- High school completed by 32 out of 100 adults
- College completed by 5 out of 100 adults
- Substandard housing twice the national average
- Infant mortality one-third higher than national average
- Two-thirds the number of doctors as compared with the nation as a whole
- Infectious disease mortality 33 percent above national average
- Widespread incidence of black lung disease
- Net loss of population from the region due to out-migration
- Erratic economic swings
- Stagnant and dying industries

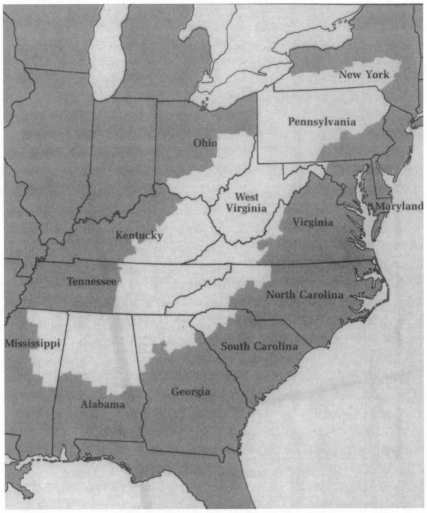

FIGURE 10-3   Territory of the Appalachian Regional Commission.

- Exportation of capital to nonresident owners accompanied by non-reinvestment in the region

The Appalachian Regional Commission is a unique federal–state entity, not a federal agency. Its executive board consists of the governors of the 13 Appalachian states, plus a federal cochairperson. Decisions of the commission must be approved by unanimous vote of the foregoing. The commission has an executive director and a small staff of about 55 employees. Its office is located in Washington, D.C. Its administrative budget is shared half by the federal government and half by the 13 states.

The raison d'être of the ARC is to focus federal and state funds upon the economic, social, and environmental upgrading of the Appalachian Region. The keystone of its program has been the planning and partial construction of some 4200 miles of new four-lane highways. These were needed both to reduce internal isolation within the region and to facilitate the movement of goods and services to and from the region. In 1960, only a single major highway, the Pennsylvania Turnpike, traversed the Appalachian Region from east to west. Two-thirds of the planned Appalachian Highway System has now been completed, at a cost of over $5 billion (75 percent federal; 25 percent state).

Aside from highway construction, the ARC has promoted diverse objectives in the region, for example:

- Public health—local health clinics, hospital improvements, expansion of medical staffs

- Education—upgrade of local schools, colleges, and vocational schools

- Environment—reduction of air and water pollution, acid mine drainage, solid waste management

- Natural hazards—mitigation of flash flood and landslide hazards

- Housing—new construction and renovation of existing housing stock

- Community development—better sewer and park systems

Decision making regarding the location and form of ARC activities is decentralized. Priorities are proposed in annual plans prepared by each state for approval by the commission. The Appalachian portion of each member state is subdivided into "local development districts" consisting of one or more counties. Altogether, there are 69 local development districts designated by states, which cover the entire Appalachian Region. These local districts have planning staff and play a key role in helping to formulate the ARC annual plan within their respective states.

ARC takes credit for promoting a significant upgrading of economic, social, and environmental conditions in the Appalachian Region. Some 430,000 new jobs have been created in the region along or near highways, of which 214,000 jobs are in manufacturing and the rest in service industries, transportation, or commerce. Sixty percent of new manufacturing plants in the region have located within 30 minutes of existing or proposed new highways.

The commission has promoted the conversion of cutover woodlands and marginal croplands to pasture and has cooperated with the Soil Conservation Service in promoting land stabilization and erosion control, and reforestation. It has initiated a mine-related hazards program and helped to win support for adoption of the 1977 Federal Surface Mine Reclamation Act. It has reduced flood hazards through installation of automated flash flood warning systems, channel clearance projects, and relocation of some chronically flood-prone properties. (Ninety-nine ARC counties are also within the jurisdiction of the Tennessee Valley Authority, which administers a local floodplain management assistance program.) ARC has also promoted the establishment of new industrial parks and has encouraged an inflow of venture capital and modernization of existing manufacturing and mining facilities. It has facilitated the development of new water, sewer, and solid waste facilities in mining communities, rapidly changing communities, and backward rural areas.

River Basin Commissions

A different experiment with federally sponsored regional planning was conducted under authority of the Water Resources Planning Act of 1965. This Act established the U.S. Water Resources Council (WRC) as a central clearinghouse in Washington, D.C. on which all federal water management agencies were represented. WRC between 1966 and its termination in 1981 made significant contributions to the methodology of water resource planning in the United States by government agencies. In particular, it designated the "100-year flood" (or 1 percent flood) as the standard "design event" for purposes of the National Flood Insurance Program. (See Chapter 12.) WRC also promulgated "Principles and Standards" for water resources planning which, for the first time, placed environmental consequences on an equal footing with economic impacts as criteria for the approval of federal water resources projects.

Title II of the Water Resources Planning Act authorized the creation of federal–state river basin commissions on the initiative of the states sharing jurisdiction over specific river basins. Six commissions were established under this authority: (1) New England, (2) Ohio River, (3) Great Lakes, (4) Upper Mississippi River, (5) Missouri River, and (6) Pacific-Northwest rivers. (These did not include other river basin commissions established under interstate compacts—for example, the Delaware, the Susquehanna, and the Colorado.)

The primary purpose of the Title II river basin commissions was to prepare plans at various levels of detail for the management of the water resources and associated lands within their respective regions. The problems studied by the commissions varied according to the hydrology and settlement characteristics of their respective basins. The New England River Basins Commission devoted much effort to studies of nonstructural floodplain management in the Connecticut River, to reduction of coastal storm hazards, and to low-head hydropower development. The Great Lakes Basin Commission was more concerned with water quality and shoreline erosion, while the Missouri RBC addressed issues relating to irrigation and navigability.

Studies prepared by each commission were funded jointly by federal and state governments and were overseen by the Water Resources Council. Unlike the Tennessee Valley Authority, the RBCs were given no power to implement their proposals. Upon their termination in 1981, the policy recommendations that they made were left to the federal, state, and local governments to pursue or to ignore.

Conclusion

States, long viewed as retarded and useless participants in the process of public land use control, have assumed a variety of roles, powers, and functions since the 1960s. They have rightly served as the lead level of government on agricultural land protection. They have responded creatively to federal incentives in coastal zone management. They have performed tolerably, and in some cases very effectively, as managers of wetlands and floodplains. "Nation-states" such as California, Florida, and New York operate a galaxy of land-related programs. Amenity-oriented states such as Vermont, Oregon, and Maine have carved out enduring state land use control functions, albeit less ambitious and effective than early "quiet revolutionaries" had hoped.

New Jersey has demonstrated that even states that are not bastions of environmentalism may engage in state land planning as in the Pinelands, the Hackensack Meadowlands, and in its fair housing and coastal laws. Other states also have served as laboratories for innovation in land use control, as in the case of coastal erosion setbacks. While often accused of being handmaidens to the federal government and neglectful parents of local governments, it is clear that many states are land use managers to be reckoned with.

Regional planning has followed a roller-coaster course during the postwar period, with its ups and downs closely related to federal priorities and funding.

References

American Law Institute. 1975. *A Model Land Development Code*. Philadelphia: American Law Institute.

Babcock, R.F., and C.L. Siemon. 1985. *The Zoning Game Revisited*. Boston: Oelgeschlager, Gunn, and Hain.

Bosselman, F., and D. Callies. 1971. *The Quiet Revolution in Land Use Control*. Washington, D.C.: U.S. Government Printing Office.

Bradshaw, M. 1992. *The Appalachian Regional Commission: Twenty-Five Years of Government Policy*. Lexington: The University of Kentucky Press.

Brooks, M.P. 1988. "Four Critical Junctures in the History of the Urban Planning Profession." *Journal of the American Planning Association* 54(2): 241–248.

Cassella, W.N., Jr. 1983. "Regional Planning and Governance: History and Politics." In *Regional Planning: Evolution, Crisis and Prospects*. G.C. Lim, ed. Totowa, NJ: Allanheld, Osmun.

Clawson, M. 1981. *New Deal Planning: The NRPB*. Baltimore: The Johns Hopkins University Press for Resources For the Future.

Conservation Foundation. 1987. *State of the Environment: A View Toward the Nineties*. Washington, D.C.: Conservation Foundation.

DeGrove, J.M. 1984. *Land Growth and Politics*. Chicago: American Planning Association Planners Press.

DeGrove, J.M., and N.E. Stroud. 1987. "State Land Planning and Regulation: Innovative Roles in the 1980s and Beyond." *Land Use Law* (March): 3–8.

Feiss, C. 1985. "The Foundations of Federal Planning Assistance." *Journal of the American Planning Association* 51 (2): 175–184.

Furuseth, O.J., and J.T. Pierce. 1982. *Agricultural Land in an Urban Society*. Washington, D.C.: Association of American Geographers.

Healy, R.G., and J.S. Rosenberg. 1979. *Land Use and the States* 2nd ed. Baltimore: Johns Hopkins Press for Resources For the Future.

Healy, R.G., and J.A. Zinn. 1985. "Environment and Development Conflicts in Coastal Zone Management." *Journal of the American Planning Association* 51(3): 299–311.

L.R. Johnston Associates. 1989. *A Status Report on the Nation's Floodplain Management Activity.* (Mimeo)

McDowell, B.D. 1983. "The Federal Role in Regional Planning: Past and Present." In *Regional Planning: Evolution, Crisis, and Prospects.* G. C. Lim, ed. Totowa, NJ: Allanheld, Osmun.

McPhee, J. 1968. *The Pine Barrens.* New York: Farrar, Straus & Giroux.

Mitsch, W.J., and J.G. Gosselink. 1986. *Wetlands.* New York: Van Nostrand Reinhold.

Nash, R.N. 1982. *Wilderness and the American Mind* 3rd ed. New Haven: Yale University Press.

National Research Council. 1990. *Managing Coastal Erosion.* Washington: National Academy Press.

Owens, D.W. 1985. "Coastal Management in North Carolina: Building a Regional Consensus." *Journal of the American Planning Association.* 51(3): 322–329.

Pinelander. 1989. "PDC Sales Good News for Landowners." 9(2): 2.

Pinelands Commission. 1989. *A Brief History of the New Jersey Pinelands and the Pinelands Comprehensive Development Plan.* (Mimeo)

Platt, R.H., H.C. Miller, T. Beatley, J. Melville, and B.G. Mathenia. 1992. *Coastal Erosion: Has Retreat Sounded?* Program on Environment and Behavior Monograph No. 53. Boulder: University of Colorado Institute of Behavioral Science.

Platt, R.H., T. Beatley, and H.C. Miller. 1991. "The Folly at Folly Beach and Other Failings of U.S. Coastal Erosion Policy." *Environment* 33(9): 6–9; 25–32.

Popper, F.J. 1988. "Understanding American Land Use Regulation Since 1970." *Journal of the American Planning Association* 54(3): 291–301.

Reilly, W. K., ed. 1973. *The Use of Land: A Citizen's Guide to Urban Growth.* New York: Thomas Y. Crowell.

CHAPTER 11

The Federal Lands:
Policies in Conflict

Introduction

The federal government of the United States owns outright about 730 million acres, or about one-third of the nation's total land and water area. This vast expanse, about the size of India, is unevenly distributed spatially. Alaska alone accounts for about 313 million acres; the balance is predominantly located in the lightly settled mountain and arid regions of the western states. Several states are substantially owned by the federal government—for example, Alaska (96 percent), Nevada (86 percent), Utah (66 percent), Idaho (63 percent), and Oregon (52 percent). Federal ownership east of the Rocky Mountains is much sparser, although most land west of the Appalachians was at one time federally owned. This chapter reviews the history and policy conflicts that have characterized management of the federal lands since the nation's founding.

The Public Domain

The vast majority of federal lands, past and present, belong to what is known as the "public domain." The public domain consists of lands that came into federal ownership in massive transfers by virtue of cession or purchase from states or a foreign nation. Excluded from the public domain are federal lands acquired by purchase or gift from private owners, as has occurred in many locations since 1960. The distinction between public domain and other federal land lies in legal technicalities: For the sake of simplicity, this discussion uses the terms "public domain" and "federal lands" interchangeably.

At the end of the Revolutionary War, the United States extended from the Atlantic to the Mississippi River, excluding Florida and the Gulf Coast, which still belonged to Spain and France. Several of the newly formed states fringed the eastern seaboard but claimed territories extending westward as far as the Mississippi. But in settlement of war debts, seven states between 1784 and 1786 ceded their claims to lands beyond the Appalachians to the national government. Thus began the public domain, and the nation's founders faced a literal embarrassment of (land) riches:

> It seems paradoxical on the face of it that a Congress too poor to own and maintain a capital, too weak to protect itself from the insults of a band of ragged mutineers, should yet be concerned with the disposal of a vast domain of over 220,000 [actually 370,000] square miles of the richest of virgin soil.   Treat 1962, p. 7.

As if this were not enough, Thomas Jefferson's Louisiana Purchase in 1803 added another 831,000 square miles, extending the nation's western limit to the Continental Divide (western boundary of the Mississippi-Missouri drainage system). This acquisition doubled the territory of the nation and tripled the public domain (Clawson 1983, 17). Later territorial cessions and purchases further expanded the public domain, which peaked in 1867 with the acquisition of Alaska. At one time or another, 1800 million acres (2.8 million square miles) have belonged to the public domain, of which 730 million acres remain today (Figure 11-1). The disposal of nearly 1100 million acres clearly was the dominant feature of federal land management until the late 19th century.

Disposal

The fate of the vast empire of unsettled public land was substantially influenced by the Land Ordinance of 1785, the most important act of the short-lived Confederation. Its chief contribution was to establish the rectangular Federal Land Survey as a means of organizing the

FIGURE II-I   Map of federal lands of the coterminous United States. Dark shaded areas are National Forests and National Parks. Light shaded areas in western states are administered by the Bureau of Land Management. *Source:* Public Land Law Review Commission.

management, disposition, and use of the new public domain. From its "point of beginning" in 1785 where the Ohio River crosses the western boundary of Pennsylvania, the federal survey has imposed its grid on the nation's hinterland to the Pacific Ocean, as far west as the Aleutian Islands, and as far south as Key West. It ultimately covered all of the continental United States except for the original 13 states, three states carved out of them (West Virginia, Kentucky, Tennessee), Texas, and parts of Ohio. (See technical description and diagram of the federal survey in Chapter 4.)

The Land Ordinance and its survey thus prepared the way for disposition and settlement of the federal lands, initially the Northwest Territories of Ohio, Indiana, Illinois, Michigan, Wisconsin, and part of Minnesota. But the federal objectives in disposing of its land were by no means settled. Competing policies advocated by Thomas Jefferson and Alexander Hamilton, respectively, proposed (1) disposal free of charge or for a modest fee to promote agrarian settlement and a buffer against Indian or foreign attack and (2) disposal at a significant price to augment the nation's meager cash reserves. The debate was further complicated by a schism within the "settlement school" between those advocating the New England pattern whereby towns were settled incrementally on the edge of the already consolidated territory versus the plantation model of extensive settlement of large units, widely spaced from each other (Treat 1962).

The Land Ordinance compromised between the Jefferson and Hamilton proposals. Settlement on the New England plan was served by the requirement that land be precisely surveyed prior to sale and that it be conveyed in parcels of 640 acres (one section) or fractions thereof, reasonably suited to agricultural settlement, at least in the Midwest. The revenue objective was served by a requirement that land be sold at public auction with a "substantial" minimum price of $1 per acre (raised in 1796 to $2!).

The disposition issue was not, however, settled by this apparently equitable solution. According to Hibbard (1965), the land disposal situation in 1800 was complicated by several factors: (1) granting of free lands to veterans of the Revolutionary War; (2) conveyance of large tracts to private companies for resale to settlers; and (3) speculation by persons who bought land cheaply from either of the two preceding classes of recipients and resold it below the prevailing federal market price. These factors undermined the revenue objective since relatively little land was purchased directly from the federal government.

An additional complication was the prevalence of illegal squatters who entered and settled federal land without any legal title. Technically law breakers, these pioneers epitomized the westward movement. During the early decades of the 19th century, support increased among northern and "western" states to grant a *right of preemption* to such settlers— that is, to allow them to buy the land for a token price before speculators could bid. The southern states through their spokesman Henry Clay opposed preemption on the ground that it would reward illegal conduct (and incidentally foster settlement from nonslave parts of the country). The Preemption Act of 1841 awarded the right to purchase 160 acres at $1.25 per acre without competition. While technically still a revenue measure, it further undermined the principle of sale to the highest bidder (Hibbard 1965).

The revenue policy was further eroded by wholesale Congressional land grants to many kinds of recipients during the mid-19th century, including public improvement companies, states, and land grant schools (Table 11-1). Grants for public improvements, including canals, national roads, and railroads, totaled 125 million acres, and grants to states for various purposes eventually totaled 328 million acres. The railroad grants, which foreshadowed contemporary grants in aid for economic development, conveyed land in a checkerboard of square-mile sections. Alternate sections were conveyed and retained within several miles of the proposed right of way. It was expected that the retained sections would become more valuable due to demand generated by access to the

TABLE 11-1   Disposition of the Public Domain
(million acres)

Total Public Domain (1781–1867)		1837
Minus: Grants to States	328	
Grants to Railroads	94	
Grants to Homesteaders	287	
Other Grants	435	
Total Dispositions (1803–1975)		1144
Remaining Public Domain (1975)		693

Source: Bureau of Land Management 1975, Tables 2 and 3.

railroad. But most settlers bought land (often to their grief) from the railroad itself and once again, hopes of revenue proved illusory.

The threadbare revenue objective was largely abandoned with the passage of the Homestead Act in 1862. After decades of controversy, the Act was finally adopted upon the secession of the southern states from the Union. It provided that settlers would receive clear title to 160 acres upon filing a claim and living on the land for a period of five years. The new policy was claimed as a victory by the western states, who foresaw a massive influx of new settlers. Statistically, it appeared to have this effect: During the decade 1870–1880, some 140,000 claims were filed involving 16 million acres of land (Hibbard 1965, 396). Altogether, nearly 300 million acres have been conveyed under the Homestead Act.

But the results were often tragic. Gates (1962) notes that during the decade following adoption of the Homestead Act, Congress granted vast areas to railroads, which they could resell to subsidize the costs of constructing a rail line through unsettled territory. This land, by definition, was the most accessible to rail service; remaining homestead sites were likely to be more isolated and of lesser quality than valley lands favored by the railroads. Furthermore, 160 acres was simply insufficient to support a family in the arid West without access to irrigation. The homily that "rainfall follows the plow" proved to be a public relations myth perpetrated by railroads and land speculators. Homesteaders either had to obtain additional land, legally or illegally, or starve. No one has described the plight of the two million homesteaders better than Wallace Stegner (1953/1982, 220–221):

> Suppose a pioneer tried. Suppose he did (most couldn't) get together enough money to bring his family out to Dakota or Nebraska, or Kansas or Colorado. Suppose he did (most couldn't) get a loan big enough to let him build the dwelling demanded by the [Homestead] law, buy a team and a sodbuster plow. . . . Suppose he and his family endured the sun and glare on their treeless prairie, and were not demolished by the cyclones that swept across the plains like great scythes. Suppose they found fuel in a fuelless country . . . and sat out the blizzards and the loneliness of their tundra-like home. Suppose they resisted cabin fever, and their family affection withstood the hard fare and the isolation, and suppose they emerged into spring again. It would be like emerging from a cave.

Spring would enchant them with crocus and primrose and prairies green as meadows. It might also break their hearts and spirits if it browned into summer drouth.

Land continued to move out of the public domain at an incredible pace during the late 19th to early 20th century. Of 1.3 billion acres in the public domain in 1850, about half were distributed to individuals by 1909 either for a price or as a free grant. Another 11 percent were granted to states for various purposes (Hibbard 1965, 529). Accompanying this massive change of ownership was much fraud and misuse of lands obtained for particular purposes. For instance, lands conveyed on condition of physical improvement by the recipient in the form of drainage, irrigation, or timber planting were frequently never used as specified. But according to Marion Clawson (1983, 25):

> The process of land disposal was a lusty affair—a headlong, even precipitous process, full of frauds and deceits, but one which transformed a great deal of land into valuable private property—and one which built a nation. Historians, political scientists, conservationists and others have frequently criticized the speed, disorder, fraud, and other undesirable features of the long disposal process. If the process had been slower, with more opportunity to learn from experience, some mistakes possibly could have been avoided. But would even worse consequences have ensued?

Retention

At the very peak of the disposal binge during the last third of the 19th century, a new conflict regarding the public domain was emerging, namely, between *disposal* and *retention* of federal lands. Prior to the Civil War, there seemed to be consensus at least that federal land should be conveyed, not retained. But by the 1860s, the effects of profligate squandering of the nation's natural resources were becoming inescapable. According to Steward Udall (1963, 66): "It was the intoxicating profusion of the American continent which induced a state of mind that made waste and plunder inevitable."

The lumber industry moved rapidly westward from Maine to

Minnesota, and on to the Pacific Northwest, stripping forests and leaving a wasteland. This in turn caused soil erosion that clogged streams and lakes. In the Rocky Mountains and California, mining fever drew thousands of fortune seekers from the East. Like the lumber industry, mining severely damaged the natural environment and left behind a swath of abandoned "boom towns," denuded hill slopes, and debris-clogged streams. The pursuit of oil and gas in the late 19th century caused equivalent devastation to many areas in the Southwest.

In 1864, George Perkins Marsh, an inquisitive Vermonter, published a seminal treatise: *Man and Nature Or, Physical Geography as Modified by Human Action* (Marsh 1864/1965). In company with Chadwick, Olmsted, and (later) Howard, Marsh was a paragon of the 19th century "versatile amateur" tradition. Lacking formal training in natural science or geography, Marsh produced the first and one of the most celebrated studies of human impacts on the natural environment. According to Lowenthal (1965, ix):

Few books have had more impact on the way men view and use land. Appearing at the peak of American confidence in the inexhaustibility of resources, it was the first book to controvert the myth of superabundance and to spell out the need for reform.... *Man and Nature* was indeed "the fountainhead of the conservation movement."

Marsh was inspired by the contemporary German geographers Alexander von Humboldt and Carl Ritter, whose research on human alteration of natural regions underlay the subsequent development of geographical inquiry in Europe and the United States (Hartshorne 1939). Marsh traveled and read widely, recording evidence, particularly from European history, of deforestation, soil erosion, loss of biological diversity, and hydrologic alteration. He related his findings with a normative, even moralistic tone that anticipated the rhetoric of the environmental movement a century later:

Man has too long forgotten that the earth was given to him for usufruct alone, not for consumption, still less for profligate waste ...
Man everywhere is a disturbing agent. Wherever he plants his food,

the harmonies of nature are turned to discords. The proportions and accommodations which insured the stability of existing arrangements are overthrown. Indigenous vegetable and animal species are extirpated, and supplanted by others of foreign origin, . . . Of all organic beings, man alone is to be regarded as essentially a destructive power . . . [against which] nature . . . is wholly impotent.

Marsh, p. 36.

Marsh's plea joined a growing chorus of lamentation against the despoliation of the nation's natural resources. It served as scientific counterpoint to the romantic yearning for a vanishing America expressed in the great Hudson River School paintings of Thomas Cole, Frederick Church, and Albert Bierstadt; the bird paintings of John James Audubon; the poetry of William Cullen Bryant, Emily Dickenson, and Henry Wadsworth Longfellow; the essays of Henry David Thoreau and Ralph Waldo Emerson; and the novels of Nathanial Hawthorne and James Fenimore Cooper (White and White 1962; Nash 1982; Stewart 1995).

In the 1880s John Muir, the wilderness mystic of the Sierra Nevada, began to fan the flames of public indignation. From his base in San Francisco, he divided his time between treks into the mountains (where he allegedly relished climbing tall trees during thunderstorms) and courting the eastern establishment through essays, poems, and lectures (Fox 1981). In 1891 he founded the Sierra Club, and his influence peaked in the Hetch Hetchy dispute two decades later.

A very different voice from the West was that of Major John Wesley Powell, one-armed geologist, geographer, ethnologist, and exemplar of scientist in service to government. Powell gained fame for his explorations of the Grand Canyon of the Colorado River in 1869 and 1871. These were followed by survey expeditions through the Colorado Plateau and the arid regions of the Columbia, Rio Grande, and Missouri river basins. His 1878 *Report on the Lands of the Arid Region* and subsequent reports of the U.S. Geological Survey (USGS), (of which he was the second director) documented the unworkability of existing national policy toward disposition of the public domain in arid areas (Stegner 1953/1982). Powell advocated the need to organize human use of western land in relation to its physical limitations, especially water. He urged that allocation of public land be based, not on political determinations in Washington, but rather on scientific appraisal of the physical resources of the area in question. The USGS topographic map system was initiated under his direction.

Powell's advocacy of large-scale dams and irrigation projects, which served as a blueprint for the future work of the Bureau of Reclamation and the Army Corps of Engineers in the West, earned Powell the disdain of today's environmentalists (e.g., Reisner 1986). But his criticism of prevailing national policies lent authority to arguments against heedless disposal of the public domain. And his insistence on a scientific basis for government decisions regarding land anticipated the modern practice of environmental impact assessment.

Gradually, the diverse voices of Marsh, Muir, Powell, and others collectively eroded the political viability of disposal per se as the public land policy. As perception of the impact of human actions on natural resources changed, so too, eventually, did the laws and policies governing such actions.

The beginning of a new *retention* philosophy may be dated to the establishment of Yellowstone Park by Congress in 1872. With spectacular scenery, lakes, water falls, wilderness, hot springs, and geysers, this two million acre preserve, carved out of the public domain, remains one of the nation's leading national parks. It was to be an exemplar for the national parks of the United States and the world (Nash 1982, 108).

This was followed in 1891 by federal legislation establishing "forest reserves," under which 40 million acres were withdrawn from the public domain. This was the beginning of the national forests, which today total 187 million acres. Also in 1891, New York State established its Adirondack Forest Preserve to be "kept forever as wild forest lands" (Nash 1982). (Much of the 6-million-acre Adirondack Park today remains in private ownership, however, with considerable development in progress: Kunstler 1989; McMartin 1994.)

Conservation fervor in the early 20th century yielded two additional federal land preservation programs. In 1903, the National Wildlife Refuge System originated with the designation of Pelican Island in Florida as a refuge by President Theodore Roosevelt. By 1984 the system had grown to include 427 units totaling more than 90 million acres. The National Park Service was established by Congress in 1916, initially to manage a variety of national battlefields and the few western parks already in existence. Its holdings now total about 75 million acres, of which 40 million are in Alaska.

Conflict and Management in the 20th Century

At the opening of the 20th century, disposal and retention were in competition as alternative public land policies. But soon to emerge was still another round in the succession of conflicts that have characterized United States public land history. This involved a schism among the retentionists themselves and, specifically, between the wilderness ethic of John Muir and his admirers on the one hand and the philosophy of "rational use of public lands" advocated by the first director of the U.S. Forest Service, Gifford Pinchot, on the other.

The conflict crystallized over the pristine Hetch Hetchy Valley on the west slope of the Sierra Nevada within the boundaries of Yosemite National Park (which had been established in 1890). The 1906 San Francisco earthquake and fire had forcefully demonstrated the inadequacy of that city's local water supply. The quest for a reliable external water source focused on Hetch Hetchy, which was proposed to be dammed and flooded. The valley, which was designated as "wilderness preserve" by Congress, would remain public land but would be physically transformed. Pinchot, a Yale-educated forester and Theodore Roosevelt's chief conservation advisor, supported the project. John Muir passionately opposed it: "Dam Hetch Hetchy! As well dam for water-tanks the people's cathedrals and churches, for no holier temple has ever been consecrated by the heart of man" (quoted in Nash 1982, 168).

The conflict that raged from San Francisco to Washington highlighted the dilemma in the management of retained public lands between preservation in their natural state versus human use. Muir's position, being absolute, was simpler in concept: "Wilderness is wilderness"—it cannot be tampered with. Pinchot, the progressive, represented the orthodox "conservation" position as the term was then used, namely that natural resources should be managed rationally to promote the greatest good for the greatest number of people. The handwriting of Powell in this doctrine is manifest (although Powell himself took little interest in forests and died in 1902) (Stegner, 354).

When the Hetch Hetchy debate erupted in 1908, President Theodore

Roosevelt was caught in the middle between his trust in Pinchot and his admiration for Muir (Nash 1982, 162–164). Ultimately the decision to dam the "cathedral" was made by President Woodrow Wilson in 1913. But in the words of Nash (p. 180): "The preservationists had lost the fight for the valley, but they had gained much ground in the larger war for the existence of wilderness."

This point was exemplified in the Echo Park Dam controversy 50 years after Hetch Hetchy. In that case, opponents led by the Sierra Club and The Wilderness Society successfully blocked construction of a Bureau of Reclamation dam in a valley within Dinosaur National Park in Utah and Colorado (Gottlieb 1993, 41). In the 1960s, the Bureau constructed the Glen Canyon Dam on the middle reach of the Colorado despite similar opposition. But this project, whose 186-mile-long impoundment is named Lake Powell after the Bureau's patron saint, was one of the last major dams to be constructed in the United States, for both economic and environmental reasons. A subsequent proposal by the Bureau to dam a portion of Grand Canyon was handily demolished by outraged environmentalists in 1966. The ill-advised Teton Dam built by the Bureau in Idaho collapsed on June 5, 1976 before its completion (Reisner, chs. 8 and 11).

Beginning in 1955, The Wilderness Society and other national organizations introduced a series of bills in Congress to create a national wilderness system within the federal lands. The Wilderness Act finally passed in 1964 in greatly reduced scope from the original hopes of its backers such as Robert Marshall: About nine million acres of federal lands were authorized to be designated as wilderness, with activities such as mining, water development, recreation, and livestock grazing limited but not entirely prohibited (Gottlieb 1993, 43).

Multiple Use

Not every tract of public land is a Hetch Hetchy or a Grand Canyon. Hundreds of millions of federal acres consist of undistinguished forests, grasslands, desert, tundra, and wetlands (Table 11-2). While most of this is "wilderness" in the sense of absence of visible human presence, even the most ardent preservationist has not called for the nonuse of *all* federal land. On the other hand, total laissez faire of the 19th century variety is scarcely a viable political position today. The era of the public domain as an unregulated commons ended with the Taylor Grazing Act of 1934, which established grazing districts in place of the chaotic and mutually destructive practice of unlimited grazing of private livestock on federal grasslands. The "open range" thus gave way to range management, as has the been the case with minerals, timber, water, recreation, and other valuable resources of the federal lands.

Thus a compromise between total control and no control is required for federal land not designated as wilderness or belonging to the National Park System. Powell and Pinchot have prevailed and resource management, as their "conservation" is now called, has been national policy since the 1920s.

But this scarcely has led to a quieting of the passions that the public domain has generated since the nation's founding. To the contrary, management of public lands has been if anything more contentious than non-management. Marion Clawson (1983, 39–59) describes the period since 1960 as one of "consultation and confrontation."

The central concept guiding public lands management since 1960 has been "multiple use." This concept was declared national policy in two Congressional acts, one concerning the Forest Service (USFS) in 1960 and the other the Bureau of Land Management (BLM) in 1964. Together these agencies account for nearly 600 million of the 730 million acres of total federal land (Table 11-2). Both acts were replaced by the Federal Lands Policy and Management Act of 1976 that further broadened federal land planning objectives. Thus, instead of listening only to its timber company constituents (who lease timber rights), the Forest Service is required to incorporate watershed management, wildlife habitat protection, and recreation into its management plans for each national forest. Similarly, BLM must weigh those needs alongside its traditional grazing, mining, and timber interests (Cutter, Renwick, and Renwick 1985, 176–7). But as Clawson (1983, 137) suggests: "The meaning [of multiple use] implied by those acts and in today's popular usage expresses a desire for a kind of management that is defined in the minds of the users rather than in specific instructions to the agencies. Almost everyone supports the general idea; it is its translation into practice that produces controversies."

Public participation is fundamental to planning procedures by federal land agencies. Draft plans are published and available for public comment, which is often negative. Public hearings are required at each step

TABLE II-2   Holdings of Major Federal Land
              Management Agencies (1980)
              (million acres)

Department of the Interior	
Bureau of Land Management	398
National Park Service	75
Fish and Wildlife Service	43
Department of Agriculture	
U.S. Forest Service	188
Other	41
Total Federal Land Ownership	745[a]

Source: Clawson 1983, Table 2-2.

[a] This total includes public domain lands shown in Table 11-1 as well as other federal lands subsequently acquired.

in the development of plans. Environmental impact statements under the National Environmental Policy Act of 1969 are required for major plans and policy initiatives, and these generate another layer of public involvement and contention. Finally, lawsuits by public interest organizations or special user groups frequently challenge and delay the implementation of proposed actions on federal lands.

An issue of particular interest to western states is that expressed in the "Sagebrush Rebellion" of the early 1980s, namely, whether states may assume control and even ownership of federal lands within their territories. Nevada in 1979 adopted a law making such a claim. While partly symbolic, this and equivalent statements reflect a frustration by states and private economic interests with federal control over the water, timber, grasslands, minerals, and wildlife located on the public domain. Closely allied to this view is the question of outright privatization of certain federal lands or resources. This idea was supported rhetorically by Secretary of the Interior James Watt during the first Reagan Administration, but with little substantive result. In the 1990s, the "wise use movement" continues to advocate greater control over federal lands and resources by local interests.

National Forests

Although they include only about 29 percent of total commercial timberlands, the national forests include over 40 percent of the timber volume and account for a large proportion of mature, higher-quality trees, particularly western conifers (Clawson 1963, 93). Western forests, mostly in federal ownership, are estimated to contain about 50 million acres of old-growth sawtimber, of which 40 percent is unexploited virgin forest—a resource virtually unknown in the eastern United States (Landsberg 1964, 162). Such ancient forests possess great attraction in terms of public recreation and wildlife habitat in their natural state, and therefore cutting is widely opposed by environmental organizations such as the Sierra Club and Friends of the Earth. On the other hand, foresters argue for increased cutting of these old stands since they grow very slowly in comparison with younger trees that would replace them. The Forest Service is thus caught in a perpetual dilemma regarding the management of its older western forests (Clawson 1983, 82).

Cutting of timber in the national forests is conducted by private companies that buy timber rights from the U.S. Forest Service. Between 1975 and 1984, sales of timber rights in national forests exceeded the volume of timber actually harvested by the buyers. The average annual volume sold during the decade was 10.8 billion board feet (U.S. Council on Environmental Quality 1984, 267). Thus, recent experience indicates that timber companies are in no hurry to harvest the timber that they have purchased as they wait for the market price to rise.

Meanwhile, foreign sources of timber products, especially Canada, continue to increase their share of U.S. domestic consumption. Domestic production and consumption of forest products each rose by about 37 percent between 1960 and 1983, but imports of these products increased by 120 percent, rising from 16 percent to 26 percent of total domestic requirements (U.S. Bureau of the Census 1985, 675). U.S. exports have risen substantially since 1960 but most of that growth occurred before 1970. Exports increased by only 3 percent per year during the 1970s and amounted to only about half of total imports in 1983. The U.S. Forest Service believes that this country will remain a net importer of forest products (Conservation Foundation 1984, 166).

The foregoing trends signify that U.S. forest resources are not unduly stressed. In fact, growing stock of timber on both public and private lands has increased by 18 percent since 1952. This reflects a growth of 56 percent in the East and 48 percent in the South, in contrast to a loss of 5 percent in the more massive but slower growing timber stock of the West (U.S. Bureau of the Census 1985, 672).

National Parks

Within the broad spectrum of federal lands conflicts since 1960, some of the most publicized and bitter disputes have involved the National Park System. In terms of acreage, national parks account for a modest portion of the total federal lands: about 75 million acres in 1984. Forty million acres of this total in Alaska were transferred to the National Park Service (NPS) by Congress for safekeeping in 1978 and are essentially inaccessible. The real park system consists of 35 million acres scattered throughout the nation, an increase of 10 million acres (40 percent) since 1960.

The National Park System is best known for its "crown jewels": the great western parks of Yosemite, Yellowstone, Rocky Mountain, Grand Canyon, Zion, Bryce Canyon, Grand Teton, Glacier, and Olympic. In the East, Acadia in Maine attracts 4.5 million visitors a year and Shenandoah receives 2 million.

Since 1960 these traditional scenic marvels have been supplemented by a variety of new kinds of NPS facilities established by Congress. Beginning with Cape Cod National Seashore in 1961, NPS now operates 10 national seashores (nine on the Atlantic and Gulf and one, Point Reyes, on the Pacific) and four national lakeshores on the Great Lakes. Seventeen national recreation areas have been established in or near urban areas, including Gateway in New York City, Golden Gate in San Francisco, and Santa Monica in Los Angeles. NPS also operates many smaller facilities including historic sites and battlefields, national monuments (including the venerable Muir Woods north of San Francisco), and miscellaneous special facilities such as an industrial museum park at Lowell, Massachusetts (Conservation Foundation 1985, ch. 2).

This varied assortment of public sites, both traditional and nontraditional, has provoked endless possibilities for conflicts over management policies of the NPS. Some place-specific and generic issues have involved:

- Water supply for the Everglades
- Off-road vehicles at Cape Cod and elsewhere
- Mining in Death Valley
- Whether to move the Cape Hatteras Lighthouse
- Clearcutting timber adjacent to national parks
- Controlling forest fires in Yellowstone and elsewhere

- Airplane flights through the Grand Canyon

- Nude bathing

- Quotas for wilderness backpacking

- Traffic and parking

- Concessions

- Land use planning in "gateway communities"

- Wildlife management

- Erosion control

- Rights of inholders and enclave communities

- Sewage and solid waste

In charting its course through these and other minefields of public contention, the NPS has little statutory guidance from Congress. The 1916 National Park Service Organic Act charged NPS: ". . . to conserve the scenery and the natural and historic objects and the wildlife therein and to provide for the enjoyment of the same in such manner and by such means as will leave them unimpaired for the enjoyment of future generations" (16 U.S.C. Sec. 1).

This mandate thus poses the eternal dilemma for NPS as to how it may both preserve the resources entrusted to it while promoting public enjoyment of them. Further guidance is provided in authorizing legislation for particular facilities such as the Cape Cod National Seashore Act of 1961. And of course NPS is subject to the National Environmental Policy Act of 1969 and its own planning regulations.

Much of the controversy swirling around the National Park System involves long-standing issues pertaining to the internal management of parks: recreation, traffic, wildlife, primitive areas, off-road vehicles, and so forth. Such issues relate to the essence of the parks, their very raison d'être—scenery, water resources, biodiversity, quiet, and solitude. Protection of these qualities arouses passionate advocacy even among members of the public and interest groups far from the scene, who may never have visited the site in question. This tradition dates back at least to Hetch Hetchy in the first decade of this century.

But users of parks have been equally outspoken on behalf of more facilities for the public, more concessions, parking, campgrounds, and opportunities for specialized pastimes. Visitorship to the National Park System quadrupled from 79 million in 1960 to 332 million in 1984. Increasing mobility of middle-class Americans has facilitated access to and pressure on the "crown jewels." Meanwhile, the newer urban-oriented facilities have attracted visitation far disproportionate to the relatively small acreage that they represent. New recreational pastimes and inventions such as snowmobiles, jet-skis, high-tech rafting, and hang-gliding create demands for special-use areas or privileges within parks. Cultural and ethnic diversity of users (a contrast to the recent past) create additional needs (for instance, bilingual signs). Handicapped and elderly users require specially designed trails and other facilities.

A separate cluster of management issues stems from the intermingling of public and private ownership in many facilities. The great western parks consist of large tracts of NPS land surrounded by other federal land managed by USFS or BLM. Private ownership adjacent to or within these parks consists largely of agricultural or timber holdings. There are few local governments to deal with except for gateway communities like Estes Park at the entrance to Rocky Mountain National Park in Colorado.

A different legal geography applies to NPS facilities elsewhere, especially the national seashores and lakeshores. Those sites were not carved out of the public domain like the western parks but instead have been acquired through negotiated purchase, condemnation, or gift from previous owners. Typically, the authorized areas of these facilities are much larger than the land actually acquired to date, since Congress almost never appropriates enough money to buy the entire park outright. The result is a hodge-podge of NPS land scattered throughout the authorized area, interspersed with private holdings and tracts owned by other federal, state, county, and municipal governments.

This crazyquilt of ownership and jurisdiction presents challenging problems for NPS management. In coastal areas, passions are especially aroused due to the high property values and scarcity of access to the shore. NPS is a mixed blessing to preexisting communities such as those affected by the Cape Cod, Fire Island, and Cape Hatteras national seashores. Federal acquisition preserves key areas from development, such as the Sunken Forest on Fire Island, a renowned ecological preserve. But the NPS mission to facilitate public usage brings traffic, crowds, pollution, and ethnic diversity to previously aloof summer enclaves.

Under such circumstances, NPS is thrust reluctantly into the local and regional planning process. At Cape Cod and Fire Island, Congress authorized NPS to intervene in local development decisions within the authorized park boundaries. Elsewhere, NPS exercises at least the same rights as any other landowner to testify in zoning proceedings and otherwise make its views known. Subdivisions, condominiums, shopping centers, and amusement parks, which are often attracted to the vicinity of national parks, may detract from the quality of the park environment. Adverse impacts include visual blight, traffic congestion, water quality degradation, littering, and reduction of natural wildlife habitat.

Sticky questions also arise where growth-inducing facilities such as roads, water lines, sewers, and electrical lines must be routed across NPS land to serve private inholdings, as at Cape Hatteras. The leverage this provides to NPS is tempered by its desire to promote harmonious relations with its nonfederal neighbors. Park management in these situations involves as much diplomacy as technical expertise on the part of park superintendents and their staffs. Cape Cod National Seashore, the archetype of the new generation of national parks, has gained nearly three decades of experience with a formal advisory committee that represents the various public and private interests of that complex region (Foster 1987).

Overriding the myriad specific disputes that influence NPS management is the paramount philosophical concern as to the purpose of the national parks. Ultimately, should they cater to the desires of the user public (however those may be defined) or should they provide a "park experience" that uplifts and refreshes those who choose to experience it (Conservation Foundation 1985, ch. 7)? Environmental lawyer Joseph Sax (1980) strongly advocates the latter option. Drawing on Thoreau and Olmsted, Sax argues that the park must offer "contemplative recreation" in contrast to "artificial recreation" (e.g., scenic vistas, not water slides):

> Engagement with nature provides an opportunity for detachment from the submissiveness, conformity, and mass behavior that dog us in our daily lives; it offers a chance to express distinctiveness and

to explore our deeper longings . . . From this perspective, what distinguishes a national park idea from a merely generalized interest in nature may be the special role that the nature park plays as an institution within a developed and industrialized society, in contrast to those traditions in which nature is offered as an alternative to society.

Sax 1980, p. 42.

Conclusion

This chapter has briefly surveyed the history and present status of federal land management (see Table 11-3). The major eras may be identified as (1) disposal—1785 to about World War I; (2) retention—1872 to the present; and (3) multiple-use management and advocacy planning—1960 to the present. Throughout the nation's history, federal land policy has generated conflicts:

- Revenue versus free disposal

- Retention versus disposal

- Preservation versus "conservation"

- Single use versus multiple use

- "Artificial recreation" versus "contemplative recreation"

Stakeholders in federal land decision making include politicians, professional land managers, private economic interests (mining, timber, water users, grazing interests, recreation providers), adjacent and inholder property owners, the environmental community, and the recreation-seeking public. Each of these major groups is in turn subdivided into subgroups of more specialized interests (such as off-road vehicle users versus backpackers).

From the beginning of the public domain in the 1780s, revenue to the public treasury has fared poorly as an object of federal land management. The shift from sale to free grant marked by the 1862 Homestead Act and its sequels marked the first retreat from a revenue policy. But land retained in federal ownership, except for national parks and designated wilderness areas, has been eligible for lease of timber, mining, grazing, and other economic rights to private interests. Clawson (1983),

TABLE II-3   Significant Events and Laws Affecting Federal
             Lands Management

1784–1785	Cession of "Northwest Territories" to national government
1785	Land Ordinance–beginning of Federal Land Survey
1787	Northwest Ordinance–organization of territorial governments
1803	Louisiana Purchase–doubled size of United States
1823–1868	Road and canal land grants
1841	General Improvement Act–land grants to 10 states
1849–1850	Swampland Acts–further grants to certain states
1850–1872	Land grants to railroads
1862	Homestead Act–free land grants to settlers
1872	Yellowstone Park established–first national park
1878	Powell Report on the arid lands
1879	U.S. Geological Survey established
1891	Forest Reserve Act–beginning of National Forest System
1902	Newlands Act–Bureau of Reclamation established
1905	U.S. Forest Service established
1908–1913	Hetch Hetchy controversy–first "environmental" battle
1911	Weeks Act–to purchase private land for national forests
1916	National Park Service established
1920	Mineral Leasing Act
1933–1940	New Deal Programs, such as TVA, SCS, CCC
1934	Taylor Grazing Act–closing of the "open range"
1953	Submerged Lands Act
1960	Multiple Use and Sustained Yield Act–U.S. Forest Service
1961	Cape Cod National Seashore Act–first national seashore
1964	Land and Water Conservation Fund Act Wilderness Act Classification and Multiple Use Act–BLM
1968	National Wild and Scenic Rivers Act National Trails Act
1970	National Environmental Policy Act Public Land Law Review Commission Report
1976	Federal Land Policy and Management Act

however, reports that federal leasing policies in general fail even to cover the administrative costs of the management agencies. The major exception is oil and gas leasing from submerged lands of the Outer Continental Shelf (OCS) which, since the late 1960s, "has produced about two-thirds of the BLM's receipts, completely overwhelming the onshore oil and gas, the timber, and especially the grazing receipts" (Clawson 1983, 91). (Much of the OCS revenue was earmarked for the Land and Water Conservation Fund to acquire additional public lands, although little is currently appropriated for that purpose.)

Recreation remains essentially a free public good with gate fees at NPS and other federal facilities either nonexistent or nominal. Long lines of expensive recreation vehicles, laden with all kinds of costly high-tech recreation gear, are admitted to the nation's parks at a cost of a few dollars per day. Concessionnaires in those parks charge substantial prices for their services and facilities with comparatively little return to the responsible federal agency (Conservation Foundation 1985, ch. 5).

Barring a drastic change in Congressional policy, there is little likelihood of a change in the foregoing policies. But the pressures for multiple usage and particularly multiple recreational use of public lands continue to mount, fueled in part by the low cost of entering federal facilities. There will certainly be much debate ahead as to the necessity of limiting access to certain facilities, through quotas, higher fees, or other means, in order to protect the quality of the park experience (as is already the case in wilderness areas). In the future, this issue, among many others, may be expected to provide much grist for continued "confrontation and consultation" regarding federal lands.

References

Bureau of Land Management 1975. *Public Land Statistics*. Washington: U.S. Government Printing Office.

Clawson, M. 1963. *Land for Americans: Trends, Prospects, and Problems*. Chicago: Rand, McNally.

——. 1983. *The Federal Lands Revisited*. Baltimore: Johns Hopkins University Press for Resources for the Future.

Conservation Foundation. 1984. *State of the Environment: An Assessment at Mid-Decade.* Washington: The Foundation.

———. 1985. *National Parks for a New Generation.* Washington: The Foundation.

Cutter, S.L., H.L. Renwick, and W.H. Renwick 1985. *Exploitation, Conservation, Preservation: A Geographic Perspective on Natural Resource Use.* Totowa, NJ: Rowman and Allanheld.

Foster, C.H.W. 1987. *The Cape Cod National Seashore: A Landmark Alliance.* Hanover, NH: University Press of New England.

Fox, S. 1981. *John Muir and His Legacy.* Boston: Little Brown.

Gates, P.W. 1962. "The Homestead Law in an Incongruous Land System." In *The Public Lands.* V. Carstenson, ed. Madison: University of Wisconsin Press.

Gottlieb, R. 1993. *Forcing the Spring: The Transformation of the American Environmental Movement.* Washington: Island Press.

Hartshorne, R. 1939. *The Nature of Geography.* Lancaster, PA: Association of American Geographers.

Hibbard, B.H. 1965. *A History of the Public Land Policies.* Madison: University of Wisconsin Press.

Kunstler, J.H. 1989. "For Sale." In *The New York Times Magazine* (June 18), 23 ff.

Landsberg, H.H. 1964. *Natural Resources for U.S. Growth.* Baltimore: Johns Hopkins University Press for Resources for the Future.

Lowenthal, D., ed. 1965. See Marsh, G.P. 1864/1965.

Marsh, G.P. 1864/1965. *Man and Nature Or, Physical Geography as Modified by Human Action.* D. Lowenthal, ed. Cambridge: Belknap Press of Harvard University Press.

McMartin, B. 1994. *The Great Forest of the Adirondacks.* Utica, New York: North Country Books.

Nash, R.F. 1982. *Wilderness and the American Mind.* New Haven: Yale University Press.

———. 1990. *American Environmentalism: Readings in Conservation History* 3rd ed. New York: McGraw-Hill.

Powell, J.W. 1878. *Report on the Lands of the Arid Region of the United States.* 45th Cong. 2d Sess. H. Doc. 73.

Reisner, M. 1986. *Cadillac Desert: The American West and Its Disappearing Water.* New York: Penguin Books.

Sax, J.L. 1980. *Mountains Without Handrails: Reflections on the National Parks.* Ann Arbor: University of Michigan Press.

Stegner, W. 1953/1982. *Beyond the Hundredth Meridian: John Wesley Powell and the Second Opening of the West.* Lincoln: University of Nebraska Press.

Stewart, F. 1995. *A Natural History of Nature Writing.* Washington: Island Press.

Treat, J.P. 1962. "Origin of the National Land System under the Confederation." In *The Public Lands.* V. Carstenson, ed. Madison: University of Wisconsin Press.

Udall, S.L. 1963. *The Quiet Crisis.* New York: Avon Books.

U.S. Council on Environmental Quality. 1984. *Environmental Quality–1984.* Washington: U.S. Government Printing Office.

U.S. Bureau of the Census. 1985. *Statistical Abstract of the United States–1985-86.* Washington: U.S. Government Printing Office.

White, M., and W. White. 1962. *The Intellectual Versus the City.* Cambridge: Harvard and M.I.T. University Presses.

CHAPTER 12 / Congress and Land Use

Introduction

Twice during the 20th century, demographic thresholds signaled major innovations in land use control practices. The 1920 census was the first to report that population of urban places outnumber rural residents. In 1960, the census found that suburbanites exceeded central city inhabitants for the first time. In both cases, the shift in the demographic center of balance–from rural to urban in 1920 and from city to suburb in 1960–closely coincided with a radical change in the structure of public authority over land use. In the earlier case, the advent of Euclidean zoning marked the assertion of municipal power in relation to private property rights. In the 1960s, the federal government, in collaboration with the states, began to reassert the powers with which it had experimented during the New Deal, and to play an increasingly significant, albeit indirect, role in shaping the contemporary American metropolitan region.

Two factors may be cited to account for the importance of the 1960 demographic threshold. First, suburban growth involved a proliferation of increasingly fragmented local governments (as discussed in Chapter 5). While these clung tenaciously to their land use prerogatives, it was gradually recognized that local units are inadequate–spatially, fiscally, and philosophically–to address metropolitan, state, and national needs. Second, spatial redistribution of population was accompanied by a shift in political power in state legislatures and in Congress. This was facilitated by the 1963 Supreme Court decision in *Baker v. Carr* (369 U.S. 186), which declared that electoral districts must be redrawn to reflect demographic shifts to ensure the principle of "one man, one vote." Thus suburbanites began to outvote as well as outnumber the central cities' inhabitants in the 1960s.

In theory, public power over private land use is vested in the sovereign states, not the federal government. And the states, as discussed in earlier chapters, have long delegated most of their authority to local municipalities and counties. The mighty federal government of the United States is powerless to interfere in a local zoning determination. States for their part have the legal power but often lack the political will to influence local actions, and they generally ignored land use entirely until the 1970s.

Between the 1960s and the late 1980s, however, the relative balance of influence over land use decisions shifted markedly from the local government toward the state and federal levels. According to Popper (1988, 291): "Two decades ago, American land use regulation consisted almost entirely of local zoning: it no longer does. Instead it has become increasingly centralized—that is, more likely to originate with regional, state and federal agencies rather than with local ones." (In 1995, however, the balance may have shifted back somewhat in the local direction.)

National Planning Before the 1960s

Federally sponsored land use planning, while alien to the Eisenhower Administration in 1960 and to the Gingrich "Contract with America" in the mid-1990s, is not unprecedented. President Franklin D. Roosevelt's New Deal during the 1930s briefly interjected the federal government into the planning and development of the nation's natural resources on a massive scale.

One of the most durable legacies of the New Deal, the Tennessee Valley Authority (TVA), was chartered by Congress in 1933 as a public corporation to focus federal resources on an impoverished and environmentally stressed region: the drainage basin of the Tennessee River. TVA is best known for its series of main stem dams that harnessed the river for power, navigation, recreation, and flood control. But TVA also developed pioneering programs in soil erosion management, reforestation, economic development, and improvement of housing, medical care, schools, and recreation. It proved to be an internationally important experiment in governmental resource management. Although no other similar agencies were established in the United States, the idea of promoting regional development through comprehensive river basin management was demonstrated (White 1969). The concept of river basin planning was further promoted through the many reports of the National Resources Planning Board (see Chapter 10).

TVA and another New Deal program, the Resettlement Administration, dabbled with the planning and construction of small "greenbelt towns" modeled on Ebenezer Howard's Garden City concepts. But only three such towns were actually built, in Maryland, Ohio, and Wisconsin (Parsons 1990).

The Soil Conservation Service (SCS) was created by Congress in 1935 in response to a national soil erosion crisis. SCS, an agency of the U.S. Department of Agriculture, fostered the establishment of soil and water conservation districts in most of the nation's counties. With SCS funding and guidance, the districts assist private landowners to improve land management and development practices. These and other New Deal programs fostered a tradition of federal funding and technical assistance to nonfederal planning and resources management agencies. Primarily however they were addressed to rural rather than urban issues.

Post-World War II America was much more interested in building than in planning. Single-family residential subdivisions proliferated with federal low interest loans and mortgage guarantees from the FHA and VA. In 1956, Congress launched the 42,500-mile Interstate Highway System that further promoted development at the fringes of metropolitan areas. These programs promoted the suburban population surge noted in the 1960 census. For central cities, Congress established the Urban Renewal Program in the Housing Acts of 1949 and 1954 to acquire, clear, and redevelop "blighted" urban land.

These federal programs and policies profoundly changed the face of metropolitan America. While technically they did not violate the doctrine that land use is a nonfederal concern, they demonstrated the immense capability of the federal government to indirectly influence–through spending, tax incentives, and technical guidelines–the use of private land. FHA regulations literally specified suburban single-family homes as the approved style of housing to be constructed with its assistance (Fried

1971, 66–70). Tying strings to federal benefits was thus a means of exerting federal influence over the form of urban development in the 1950s, whether or not so recognized at the time.

Rumblings of Dissent

Who would have predicted in the complacent 1950s the turmoil of the 1960s: the civil rights movement, the anti-Vietnam War movement, and– more genteel but ultimately powerful–the rebirth of the conservation movement, which laid the foundation for the environmental movement of the 1970s. The role of the conservation/environmental activism of the 1960s recalls two earlier periods when public outcry yielded new laws and policies. The first was the mid-19th century reaction to despoliation of the public domain, which led to the beginning of retention and preservation of such lands, in contrast to disposal of them. Second, the progressive crusade against "urban congestion" of the early 1900s in its turn prompted the advent of city planning and zoning.

An important exception to the prevailing euphoria concerning "growth" during the 1950s was the 1955 Wenner-Gren Conference held at Princeton on "Man's Role in Changing the Face of the Earth." (Thomas 1956). This symposium marked a scholarly watershed as significant as that defined by George Perkins Marsh a century earlier (to whom *Man's Role* was dedicated). Seventy-six distinguished scholars described "the multiple impacts of human beings as agents of vast and often fearsome change in the world" (Kates 1987, 529). Like Marsh, *Man's Role* focused on degraded "landscapes" of the world: soils, forests, water, biotic species, with new attention to cities, climate, and wastes.

Lewis Mumford (1956), one of the conference convenors, sounded a tocsin of the coming environmentalism, noting that modern metropolitan development tends:

> ... to loosen the bonds that connect [the city's] inhabitants with nature and to transform, eliminate, or replace its earth-bound aspects, covering the natural site with an artificial environment that enhances the dominance of man and encourages an illusion of complete independence from nature (p. 386).

Within a century, the economy of the Western world has shifted from a rural base harboring a few big cities and thousands of villages and small towns, to a metropolitan base whose urban spread ... is fast absorbing the rural hinterland and threatening to wipe out many of the natural elements favorable to life which in earlier stages balanced off against the depletions of the urban environment (p. 395).

Mumford's concern was geographically cosmic and not based on study of any particular urban region (although he had a love-hate relationship with New York City). By contrast, the French geographer Jean Gottmann (1961) published the classic study of the urbanized northeastern seaboard of the United States, which he named *Megalopolis*. This region was loosely defined by Gottmann as a series of connected metropolitan areas extending from southern Maine to Virginia. He included all adjacent counties having a minimum average density of 600 people per square mile, which included a lot of still-rural land. It also included several of the nation's leading cities: Boston, New York, Philadelphia, Baltimore, and Washington, D.C. Contrary to Mumford, Gottmann revered large-scale urbanization: "Because of its concentration of people, wealth, and economic activities, Megalopolis stands out on the map of the present world as a stupendous monument erected by titanic efforts" (Gottmann 1961, 23).

Gottmann examined the history, geographical functions, linkages, and land use patterns that characterized this vast region. His findings were more sanguine than most later metropolitan studies: poverty, pollution, and politics were not his primary concerns. But with respect to the "symbiosis of urban and rural," his findings reinforced more polemical writers:

In Megalopolis the fully urbanized and built-up sectors are many and of impressive size, but there still remains a great deal of thinly occupied space devoted to woods, fields, and pasture. ... On closer examination, however, we shall find that present and future use of these green spaces within Megalopolis is completely dependent on the march of urbanization. We shall also discover that, while the actual crowding is still localized and open land is available on a much larger scale than is usually recognized, present trends indicate an urgent need for new policies if Megalopolitan populations are not to find themselves even more fenced in than are the people in other highly urbanized regions of the world (p. 218).

Megalopolis strengthened public perception of a new kind of region characterized by a high degree of functional interdependence, yet fragmented by political boundaries. His penultimate chapter, "Sharing a Partitioned Land," was devoted to the need for intergovernmental cooperation in solving the problems of Megalopolis and its analogues elsewhere. (For a comparison of Megalopolis with its British counterpart, see Clawson and Hall 1973.)

The manifesto of the 1960s urban conservation movement was a short, punchy essay entitled "Urban Sprawl" by sociologist William H. Whyte, Jr. (1958). Whyte, an acute observer and critic of American land development, argued that zoning had failed to promote orderly and efficient use of land. He portrayed the results of recent land development as wasteful, costly to provide with public services, and aesthetically a disaster. Over three decades, Whyte has promoted new techniques to improve land development practices and save open space (e.g., Whyte 1959, 1968, 1988).

The perceived loss of open space prompted an outpouring of scholarly and civic reports by many respected organizations, for example, the Committee for Economic Development (1960), the Urban Land Institute, the New York Regional Plan Association, and Resources for the Future (Wingo 1963). "Open space" was to the conservationists of the Kennedy/Johnson era what "congestion" was to the progressives of Theodore Roosevelt's time. Congress responded to these concerns with a cornucopia of new laws concerning open space, urban development, and public lands (Table 12-1), several of which have been mentioned earlier.

The "rumblings of dissent" that began with the *Man's Role* symposium in 1955 extended well beyond urban planning issues to broader ecological and environmental concerns during the 1960s. An important source of inspiration to the general public was the American tradition of natural history writing for the nonscientist as pioneered by Thoreau's *Walden*, Henry Beston's *The Outermost House* and by the many writings of John Burroughs (Stewart 1995). The tradition continued in the 1960s

TABLE 12-1   Selected Federal Laws of the 1960s Concerning
Cities and Land Use

1961	Cape Cod National Seashore Act (PL 87-126)
1963	Outdoor Recreation (PL 88-29)
1964	Wilderness Act (PL 88 577)
	Civil Rights Act (PL 88-352)
1965	Appalachian Regional Development Act (PL 89-4)
	Land and Water Conservation Fund Act (PL 88-578)
	Department of Housing and Urban Development Act (PL 89-174)
	Highway Beautification Act (PL 89-285)
	Water Resources Planning Act (PL 89-80)
1966	Historic Preservation Act (PL 89-665)
	Department of Transportation Act (PL 89-670)
	Demonstrations Cities ("Model Cities") Act (PL 89-754)
1968	Civil Rights Act (PL 90-284)
	Fair Housing Act (Title VII)
	Housing and Urban Development Act (PL 90-448)
	Urban Mass Transportation (Title VII)
	New Communities Act (Title IV)
	National Flood Insurance Act (Title XIII)
	Interstate Land Sales Act (Title XIV)
	Wild and Scenic Rivers Act (PL 90-542)
	National Trails System Act (PL 90-543)

(N.B. Subsequent amendments to these acts are not listed. Consult U.S. Code Annotated for current versions.)

with Edwin Way Teale, Joseph Wood Krutch, Edward Abbey, and this writer's father, Rutherford Platt (1966).

The science of ecology itself was relatively new, having originated in the work of botanist Henry Cowles at the Indiana Dunes in the early 1900s (Engel 1985). Aldo Leopold in *A Sand County Almanac* (1949/ 1966) synthesized concepts of ecological succession and process with George Perkins Marsh's view of man as an agent of environmental disturbance. Leopold proposed a "land ethic" to guide human use of natural resources. This urged that humans live in harmony rather than in conflict with the biosphere of which they are a part. *A Sand County Almanac*, republished in 1966 and again in 1989, became the holy scripture of environmentalism.

The book that finally ignited the environmental movement was

Rachel Carson's *Silent Spring* (Carson 1962; Stewart 1995, ch. 8). Carson was already well established as a natural history writer for her books *The Edge of the Sea* and *The Sea Around Us*. In *Silent Spring*, written as she battled cancer, she warned against the pernicious and irreversible effects of introducing DDT and other hazardous chemicals into the environment and thus the food chain:

> The most alarming of all man's assaults upon the environment is the contamination of air, rivers, and sea with dangerous and even lethal materials. This pollution is for the most part irrecoverable; the chain of evil it initiates not only in the world that must support life but in living tissues is for the most part irreversible. In this now universal contamination of the environment, chemicals are the sinister and little-recognized partners of radiation in changing the very nature of the world—the very nature of its life.
>
> Carson 1962, p. 6.

This powerful book marked the advent of the politics of ecology on the national scene. Subsequent contributions included Barry Commoner's *The Closing Circle* (1971), the Teals' *Life and Death of the Salt Marsh* (1969), Garret Hardin's article "The Tragedy of the Commons" (1968), Edward Abbey's *Desert Solitaire* (1968), Ian McHarg's *Design with Nature* (1968), John McPhee's *The Pine Barrens* (1968) and "Encounters with the Archdruid" (1971), as well as the photographic essays of Eliot Porter featured in Sierra Club publications.

Coinciding with the "Age of Aquarius" and the Antiwar Movement, the environmental movement attracted an unlikely alliance of "flower children," concerned scientists, journalists, public interest lawyers, ladies and men in tennis shoes, and Richard M. Nixon. Its troubadour was Pete Seeger, whose sloop "Clearwater" became both a symbol and an organization for environmental protest. The movement's success was both a cause and an effect of the rising influence and affluence of national environmental organizations such as the Sierra Club, National Wildlife Federation, Friends of the Earth, and the National Resources Defense Council (Gottlieb 1993). New journals were started, such as *Environment, Environmental Action,* and *Environmental Management.* Conferences were held by the dozens, and media reporters and environmental activists avidly courted each other. Many politicians quickly joined the environmental crusade and a multitude of laws were passed.

The Environmental Decade of the 1970s

It may have appeared to some observers at the end of the 1960s that Congress, with a conservative Republican in the White House, was unlikely to adopt more laws on the environment, for example:

> And what about the future? There is some indication that the close of the Ninetieth Congress late in 1968 may mark the end of this remarkable period in the history of conservation politics in the United States. Some members of Congress, as well as of the new Republican Administration, have suggested that we are reaching the end of a long wave of significant and highly visible progress, and that the widely hailed "environmental crisis" has, in a certain sense, passed the peak of critical national interest and public concern.
>
> Cooley and Wandesforde-Smith, eds. 1970, p. xvi.

But in the clear light of hindsight we can now view the conservation movement of the 1960s as merely a prelude to the environmental revolution of the 1970s. The former was the larval stage, so to speak; and the latter, the butterfly.

The "federal environmental decade" was inaugurated symbolically by the first Earth Day, April 15, 1969, and by the signing of the National Environmental Policy Act on January 1, 1970. Also in 1970, the creation of the U.S. Environmental Protection Agency (EPA) consolidated several existing federal environmental programs and provided an administrative umbrella for many new initiatives soon to be legislated by Congress.

The new environmental laws of the 1970s (Table 12-2) did not merely refine the conservation measures of the 1960s. They enlarged both the range of problems addressed through federal programs and the spectrum of means by which such problems were to be attacked. In air and water pollution, the federal role shifted from a timid reliance on state programs to direct setting and enforcement of national standards. Other new federal laws addressed such problems as noise, pesticides, solid and hazardous wastes, floodplain management, wetlands, mining reclamation, drinking water, occupational safety, ocean dumping, oil spills, and coastal management.

Constitutionally, these new programs relied on a broadened interpretation of federal powers, particularly the commerce clause, which grants Congress the power to "regulate commerce . . . among the several states"

TABLE 12-2   Selected Federal Environmental Laws Since 1970

1970	National Environmental Policy Act (PL 90-190)
	Environmental Quality Improvement Act (PL 91-224)
	Clean Air Act Amendments (PL 91-604)
	Resources Recovery Act (PL 91-512)
	Occupational Health and Safety Act (PL 91-596)
1972	Federal Water Pollution Amendments (PL 92-500)
	Noise Control Act (PL 92-574)
	Coastal Zone Management Act (PL 92-583)
	Federal Environmental Pesticide Control Act (PL 92-516)
	Marine Protection, Research. and Sanctuaries Act (PL 92-532)
1973	Flood Disaster Protection Act (PL 93-234)
	Endangered Species Act (PL 93-205)
	Safe Drinking Water Act (PL 93-523)
1976	Resources Conservation and Recovery Act (PL 94-580)
	Federal Land Policy and Management Act (PL 94-579)
	Surface Mining Control and Reclamation Act (PL 95-87)
	Toxic Substances Control Act (PL 94-469)
1977	Soil and Water Resources Conservation Act (PL 95-102)
1980	Comprehensive Environmental Response Compensation and Liability Act (PL 96-510) ("Supervened")
1982	Coastal Barrier Resources Act (PL 97-348)
1984	Hazardous and Solid Waste Amendments (PL 98-616)
1985	Food Security Act (PL 99-198)
1986	Superfund Amendments and Reauthorization Act (PL 99-499)

(N.B. Subsequent amendments to these acts are not listed. Consult U.S. Code Annotated for current versions.)

(U.S. Constitution, Art. I, Sec. 8). The emission of pollution by vehicles or in economic production of goods for sale in interstate commerce has been held in many court decisions to justify federal pollution regulations. Also, the movement of air and water across state lines itself gives rise to a federal interest in controlling the pollution that they convey (Dolgin and Guilbert 1974, 22–27).

Thus, the environmental reforms of the 1970s redefined the meaning of federalism—the relative balance of power between the federal government on the one hand and states and local governments on the other.

Like the New Deal in the 1930s, this marked an irreversible enlargement of the federal role. (Even the antiregulatory ideology of the Reagan Administration failed to dismantle the environmental programs started during the 1970s, although it did damage some of them through neglect and mismanagement.) In a parallel development, certain states redefined their relationships with local governments during the 1970s as well (see Chapter 10).

The shift in rhetoric from "urban sprawl" in the 1960s to "environmental deterioration" in the 1970s signified a subtle change in political and geographical emphasis. While cities had occupied central stage in the earlier wave of new federal programs, the environmental movement expanded the area of concern to the entire nation with a consequent downgrading of strictly urban concerns such as housing and transportation. (This geographical enlargement would extend to the entire planet in the 1980s, with reference to global warming, stratospheric ozone depletion, acid rain, and tropical deforestation.) With the inauguration of the Republican presidency of Richard Nixon in January, 1969, the urban and community development agenda of the Democrats under Presidents Kennedy and Johnson was substantially dismantled.

In the process, political influence shifted from urban planners in the 1960s to ecologists, chemists, and climatologists in the next two decades. A foretaste of the imminent shift in geographic and disciplinary emphasis was provided in two major publications that appeared in 1965. The first was a special issue of *Scientific American* on "Cities," featuring articles by some of the leading urban scholars of the day. The second was a volume entitled *Future Environments of North America* (Darling 1965). The latter, the proceedings of a conference dominated by natural scientists, largely ignored cities, even though they would be the "future environment" for over three-quarters of North Americans.

The cover of *Time* for February 2, 1970 was emblazoned: "Environment: Nixon's New Issue." In cooperation with Congress, the Nixon Administration presided over adoption of the National Environmental Policy Act, the far-reaching amendments to the federal air and water quality acts, and the creation of the Environmental Protection Agency. Even a national land use policy act was nearly achieved: the federal Coastal Zone Management Act of 1972 was the survivor of many bills filed on that topic. The laws passed between 1970 and 1976 have served the nation well in many respects over the past two decades. Collectively, they comprised a massive and creative legal response to the findings of environmental scientists and the common sense of the average voter.

The National Environmental Policy Act

The National Environmental Policy Act (NEPA) was the keystone of federal environmental reforms of the 1970s. NEPA united both a statutory declaration of national commitment to a safer, healthier environment with a new decision-making procedure applicable to all federal agencies. It also created a new agency, the U.S. Council on Environmental Quality, to administer the new policy and procedures established by the Act.

NEPA reflected a perception that the federal government should get its own house in order before, or at least while, it sought improvement in nonfederal activities affecting the environment. Federally sponsored domestic and military construction programs of the 1950s and 1960s were accompanied by widespread land degradation, air and water pollution, habitat destruction, and aesthetic blight. Also, federal licensing and regulatory authorities were deemed to be administered in disregard of environmental consequences of proposed actions. According to the first Annual Report of the U.S. Council on Environmental Quality (1970, 191), harmful environmental impacts arise from:

> a myriad of federal loans, grants, projects, and other programs enacted for specific public purposes.... The most significant federal activities include the highway, airport, and mass transit programs, the sewer and water grant programs, ... the location of Federal facilities, and water resource projects.

In addition to federal spending programs, environmental neglect was charged in the administration of diverse federal licensing and regulatory activities involving, for example, pesticide usage, offshore oil and gas leasing, nuclear and fossil fuel power plant siting and design, discharges into navigable waters, and federal land management. Some notable controversies involving federal actions during the 1960s included:

- The proposal by the Bureau of Reclamation to dam portions of the Grand Canyon

- A proposed 39-square-mile jetport to be built just north of Everglades National Park in Florida

- The Cross-Florida Barge Canal initiated (but never completed) by the Army Corps of Engineers

- Competing proposals for a national park and a federally funded harbor in the Indiana Dunes on Lake Michigan (Platt 1972; Engel 1985)

- The 1969 oil spill disaster in Santa Barbara Channel (Baldwin 1970)

- Innumerable conflicts over the siting and design of Interstate Highways, for example, Franconia Notch, NH; San Francisco's Bay Freeway; New Orleans; Boston; Seattle; and so forth

- The Rampart Dam proposal for the Yukon River in Alaska

- The North American Water and Power Alliance (NAWAPA) proposal to impound massive quantities of water from British Columbia for diversion to arid regions of the United States and Canada (Reisner 1986)

There were precedents for a requirement, as adopted in NEPA, that adverse effects of a proposed action be identified before a federal action is taken. The Fish and Wildlife Coordination Act of 1958 required that any proposal to impound, divert, deepen, or otherwise control or modify any stream or water body under the auspices of a federal project or permit must be reviewed by the U.S. Fish and Wildlife Service (FWS) of the Department of the Interior. The objective of this review is "the conservation of wildlife resources by preventing loss of and damage to such resources." The FWS cannot veto directly a project that would endanger wildlife habitat, but its comments are appended to the report to Congress or other authorizing agency. The proposed Rampart Dam in Alaska was an example of a project abandoned due in part to foreseeable impacts on wildlife habitat.

Another precedent was Section 4(f) of the Department of Transportation Act of 1966, which limited the encroachment of DOT projects on preserved open spaces. It prohibited approval of a project that

"... requires the use of any publicly owned land from a public park, recreation area, or wildlife and waterfowl refuge of national, state or local significance ... unless (1) there is no feasible and prudent alternative ... and (2) such program includes all possible planning to minimize harm ... " to such areas.

This doctrine as expressed in the pertinent laws applied to federally assisted highways, mass transportation facilities, and airport development. Section 4(f) provided a basis for several challenges to federal transportation projects prior to NEPA. In *Citizens to Preserve Overton Park v. Volpe* 401 U.S. 402, 1971, the U.S. Supreme Court directed DOT to reevaluate a proposed alignment of Interstate 40 through a Memphis park. Although the alternative was to cut through urban neighborhoods, the park was eventually spared.

NEPA, like the Declaration of Independence, is short, clear, and bold. It first states the intent of Congress: "... to foster and promote the general welfare, to create and maintain conditions under which man and nature can exist in productive harmony, and fulfill the social, economic, and other requirements of present and future generations of Americans" (PL 91-190, Sec. 101(a)). This is followed by a series of rhetorical goals.

To add force to its rhetoric, NEPA requires all federal agencies to prepare "detailed statements" disclosing potential environmental consequences of their proposed actions. The requirement applies to any proposed "major federal actions significantly affecting the quality of the human environment," for example: (1) direct federal actions such as the siting of federal facilities, (2) funding commitments for nonfederal activities, (3) federal licensing and permits, and (4) proposals for federal legislation.

Environmental Impact Statements

An "environmental impact statement" (EIS) must be prepared and circulated to all interested agencies, organizations, and individuals prior to the final agency decision concerning the proposed action. Section 102(c) of the act requires an EIS to consider:

1. The environmental impact of the proposed action

2. Adverse environmental effects which cannot be avoided should the proposal be implemented

3. Alternatives to the proposed action

4. The relationships between local short-term uses of man's environment and the maintenance and enhancement of long-term productivity

5. Any irreversible and irretrievable commitments of resources which would be involved in the proposed action should it be implemented

Many early EISs were excessively long and detailed, impeding their usefulness. Environmentalists complained that some agencies engaged in overkill to bury opposing views in prolixity. The agencies, on the other hand, responded that they were only trying to avoid being sued for producing an insufficient EIS. In 1978, CEQ issued new regulations to refine the EIS preparation process (40 *Code of Federal Regulations* Parts 1500–1508). The policy of "scoping" was introduced whereby affected agencies would agree in advance as to environmental issues to be addressed and the level of detail to be devoted to each.

Even with the 1978 refinements, NEPA has generated a mountain of paperwork. Between 1978 and 1984, a total of 6689 draft and final EISs were filed by federal agencies (U.S. Council on Environmental Quality 1984, Table A-69). Two-thirds of these were submitted by the major construction agencies: U.S. Department of Transportation–1474 statements; Army Corps of Engineers–1062; Department of Housing and Urban Development–843; and Department of Agriculture–816.

The purpose of all of this effort has been to "provide full and fair discussion of significant environmental impacts and ... inform decision makers and the public of the reasonable alternatives which would avoid or minimize adverse impacts" (40 CFR sec. 1505.1). Unlike Section 4(f) of the DOT Act, NEPA includes no directive to disapprove actions deemed likely to produce avoidable adverse consequences. Rather, its impact has been indirect, through the political process and through the courts.

Political response to an EIS involves a variety of pressures that may bear on the decision agency. These include formal objections from sister agencies; from members of Congress, governors, mayors, and other elected officials; by environmental organizations and residents of the area to be affected; and adverse publicity in the public media. These various forms of pressure, fueled by the mandatory disclosures of the EIS,

may lead to funding cuts or other sanctions by Congress, to a presidential veto, or simply to modification or cancellation of the project by the
decision agency. Or they may produce no change at all, leaving the project to proceed as proposed.

Probably the more profound effects of NEPA have occurred through
lawsuits challenging particular EISs. Hundreds of legal challenges based
on NEPA grounds have been filed by environmental organizations and
other objectors since the early 1970s by parties objecting to proposed
federal actions. NEPA does not prohibit unwise federal actions but
requires full disclosure of adverse implications. Therefore, lawsuits generally challenge the sufficiency of such disclosures in an EIS or demand
that one be prepared where it has not been.

Delay is a common motive in filing a NEPA lawsuit. Years may pass
pending the outcome of (1) preliminary hearings, (2) a decision at the
trial level, and (3) appeals. The defendant agency is precluded from
approving the disputed action until final resolution or settlement is
reached. Delay adds to the cost of the project in addition to the costs of
the litigation itself and may result in its abandonment or substantial
modification.

The Sears Island Case

To take one example among many, Maine in 1978 proposed to construct
a small bulk cargo port on Sears Island at the head of scenic Penobscot
Bay (Figure 12-1). A federal permit to "dredge and fill" in estuarine wetlands was granted, and certain federal funds were committed to the project. The responsible agencies prepared "environmental assessments"
(EAs) but concluded that a full-scale EIS would not be needed. Upon
suit by the Sierra Club, the federal Court of Appeals in Boston ordered
that an EIS be prepared and enjoined the start of construction (*Sierra
Club v. Marsh* 769 F.2d 868, 1985). A draft and final EIS were duly prepared by the relevant federal and state agencies and circulated for
review.

The Boston regional office of the U.S. Environmental Protection
Agency and the Fish and Wildlife Service joined the Sierra Club in
raising further questions as to the adequacy of the EIS, especially in its
consideration of the alternative location of the proposed port at Mack
Point, where an existing port now exists a few hundred yards from Sears

FIGURE 12-1   Map of Sears Island, Maine, and site of proposed bulk cargo terminal.

Island. The Sierra Club returned to court to make that objection and, further, to argue that the EIS narrowly addressed only the *direct* impacts to the site of the proposed port, while ignoring *secondary* effects on the rest of the still-undeveloped Sears Island and Penobscot Bay. An underlying economic issue, not covered by NEPA, was the lack of any interest by shippers in using the Sears Island facility if it were built, making it likely to be a "white elephant" (Platt 1987). After further refinements were made in the EIS, in 1992 it was discovered that the proposed project would impinge on not only tidal wetlands, but also some 200 acres of freshwater wetlands on Sears Island that had not previously been noticed! The courts ordered further revision of the EIS to consider these "new" wetlands.

As of 1995, the Sears Island case has so far generated at least 10 federal court opinions and the project is still on hold except for the causeway, which was constructed in 1987. Port advocates blame the Sierra Club and EPA for using NEPA litigation to obstruct development in an economically depressed area of the state. Others, however, suggest that the 900-acre undeveloped Sears Island could better be used as a state park, which would also generate construction and economic benefits. (Even some of the townspeople of Searsport, Maine where the port would be located have begun to question the wisdom or need for the project: *The Boston Globe*, April 23, 1995.)

NEPA is poorly adapted to fostering a broader regional planning perspective and it certainly cannot force states to spend money for parks. But NEPA sometimes may be useful to suspend a project long enough to allow the entire plan to be reconsidered. The Environmental Law Institute (1989, 10060) praised NEPA as "Congress's first modern environmental law [which] has set the tone for the complex superstructure of federal environmental law that was to follow." But on the other hand, Lynton K. Caldwell (1989), who participated in the drafting of the original NEPA in the late 1960s, urges that a constitutional amendment on the environment would offer more reliable protection than the statute alone, whose application has often been swayed by politics.

Coastal Zone Management

The tidal and Great Lakes shorelines of the United States extend about 58,000 miles (National Oceanic and Atmospheric Administration 1975).

These shorelines include many different geomorphic types, of which the following are representative (National Research Council 1990):

- crystalline bedrock (central and northern Maine)

- eroding bluff (outer Cape Cod, Great Lakes)

- pocket beach (southern New England, Pacific Coast)

- strandplain beach (Myrtle Beach, South Carolina)

- coastal barriers (Long Island, New York to Texas)

- coral reef and mangrove (south Florida)

- coastal wetland (Louisiana)

Coasts also vary as to type and intensity of human usage and modification. Coastal settlements include (1) totally urbanized industrial, port, and resort developments; (2) medium-density, older summer colonies, often converted to year-round use and higher-density condominiums; (3) still-picturesque fishing and artist villages becoming "yuppified"; and (4) new megadevelopments like Hilton Head, South Carolina, or Amelia Island Plantation, Florida.

Public or quasi-public agencies own extensive tracts of unspoiled or less-developed coastal lands. The National Park Service operates 10 national seashores, four national lakeshores, and several other coastal recreation facilities. Other undeveloped shorelines are included in units of the National Wildlife Refuge System or are owned by the military. There are 18 National Estuarine Sanctuaries in 15 states under the administration of the National Oceanic and Atmospheric Administration (NOAA). Some key ecological sites on the coast have been preserved by private organizations such as The Nature Conservancy (for instance, the Coastal Reserve in Virginia) and the various Audubon Societies.

Of course, not all privately owned shorelines are developed. Some areas remain undeveloped due to isolation, personal preference of the owner, or some form of development restriction. Certain undeveloped and privately owned coastal barriers were placed off limits to flood insurance and other federal growth incentives by the Coastal Barrier Resources Act of 1982. But accessible private shore frontage tends to be extremely valuable for development and usually is densely built-up.

Though limited in geographic extent, coastal areas encompass much of the nation's population growth: Eight of the 10 largest metropolitan areas are situated on tidal waters or the Great Lakes. The aggregate population of counties substantially within 50 miles of coasts grew from 92.7 million in 1960 to 129.5 million in 1988, comprising slightly over half the nation's total population (U.S. Bureau of the Census 1991, Table 34).

Both within and outside metropolitan areas, coasts are "awash with disputes" (Conservation Foundation 1977). They are the scene of intense competition between public and private interests, between economic and environmental values, and between diverse land and water uses: residence, business, industry, transportation, recreation, fisheries, and natural habitat. The results are sometimes mutually conflicting as in the case of the Indiana Dunes where 50 years of controversy yielded a national lakeshore wrapped around a major industrial complex, to the detriment of both (Platt 1972).

Vast areas of estuarine wetlands and related natural habitat have been lost to filling, dredging, pollution, and land subsidence (Frayer et al. 1983; Dahl and Johnson 1991; see Chapter 1). Tidal freshwater wetlands and mangrove habitat also have sustained losses at the hands of developers. Coastal wetland losses endanger commercial and sport fisheries and impair other natural functions of wetlands such as bird habitat, water purification, and protection against wave damage (Mitsch and Gosselink 1986, ch. 16).

Another concern is the vulnerability of coastal development, especially on low-lying barrier beaches, to natural hazards including hurricanes, northeasters, erosion, landslides, and tsunamis. Often the very physical characteristics that attract humans to the shore are directly responsible for potential disaster. Pacific Coast residents seeking ocean views build on unstable slopes that collapse during heavy winter rains. Atlantic and Gulf coast barrier residents of "cities on the beach" (Platt, Pelscarski, and Burbank 1987) may be entirely stranded at times of storm surge, unable to flee to the mainland across an impassable causeway. Cottages on the Great Lakes cling to the rim of eroding bluffs and are undermined during periods of high lake levels. The experience of the "Great 1938 Hurricane" in New England, several others in the 1950s and 1960s, and the catastrophic Hurricane Camille in 1969 signaled even greater losses in the future as the coasts fill up with homes. In 1989, Hurricane Hugo damaged or destroyed nearly all of several hundred shorefront homes lining the coastal barriers near Charleston, South Carolina (Figure 12-2) (Platt, Beatley, and Miller 1991). The growing awareness of coastal hazards, focused by a succession of disastrous hurricanes and northeasters, has yielded a diverse array of public responses, including structural protection, beach and dune restoration, setback laws, and incentives to retreat from the water's edge (Figure 12-3) (Platt 1994).

The Federal Coastal Zone Management Act

The federal Coastal Zone Management Act (CZMA) (PL 92-583) arose from the ashes of more than 320 land and water management bills filed in the Ninety-first and Ninety-second Congresses (U.S. Congress 1973). The rancor surrounding various proposals for a National Land Use Policy Act apparently could not withstand the charm of the seacoast. The CZMA passed the Senate by a vote of 68 to 0 and the House by 376 to 6 and has continued to enjoy strong Congressional support even in the face of hostility from the White House.

The CZMA was another product of the wave of federal activism that

FIGURE 12-2   Reconstruction of expensive homes on the eroding barrier island of Isle of Palms, South Carolina a year after Hurricane Hugo (1990).

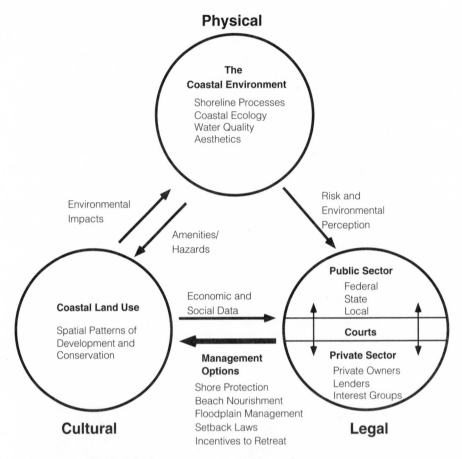

FIGURE 12-3   Model of response to coastal hazards.

yielded NEPA and other legislation listed in Table 12-2. The specific idea for a federal CZM program was proposed by the Commission on Marine Science, Engineering, and Resources (1969) (the Stratton Commission). Another influence was the Model Land Development Code (discussed in Chapter 10). A few states had adopted their own coastal management laws before CZMA was enacted in 1972, notably California, Washington, and Rhode Island. These provided models for what the federal act might encourage other coastal states to do.

The CZMA is an experiment in creative and dynamic federalism (Godschalk 1992). It tries to strike a balance between direct federal regulation of the coast (politically unpalatable) and simply generating endless studies that no one implements. It supports *state* planning and management programs subject to *federal* guidelines. It seeks to achieve its objectives by working with and through coastal states and territories and granting much latitude for them to develop programs consistent with their particular physical, settlement, and political characteristics.

But the CZM act sought to ensure federal influence over the scope and content of state plans. Short-term funding was extended to coastal states to help them prepare plans (Section 305). For states to continue to receive funding toward the implementation of their plans, the latter must be approved by the Office of Ocean and Coastal Resource Management (OCRM), a unit of the National Oceanic and Atmospheric Administration (NOAA). Plan approval has required prolonged negotiation between federal and state coastal officials over the scope and provisions of each state plan, which has generally yielded valuable results (Matuszeski 1985). As of 1995, 29 of the 35 eligible coastal states and territories were receiving federal funds to administer their approved state plans.

The objectives of the CZM program are extremely broad. The original 1972 act specified diverse and often incompatible coastal activities to be considered, such as ". . . industry, commerce, residential development, recreation, extraction of mineral resources and fossil fuels, transportation and navigation, waste disposal, and harvesting of fish, shellfish, and other living marine resources, wildlife . . ." Subsequent amendments added more concerns: public access to beaches and coastal waters, natural hazard reduction, energy development, estuarine research, and protection of cultural and natural landmarks (Beatley, Brower, and Schwab 1994).

The first step in coastal zone planning was for each state to designate its "coastal zone." The Act defined the coastal zone to include "coastal waters . . . and the adjacent shorelands . . . strongly influenced by each other and in proximity to the shorelines of the several coastal states." The offshore boundary was set by the Act as the seaward limit of state sovereignty (generally three miles from mean high water along ocean shorelines). The inland boundary was to be designated by each state. A combination of physical and cultural reference lines (for example, elevation contours and coastal roads) were employed in most cases.

Within its coastal zone, each state was required to identify "permissible land and water uses" and "areas of planning concern" within which special restrictions would apply. All this sounded suspiciously like "state zoning," a notion stoutly opposed by most local governments. States therefore have been compelled to walk a tightrope between adopting significant restrictions on the use of coastal land as specified in federal guidelines while minimizing interference with the prerogatives of local governments and private owners. (See discussion of *Nollan v. California Coastal Commission* and *Lucas v. South Carolina Coastal Council* in Chapter 8 and state programs in Chapter 10).

The CZMA further required as a condition of plan approval that states exercise some form of control over important coastal land use decisions through at least one of the following methods:

a. State establishment of criteria and standards for local implementation, subject to administrative review and enforcement of compliance

b. Direct state land use and water use planning and regulation

c. State administrative review . . . of all development plans, projects, or . . . regulations (Sec. 306(e))

Satisfying this requirement was no simple task: "Arrayed against those options was the nearly overwhelming complexity of 35 sets of state laws" (Matuszeski 1985, 270). Some states offered comprehensive coastal management laws that they had adopted either before or after the federal CZM Act–for example, California, Washington, Rhode Island, North Carolina, and Michigan. Others, such as Massachusetts, however, in the absence of a single coastal law, offered a "network" of statutes, regulations, and executive orders that individually addressed such issues as coastal wetlands, facility siting, beach access, pollution abatement, and hazard protection.

Federal versus state control over the leasing and development of offshore oil and gas reserves has provoked much legal and political controversy. Coastal states control oil and gas within their own areas of jurisdiction (usually three miles seaward of the mean high-water line), and many have refrained from developing such resources. Beyond that limit, seabed resources of the "outer continental shelf" (OCS) are federal property, under the jurisdiction of the federal Bureau of Land Management (BLM). Revenue from federal offshore oil and gas development is earmarked for the Land and Water Conservation Fund, as discussed in Chapter 10. Nevertheless, proposed lease sales and further development of OCS resources have been vigorously opposed by environmentalists and certain state governments.

Section 307 of the CZM Act requires that federal actions be "consistent with approved state management programs." Thus state CZM plans may theoretically "veto" federal activities, a reversal of the normal federal–state relationship. The U.S. Supreme Court in *Secretary of the Interior v. California* 464 U.S. 310, 1984 held that Section 307 did not apply to federal lease sales but would limit subsequent exploration, development, and production of OCS oil and gas resources in accordance with state plans. Congress in 1990 amended Section 307 of the act to overturn that decision and to clarify that "all federal agency activities, inside or outside the coastal zone, are subject to the consistency provisions of the CZM act if they affect natural resources, land uses, or water uses in the coastal zone" (Godschalk 1992, 110).

The federal CZM program has been popular with recipient states, which have successfully lobbied in Congress for continuation of funding. However, the substantive results of the program are difficult to evaluate:

Congress decided, for a variety of reasons, not to prescribe for the nation's coastline substantive federal standards of the type contained in contemporaneous pollution control laws, but rather to encourage each coastal state to set up a rational comprehensive process for making decisions about coastal resources. . . . [B]ecause of this lack of federal standards, it is impossible to evaluate rigorously the federal program's national impact on the protection of the coastal environment or on the rate of coastal development.

Healy and Zinn 1985, p. 308.

The CZM program is also difficult to evaluate due to its multiplicity of objectives—environmental, economic, social—and the complexity of federal-state-local-private interaction from which identifiable results emerge. Thus, the preservation of coastal wetlands, for example, may result from the CZM program, but may equally be attributable to the federal wetlands program (Sec. 404 of the Clean Water Act), to state or local laws, or to private actions. Nevertheless, federal CZM officials are not bashful in claiming credit for a variety of specific improvements in coastal management (for example, Office of Ocean and Coastal Resource Management 1988).

Apart from individual projects, the CZM program may fairly be credited with fostering a variety of new state laws, regulations, and bond issues concerning coastal management. An important example is the adoption of coastal setback requirements for new construction in 13 states (National Academy of Sciences 1990; Platt et al. 1992). [The U.S. House of Representatives in 1991 adopted H.R. 1236, which would have added erosion setbacks to the National Flood Insurance following the model of North Carolina's Coastal Area Management Act. However, coastal property owner interests successfully blocked the measure in the Senate and the National Flood Insurance Reform Act of 1994 (PL 103-325) requires only a study of coastal erosion by the Federal Emergency Management Agency.]

Overall, the federal CZM program has facilitated an upgrading of state capabilities to plan and administer coastal planning. The program is sometimes viewed as timid (as in the Sears Island dispute mentioned earlier, in which federal and state CZM officials were conspicuously silent). But, in balance, it has strengthened state skills and confidence in confronting coastal disputes, and may indirectly have contributed to upgrading the management of noncoastal resources as well.

The National Flood Insurance Program

National Effects of Floods

Riverine and coastal disasters inflict an ever-rising toll of economic, social, and emotional costs on the United States. Damage data is very inexact, but one study estimates that the per capita cost of floods to public and private property was almost 2.5 times greater for the period 1951 to 1986 as from 1916 through 1950 (Federal Interagency Floodplain Management Task Force [FMTF] 1992, 18). More recently, Hurricane Hugo alone in 1989 caused approximately $7 billion in flood, wind, and other damage in Puerto Rico, the Virgin Islands, and the Carolinas. The Midwest Floods of 1993 inflicted an estimated $12–16 billion in agricultural and urban damage, including $4.2 billion in direct federal disaster assistance costs and $1.3 billion from federal insurance programs (Interagency Floodplain Management Review Committee 1994, 15 and 22).

The geographic area flooded varies according to the magnitude of the storm causing the flood. This presents the issue as to whether public programs should address only the area frequently flooded or should extend more widely to areas flooded only rarely. The federal government is chiefly concerned with hazards within the "100-year floodplain," namely the area with a probability of at least 1 percent of being flooded in any given year. (See Chapter 9 for discussion of the physical nature of floodplains.) This standard represents a compromise between very frequent and the most rare catastrophic events. Although it sounds fairly remote, a 100-year flood has a 26 percent chance of occurring during the lifetime of a 30-year mortgage. And only the outer edges of the 100-year floodplain have a risk as low as 1 percent per year: closer to the stream channel the risk is progressively higher.

The total land area within 100-year floodplains is approximately 150,000 square miles (94 million acres) or about 7 percent of the nation's land area (Federal Emergency Management Agency [FEMA] 1994, 3). Over 90 percent of these flood hazard areas are rural, but some 3.5 to 5.5 million acres of floodplain are urbanized (FMTF 1992, 16). In 1975, 6.4 million dwelling units were estimated to be located in flood hazard areas nationally (U.S. Congress 1975, 127). Urban floodplains also contain industrial and commercial infrastructure—highways, airports, bridges, water and sewer treatment plants, and electrical facilities (Figure 12-4). Thus the disruptive effects of floods may extend far beyond the area actually under water when these facilities are disabled. Also, storm drainage backup accounts for extensive problems in many metropolitan areas such as Chicago, Atlanta, and Houston.

Flash floods pose special difficulties for public flood response. Unlike gradual riverine floods that develop slowly and may allow days of notice to evacuate downstream areas, flash floods crest within hours or even minutes after a heavy deluge, thus endangering both lives and property. Flash floods are very destructive in narrow, steep canyons or valleys, as in the Rocky Mountains and Appalachia. The 1976 Big Thompson Canyon flood in Colorado was described as a "wall of water" carrying boulders, trees, cars, building debris, and bodies (Gruntfest 1987). Flash floods also strike small watersheds in urban areas where paving and sewering of natural land surfaces convey runoff directly to local streams, converting them into raging and destructive torrents.

Clearly, much of the flood problem stems from human encroachment on natural floodplains. Floods have long been regarded as "acts of God" or, paradoxically, natural phenomena to be controlled by human

FIGURE 12-4   The 1979 Pearl River Flood at Jackson, Mississippi. State Coliseum, industrial, and commercial buildings built in area "protected" by flood control were inundated by overtopping of levees.

intervention. Floodplains attract development despite the risk involved because they offer level building sites favorably located near waterways, highways, and other arteries of commerce. If properly situated and engineered, certain types of buildings may be compatible with occasional flooding. Wise use rather than nonuse of floodplains has long been a national objective. But too often, encroachment has simply proceeded in ignorance or disregard of flood hazards. Also, the private investor may fairly conclude that if the site is unsafe, "the government" will offer protection against loss.

Structural Flood Control

In the 1936 Flood Control Act, Congress undertook to do exactly that. Motivated by a rash of serious floods in the midst of the Great Depression, the act launched a $10-billion, 30-year effort to control flooding through the construction of dams, reservoirs, levecs, diversion channels, and coastal protection works. Depending on the location, the major construction agencies have included the U.S. Army Corps of Engineers, the Bureau of Reclamation, and the Tennessee Valley Authority. Since 1954, the Soil Conservation Service of the Department of Agriculture under P.L. 83-566 has supplemented the large dam-building efforts of these agencies with conservation and flood control projects for small rural watersheds.

Flood control thus joined river and harbor improvements as the object of Congressional generosity, and of competition among members of Congress for projects to be located in their districts or states. (The next generation would have its interstate highways and military bases.) States and local governments were only required to provide land, flowage easements, and future maintenance, with the project costs otherwise covered by Congress.

Federal water development projects including flood control works may only be approved: "... if the benefits to whomsoever they may accrue are in excess of the estimated costs. ..." (33 USC sec. 701a). Like NEPA 35 years later, the requirement of a favorable benefit/cost ratio generated elaborate economic evaluation procedures and even more elaborate ways of ensuring that the benefits would indeed exceed the costs. This was sometimes accomplished by assigning extravagant economic value to potential recreation opportunities of proposed reservoirs.

In the case of many projects, especially urban levees, the chief benefit would be the protection of buildings in the floodplain from flooding. Herein lay a fallacy of federal efforts to alleviate flood losses through flood control projects. Such projects made economic sense only if they protected buildings from flooding. The more buildings protected, the more favorable the B/C ratio. Thus, structural flood control implicitly was intended to attract *more building* in "protected" floodplains. Although future construction technically was not counted as a "benefit" in project justification, little effort was made to restrain further building in areas behind levees or downstream from flood control reservoirs. The projects themselves gave an illusion of safety to new investments in floodplains. The Corps of Engineers in 1993 claimed that its flood control structures in the Mississippi-Missouri valleys saved $19.1 billion in additional losses (IFMRC 1994, 21).

But flood control projects are designed to a particular level of safety. Floods that exceed that design level can overtop a levee or overwhelm the storage capacity of a reservoir, creating havoc in the "protected" floodplain. A classic example occurred in Jackson, Mississippi where the Corps of Engineers constructed levees and channelized the Pearl River during the 1960s. New commercial and public buildings constructed in the floodplain behind the levee were inundated by up to 14 feet of water when the river overtopped the levee in April 1979 (Figure 12-4) (Platt 1982). Overtopping of levees was blamed for at least 40 percent of the losses from Tropical Storm Agnes in 1972 (White 1975, 10). Earlier studies by White and others (1958; 1964) indicated that average annual flood losses may actually be *increased* by the federal flood control program due to the failure to limit new development in areas protected against ordinary flooding but still vulnerable to catastrophic events.

Flood control projects may inadvertently worsen flood hazards by altering natural processes. A flood control dam blocks sediments from reaching the lower river. This creates a siltation problem behind the dam, reducing storage capacity, and may cause increased bank erosion downstream at times of high flow as the stream seeks to dissipate its excess energy. Where silt does reach the lower river from tributaries, the elimination of lower-magnitude floods due to flood control projects allows the stream channel to silt up during periods of low flow without being periodically scoured, leading to increased flood risk downstream than under natural conditions.

Haphazard local protection measures also may exacerbate flooding, as when property owners or a municipality, in protecting themselves, transfer the problem to a cross-stream or downstream neighbor. Similarly, coastal jetties and groins may cause downdrift shorelines to erode due to lack of sand supply.

Federal response to the flood problem has been episodic (Burby and French 1985, 6). Consistent with the model in Chapter 2, new laws, policies, and initiatives have tended to follow closely major floods or series of floods, as perceived by policy makers with the help of expert advice (Table 12-3).

A major turning point in federal flood policy occurred in the mid-1960s following a series of disasters that were driving federal disaster relief costs to over $1 billion annually. After Hurricane Betsy in 1965, Congress called for a study on the feasibility of a federal flood insurance program. At the same time, the Bureau of the Budget formed a Task Force on Federal Flood Control. These two studies (U.S. Congress 1966a

TABLE 12-3   Chronology of Major Flood Events and Public Response

Year	Flood Disaster	New Law or Study
1927	Lower Mississippi	Lower Miss. Flood Control Act, 1928
1936	Eastern river basins Ohio-Mississippi	Flood Control Act, 1936
1938	New England	Flood Control Act, 1938
1944	Hurricane–Florida	Flood Control Act, 1944
1954	New England hurricanes	
1955	New England hurricanes	PL 84-71–structural protection
1961	Southwest and Midwest	Corps Flood Information Program Senate Select Comm. Report
1962	Atlantic Coast	PL 87-874–structural protection
1965	Hurricane Betsy Upper Mississippi	SE Hurricane Relief Act, PL 89-339
1966		House Doc. 465 HUD Report on Flood Insurance
1968		National Flood Insurance Act, PL 90-448, Title XIII
1969	Upper Mississippi Hurricane Camille	
1972	Tropical Storm Agnes Rapid City flash flood	
1973	Upper Mississippi	Flood Disaster Protection Act, PL 93-234
1974		Federal Disaster Relief Act, PL 93-288
1975	Mid-Atlantic	
1978	Northeaster–N. E.	
1979	Hurricane Frederic Pearl River flood Red River	
1980	Hurricane David	OMB Flood Mitigation Directive
1981		Sheaffer and Roland Report
1982		Coastal Barrier Resources Act
1985-86	Great Lakes flooding Southeast coastal floods	Upton-Jones amendment to NFIP
1988		Federal Disaster Relief Amendments
1989	Hurricane Hugo	
1990		NRC Coastal Erosion Report
1992-93	Northeasters–mid-Atlantic	
1993	Mississippi/Missouri	"Sharing the Challenge" Report
1995	California winter floods	

and 1966b) were directed respectively by Marion Clawson and Gilbert White.

The White task force questioned the wisdom of exclusive reliance on structural flood control in view of the limitations cited in the foregoing. Instead, it proposed a multi-means approach to flood hazards (U.S. Congress 1966b; White 1975, Table II-1) including:

- *Flood control works*, where economically justified and where benefited interests share the full costs of construction

- *Floodproofing* of existing structures or new structures that must be built in floodplains

- Improvement of *forecast* and *warning* systems

- *Land use management*, including floodplain zoning and land acquisition

- *Flood insurance* provided at affordable rates by the federal government but subject to community floodplain management to control further development in hazard areas

- *Relief and rehabilitation* following a flood disaster

The White task force further urged caution in the establishment of a national flood insurance program:

A flood insurance program is a tool that should be used expertly or not at all. Correctly applied, it could promote wise use of floodplains. Incorrectly applied, it could exacerbate the whole problem of flood losses. For the Federal Government to subsidize low premium disaster insurance . . . would be to invite economic waste of great magnitude. Further, insurance coverage is necessarily restricted to tangible property; no matter how great a subsidy might be made, it could never be sufficient to offset the tragic personal consequences which would follow enticement of the population into hazard areas (U.S. Congress 1966b, p. 17).

The task force report was forwarded to Congress by President Lyndon Johnson together with Executive Order 11296 directing federal agencies to evaluate flood hazards before funding new construction or the purchase or disposal of land. Congress then adopted the National Flood Insurance Act of 1968 (P.L. 90-448, Title XIII).

The National Flood Insurance Program: A New Approach

The National Flood Insurance Program (NFIP) has been the mainstay of federal response to floods since the early 1970s. It represents a dramatic departure from the long-standing reliance on structural flood control projects. Instead, the NFIP offers an array of nonstructural forms of response to flood hazards including (1) floodplain mapping; (2) floodplain management; (3) flood insurance; and, to a modest extent (4) floodplain land acquisition.

The NFIP is really two programs rolled into one. First, it seeks to reallocate a portion of the costs of floods from the victims themselves and federal taxpayers (who fund disaster relief) to all property owners in hazard areas through the mechanism of insurance. Flood insurance has been unavailable from private insurers because flood losses, when they occur, are catastrophic and require billions of dollars of reserves. The NFIP, operating through private insurance companies, provides insurance against flood damage to buildings and their contents. Routine claims and administrative costs are paid out of insurance premiums (which are subsidized for older structures and actuarial for new ones, as explained in the following). If a multi-billion-dollar hurricane occurs, the NFIP is backed up by the federal Treasury.

Second, the NFIP promotes floodplain management to limit flood risk to new construction along the nation's rivers and shorelines. As noted in the White report, unless new encroachments are controlled, the NFIP could inadvertently subsidize new floodplain development. But the idea of federal control over land use in floodplains has always been politically unviable. Therefore, a clever backdoor approach is employed by the NFIP. It does not impose mandatory national land use standards, equivalent to EPA's air and water quality standards. Instead it establishes minimum standards for local adoption as a condition to the availability of flood insurance within a given community. Communities are free to ignore the floodplain management guidelines and deny flood insurance to owners of property at risk within their jurisdictions.

At first, the NFIP began with a whimper: Only four communities entered the program and 20 policies were sold during its first year. Two obstacles impeded its progress. First, most communities lacked detailed maps of their flood hazard areas on which land use regulations could be based. Second, few property owners were interested in buying flood insurance; thus there was little incentive for communities to adopt politically unpopular floodplain regulations in order to enter the program.

To address the first problem, the NFIP has spent $1 billion over two decades mapping the nation's floodplains at a scale suitable for local land use regulations (1 to 400). Unlike the Coastal Zone Management Program, which has funded states to prepare their own maps, the Federal Emergency Management Agency (FEMA), which administers the NFIP, has directly prepared flood hazard maps under contract with other federal agencies and private engineering firms. The maps are based on standard engineering models of stream flow and coastal flooding (HEC-2 and SLOSH are the usual models). Using available hydrologic or oceanographic data, the models estimate the elevation of the 100-year flood at specific points along a stream or coast. Elevation data are then converted to estimates of the geographic extent of the floodplain, using topographic data. These calculations are of course subject to several sources of error (Dingman and Platt, 1977). The typical NFIP map depicts the 100-year floodplain ("base flood" in NFIP jargon) and also in some cases a "floodway," a "coastal high hazard area" (on open ocean coasts), and a 500-year floodplain. They also provide data on the level of risk from which actuarial insurance rates may be calculated (Figure 12-5).

NFIP maps are prepared for individual political units: municipalities or unincorporated portions of counties. Prior to completion of a map study, a community may qualify for provisional participation in the NFIP. Once the map is complete and opportunity for appeal of errors has been provided, the map is formally published. From the date of publication, the community has one year to adopt full-scale floodplain management measures or lose all NFIP benefits.

The other obstacle, buyer resistance, was addressed in the Flood Disaster Protection Act of 1973 (PL 93-234), which closely followed Tropical Storm Agnes (Table 12-3). This Act required that anyone borrowing money from a federal or federally related source for purchase or improvement of a structure in a floodplain identified by the NFIP must

FIGURE 12-5   Excerpt from flood insurance rate map for Boulder, Colorado. (Dark area is regulatory 100-year floodplain; light gray is 500-year floodplain). *Source:* Federal Emergency Management Agency.

purchase a flood insurance policy. Since many lending institutions are insured or regulated by federal agencies, this covered a large proportion of mortgage loans involving flood-prone structures.

With these two midcourse corrections, the NFIP began to grow rapidly. By 1975, 9600 communities had joined and a half-million policies were in effect. By 1990, of nearly 22,000 communities in which flood hazards had been identified, 18,200 had joined the NFIP and 16,470 of those had satisfied the minimum federal standards for floodplain management (Federal Interagency Floodplain Management Task Force 1992.) By 1995, a total of 2.9 million policies were in effect, covering about $200 billion in flood-prone property. Also the program has been self-supporting (funded out of premiums) since 1987.

Flood Loss Reduction under the NFIP

These impressive statistics on the expansion of the NFIP provide no evidence as to whether the program has affected the national level of flood losses for better or worse. As mentioned earlier, average annual losses continued to rise during the 1970s and 1980s, but perhaps less than if the NFIP did not exist. Also, the impact of NFIP would be felt gradually as new structures are built to NFIP standards and older ones are destroyed or upgraded. It is therefore not simple to evaluate the effectiveness of the NFIP in terms of flood loss reduction. But we can at least understand how it operates.

The NFIP seeks to reduce flood losses to structures in two ways: (1) by charging actuarial rates for new or substantially improved structures and (2) by setting minimum standards for local regulation of development and redevelopment in floodplains. These are intended to be mutually supportive.

Actuarial rates are insurance premiums calibrated to the assumed level of risk to which a structure is exposed. Thus, a greater likelihood of loss would necessitate a higher premium. Actuarial rates are charged for flood insurance on "new construction" (started after the community entered the NFIP). Older buildings may be insured to a specified amount at a nonactuarial, subsidized rate. This means that structures existing when a community entered the program may be insured at low rates unrelated to risk, whereas new structures must be built safely to avoid prohibitively high rates (and unavailability of federally related financing if flood insurance is not purchased). There is a strong incentive, therefore, for new structures to be located and designed so as to minimize the actuarial rate charged. Elevation of coastal structures is the most conspicuous example: the higher the ground-floor elevation, the lower the flood insurance premium. The Atlantic and Gulf shorelines are lined with post-NFIP structures standing high in the air atop substantial pilings. This in part reflects the influence of actuarial rates, and in part the effect of local minimum elevation requirements pursuant to NFIP floodplain management standards.

Land use and building regulations in floodplains were rare before 1970. In the mid-1950s, Hoyt and Langbein (1955, 95) noted: "Floodplain zoning, like almost all that is virtuous, has great verbal support, but almost nothing has been done about it." Murphy (1958) surveyed national experience with local floodplain management and found only about 50 communities with a local program. The negative outcome in the *Morris County* case (discussed in Chapter 9) reflected the lack of experience and judicial support for floodplain and wetland regulations in the early 1960s. The judicial outlook brightened considerably however with the *Turnpike Realty* and *Just* decisions in 1972.

The NFIP entered the turbulent waters of floodplain management cautiously. Section 1361 of the Act mandates the development of federal criteria for state and local measures to

- "Guide the development of proposed construction away from locations which are threatened by flood hazards;"

- "Assist in reducing damage caused by floods;" and

- "Otherwise improve the long-range land management and use of flood-prone areas."

Such criteria were finally published in 1976 and have been relatively unchanged ever since (44 *Code of Federal Regulations* Secs. 60.3 et seq.). They specify progressively more stringent levels of floodplain management to be satisfied by local communities as the NFIP provides more detailed flood hazard data. The fundamental requirement is that when elevations of the local 100-year flood are determined, the community must require the lowest floor of new residential construction to be at or above that elevation. New commercial structures must be elevated or designed to withstand flood damage ("floodproofed") to that level. This dovetails with the actuarial rate incentive mentioned in the foregoing. (Other technical requirements are not discussed here.)

Tighter control is required in areas delineated by the NFIP as "floodways" or "coastal high hazard areas." A *floodway* is the inner portion of a riverine floodplain adjoining the channel, which experiences frequent and sometimes fast-moving inundation. (See Figure 9-4.) No structures are to be permitted in such areas that "would result in any increase in flood levels within the community . . ." during the 100-year flood. Some states and communities have simply banned all new development in floodways.

Coastal high hazard areas ("V zones") along many open ocean coastlines are defined by the estimated reach of a three-foot breaking wave during a 100-year storm. Such areas are indeed hazardous and also are often subject to increasing risk due to coastal erosion. Nevertheless, the NFIP does not prohibit new construction in V zones. New structures must be landward of mean high tide and must be elevated above the estimated reach of waves during a 100-year storm surge. Also, "man-made alteration" of dunes or mangrove stands is prohibited in V zones. Subject to these minimal requirements, new buildings may be constructed in V zones and insured by the NFIP. Like the flood control program, if the design limits of NFIP floodplain management criteria are exceeded, the resulting loss to structures allowed in the hazard area may be greater than if insurance were not available and investors stayed away from the water's edge.

Another issue is consistency of effort and level of effectiveness from one community to another. In 1979 and 1983, researchers at the University of North Carolina surveyed the floodplain management practices of local governments in the NFIP (involving 1415 and 956 respondent communities, respectively) (Burby and French 1985). They found a wide diversity in the means used to meet or exceed NFIP floodplain management standards. Smaller communities were less likely to employ even the basic tools of minimum elevation and zoning. Since 1993, the NFIP has offered lower insurance premiums to communities that voluntarily exceed the basic national standards for floodplain management under its "Community Rating System." It is too soon to determine the effectiveness of this approach in raising the level of effort by local communities in managing their flood hazard areas.

The Need for Orchestration

Ironically, the nation's response to floods has shifted from being excessively narrow in approach and agency mission, to its present state in which it is perhaps overly diffuse. Responsibilities and authority are fragmented among the federal, state, regional, and local levels of government. Federal flood-related efforts alone are diffused among 27 agencies and nine program purposes (Federal Emergency Management Agency 1986, VII-2). The NFIP is the cornerstone of federal response, but many functions, such as flood prediction and warning, mapping, and emergency planning, cross program and agency boundaries. Following the original call for coordination (U.S. Congress 1966b), various blueprints for a "Unified National Program on floodplain management" have been prepared by the U.S. Water Resources Council (1976) and FEMA (1986; 1994). A "unified national program" for managing flood losses has been an elusive goal. In 1989, the National Review Committee on Floodplain Management (1989) concluded that "there is no truly unified national program . . ." and further:

> There is no central direction for the Unified National Program. No agency has the charter or capability to carry it out in its entirety, and no agency has authority for assuring coordination of the numerous programs targeted on its objectives. There are serious overlaps, gaps, and conflicts among programs aimed at solving the same problem.

The Coastal Barrier Resources Act

In the case of coastal barriers, Congress was persuaded by research that various federal programs were hopelessly at loggerheads and decided to cut through the bureaucratic muddle. Coastal barriers are elongated spits or islands, composed mainly of sand, which fringe much of the Atlantic and Gulf coastlines (Figure 12-6). In a natural state, they provide important habitat for marine life and birds, and dramatic expanses of beach, dune, and salt marsh. When developed, they are exposed to the destructive force of hurricanes and winter storms that sometimes overwash an entire barrier. They also tend to erode readily when beach material is obstructed and in response to sea level rise.

The Coastal Barrier Resources Act of 1982 (PL 97-348) declared that: "Coastal barriers contain resources of extraordinary scenic, scientific, recreational, natural, historic, archeological, cultural, and economic importance, which are being irretrievably damaged and lost due to development on, among, and adjacent to such barriers." The Act further stated that federal assistance was contributing to "the loss of barrier resources, threats to human life, health, and property, and the expenditure of millions of tax dollars each year . . ."; and therefore: "A program of coordinated action by Federal, State, and local governments is critical to the more appropriate use and conservation of coastal barriers."

To effectuate such a program, the Act established a Coastal Barrier Resources System (CBRS) within which certain federal benefits would

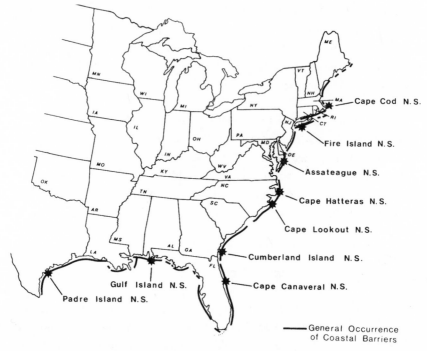

FIGURE 12-6   Location of coastal barriers and national seashores on Atlantic and Gulf of Mexico shorelines. *Source:* Federal Register, 47:158, August 1982.

be withheld. The CBRS was based on an inventory of nonpublic, non-protected, undeveloped coastal barriers prepared by the Department of the Interior (Figure 12-7). These included 186 geographic units extending along 656 miles of oceanfront shoreline (about 24 percent of the total U.S. barrier coastline along the Atlantic and Gulf of Mexico) (Platt et al. 1987). The CBRS was expanded in 1990 to include 560 units comprising 1.3 million acres extending along 1200 shoreline miles (Beatley et al. 1994, 90).

Within the CBRS, the Act prohibits most federal incentives to growth including flood insurance, road and bridge funds, sewer and water construction, and beach protection. Areas within the CBRS may still be developed without federal involvement if local law allows. But the denial of flood insurance and other federal benefits is an innovative approach to slowing growth in sensitive areas (Kuehn 1984). It is also a bold, if

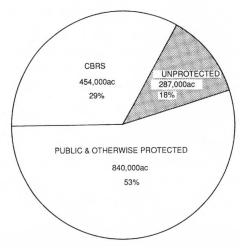

FIGURE 12-7   Status of Atlantic and Gulf Coast barriers, 1987. CBRS is Coastal
Barrier Resources System. All coastal barriers: 1.6 million acres.

fairly crude, method of "orchestrating" federal policies for specified geographical circumstances.

Federal Wetlands Programs

Many floodplains are also wetlands and vice versa, although the two are
not synonymous. Despite extensive areas of geographical overlap, federal programs concerning wetlands have evolved independently from
those addressing floods. Each involves a different set of statutes, agencies, goals, procedures, and terminology. The need for coordination of
federal floodplain and wetland management efforts with each other and
with the Coastal Zone Management Program has been strongly urged
(Kusler and Larson 1993; Myers and White 1993; Interagency Floodplain Review Committee 1994).

As discussed in Chapters 1 and 9, wetlands comprise an important
subset of the total land and water resources of the United States. The
term encompasses a variety of ecological and hydrological regimes generally characterized by (1) the presence of water, (2) predominance of
saturated hydric soils, and (3) prevalence of vegetation adapted to wet

conditions (hydrophytes) (Mitsch and Gosselink 1986, 15–16). Many kinds of physical features share these broad characteristics–for example, red maple swamps and black spruce swamps in the northern states (associated with glaciation); estuarine salt marshes behind coastal barriers; bottomland hardwood forests in the lower Mississippi Valley; prairie potholes in the Great Plains; playa and riparian wetlands in the West; and wet tundra in Alaska (Tiner 1984, vii). Depending on their physical type, size, and location, wetlands provide many natural values including habitat for flora and fauna; natural flood detention (inland wetlands) or shoreline buffering (coastal wetlands); aquifer recharge and pollution filtration; scenic beauty; and open space (Kusler 1983; Mitsch and Gosselink 1986).

Since 1937, Congress has supported the acquisition, restoration, and maintenance of wildlife areas including wetlands under the Pittman-Robertson Act (16 USCA Sec. 66a). This Act authorizes grants of up to 75 percent of the cost of projects from excise taxes on firearms and ammunition. The 1950 Dingell-Johnson Act (16 USCA Sec. 777) similarly has supported wetland acquisition for fish habitat restoration. The 1958 Fish and Wildlife Coordination Act mentioned earlier required consideration of impacts on wetlands and other wildlife habitat before a federal water development project could be approved.

The National Wetlands Inventory

A long-standing federal activity has been to identify the types, extent, and distribution of wetlands and to estimate their rates of change. The U.S. Department of Agriculture (USDA) conducted crude surveys of wetlands as early as 1906 and 1922 to see how much cropland could be created by draining wetlands. The first conservation-oriented wetland survey was conducted during the mid-1950s by the U.S. Fish and Wildlife Service (FWS) (1956).

In 1974, FWS launched the National Wetlands Inventory (NWI), a massive project to classify and map virtually all the nation's wetlands. The NWI uses color-infrared aerial photography at scales ranging from 1:60,000 to 1:130,000. Wetland data thereby obtained is superimposed on conventional topographic base maps of 1:24,000 and smaller scales (Mitsch and Gosselink, 471) (Figure 12-8). As of the mid-1990s, NWI maps have been prepared for most areas of the nation at a scale of

FIGURE 12-8   Excerpt from a National Wetlands Inventory map. Abbreviations refer to various types of wetlands. *Source:* U.S. Fish and Wildlife Service.

1:25,000. Increasing numbers of these maps are being digitized for use in geographic information systems. The maps are explicitly not intended to be used directly for wetlands regulation. Unlike NFIP flood hazard maps, they have no legal weight. (And they are often difficult to decipher.)

Measuring rates of wetland loss is hampered by differing definitions from one survey to another as well as by technical inaccuracy of measurement techniques. The NWI has estimated total wetlands in the early 1980s to comprise about 99 million acres in the lower 48 states, of which 93.7 million were inland freshwater wetlands and the rest coastal (Frayer et al. 1983). This represented a loss since the mid-1950s of approximately 14.8 million acres of freshwater wetlands and 482,000 acres of saltwater wetlands (Figure 12-9) (Conservation Foundation 1988).

Nationally, approximately one-fourth of wetlands are fully protected under public ownership. Extensive areas of salt marsh are contained within National Seashores and National Wildlife Refuges. Other federal, state, and local land holdings include diverse types of wetlands. Certain wetlands are owned by private conservation organizations such as the Nature Conservancy, the Massachusetts Audubon Society, and the National Audubon Society. The remaining wetlands are privately owned and in many areas are ripe for drainage or filling for development. There is little technical difficulty in filling or dredging wetlands, and alteration is practically irreversible. Governmental intervention in the private land market through wetland regulatory programs has sought to moderate this process.

The Section 404 Program

Section 404 of the Federal Clean Water Act (33 USCA Sec. 1344) is the basis for the federal wetlands regulatory program, even though the term "wetland" does not actually appear in the law. The law regulates dredge and fill in "waters of the United States" but the latter have been construed to include bottom and hardwood forests, mangrove swamps, and prairie potholes that are dry most of the year. The program is administered jointly by an uneasy alliance between the U.S. Army Corps of Engineers (COE) and the U.S. Environmental Protection Agency (EPA). Also, the U.S. Fish and Wildlife Service of the Department of the Interior and the National Marine and Fisheries Service of the Department of Commerce are notified of 404 applications and given opportunity to offer their own recommendations regarding their respective agency interests in a particular wetland.

Section 404 was enacted in 1972 as part of extensive amendments to the Federal Water Pollution Control Act, later renamed the Clean Water Act. It was intended to supplement the COE's existing authority under

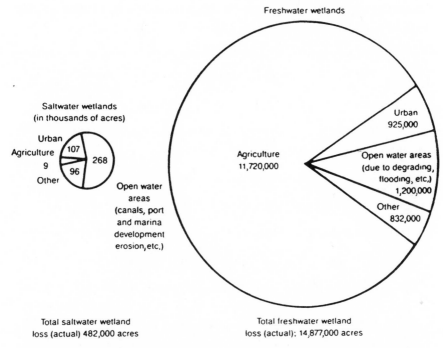

Freshwater wetlands

Saltwater wetlands
(in thousands of acres)

Urban
Agriculture 107
9   268
Other 96

Open water
areas
(canals, port
and marina
development
erosion, etc.)

Agriculture
11,720,000

Urban
925,000

Open water areas
(due to degrading,
flooding, etc.)
1,200,000

Other
832,000

Total saltwater wetland
loss (actual) 482,000 acres

Total freshwater wetland
loss (actual): 14,877,000 acres

FIGURE I2-9 Wetlands conversions: mid-1950s to mid-1970s. *Source:* Conservation Foundation, 1988. Reproduced by permission.

Section 10 of the 1899 Rivers and Harbors Act (33 USCA Sec. 403) to prohibit "unauthorized obstruction or alteration of any navigable water of the United States" in the absence of a permit from the COE. In 1968, the COE amended its Section 10 regulations to require permit reviews to consider: ". . . the effect of the proposed work on navigation, fish and wildlife, conservation, pollution, aesthetics, ecology, and the general public interest." The denial of a permit to fill 11 acres of mangrove swamp under these criteria was upheld by a Federal Court of Appeals in *Zabel v. Tabb* 430 F.2d 199 (5th Cir., 1970).

But when Section 404 was adopted in 1972, the Corps interpreted its authority as extending only to traditional "navigable waters." This narrow interpretation of "waters of the United States" in Section 404 was invalidated in *Natural Resources Defense Council v. Callahan* 392 F. Supp. 685 (D.C., 1975), which held that the phrase was intended by Congress to apply broadly to include wetlands.

The geographic reach of the Section 404 program was eventually defined by the Corps of Engineers administratively to include a wide range of land–water features:

- "Navigable waters" (including waters which once were navigable or that could be made navigable, and including all tidal waters)
- All interstate waters including interstate wetlands
- All other waters . . . the use, degradation, or destruction of which could affect interstate or foreign commerce
- Impoundments of waters described above
- Tributaries of waters described above
- The territorial sea
- Wetlands adjacent to the waters described above" (33 CFR 323.2)

The term "wetlands" was specifically defined by the Corps to include:

Those areas that are inundated or saturated by surface or ground-water at a frequency and duration sufficient to support, and that under normal circumstances do support, a prevalence of vegetation typically adapted for life in saturative soil conditions. Wetlands generally include swamps, marshes, bogs, and similar areas (33 Code of Federal Regulations, Subpart E).

One might expect that the jurisdiction of Section 404 (that is, an area where a permit is required for dredge or fill) would be determined according to the maps of the National Wetlands Inventory. No such direct connection between the NWI and Section 404 has been established however. The Corps' permit jurisdiction under 404 must be established by site visit in most cases. NWI maps are indicative of areas that probably fall under 404 jurisdiction.

Parties subject to 404 are defined broadly to include "any individual, commercial enterprise, organization, or governmental agency" that intends to construct or fill in areas covered by Section 404. Even federal agencies other than the COE itself must obtain a permit. The Corps' 404 review process is illustrated in Figure 12-10.

As stated above, the Section 404 Program is jointly administered by the Army Corps of Engineers and the U.S. Environmental Protection

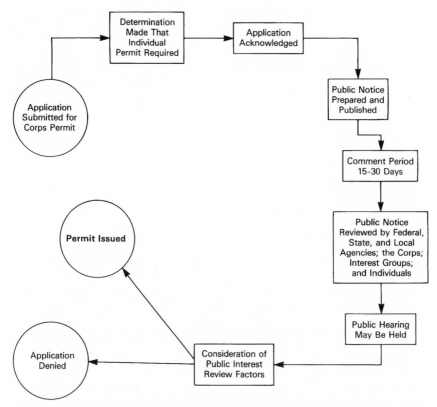

FIGURE 12-10   Approval process for Section 404 Federal wetlands permit. *Source:* U.S. Army Corps of Engineers.

Agency. While the former receives permit applications and performs a "public interest review," its decision in each case must conform to "environmental guidelines" issued by EPA under Section 404(b)(1) (found at 40 CFR, Part 230). These guidelines specify additional policies and procedures to be followed by the Corps. It is unusual for one federal agency to have statutory authority over the administrative actions of another. Furthermore, EPA has the right to review any case submitted to COE and, if it wishes, to veto a permit that has already been issued by the latter. Furthermore, EPA may utilize "advance identification" to prohibit COE permits in specified wetlands (Platt 1987).

The EPA Guidelines articulate two key management concepts: "water dependency" and "mitigation." *Water dependency* refers to activities that require access or proximity to water to fulfill their purpose—for example, marinas or fishing docks. For activities that are not water dependent, it is presumed that an alternative nonwetland site is available unless the applicant proves otherwise.

Mitigation refers to actions that minimize adverse effects of fill or discharge into regulated areas. EPA's guidelines specify a series of remedial measures to reduce the effects of the proposed fill. These address:

1. Location of the discharge

2. Type of material to be discharged

3. Control of the material after discharge

4. Dispersion of material

5. Adapting discharge technology to the needs of the site

6. Restoration of alternative degraded sites (40 CFR, Subpart H)

The last of these options has introduced a number of experiments with the rehabilitation of degraded wetlands and, in a few cases, attempts to create entirely new wetlands to offset the loss of areas to be dredged or filled.

Both of these concepts were applied in a landmark case involving a proposal to fill part of "Sweedens Swamp" in southeastern Massachusetts for a regional shopping mall in the mid-1980s. After considerable deliberation, the Army Corps of Engineers concluded that the only alternative site was owned by a competing shopping center developer. It issued a Section 404 permit for the project contingent on the creation of substitute wetland habitat on a tract two miles from the project site. The EPA then vetoed the permit under its 404(c) authority, finding that the alternative site could have been purchased by the developer and that the proposed mitigation by creating a replacement wetland was unreliable. On appeal, the Federal District Court in Boston upheld the EPA as acting reasonably on the basis of its administrative expertise (*Bersani v. Robichaud* 850 F.2d 36, 1988).

Assessment of the 404 Wetlands Program, like the Coastal Zone Management and National Flood Insurance Programs, is difficult at a national scale. Most 404 permit applications are approved: Of 11,000 applications received annually, COE denies only about 3 percent. However, of those approved, about one-third are modified from their original form and 44 percent of the 11,000 applications are withdrawn without action (Baldwin 1987).

Some wetland conversions slip through the 404 net, either legally or illegally. Agricultural drainage of wetlands and several other activities are exempted by statute or "general permit" from 404 review. In states that have their own wetland laws, the state review may serve as a substitute for COE review in minor cases. In other cases, state and federal reviews may both be required. And in really important cases, an EIS may be required to justify a federal 404 permit. (See discussion of Sears Island, Maine earlier in this chapter.)

Section 404 compliance is a cumbersome and often time-consuming process. Sometimes it duplicates state or local reviews and can be used as a lever for tying up unpopular projects in court. It is not an effective substitute for preserving key wetlands through acquisition. Nor is it a surrogate for advance comprehensive planning at a state or regional level (Platt 1987). It is however a "Rube Goldbergian" attempt to impose a de facto national wetlands policy through the medium of water pollution legislation where federal jurisdiction is stronger than on dry land. In 1995, it faces widespread criticism and threats of Congressional revision or termination.

Endangered Species: Habitat Conservation Plans

The Endangered Species Act of 1973 (ESA) (16 USCA secs. 1631–1643) represents the cornerstone of federal efforts to protect endangered or threatened flora and fauna (Beatley 1994a; 1994b). It has been called "the nation's toughest environmental law, a measure so strict that it can stop a $100 million dam project to protect a rare fish or ban logging on millions of acres of federal land to save an owl" (*Boston Globe* 1993). The ESA has also been assailed by many critics as rigid and inflexible (Beatley 1994a, 10).

Congress had expressed interest in protecting wildlife in several earlier laws before the ESA. For example, the Lacey Act of 1900 restricted interstate trade and transport of specified wildlife, and the Fish and Wildlife Coordination Act of 1958 required review of the wildlife habitat impacts of proposed federal water projects by the Fish and Wildlife

Service. Endangered species laws passed in 1966 and 1969, although lacking regulatory teeth, established a list of endangered species and generally laid a framework for later federal efforts.

The intent of Congress in adopting the ESA was:

> ... to provide a means whereby the *ecosystems upon which endangered species and threatened species depend may be conserved,* to provide a program for the conservation of such ... species and to take such steps as may be appropriate to achieve the purposes of ... treaties and conventions.
>
> (ESA, sec. 2b; emphasis added)

This statement implies that land use planning and regulation will be utilized to conserve "ecosystems" and thus the species that depend upon them. Significantly, the act applies to privately owned land as well as public land—a source of much controversy.

Two tiers of species, "endangered" and "threatened," are listed under procedures established by the ESA. An "endangered species" is one that "is in danger of extinction throughout all or a significant portion of its range," while a "threatened species" is one that "is likely to become an endangered species within the foreseeable future (ESA, sec. 3). More than 950 domestic animal and plant species have been listed as endangered or threatened, and some 3900 additional species have been classified as candidates for possible future listing. Nearly two-thirds of all mammals are either listed or are candidates, along with 14 percent of birds, 12 percent of plants, and 10 percent of fish (*New York Times* 1995). A few species, notably the American bald eagle and the American alligator, have been delisted due to the recovery of their populations. A handful of listed species are believed to have become extinct since the ESA was adopted in 1973.

The act is administered by the Fish and Wildlife Service (FWS) and the National Marine Fisheries Service (NMFS) with respect to terrestrial and aquatic species, respectively. They are charged with the preparation of a "species recovery plan," which evaluates the status of a particular species and identifies goals and actions necessary to promote its recovery. In furtherance of such plans, federal agencies are required to consult with FWS and NMFS to "insure that any action authorized, funded, or carried out by such agency is not likely to jeopardize the continued existence of any endangered species or threatened species or result in the destruction or adverse modification of critical habitat of such species. . . ." (ESA, sec. 7(a)(2)). The listing of a species and its habitat is a scientific determination by the responsible agencies that is often the subject of heated dispute.

The ESA prohibits anyone from "taking" any listed species. Section 3(19) broadly defines "taking" (not to be confused with the "taking issue" discussed in Chapter 8) to include actions that: ". . . harass, harm, pursue, hunt, wound, kill, trap, capture, or collect, or attempt to engage in any such conduct." Thus activities such as land development or timber cutting that destroy habitat of listed species may lead to civil or criminal prosecution (Beatley 1994b, 231).

It is frequently charged that ESA is used as a tool to block land use changes or development that cannot otherwise be prevented. Completion of the Tellico Dam in Tennessee was halted temporarily after FWS listed the tiny snail darter fish—believed to be found only in the valley about to be flooded—as endangered. In an appeal to the U.S. Supreme Court by the Tennessee Valley Authority, the ESA was upheld despite the plea that the dam was largely completed by the time the species was listed (*TVA v. Hill* 98 S. Ct. 2279, 1978). Congress then amended the act to establish an interagency "endangered species committee" to review applications for exemptions from the act. This committee (known as the "God Committee") rejected an appeal to delist the snail darter, but the Tellico Dam was later completed under a Congressional exemption.

Other controversial applications of the act have included limitations on logging of old-growth forests in the Pacific Northwest to protect the northern spotted owl, the temporary closing of public bathing beaches along the Atlantic Coast to protect nesting habitat for the piping plover, and proposed limits on development in the Florida Keys to protect the diminutive key deer. (In 1995, the U.S. Supreme Court rejected by a vote of 6 to 3 a challenge by timber interests claiming that logging on private land should not be restricted under the ESA. See *Babbitt v. Sweet Home Chapter of Communities for a Greater Oregon*, no. 94-859 decided June 29, 1995.)

In 1982, Congress amended ESA to permit limited "takes" of designated habitat and species pursuant to the development of a "habitat conservation plan" (HCP) for a particular area. An HCP requires a formal planning process involving all interested parties—for example, landowners, developers, local governments, state and federal wildlife agencies, and environmental organizations. This process seeks to achieve an agreement among all parties that specifies (1) the impacts that will result from proposed land use changes, (2) steps to be taken to minimize and mitigate such impacts and funding to implement those steps, and (3) alternatives to the "taking" and why they were not adopted. Nearly 100 HCPs are in various stages of preparation although few have been put into operation (Beatley 1994a, 20).

Among several case studies of habitat conservation plans documented by planner Timothy Beatley, one of the most ambitious has been the HCP completed in 1985 to protect the Coachella Valley lizard in a rapidly urbanizing portion of the Southern California desert. The Coachella Valley is a region of about 100 square miles of windblown sand and rocky alluvial deposits. The valley is attracting many desert resorts and spillover development from the Los Angeles urban area. The Coachella Valley fringe-toed lizard requires blowsand habitat, which has been reduced by at least half in the region due to irrigated agriculture, urban development, and highway construction. The lizard was listed as "threatened" under ESA in 1980 but, in the face of political opposition, only 20 square miles of critical habitat were designated. The lizard was also listed by California under its state ESA.

In 1983, a proposed 433-acre, 1300-unit development near Palm Desert sparked a confrontation between economic growth and habitat protection. Faced with penalties under the ESA, the developers joined in a two-year process with federal, state, local, and environmental interests to negotiate a habitat conservation plan for the lizard. Upon approval by the FWS, development could proceed.

The resulting HCP, as approved in 1986, designated three areas of desert habitat to be preserved, comprising a total of 16,700 acres of which 7800 acres is suitable habitat for the lizard. Conservation of habitat areas on adjacent public lands brings the total area of lizard habitat to 12,300 acres or about 26 percent of the remaining unshielded blowsand desert (Beatley 1994b, 242). Purchase of privately owned portions of the preserve has been spearheaded by The Nature Conservancy under a $25 million acquisition plan. Of that amount, $7 million was expected to be derived from developer impact fees and the rest from federal and state sources. Most of the acquisition was completed by 1994.

The Coachella Valley HCP was a success in terms of achieving consensus on a complex plan for habitat preservation amid extreme development pressure. The acquisition of nearly 17,000 acres of prime desert habitat will of course support other species besides the lizards, as well as passive human enjoyment as well.

But biologists differ as to whether the lizard will survive on the relatively small patches of habitat to which it is relegated under the HCP. And a larger planning perspective asks whether bolder efforts to redesign and channel growth must be devised:

> The Coachella Valley plan, like most others, does not challenge development trends, but rather accepts them, seeking to find a conservation solution that allows these growth patterns to continue. Yet, part of the logical long-term solution might be to reconsider seriously and fundamentally the current development patterns and to make adjustments to allowable densities and uses, and so reduce the overall extent of habitat loss. Need development projects be as large or as sprawling as they are? Can units be smaller and development more compact and contiguous? Can recreational amenities such as golf courses be scaled back to better conserve limited land [and conserve scarce water in the desert]? These types of land use and growth assumptions were not, however, explicitly addressed in the Coachella Valley habitat conservation plan.
>
> (Beatley 1994b, 248)

As of mid-1995, the future of the Endangered Species Act appears troubled. It is a prime target of property rights and "wise use" activities, particularly in the West. It is widely accused of being overly concerned with the protection of butterflies, birds, lizards, rats, and plants at the expense of human economic activities. It is often viewed as a subterfuge for blocking land use changes where no other legal mechanism is available. While the U.S. Supreme Court granted a reprieve to ESA in the *Sweet Home* case, as mentioned above, legislative efforts are pending at this writing to amend or abolish the act (*New York Times* 1995).

Agricultural Land

Agriculture has been a national concern since the debate between Jefferson and Hamilton regarding the disposition of the incipient public domain. The most visible and controversial federal agricultural programs of the 20th century are those concerned with price supports and subsidies for selected crops. While those programs indirectly influence land usage and cropping practices in various regions, they are beyond the scope of this discussion. But Congress has addressed the conservation of agricultural land more directly in a series of measures beginning with the creation of the Soil Conservation Service of the U.S. Department of Agriculture in 1935. Another federal role has been to sponsor large-scale irrigation projects in arid western states beginning with the establishment of the Bureau of Reclamation in 1902.

In the 1970s and 1980s, several new initiatives were taken in response to mounting concern regarding stewardship of the nation's land resources for the production of food and fiber. The principal issues have been (1) the conversion of productive farmland to urban development and other irreversible and nonagricultural uses, and (2) the loss of topsoil due to water and wind erosion. Federal response has taken the form chiefly of a series of inventories documenting the extent and condition of agricultural lands and, through the Food Security Act of 1985, a bold initiative to remove large areas of highly erodible lands from production.

The Cropland Base and Productivity

As discussed in Chapter 1, cropland is the most sensitive and valuable of the nation's rural land resources. Estimates of the extent of cropland and its variation over time are based on periodic inventories of agricultural land conducted by the U.S. Department of Agriculture (USDA). Land is classified according to its actual usage at a given time (for example, harvested crops, pasture, forest, range) and according to its physical suitability for various uses, particularly crops. The physical advantages and limitations of specific land are assessed by means of the Land Capability Classification (LCC) of the USDA Soil Conservation Service. The LCC, which has been in use since the mid-1960s, rates soils in terms of adequacy of moisture; capacity to hold moisture without waterlogging; susceptibility to erosion; freedom from excessive alkalinity, acidity, and salinity; stoniness; and climatic variables (Furuseth and Pierce 1982, 20). The LCC classes are listed in Table 12-4. Cropland is predominant on the Class I–III soils, but some crop cultivation is attempted on lower-level soils as well. Also, some of the higher-level soils are actually in forest, range, or pasture condition rather than crops.

TABLE 12-4   U.S. Soil Conservation Service Land Capability
Classification

Capability Classes	
Class I	Soils with few limitations that restrict their uses.
Class II	Soils which have moderate limitations that reduce the choice of plants or that require moderate conservation practices.
Class III	Soils that have severe limitations that reduce the choice of plants, require special conservation practices, or both.
Class IV	Soils having very severe limitations that reduce the choice of plants, require very careful management, or both.
Class V	Soils that are not likely to erode but have other limitations, impractical to remove, that limit their use largely to pasture, range, woodland, or wildlife.
Class VI	Soils having severe limitations that make them generally unsuited to cultivation and limit their use largely to pasture or range, woodland, or wildlife.
Class VII	Soils which have very severe limitations that make them unsuited to cultivation and that restrict their use largely to pasture or range, woodland, or wildlife.
Class VIII	Soils and landforms with limitations that preclude their use for commercial plants and restrict their use to recreation, wildlife, water supply, and esthetic purposes.

Source: Furuseth and Pierce 1982, Table 2 (derived from U.S. Soil Conservation Service).

The 1977 National Resources Inventory (NRI) estimated the total acreage of land that was or could be used for the production of crops—the "cropland base"—to be 540 million acres. This included 413 million acres of readily available "cropland" and 127 million acres of "potential cropland," which would require substantial investment to convert it from other uses (Figure 12-11) (National Agricultural Lands Study 1981).

The USDA also identified 345 million acres as "prime farmland" on which crops can be produced for the least cost and with the least damage to the resource base (USDA Economic Research Service 1984). Of that total, 230 million acres were in cropland and the rest in other rural status (Figures 12-12 and 12-13) (USDA 1981, 5).

American farmers have steadily raised the productivity of the nation's land. In 1956, it was estimated that the doubling of American agricultural output that characterized the first half of the 20th century would be repeated in the second half (Harris 1956). The U.S. Farm Output Index

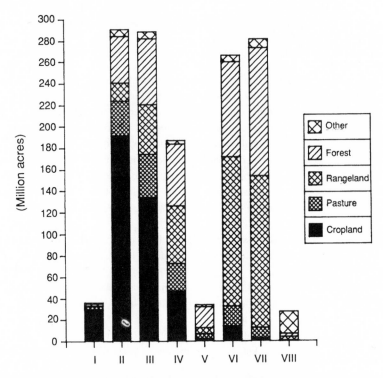

FIGURE 12-II Use of nonfederal rural land by soil capability class. *Source:* U.S. Department of Agriculture, 1987.

in fact rose by 54 percent in 30 years from 76 in 1960 to 117 in 1990 (1977 = 100) (U.S. Bureau of the Census 1991). This increase occurred without any net increase in harvested acreage, which in fact declined from 392 million acres in 1959 to 340 million in 1992 (Table 1-1). While much of the rise in productivity before 1950 resulted from mechanization, the post-1950 rise has resulted largely from the wider use of irrigation, artificial fertilizer and pesticides, and genetic improvements. Meanwhile, inputs of labor per unit of production have steadily declined, thus dramatically raising the productivity of farm labor (Conservation Foundation 1985, 154–157). (See Figure 12-14.)

As stated in Chapter 1, estimates of total cropland are fairly inexact and difficult to compare over time. Also, national estimates of total cropland mask regional variations in the quality of land under cultivation. As prime land is lost in the Northeast and north central states, acreage of lower quality requiring drainage or irrigation and heavy use of pesticides has been brought into production in the South and Southwest. While the

America's Land Base in 1977
(Million acres)

Uses of the Cropland Base in 1977
(Million acres)

Note: Unless otherwise specified, all data and references to the United States or to the "U.S. agricultural land base" in this report refer to the 50 states. In discussions based on Census of Agriculture and farm production regions, Alaska and Hawaii are excluded from the Western Region and U.S. totals.

FIGURE 12-12   America's land base in 1977. *Source:* National Agricultural Land Study, 1981.

number of acres may appear to be unchanged, the average quality of land in production is thus diminished (Batie and Healy 1983).

Within each region much land shifts into and out of cropland usage over time. When prices are high, as in the late 1970s, marginal land is planted in crops despite severe limitations, such as steep slopes, erodibility, aridity, wetness, or poor soil quality. The total "harvested cropland" was thus temporarily boosted (for example, from 330 million acres in 1975 to 391 million acres in 1981 due to high export demand), but marginal lands brought into production when prices are high may be just as quickly dropped. By 1992, the total estimated supply of cropland was 340 million acres, nearly what it was in 1975.

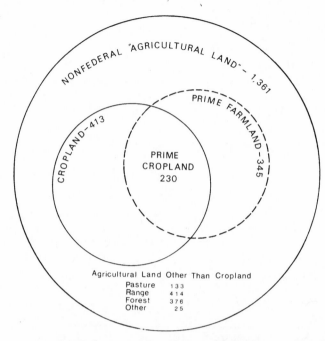

FIGURE 12-13   Utilization of nonfederal agricultural land, 1977 (millions of acres). *Source:* Platt, 1985, fig. 2. Reproduced by permission of Association of American Geographers.

Urbanization of Agricultural Land

Concern about farmland conversion is largely a post-1960 phenomenon. The primary farmland issue of the 1930s was overpopulation of land, which was desiccated in some regions by drought, inundated elsewhere by floods, and widely eroding. President Roosevelt's National Resources Board (1934) urged that 75 million acres of marginal land be removed from agricultural usage and the impoverished inhabitants relocated elsewhere. Ironically, the Board urged certain public measures that today are proposed to *retain* land in farming—for example, land use zoning, purchase of easements, and tax incentives (Platt 1985, 434).

The past three decades, however, have witnessed a wordy, sometimes acrimonious, and often confusing debate over the impact of urbanization on agricultural land. The U.S. Department of Agriculture (1987, 3–9) has estimated that in the 1980s approximately 900,000 acres per year were

FIGURE 12-14   Resources used in agricultural production: 1964–1983.
Source: Conservation Foundation, 1985. Reproduced by permission.

paved, flooded, or built over, of which perhaps one-third was prime farmland. But land use scholars have differed on the significance of this trend and whether federal, state, or local intervention is justified.

Much of the problem has been a confusion of objectives. Crosson and Haas (1982) identify two dimensions of the farmland adequacy issue: (1) the role of the land in producing food and fiber, which they term the "capacity issue"; and (2) the role of the land in producing intangible values, which they label the "amenity issue." The latter may preferably be termed the "land planning issue," since more than amenity is involved. In any event, these two issues have often been argued at cross purposes.

The distinction between food production and land planning was recognized by Clawson (1963, 16 and 61), who estimated that the nation could feed 10 to 20 times its existing population, but that urban growth was "withdrawing" twice as much land from rural use as was actually needed for urban purposes, generating harmful externalities such as visual blight, water pollution, and adverse fiscal impacts.

The USDA Soil Conservation Service (1977) stirred up a professional uproar with its *Potential Cropland Study* (PCS), which reported a net annual loss of about 675,000 acres of cropland to nonfarm purposes. The PCS was followed by a swarm of additional studies including the National Agricultural Lands Study (NALS) and the National Resource Inventories of 1977 and 1982, among others. The NALS, a joint venture of the USDA and the Council on Environmental Quality, was a highly publicized and polemical exploration of "the economic, environmental, and social consequences of agricultural land conversion and methods used to attempt to restrain and retard conversion" (National Agricultural Lands Study 1981). The report, issued in the waning hours of the Carter Administration, was weakened by fiscal, methodological, and ideological difficulties (Brewer and Boxley 1981; Fischel 1982).

NALS, however, did accomplish several tasks: (1) It documented regional differences in farmland conversion; (2) it inventoried farmland protection measures by states and local governments; and (3) it identified 90 federal programs that contribute to farmland conversion (Platt 1985). The latter findings supported adoption of the Farmland Protection Act of 1981 (PL 97-98, Subtitle 1), which required all federal agencies to: ". . . develop criteria for identifying the effects of Federal programs on the conversion of farmland to nonagricultural uses . . . [and] consider alternative actions, as appropriate, that could lessen such adverse effects. . . ." This law was little noticed. During the Reagan Administration, the impact of urbanization on farmland ceased to be a federal concern and was left to the states and local governments.

Soil Erosion

Congress in the 1930s and again in the 1980s was aroused by the specter of widespread degradation of rural land through soil erosion. Soil erosion is the rapid weathering of the soil mantle through the action of water, wind, or both. Water-caused erosion occurs in several forms: (1) overland sheet flow caused by rainfall or rapid snowmelt; (2) rill and gully formation whereby overland flow becomes concentrated into distinct pathways or channels of diverse size; and (3) streambank caving at times of high water.

Water-caused erosion is most serious in hilly or rolling agricultural regions in the Midwest, south central, and southeastern states. Soil erosion by water not only degrades the source land surface but also causes deterioration of water quality and sedimentation of reservoirs, river channels, and harbors downstream (Clark, Haverkamp, and Chapman 1985).

Wind erosion, which scours exposed topsoil to form dust clouds, is characteristic of the west central states, especially the High Plains. The infamous "Dust Bowl" of that region prompted Congress in a unanimous vote to establish the Soil Conservation Service (SCS) in 1935. The formation of the Tennessee Valley Authority in 1933 was also motivated in part by perception of excessive soil erosion on that region's hilly farmlands.

SCS has never engaged in federal land use regulation for erosion-prone areas. Instead, its modus operandi has been to fund and otherwise assist "soil and water conservation districts," which were ultimately established in nearly all the nation's counties. These districts are corporate entities established under state, not federal, law. SCS assists the districts, technically and financially, to prepare and carry out plans for the mitigation of erosion and protection of farmland within their respective counties. In practice, SCS, state, and county officials all work cooperatively with local landowners to promote better land use practices such as contour plowing, terracing, and conservation tillage.

Nevertheless, the National Resources Inventories of 1977 and 1982 revealed a shocking level of soil erosion still afflicting U.S. agricultural land. The 1982 survey disclosed that 25 percent of the nation's cropland, or 105 million acres, was subject to sheet and rill erosion at rates exceeding natural soil replenishment. Wind erosion was affecting 14 percent of cropland, or 67 million acres (some of which was also subject to water-induced erosion). For all nonfederal land, water erosion affected nearly 200 million acres and wind erosion, 90 million acres (U.S. Department of Agriculture 1987, figure 5). Over one-half of the water-induced erosion occurs in the Corn Belt and northern plains, the nation's primary rainfall-based grain region (Clark, Haverkamp, and Chapman, 5).

What does this signify in terms of loss of productivity? One estimate is that sheet and rill erosion alone, based on the rate in 1977, is removing the equivalent of about 1 million acres per year from the cropland base, with another quarter-million acre-equivalents removed by wind. This would add up to about 62 million acres of lost productivity over 50 years, assuming constant rates of loss (Sampson 1981, 131). This is considerably higher than the estimated rate of loss of cropland to urbanization. Of course, erosion losses are actually much more widely distributed and more gradual in any given location than this formulation would indicate. It is merely a device for describing the effects of incremental losses spread over more than 125 million acres.

The Food Security Act of 1985 (PL 99-198) launched a new assault on soil erosion. First, it required SCS to identify "highly erodible" land and to develop conservation plans for such areas in cooperation with state and local interests by 1990. Landowners who failed to conform with such conservation plans were ineligible for USDA crop and other subsidies. Over 100 million acres of marginal land have been covered by such plans.

The act also established the Conservation Reserve Program, under which USDA is authorized to lease highly erodible land from private owners to remove it from crop usage and to convert it back to grassland or woodland. About 23 million acres were signed up by mid-1988 (Brown 1989, 48).

The act also denies federal agricultural benefits to landowners who grow crops on highly erodible land that is plowed for the first time after the date of the Act (known as the "sodbuster law"). A parallel provision denies benefits to owners who grow crops on newly drained wetlands ("swampbuster"). (Both of these provisions are under challenge in 1995.)

In summary, federal agricultural land management efforts focused on urbanization in the 1970s and soil erosion in the 1980s. The former chiefly involved studies of trends in land usage with encouragement of nonfederal programs to retard urban encroachment on prime farmland. The soil erosion problem has been addressed chiefly through economic incentives and disincentives. In neither area has Congress grasped the nettle of federal regulation of agricultural land.

Solid and Hazardous Waste Management

Earlier sections of this chapter have examined the federal role in diverse land management contexts: the coastal zone, floodplains, wetlands, and agricultural land. Although differing in terms of objective and form of federal involvement, each of those topics was geographically selective. The federal policy or program was directed to a particular land type, distinguished by its physical and human-usage characteristics. To the extent that public authorities have intervened in the private land market in those areas, such actions have been based on a perception of their specific geographic attributes, for example, ecological characteristics, scenic amenity, hazardousness, resource productivity, and so forth.

Public response to the problem of solid and hazardous waste management is of a different nature. Here the focus of attention is not on particular types of land (although some sites are clearly better or worse than others for waste disposal), but rather on the activity—production and disposition of waste—that generates the problem. Furthermore, the nature and degree of governmental response also vary greatly with the type of waste considered, ranging from mundane garbage and sludge to exotic and lethal chemical, biological, and radiological wastes. The selection of a management option must also consider the need to avoid transferring the problem to a different medium—air to water—which would subvert national pollution abatement goals for those resources. The practice of ocean dumping of solid and liquid wastes, for example, a long-time practice of coastal cities, has been substantially limited by the Marine Protection, Research, and Sanctuaries Act of 1972 and may be totally banned in the United States by the end of the century. This throws the solid waste disposal problem back "on shore." And lurking in ambush for any site-specific proposal is the growing phenomenon of "NIMBY"—not in my backyard.

The management of solid and hazardous wastes thus presents complex policy issues that impinge both on the conduct of economic activities that generate the wastes and on geographic resources that receive them. The following discussion considers first the problem of ordinary solid waste as a land use issue, followed by a brief review of federal efforts to prevent or remedy public health hazards due to unsafe disposal of toxic and hazardous wastes.

Conventional Solid Wastes

The United States probably leads the world as a throw-away economy, although Western Europe and Pacific Rim countries have expanded their capacity to generate (and sometimes reuse) wastes. The United States in the late 1980s was estimated to produce about 160 million tons of conventional trash and garbage, or about 3.5 pounds per capita per day (U.S. Environmental Protection Agency 1988, 81). This 160 million tons of household waste includes food and yard wastes, packaging, newsprint and catalogues, polystyrene containers, and miscellaneous other unwanted household items. Paper products account for 41 percent of the total and plastics, 30 percent. A small but dangerous proportion of this total consists of hazardous household products such as paint, cleaning agents, pesticides, medicines, petroleum products, and organic compounds. One year's total of such household wastes, if accumulated in one place, would reach ". . . 30 stories high over 1000 football fields, enough to fill a bumper-to-bumper convoy of garbage trucks halfway to the moon" (*Newsweek* November 27, 1989, 67).

This gargantuan pile of refuse in fact is only the tip of the solid waste iceberg. Collected municipal waste plus sewerage sludge comprise only about 3 percent of total U.S. solid waste production. The EPA estimates a total annual waste burden of 6 billion tons, half generated by agriculture, 39 percent in mining operations, 6.4 percent by industrial production, and 1.2 percent by utilities (U.S. Environmental Protection Agency 1988, 79; Conservation Foundation 1987, 107–115). Of course, this may overstate the issue since much of the agricultural "wastes" may be beneficially applied to land as manure, and mining overburden may be returned to excavations to restore the natural land surface (as now widely required under the federal Surface Mining Control and Reclamation Act and its state counterparts). But even excluding these two sources from the total leaves about 642 million tons of municipal, industrial, and utility wastes annually—or about 5350 pounds annually per capita (or 14.6 pounds daily per capita), which would easily reach beyond the moon!

But for new laws, programs, and policies at each level of government over the past two decades, the total quantity of waste would be much greater, and in fact it was greater in 1970 than at present. In that year, the new U.S. Council on Environmental Quality (CEQ) (1970) estimated a total volume of 190 million tons of collected residential waste, representing a daily average of 5 pounds per capita as compared with 3.5 pounds currently. Although intertemporal comparisons are approximate due to differences in definition and estimation method, it appears that collected residential waste has been reduced both absolutely and per capita since 1970 through a variety of measures such as state "bottle bills" and newspaper recycling efforts. (Some of the apparent gain, however, may be attributable to the proliferation of garbage disposals, which convey food wastes to the wastewater stream and thus are not "collected solid waste" except for the portion that becomes sewage sludge.)

Aside from the total quantity of conventional solid waste, which remains immense, the most pronounced difference since 1970 has occurred with respect to land disposal practices. In that year, over three-fourths of all collected solid wastes (146 million tons) was deposited in open dumps, which numbered about 14,000 nationally (CEQ 1970, 110–111). Such dumps were notorious blights and health hazards on the outskirts of American cities and small towns. Most were operated privately or by municipal governments, with no federal or state management standards. The average dump was a clearing in a field or woods or perhaps a filled wetland where trash and garbage was simply piled. Combustible material was burned to reduce its volume, thus emitting smoke and other air pollutants. Precipitation on dumps conveyed biological and chemical pollutants into nearby surface waters or into groundwater in the form of "leachate." Surrounding areas were affected by numerous unpleasant externalities such as windborne trash, odors, rats and other vermin, visual blight, and vehicular traffic.

The first Congressional recognition of the growing problem of solid waste and the hazards of open dumps was expressed in the Solid Waste Disposal Act of 1965, an amendment to the still-primitive federal air pollution law. This act noted a "rising tide of scrap, discarded and waste materials," and the adverse effects of "inefficient and improper methods of disposal." In response to this perception, Congress declared solid waste disposal to be a federal concern for the first time: ". . . that while the collection and disposal of solid wastes should continue to be primarily the function of state, regional, and local agencies, the problems of waste disposal ... have become a matter national in scope and in concern. . . ."

The role of the federal government was only tentative at first. It was somewhat enlarged in the Resource Recovery Act of 1970, which strengthened the 1965 law that mandated the development of "guide-lines for solid waste collection, transport, separation, recovery, and dis-posal systems" (Sec. 101). The term "guidelines" marked the beginning of a shift from merely encouraging nonfederal authorities to upgrade their programs to imposing direct federal regulation of land disposal practices. Such direct regulation emerged during the 1970s under the Clean Air Act, which required states to ban burning of open dumps, and the Clean Water Act, addressing the problem of leachate pollution of sur-face- and groundwater. The new Environmental Protection Agency assumed responsibility for federal solid waste efforts after 1970.

By 1980, the smoldering open dump was rapidly disappearing from the American landscape, except in rural areas. In its place, federal and state policy favored the *sanitary landfill*. Design requirements for sani-tary landfills have included impermeable liners to prevent leachate from entering groundwater. Modern landfills also provide for the venting or capture of methane, which is sometimes used as an energy source for heating or electrical generation. The proportion of collected municipal wastes deposited in sanitary landfills rose from 13 percent in 1970 (CEQ 1970, 111) to about 85 percent in 1987 (Conservation Founda-tion 1987, 111).

But the era of the sanitary landfill itself is soon to end. The number of such facilities declined from 16,000 in 1984 to only about 6000 in 1989 (*Newsweek* November 27, 1989, 70). Existing landfills in many areas are rapidly being filled to capacity, leaving rounded grassy hills known in some places as "Mount Trashmore." The safe closing of sani-tary landfills with proper provision for methane venting and monitoring of groundwater is a major concern of EPA. But even more perplexing is what to do with the trash as available landfill capacity shrinks. Modern sanitary landfills typically have been regional facilities of considerable size, generating much truck traffic and depressing property values in their localities.

Neighboring property owners and entire communities object to receiving trash from other municipalities: Sanitary landfills are classic examples of "locally unwanted land uses" (LULUs), which are stoutly resisted by NIMBYites everywhere. Connecticut has had no new land-fills established since 1978. Facilities in New Jersey declined from 310 in 1977 to 128 in 1984 (Conservation Foundation 1987, 111). The saga of the infamous garbage barge from Islip, New York, which wandered the oceans in 1987 looking in vain for a place to unload before returning to Islip—still loaded—symbolized the growing solid waste crisis.

Beyond landfills, two options for disposal of certain wastes are incineration and land treatment. Primitive incinerators of course are outlawed, since they are major sources of air pollution. Modern state-of-the-art resource recovery incinerators utilize extremely high temperatures (1800 degrees F.) for efficient combustion and employ sophisticated air pollution emission controls. Heat produced by the combustion is used to generate either steam or electricity. In 1987, some 70 such facilities were in operation nationally, as compared with 20 in 1977; these handled 4 to 5 percent of total municipal wastes including sludge (Conservation Foundation 1987, 113). In 1989, Connecticut had five such plants in operation, handling 60 percent of the state's refuse. Another five plants were operative in New Jersey, Long Island, and Westchester County, New York, with another 21 plants proposed for the region (*The New York Times* February 12, 1989, 24). Nevertheless, even these facilities leave one-quarter of the total weight of trash in the form of highly toxic ash, which must be landfilled or processed for recycling. (Disposal at sea is increasingly restricted by EPA.)

Land treatment is the application of organic wastes to farmland or other rural land in order to recycle the nutrients into some form of biotic productivity. This is a modern version of the ancient practice of spreading raw human wastes on agricultural fields surrounding urban settlements. Such techniques are said to "close the nutrient cycle." Direct application of partially treated wastewater from a municipal sewage system to farmland has been practiced in several locations in the United States. The primary purpose of such systems is to provide a high degree of "renovation" or pollution abatement of the wastewater before it returns to streams or coastal waters. A secondary objective is to enhance the productivity of farmland and reduce dependence on commercial fertilizers. The development of land treatment systems, however, has been impeded by concerns as to the public health effects of industrial pollutants and viruses that may reach agricultural crops. It has become more common to apply wastewater to forests, golf courses, wetlands, and other lands not yielding products entering the human food chain.

Nutrients may be recaptured from sewage treatment through the reprocessing and land application of sludge, a semi-solid by-product of the nation's 15,000 sewage treatment plants. Sludge is often handled as a solid waste and either deposited in landfills or incinerated after dewatering. Increasingly, however, sludge is being converted into various forms of usable fertilizer to be applied to land in place of standard commercial fertilizers.

A comprehensive approach to solid waste management must employ a broad variety of strategies including, but not limited to, landfills, incineration, and land application. Four categories of techniques applicable to the problem include (1) reduction in the amount of waste generated; (2) waste treatment; (3) waste containment; and (4) waste dispersal (Conservation Foundation 1987, 433). The first option is receiving increasing emphasis in many states that either mandate or facilitate recycling of certain materials to prevent them from entering the waste stream. Bottle bills requiring deposits on beverage containers are in this category. The amount of paper recovered from U.S. municipal waste rose from 13 million tons in 1985 to 26 million tons in 1993. Waste engine oil is sometimes recycled or converted into other petroleum-based products. Even ash from incinerators can be converted into paving material. As landfill space dwindles and transportation costs escalate, mandatory separation and recycling of wastes is increasingly prevalent and, as of 1995, increasingly profitable as the demand for recycled materials expands globally (Young 1995).

Congress has generally let the states choose their own strategies in dealing with conventional wastes, subject to minimum standards for landfills, air quality, and water quality. Hazardous and toxic wastes, however, are another story.

Hazardous and Toxic Substances

The United States, like other high-technology societies, was shockingly slow to recognize the risks to life, health, and property associated with the careless use and disposal of chemical and other hazardous substances. Not until the mid-1970s, when immense actual and potential damage had already been caused, was remedial legislation adopted by Congress. And it was well into the 1980s before this legislation, as subsequently amended, began to exert some impact on the management and disposal of hazardous substances. As with so many other legal reforms discussed in this book, the necessary prerequisite was a heightened understanding, perception—and indeed fear—of the magnitude of the threat to the physical environment and human health.

For one class of hazardous chemicals–pesticides–Rachel Carson's *Silent Spring* (1962) sounded a clear warning. Her disclosures regarding DDT and other agricultural poisons helped to ignite the environmental movement, generally, and reform of federal pesticide law, in particular. The CEQ's first Annual Report (1970) devoted 10 pages to pesticides, with a direct reference to *Silent Spring*, but mentioned no other types of hazardous substances. Where was the Rachel Carson for asbestos, mercury, PCBs, lead, vinyl chlorides, radioactive wastes, hospital wastes, and dozens of other hazardous substances? In recognition of this void in public awareness, the CEQ itself prepared a brief report on the problem entitled *Toxic Substances* (CEQ 1971). It concluded that regulatory mechanisms to protect the public health from a wide variety of chemical hazards were inadequate. While not as charismatic as Carson's book, this report was a major impetus to the adoption in 1976 of the Toxic Substances Control Act (TSCA). Citing the CEQ report, the committee report on that law noted that:

> It is estimated that there are presently 2 million recognized chemical compounds in existence with nearly 250,000 new compounds produced each year. . . . approximately 1000 new chemicals will find their way into the marketplace and subsequently into the environment through use or disposal. As the chemical industry has grown, we have become literally surrounded by a man-made chemical environment. (*U.S. Code, Congressional and Administrative News*, "Legislative History of PL 94-469", p. 4493.)

TSCA directed the EPA to test potentially hazardous substances, particularly those thought to be carcinogens. The Act also requires labeling of such substances to disclose risks to the user or the public.

The Resource Conservation and Recovery Act (RCRA) also was adopted in 1976. RCRA marked a major expansion of the earlier federal solid waste legislation and the first explicit Congressional action on hazardous wastes. According to Rodgers (1988, 510), RCRA

> . . . prescrib[ed] in 45 pages a regime for the management of solid and hazardous wastes that included many features (grants, planning, compliance orders, citizen suits, imminent hazards) borrowed from the Clean Air and Clean Water Acts. For the first time, in 1976, serious regulatory measures appeared in the federal law–a

qualified prohibition on the open dumping of solid or hazardous wastes, and the initiation (in a mere 7 pages in Subtitle C) of the famed "cradle to grave" regime for the control of hazardous wastes.

The "cradle to grave" provision instituted a system of manifests or documentation to accompany designated hazardous materials through each stage of their "lifetime": manufacture, transport, use, and disposition. This allows federal and state authorities to track the quantities and location of hazardous substances and to monitor their safe disposal. It also requires generators of hazardous materials to certify that they are minimizing the amount and toxicity of their waste, and that the method of treatment, storage, or disposal they have chosen will minimize the risk to human health and the environment. The implementation of this system, however, was to be delayed and frustrated for years by problems of definition, accountability, and the immense number of generators involved. Inevitably, considerable quantities of wastes continued to be dumped illegally down drains or wells, in fields, or on highways.

The magnitude of the problem in terms of volume of hazardous materials to be managed was vastly underestimated at first. Estimates of total amounts of such substances–defined by the U.S. EPA (1986, 5) to include ignitable, corrosive, reactive, or toxic materials–had risen from 9 million metric tons in 1973, to between 27.5 and 41.2 million metric tons in the 1976 RCRA hearings, to 150 million metric tons in 1984, to 260 million metric tons in subsequent studies (Rodgers 1988, 519). This expansion reflects in part a broadening of the definition of "hazardous substances" to include additional materials, and in part the discovery that some materials are more abundant than originally recognized. In 1988, EPA estimated that there were some 3000 facilities handling a total of 275 million metric tons of RCRA hazardous wastes (EPA 1988, 85).

RCRA was significantly amended in 1980 and 1984. The former comprised a retrenchment with the exemption of several classes of wastes from the terms of the Act. But the 1984 Hazardous and Solid Waste Amendments (HSWA) (PL 98-616) was an important midcourse correction that greatly strengthened RCRA. This included a major revision and tightening of the "cradle to grave" regulations for tracking hazardous materials. It extended RCRA's coverage to "small generators" of hazardous wastes, adding some 100,000 firms producing between 220 and 2200 pounds of hazardous waste monthly to the 15,000 large generators (U.S. EPA 1988, 89). It initiated regulations for leaking underground storage tanks ("LUSTs"), which were estimated to number about 400,000 out of a total of 5 to 6 million underground tanks for storing petroleum products or hazardous chemicals (U.S. EPA 1988, 102). And land disposal of certain hazardous wastes was totally prohibited. Rodgers (p. 510) describes the 1984 HSWA as "passionate, confident, and demanding."

Superfund

RCRA applies prospectively to hazardous wastes from the time of their generation until their final disposition. A major gap in its coverage was the problem of wastes already discarded improperly–in pits, lagoons, injection wells, or leaking containers strewn on the ground behind chemical plants. National perception was finally directed to this issue by the tragic disclosures of the Love Canal disaster in Niagara Falls, New York.

Love Canal was an artificial ditch dating back to the late 19th century that was used for decades as a waste dump by the Hooker Chemical Co., which owned it. In 1977, signs of desperate problems began to appear in the residential neighborhood that bordered the canal. Children were born with birth defects, high rates of cancer were prevalent, and foul-smelling chemical wastes oozed through basement walls and formed puddles in yards and playgrounds. After much denial by Hooker, the City of Niagara Falls, and the County Health Commissioner, the crisis was finally addressed by state and federal authorities. A preliminary investigation led to the declaration of a "major disaster" by President Jimmy Carter in August 1978, the first such declaration for a technological disaster (Brown 1979). The state, with the help of federal funds, then acquired the homes and assisted the relocation of 237 families from the vicinity. The canal was sealed off and a remedial drainage project initiated. Subsequently, it became apparent that the chemicals had spread much further through the ground than originally estimated. And the brew of toxic chemicals was found to contain, in addition to benzene and a dozen other carcinogens, a measurable amount of the most deadly chemical ever synthesized: dioxin. The Love Canal Homeowners Association campaigned for further public assistance. Eventually, more than 600 homes were acquired.

Media attention soon disclosed many other chemical waste horrors lurking in America's industrial backyards. Woburn, Massachusetts was characterized as "a tangle of dumps and disease" (*Boston Globe* 1980). Times Beach, Missouri was found to be contaminated by dioxin contained in oil used to resurface the streets. (The entire town was bought by the Federal Emergency Management Agency and its residents relocated.) Even the staid journal *Science* (Maugh 1979) described Love Canal and its counterparts as "an environmental time bomb gone off."

Seldom can a legislative enactment be attributed so directly to a traumatic jolt in public environmental perception. In 1980, within months after the second round of Love Canal findings, Congress adopted the Comprehensive Environmental Response, Compensation, and Liability Act (CERCLA) (PL 96-510), commonly known as "Superfund." The Act's purpose was: "To provide for liability, compensation, cleanup, and emergency response for hazardous substances released into the environment and the cleanup of inactive hazardous waste sites" (Sec. 2).

The Act authorized $1.6 billion over five years for a comprehensive program to clean up the worst abandoned or inactive waste dumps in the nation (U.S. EPA 1988, 80). The funds were to be derived from an excise tax on the sale or use of petroleum and 42 chemicals used commercially to produce hazardous substances. States must provide at least 10 percent of cleanup costs for a site within their jurisdictions. Wherever a "responsible party" could be identified either they would be required to perform remedial actions themselves, or the government would do so and sue them for the costs plus penalties. In 1986, Superfund was reauthorized by PL 99-499 and expanded to a potential funding level of $8.5 billion.

"Throwing money at the problem" was a necessary but not sufficient (or efficient) response to the threat of hazardous waste contamination. Since the problem of abandoned waste dumps had only recently been recognized, no accurate inventory of the location, size, and contents of such sites had been compiled. By definition, such sites tend to be concealed and often below ground where wastes have been buried or injected into groundwater. Furthermore, it was often very difficult and dangerous to ascertain which of several hundred hazardous substances were present at any given site. A massive task for the EPA during the 1980s was to identify sites and to allocate cleanup resources. Some 19,300 sites were identified as potentially eligible for Superfund by the end of 1984: By late 1989, this list had grown to over 31,500 sites nationally. EPA has conducted preliminary assessments on most of these. Based on evaluation of a complex array of risk factors, the "worst" sites are placed on a National Priorities List (NPL), which qualifies them for Superfund cleanup, eventually. By late 1989, over 1200 sites were listed on the NPL. The Office of Technology Assessment (1989, 6) has estimated that as many as 9000 additional sites are eligible for the NPL, and the potential cost to all parties of cleaning them up could amount to $500 billion over several decades.

Meanwhile, actual progress in implementing the goals of the 1980 CERCLA and its 1986 amendments has been slow. The startup of Superfund was impeded by controversy surrounding the actions or nonactions of President Reagan's first EPA Administrator Ann Burford and her Superfund deputy, Rita Lavelle. By 1985, EPA had cleaned up only six sites, with questionable success (*Time* 1985).

By 1988, EPA reported that it had initiated over 1000 short-term remedial actions (such as fencing), but that only 200 sites had been investigated in detail and long-term cleanup initiated on about 140 sites (EPA 1988, 83 and 95). By 1995, about 300 sites were completed.

A permanent cleanup of a hazardous waste site is immensely difficult and costly. Obviously, risks to the cleanup workers and to the surrounding area must be minimized. Removal of wastes to another location may simply transfer the problem elsewhere unless the receiving site is properly located and designed. Few approved hazardous waste sites were available. Other than removal to land disposal sites, management options are complex and expensive. They include destruction through thermal, biological, or chemical treatment; stabilization; and engineering controls, institutional controls, or natural treatment (Office of Technology Assessment [OTA] 1989, 45). A management approach must be formulated individually for each site with the participation of all levels of government and affected private interests. Also involved in the decision process for each site are a variety of professional consultants—for example, chemists, soil scientists, biologists, hydrologists, and, of course, lawyers.

The Office of Technology Assessment (1989, 3) has identified a

"Superfund syndrome" that impedes progress in making the program work effectively. This is a state of "constant confrontation" among the interested parties, produced by the high economic costs, the scientific uncertainties, the emotionalism, and what OTA considers to be "excessive flexibility" in Superfund implementation: "Unless everyone breaks out of the Superfund syndrome, most cleanups will seem to do too little or too much. Billions will be spent. Hardly anyone will be satisfied. Hardly anyone will feel treated fairly. Hardly anyone will seem in control."

Cleaning up Superfund sites and the location of new storage, treatment, and disposal facilities inherently pose geographical as well as legal and public health issues. At the heart of the problem is the pervasive issue of externalities: Each site poses potential off-site risks to the surrounding area, as in the possibility of groundwater pollution. Even where actual risks are minimized through appropriate treatment and facility design, a zone of perceived risk may extend widely beyond the area of actual risk. Such spatial distribution of actual or perceptual risks apply not only to the sites of generation, use, and disposal, but also in linear form along the routes of transport (highway, rail, barge) of hazardous substances (Zeigler, Johnson, and Brunn 1983).

Recognition of the spatial patterns of opposition (NIMBYism), whether or not limited to actual zones of risk, is essential. Ultimately the resolution of the Superfund syndrome will depend on (1) effectively reducing the actual risks of hazardous wastes through proper management practices and (2) allaying the fears of those who perceive themselves and their property values to be at risk, through public involvement, education, and, in appropriate cases, compensation.

Surface Mine Reclamation

This chapter concludes with a brief summary of federal involvement in a regionally specific land use activity: surface mining of coal. Coal strip mining, as distinct from deep tunnel mining, accounts for about 60 percent of U.S. coal production. This technique involves stripping away topsoil and rock overburden to reach coal deposits within a few hundred feet of the surface. As compared with tunnel mining, strip mining

reduces labor costs through large-scale mechanization and is less hazardous to those working in the mine: Black lung disease, cave-ins, and
explosions are rare in surface mining.

But surface mining without reclamation leaves the land devastated
with alternating excavations and piles of infertile overburden. All agricultural use of the site is extinguished and its capability to support biotic
communities is greatly modified. The spoil heaps are inherently unstable
formations and occasionally may collapse into debris flows. The failure
of a spoil dam was responsible for heavy loss of life downstream in the
1973 Buffalo Creek, West Virginia disaster. Another problem is sulfuric
acid pollution of streams draining out of strip-mined lands, which de-
stroys fish and plant life and poses a public health hazard. In the early
1970s, the federal Bureau of Mines estimated that the United States had
some 2 million acres of unreclaimed and unproductive strip-mined lands
(Hibbard 1978, 296). In 1977, surface mining of coal was disrupting some
4000 acres of land every week (U.S. Congress 1977, 3).

Environmental and energy policies clashed head on in the mid-1970s.
On the one hand, coal strip mining was degrading the land and water
resources of extensive territories in Appalachia, the Midwest and western plains states. On the other hand, the Middle East oil price rises of
1974 compelled the nation to expand reliance on its domestic energy
sources, including coal. The need, therefore, was to facilitate expansion
of strip mining operations while regulating the mining industry to com-
pel responsible management and reclamation of strip-mined lands.

Like most land use issues, the regulation of strip mining before 1976
was left to the states. In fact, 48 states had adopted laws to regulate strip
mining by the mid-1970s (Hibbard 1978, 297). But the stringency of
requirements and the level of enforcement effort varied widely among
states. Furthermore, mining companies could play one state off against
another by threatening to close their mines in a state that proposed to
"get tough." Against the customary objections to federal intervention in a
land use problem, this inconsistency among state programs was a major
argument for a national approach. Federal jurisdiction was also invoked
on the basis of the pollution of surface waters from mine drainage. In the
west, much of the coal accessible to strip mining lay beneath federal
lands, which offered a further justification for a federal surface mining
law. (Platt, Macinko, and Hammond 1983, 144).

An epic legislative battle in Congress culminated in the Surface Mining Control and Reclamation Act of 1977 (PL 95-87). According to the Act's chief sponsor, Representative Morris K. Udall:

> It took six years of tenacity and bitter debate to pass Public Law 95-87. The history of the Act would serve as a textbook for any national legislator desiring to thwart the clear will of the majority of the Congress. . . . a legislative endeavor involving 183 days of hearings and legislative consideration, 18 days of House action, three House-Senate Conferences and Reports, two Presidential vetoes, approximately 52 recorded votes in the House and Senate, and the machinations (and statesmanlike conduct) of three Presidents is an activity ripe for scholarly analysis, let alone the stuff for a pretty good novel.
>
> Udall 1979, p. 554, as quoted in Platt, Macinko, and Hammond 1983, p. 145.

The result was an 88-page law that established a national program for regulating surface mining and the surface effects of underground mining. It addressed three phases of mining activities: (1) preliminary planning, (2) mining operations, and (3) restoration of the disturbed land. The fundamental purpose of the Act was to require that topsoil and other overburden be stockpiled for replacement on excavated land that was to be returned to its original contours and level of productivity. The statute and its extensive regulations articulate mandatory national performance standards for strip mining.

But like RCRA, the federal surface mining law relies on states to adopt the national standards into their own laws and thereafter enforce them, subject to federal surveillance. Thus, the facade of state authority is maintained and the federal role is exercised indirectly, but forcefully.

Conclusion

This long chapter has reviewed selected federal policies and programs relating to nonfederal land use since the 1930s. Before the New Deal, the federal role in natural resource policy was largely confined to the disposition and management of the public lands and the development of water resources. The federal budget and bureaucracy expanded massively during the Depression to administer the array of new public works programs. Progressive concepts of managing natural resources to benefit the American people underlay such New Deal innovations as the Tennessee Valley Authority, the Soil Conservation Service, and the National Resources Planning Board.

The federal government grew even larger during World War II. But the conservative mood of the 1950s largely trimmed back the planning and resource management programs of the New Deal. City and regional planning however were promoted by federal funding for urban renewal and "701 plans." But Congress took little interest in the results of these activities and totally ignored the quality of the nation's environment until the late 1960s.

Beginning with the 1955 Symposium on "Man's Role in Changing the Face of the Earth" and culminating with Rachel Carson's *Silent Spring*, a growing chorus of dissent challenged the laissez faire policies of postwar growth. In response, Congress (and a Republican President) outdid the New Deal in creating new agencies, programs, mandates, and funding commitments to restore and protect the nation's land, air, and water resources.

Twenty-five years after the National Environmental Policy Act, a newly elected Republican majority in Congress under the "Contract with America" has announced its intent to repeal or at least diminish many of the programs described in this chapter. A vocal constituency demands that private property rights should prevail over public goals, unless compensation is paid to the affected owners. Public polls however indicate that the American people still strongly support federal intervention to protect environmental quality. How these conflicting views of the balance of public and private welfare will be reconciled will undoubtedly be one of the defining issues of the rest of the decade and beyond.

References

Abbey, E. 1968. *Desert Solitaire*. New York: Simon and Schuster.

Baldwin, M.F. 1970. "The Santa Barbara Oil Spill." In *Law and the Environment* M.F. Baldwin, Jr. and J.K. Page, Jr., eds. New York: Walker and Co.

——. 1987. "Wetlands: Fortifying Federal and Regional Cooperation." *Environment* 29(7): 16–20; 39–43.

Batie, S.S., and R.G. Healy. 1983. "The Future of American Agriculture." *Scientific American* 248(2): 45–53.

Beatley, T. 1994a. *Habitat Conservation Planning: Endangered Species and Urban Growth.* Austin: University of Texas Press.

———. 1994b. "Reconciling Urban Growth and Endangered Species: The Coachella Valley Habitat Conservation Plan." In *The Ecological City: Preserving and Restoring Urban Biodiversity.* R. H. Platt, R. A. Rowntree, and P. Muick, eds. Amherst: University of Massachusetts Press, 231(-)250.

Beatley, T., D.J. Brower, and A.K. Schwab. 1994. *An Introduction to Coastal Zone Management.* Washington, D.C.: Island Press.

Beston, H. 1949. *The Outermost House.* New York: Rinehart.

Boston Globe. 1980. "Woburn: A Tangle of Dumps and Disease." June 28: 1 and 18.

———. 1993. "A Tough Environmental Law May Get Tougher." Jan. 4, pp. 1 and 12.

Brewer, M.F., and R.F. Boxley. 1981. "Agricultural Land: Adequacy of Acres, Concepts and Information." *American Journal of Agricultural Economics* 63: 879–888.

Brown, L.R. 1989. "Reexamining the World Food Prospect." In *State of the World–1989.* L.R. Brown, ed. Washington, D.C.: Worldwatch Institute.

Brown, M.H. 1979. "Love Canal and the Poisoning of America." *The Atlantic.* Vol. 244 (December): 33–47.

Burby, R., and S. French. 1985. *Flood Plain Land Use Management: A National Assessment.* Boulder: Westview Press.

Caldwell, L.K. 1989. "A Constitutional Amendment for the Environment." *Environment* 31(10): 6–11, 25–28.

Carson, R. 1962. *Silent Spring.* Boston: Houghton Mifflin.

Clark, E.H. II, J.A. Haverkamp, and W. Chapman. 1985. *Eroding Soils: The Off-Farm Impacts.* Washington, D.C.: The Conservation Foundation.

Clawson, M. 1963. *Land for Americans.* Chicago: Rand McNally.

Clawson, M., and P. Hall. 1973. *Planning and Urban Growth: An Anglo-American Comparison.* Baltimore: The Johns Hopkins University Press for Resources for the Future.

Commission on Marine Science, Engineering, and Resources. 1969. *Our Nation and the Sea.* Washington, D.C.: U.S. Government Printing Office.

Committee for Economic Development. 1960. *Guiding Metropolitan Growth.* Washington, D.C.: The Committee.

Commoner, B. 1971. *The Closing Circle.* New York: Knopf.

Conservation Foundation. 1977. "The Coasts Are Awash with Disputes." *Conservation Foundation Letter* (March).

———. 1985. *State of the Environment: An Assessment at Mid-Decade.* Washington, D.C.: The Conservation Foundation.

———. 1987. *State of the Environment: A View Toward the Nineties.* Washington, D.C.: The Conservation Foundation.

———. 1988. *Report of the National Wetland Forum.* Washington, D.C.: The Conservation Foundation.

Cooley, R.A., and G. Wandesforde-Smith, eds. 1970. *Congress and the Environment.* Seattle: University of Washington Press.

Crosson, P.R., and R.B. Haas. 1982. "Agricultural Land." In *Current Issues in Natural Resource Policy.* P.R. Portney and R.B. Haas, eds. Washington, D.C.: Resources for the Future.

Dahl, T.E., and C.E. Johnson. 1991. *Status and Trends of Wetlands in the Conterminous United States, Mid-1970s to Mid-1980s.* Washington: U.S. Department of the Interior, Fish and Wildlife Service.

Darling, F.F., ed. 1965. *Future Environments of North America.* Garden City: The Natural History Press.

Dingman, M.L., and R.H. Platt. 1977. "Floodplain Zoning: Implications of Hydrologic and Legal Uncertainty." *Water Resources Research* June: 519–523.

Dolgin, E.L., and T.G.P. Guilbert. 1974. *Federal Environmental Law.* St. Paul: West Publishing Co.

Engel, R. 1985. *Sacred Sands: The Struggle for Community in the Indiana Dunes.* Middetown, CT: Wesleyan University Press.

Environmental Law Institute. 1989. "News and Analysis." *Environmental Law Reporter* 19: 10060.

Federal Emergency Management Agency. 1985. *FEMA Floodplain Community Report: State Ranking, 1985.* Washington, D.C.: FEMA.

———. 1986. *A Unified National Program for Managing Flood Losses.* Washington: FEMA.

———. 1994. *A Unified National Program for Floodplain Management–1994.* Washington, D.C.: Federal Emergency Management Agency.

Federal Interagency Floodplain Management Task Force. 1992. *Floodplain Management in the United States: An Assessment Report. Vol. 1–Summary.* Washington: Federal Insurance Administration.

Fischel, W.A. 1982. "The Urbanization of Farmland: A Review of the National Agricultural Lands Study." *Land Economics* 58: 236–259.

Frayer, W.E., T.J. Monahan, D.C. Bowden, and F.A. Graybill. 1983. *Status and Trends of Wetlands and Deepwater Habitats in the Conterminous United States: 1950s to 1970s*. Fort Collins: Colorado State University, Department of Forest and Wood Sciences.

Fried, J.P. 1971. *Housing Crisis U.S.A.* New York: Praeger.

Furuseth, O.J., and J.T. Pierce. 1982. *Agricultural Land in an Urban Society*. Washington, D.C.: Association of American Geographers.

Gottlieb, R. 1993. *Forcing the Spring: The Transformation of the American Environmental Movement*. Washington, D.C.: Island Press.

Godschalk, D.R. 1992. "Implementing Coastal Zone Management: 1972-1990." *Coastal Management* 20: 93–116.

Gottmann, J. 1961. *Megalopolis*. Cambridge: The M.I.T. Press.

Gruntfest, E.C. 1987. *What We Have Learned Since the Big Thompson Disaster*. Special Pub. no. 16. Boulder: University of Colorado, Natural Hazards Research Center.

Hardin, G. 1968. "Tragedy of the Commons." *Science* 162: 1243–1248.

Harris, C.D. 1956. "The Pressure of Residential–Industrial Land Use." In *Man's Role in Changing the Face of the Earth*. W.L. Thomas, Jr., ed. Chicago: University of Chicago Press.

Healy, R.G., and J. Zinn. 1985. "Environment and Development Conflicts in Coastal Zone Management." *Journal of the American Planning Association* 51(3): 299–311.

Hibbard, W.R., Jr. 1978. "Environmental Impact of Mining." In *Sourcebook on the Environment*. K.A. Hammond, G. Macinko, and W.B. Fairchild, eds. Chicago: University of Chicago Press.

Hoyt, W.G., and W.B. Langbein. 1955. *Floods*. Princeton: Princeton University Press.

Interagency Floodplain Management Review Committee. 1994. *Sharing the Challenge: Floodplain Management into the 21st Century*. Washington: U.S. Government Printing Office.

Kates, R.W. 1987. "The Human Environment: The Road Not Taken, The Road Still Beckoning." *Annals of the Association of American Geographers* 77(4): 525–534.

Kuehn, R.R. 1984. "The Coastal Barrier Resources Act and the Expenditures Limitation Approach to Natural Resources Conservation: Wave of the Future or Island Unto Itself?" *Ecology Law Quarterly* 11(3): 583–670.

Kusler, J.A. 1983. *Our National Wetland Heritage*. Washington, D.C.: Environmental Law Institute.

Kusler, J.A., and L. Larson. 1993. "Beyond the Ark: A New Approach to U.S. Floodplain Management." *Environment* 35(5): 6–11, 31–34.

Leopold, A. 1949/1966. *A Sand County Almanac.* New York: Oxford University Press.

Marsh, G.P. 1864/1975. *Man and Nature: Physical Geography as Modified by Human Action.* D. Lowenthal, ed. Cambridge: Belknap Press of Harvard University Press.

Matuszeski, W. 1985. "Managing the Federal Coastal Programs: The Planning Years." *Journal of the American Planning Association* 51(3): 266–274.

Maugh, T.H. 1979. "Toxic Waste Disposal a Growing Problem." *Science* 204 (May 25): 819–824.

McHarg, I. 1968. *Design with Nature.* Garden City, N.Y.: Natural History Press.

McPhee, J. 1968. *The Pine Barrens.* New York: Farrar, Straus, and Giroux.

McPhee, J. 1971/1976. "Encounters with the Archdruid." In *The John McPhee Reader.* W.L. Howarth, ed. New York: Random House Vintage Books.

Mitsch, W.J., and J.G. Gosselink. 1986. *Wetlands.* New York: Van Nostrand Reinhold.

Mumford, L. 1956. "The Natural History of Urbanization." In *Man's Role in Changing the Face of the Earth.* W.L. Thomas, Jr., ed. Chicago: University of Chicago Press.

Murphy, F.C. 1958. *Regulating Flood-Plain Development.* Monograph no. 56. Chicago: University of Chicago Department of Geography.

Myers, M.F., and G.F. White. 1993. "The Challenge of the Mississippi Flood." *Environment* 35(10): 6–9, 25–35.

National Agricultural Lands Study. 1981. *Final Report.* Washington, D.C.: U.S. Government Printing Office.

National Oceanic and Atmospheric Administration. 1975. "The Coastline of the United States." Washington, D.C.: U.S. Government Printing Office.

National Research Council. 1990. *Managing Coastal Erosion.* Washington, D.C.: National Academy Press.

National Resources Board. 1934. *Final Report.* Washington, D.C.: U.S. Government Printing Office.

National Review Committee on Floodplain Management. 1989. "Action Agenda For Managing the Nation's Floodplains." (mimeo: Natural Hazards Center, University of Colorado, Boulder).

Newsweek. 1989. "Buried Alive." November 27: 67–75.

New York Times. 1989. "Why the Garbage Is Never Gone." February 12, Sec. 7: 24.

———. 1995. "Future of Endangered Species Act in Doubt as Law is Debated." May 16, p. C4.

Office of Ocean and Coastal Resource Management. 1988. *Coastal Management: Solutions to Our Nation's Coastal Problems.* Technical Assistance Bulletin no. 101. Washington, D.C.: Office of Ocean and Coastal Resource Management.

Office of Technology Assessment. 1989. *Coming Clean: Superfund Problems Can Be Solved.* Washington, D.C.: U.S. Government Printing Office.

Parsons, K.C. 1990. "Clarence Stein and the Greenbelt Towns: Settling for Less." *Journal of the American Planning Association* 56(2): 161–183.

Platt, R.H. 1972. *The Open Space Decision Process: Spatial Allocation of Costs and Benefits.* Research Paper no. 142. Chicago: University of Chicago Department of Geography.

———. 1978. "Coastal Hazards and National Policy: A Jury-Rig Approach." *Journal of the American Institute of Planners* 44(2): 170–180.

———. 1982. "The Jackson Flood of 1979: A Public Policy Disaster." *Journal of the American Planning Association* 48(2): 219–231.

———. 1987. "Coastal Wetland Management: The Advance Designation Approach." *Environment* 29(9): 16–20, 38–43.

———. 1985. "The Farmland Conversion Debate: NALS and Beyond." *The Professional Geographer* 37(4): 433-442.

———. 1994. "Evolution of Coastal Hazard Policies in the United States." *Coastal Management* 22: 265–284.

Platt, R.H., S.G. Pelczarski, and B.K.R. Burbank, eds. 1987. "Cities on the Beach: An Overview." In *Cities on the Beach: Management Issues of Developed Coastal Barriers.* Research Paper no. 224. Chicago: University of Chicago Department of Geography.

Platt, R.H., T. Beatley, and H.C. Miller. 1991. "The Folly at Folly Beach and Other Failings of U.S. Coastal Erosion Policy." *Environment* 33(9): 6–9, 25–32.

Platt, R.H., et al. 1992. *Coastal Erosion: Has Retreat Sounded?* Program on Environment and Behavior Monograph no. 53. Boulder: University of Colorado Institute of Behavioral Science.

Platt, R.H., G. Macinko, and K. Hammond. 1983. "Federal Environmental Management: Some Land Use Legacies of the 1970s." In *United States Public Policy: A Geographical View.* J. W. House, ed. Oxford: Clarendon Press.

Platt, R. (Sr.). 1966. *The Great American Forest.* Englewood Cliffs, N.J.: Prentice-Hall.

Popper, F.J. 1988. "Understanding American Land Use Regulation Since 1970: A Revisionist Interpretation." *Journal of the American Planning Association.* 54(3): 291–301.

Reisner, M. 1986. *Cadillac Desert.* New York: Penguin.

Rodgers, W.H., Jr. 1988. *Environmental Law: Vol. 3–Pesticides and Toxic Substances.* St. Paul: West Publishing Co.

Sampson, R.N. 1981. *Farmland or Wasteland: A Time to Choose.* Emmaus, PA: Rodale Press.

Scientific American 1965. "Cities."(Special Issue)

Stewart. F. 1995. *A Natural History of Nature Writing.* Washington: Island Press.

Teal, J., and M. Teal. 1969. *Life and Death of the Salt Marsh.* New York: Ballantine Books.

Time. 1985. "A Problem That Cannot Be Buried." October 14: 76–84.

Thomas, W.L., Jr., ed. 1956. *Man's Role in Changing the Face of the Earth.* Chicago: University of Chicago Press.

Tiner, R.W., Jr. 1984. *Wetlands of the United States: Current Status and Recent Trends.* Washington, D.C.: U.S. Government Printing Office.

Udall, M.K. 1979. "The Enactment of the Strip Mining Control and Reclamation Act of 1977 in Retrospect." *West Virginia Law Review* 81(4): 553–557.

U.S. Bureau of the Census. 1991. *Statistical Abstract of the United States: 1991.* Washington, D.C.: U.S. Government Printing Office.

U.S. Congress. 1966a. *Insurance and Other Programs for Financial Assistance to Flood Victims.* (89th Cong., 2d Sess.). Washington: U.S. Government Printing Office.

———. 1966b. *A Unified National Program for Managing Flood Losses.* House Document 465. (89th Cong., 2d Sess..) Washington, D.C.: U.S. Government Printing Office.

———. 1973. *National Land Use Policy Legislation, 93rd Congress: An Analysis of Legislative Proposals and State Laws.* (Prepared by the Library of Congress Congressional Research Service for the Senate Committee on Interior and Insular Affairs.) (93rd Congress, 1st Session.) Washington, D.C.: U.S. Government Printing Office.

———. 1975. *Oversight on Federal Flood Insurance Programs.* (Senate Committee on Banking, Housing, and Urban Affairs). (94th Congress, 1st Session). Washington, D.C.: U.S. Government Printing Office.

———. 1977. *Hearings on the Surface Mining Control and Reclamation Act of 1977 before the House Committee on Interior and Insular Affairs.* (95th Congress, 1st Session.) Washington, D.C.: U.S. Government Printing Office.

U.S. Council on Environmental Quality. 1970. *Environmental Quality*. Washington, D.C.: U.S. Government Printing Office.

——. 1971. *Toxic Substances*. Washington: U.S. Government Printing Office.

——. 1984. *Environmental Quality*. Washington: U.S. Government Printing Office.

U.S. Department of Agriculture. 1987. *The Second RCA Appraisal: Soil, Water, and Related Resources on Nonfederal Land in the United States*. Washington, D.C.: U.S. Department of Agriculture.

——. 1981. *America's Soil and Water Conditions and Trends*. Washington: U.S.D.A.

——, Economic Research Service. 1984. *U.S. Cropland, Urbanization, and Land Ownership Patterns*. Washington, D.C.: U.S. Government Printing Office.

U.S. Department of Agriculture, Soil Conservation Service. 1977. *Potential Cropland Study*. Statistical Bulletin no. 578. Washington, D.C.: U.S. Department of Agriculture, Soil Conservation Service.

U.S. Environmental Protection Agency. 1986. *Solving the Hazardous Waste Problem*. Washington, D.C.: Environmental Protection Agency.

——. 1988. *Environmental Progress and Challenges: EPA's Update*. Washington, D.C.: U.S. Government Printing Office.

U.S. Fish and Wildlife Service. 1956. *Wetlands of the United States*. Circular 39. Washington, D.C.: U.S. Government Printing Office.

U.S. Water Resources Council. 1976. *A Unified National Program for Floodplain Management*. Washington: The Council.

White, G.F., et al. 1958. *Changes in Urban Occupance of Flood Plains in the United States*. Research Paper no. 57. Chicago: University of Chicago Department of Geography.

——. 1964. *Choice of Adjustment to Floods*. Research Paper no. 93. Chicago: University of Chicago Department of Geography.

——. 1969. *Strategies of American Water Management*. Ann Arbor: University of Michigan Press.

——. 1975. *Flood Hazard in the United States*. Monograph no. NSF-RA-E-75-006. Boulder: University of Colorado Institute of Behavioral Science.

Whyte, W.H., Jr. 1958. "Urban Sprawl." In *The Exploding Metropolis*. Editors of *Fortune*, eds. Garden City: Doubleday Anchor.

——. 1959. *Securing Open Space for Urban America: Conservation Easements*. (Technical Bulletin no. 36). Washington, D.C.: Urban Land Institute.

——. 1968. *The Last Landscape*. Garden City, NY: Doubleday.

——. 1988. *City: Rediscovering the Center*. New York: Doubleday.

Wingo, L., Jr., ed. 1963. *Cities and Space: The Future Use of Urban Land*. Baltimore: The Johns Hopkins Press for Resources for the Future.

Young, J.E. 1995. "The Sudden New Strength of Recycling." *Worldwatch Magazine* July-August: 20–25.

Ziegler, D.J., J.H. Johnson, Jr., and S.D. Brunn. 1983. *Technology Hazards*. Washington, D.C.: Association of American Geographers.

Conclusion: Successes, Failures, and Fundamentals

This book has reviewed the evolution of public controls over land use in the United States from feudalism to federalism.

The overriding theme of the book has been the tendency of a capitalist society, through its various levels and instruments of public authority, to intervene in the private land economy only in response to perception of socioeconomic or environmental dysfunction or "problem." Such perception is derived from the recognition of economic, social, or environmental harm arising from particular land use and building practices. The external effects ("externalities") of such practices may adversely affect the use, economic value, and ecological integrity of other land, either proximate to or distant from the point of origin, depending on the geographic nature and extent of the effect considered—such as downstream occupants of a floodplain, downwind residents in an airshed, or households seeking new residential opportunities in a regional housing market. The nature and spatial extent of an externality may vary from local traffic congestion and fiscal imbalance to a regional soil erosion problem, to a nationwide proliferation of abandoned toxic waste dumps, or to global warming. Avenues of legal response to these geographical externalities have included, respectively, local "growth management" policies, soil erosion control programs, the Superfund Program, and proposals (as yet uneffectuated) for limits on deforestation and carbon dioxide emissions.

Clearly this process of societal response to perceived threat is highly uneven in its application and effectiveness, and often leads to conflict among policies and measures instituted by individual units or different levels of public authority. Adverse externalities arise from the inconsistent perceptions and actions of municipalities, states, and nations as they do from the actions of individual property owners. These include, for example, the distorting of housing markets and the economic and environmental costs of long-distance commuting, due in part to municipal zoning and slow growth policies. Furthermore, attempts to solve social problems through manipulation of the spatial arrangement of land use may only address the visible tip of the iceberg. For example, programs to mandate or facilitate "affordable housing," while commendable in purpose, do little to alleviate underlying conditions of poverty.

It has been three centuries since the "first modern building law"–the Act for Rebuilding London of 1667–and 150 years since the first general sanitary laws appeared in England and the United States. Eight decades have elapsed since the First National Conference on City Planning and Congestion in 1909, seven decades since the *Euclid* decision, and 25 years since NEPA and the first Earth Day. What has all this legacy of societal response to inefficiency in the private land market accomplished, and where do we stand today?

A statistical response to this question is difficult since hard data is unevenly available and subjective value judgments are unavoidable. But some generalizations may be drawn from accounts by writers and journalists, from recent research findings (some of which are cited in Chapters 8 through 12), and from anecdotal evidence.

Like the proverbial blind men describing the elephant, describing the present state of metropolitan and rural land use must depend on what is viewed and by whom. The contemporary U.S. landscape is a mosaic of public policy successes and failures, some of which change character depending on the function, scale, and location considered. Let us optimistically begin with some successes, as viewed by some beholders at least, before turning to the failures. (In the spirit of "the cup is half empty/half full," some topics appear on both lists.)

1. Central business districts (CBDs) of many cities have new vitality, architectural distinction, cultural diversity, and economic viability due to a combination of public and private innovations in the design and use of urban space. The public plaza (indoor or outdoor) has become a standard fixture of new commercial construction since the 1960s due to zoning incentives. If suitably designed, such spaces promote street life, civic pride, and urbanity (Whyte 1988). Skywalks, underground shopping concourses, lobby exhibit areas, and public art help to enliven downtowns. Even medium-sized cities such as Hartford, Connecticut; Portland, Oregon; Charlotte, North Carolina; or San Antonio, Texas offer a cosmopolitan ambience to those who work, visit, or increasingly reside in their CBDs.

2. Meanwhile, new *outlying regional centers* (Garreau's "Edge Cities") are challenging the dominance of the older CBDs in many metropolitan areas. Houston's Galleria, Atlanta's Perimeter Mall and Cumberland/Galleria Mall, and South Coast Plaza in Orange County, California are prototypes of 21st century urbanization. These complexes, situated at strategic crossings of metropolitan highways, contain opulent retail shops, millions of square feet of office space, major hotels, restaurants, and convention facilities, all interconnected by climate-controlled pedestrian concourses. Emerging in tandem with these super-regional malls and office parks are new residential developments ranging from row houses at densities of 10 or more per acre, to high-rise condominiums and single-family "estate homes" in elite, manicured, gated subdivisions. According to the trickle down theory of housing markets, as embraced by the Federal District Court in the *Petaluma* decision (Chapter 9), the proliferation of these high-cost new communities should be opening up new housing opportunities in slightly older, less opulent neighborhoods to the upwardly mobile elements of the middle class.

3. American cities have become increasingly accessible to *handicapped* individuals due to federal and state building requirements applicable to new construction as well as renovation of older structures. Commercial, governmental, transportation, educational, cultural, and religious facilities are now widely usable by mobility-impaired persons.

4. *Historic preservation* has accomplished much over the past three decades to protect and enhance much of the nation's cultural heritage. National and state registers of historic landmarks list thousands of structures and sites of special historic or architectural importance. Not all of these have been saved from destruction or alteration, but many have been. Beginning with the Battery District of Charleston, South Carolina, and New Orleans' French Quarter, historic districts have been widely established under federal, state, or local laws that regulate in minute detail the exterior appearance of structures. Through late 1995, New York City alone has designated 1021 individual structures and 66 historic districts.

Many historic properties have been acquired by public agencies or private nonprofit foundations for permanent preservation. In older communities that have experienced economic transition, many commercial structures such as mills, railroad depots, wharfs, and warehouses have been "adaptively reused" as retail outlets, restaurants, offices, condominiums, and new kinds of manufacturing space. This process has been fostered in part by public tax credits and other legal and financial incentives.

5. Many of the nation's *older bedroom suburbs* are aging gracefully. These paragons of the Garden City influence and Euclidean zoning still offer large older homes, shady quiet streets, mature landscaping, good schools, ample water and sewerage service, parks, hospitals, commuter trains, and other amenities. While most such communities remain largely white, some have accepted and even facilitated a certain degree of racial integration by middle-class nonwhite families. In a few suburbs such as Oak Park and Park Forest, Illinois this process has been voluntary and proactive; elsewhere it has resulted from federal or state fair housing legislation or has not occurred at all. By and large, these communities continue to embody the American Utopia, as subsidized by the federal tax code through deductions for mortgage interest and local taxes.

6. Since 1960, many *natural sites and open spaces* have been protected through public measures. Since 1965 the federal Land and Water Conservation Fund (LWCF) has allocated over $3 billion for matching grants to states and local governments for the purchase and improvement of open land (although this program was greatly reduced in the 1980s). The acreage in the National Park System, excluding Alaska, has increased by 40 percent since 1960, reflecting the establishment of 14 new national seashores and lakeshores, several national recreation areas, and many other new facilities. The National Forests and National Wildlife Refuge Systems have been augmented by new land purchases funded by the LWCF. Several million acres of federal land have been classified as "wilderness" areas under the 1964 Wilderness Act. Altogether, "the acreage of America held in preservation has risen steadily during this century and now amounts to more than two times the area of California" (Easterbrook 1995, 40).

Private nonprofit organizations, from The Nature Conservancy at the national level to local land trusts, have bought or accepted gifts of thousands of acres of natural land. Land philanthropy by private owners has been encouraged by federal income tax deductions for the value of such gifts.

7. As contemporary sequels to Olmsted's Emerald Necklace Plan for Boston, stream corridors and coastlines are receiving increasing attention as multifunction resource systems. *"Greenways"* have been established along hundreds of metropolitan streams–for example, in the Bay Area of California; Boulder, Colorado; Portland, Oregon; Seattle, Atlanta, San Antonio, Denver, and St. Louis (Platt, Rowntree, and Muick 1994). The greenway approach to resource management combines several public objectives: water quality improvement, protection of riparian and fish habitat, public recreation, flood hazard reduction, and visual separation of urban districts. Means used to effectuate greenways include public acquisition, regulation, and financial incentives.

8. The $30 billion federal *sewage treatment* program established in 1972 has significantly contributed to the improvement of surface water quality in many urban areas. In 1972, only one-third of the bodies of water in the United States were safe for fishing and swimming; today nearly two-thirds are safe (Easterbrook 1995, 39).

9. Federal and state *coastal zone and wetlands* programs have sought to improve public access and protect natural resources in coastal areas, although extremely high property values, subsidized by federal incentives, continue to deter public management of the nation's shorelines in many states. The rate of wetland loss nationally has been slowed, especially due to urban development. Most coastal saltmarshes have been protected under federal, state, and local regulatory programs.

10. Although *coastal* shorelines continue to be developed, state and local policies, guided by the National Flood Insurance Program, are regulating the location, elevation, and use of new or rebuilt structures in many *riverine* floodplains. In the aftermath of the Midwest Floods of 1993, the federal government acquired and demolished more than 8000 low-cost floodplain structures to enable their owners to move to higher ground. Even along coasts, the NFIP has

at least influenced new structures to be elevated above estimated 100-year storm levels (although erosion may eventually leave them stranded in the surf).

11. Smoldering garbage dumps, commonplace in the 1960s, have largely been abolished by solid waste management laws, although their toxic contents may continue to pose a threat to groundwater. *Sanitary landfills* have replaced dumps as the approved method of land disposal of solid waste. These are themselves being replaced by energy recovery incinerators, materials recycling programs, composting, and other approaches to waste management. More than 20 percent of municipal wastes are now being recycled (Easterbrook 1995, 39).

12. *Agricultural protection laws* and policies in several states have apparently slowed the rate of conversion of prime farmland to nonagricultural uses.

The foregoing represent some accomplishments of national, state, and local land use laws and programs over the past several decades. While no arena of land use policy can be deemed an unqualified success, these have been areas of significant progress or at least slowing of deterioration. There is, however, a dark side to the U.S. landscape in the 1990s that represents a legacy of public policy failures or chronic neglect:

1. The same central cities whose downtowns and wealthier suburbs flourished in the 1980s have experienced continued deterioration of their inner city, *low-income neighborhoods*. The urban renewal programs of the 1950s and 1960s left a patchwork of now-dilapidated housing projects, vacant lots, and surviving tenement buildings, many of which are now abandoned except by crack cocaine dealers. While these neighborhoods retain basic public services—water, sewerage, streets, parks—which are being replicated in outlying areas at great public cost, the condition of inner city public facilities, particularly schools, is generally abysmal.

2. As discussed in Chapter 8, 50 years of *public housing* programs has yielded only about one million family units and 375,000 elderly units

nationally–in comparison with 31.7 million people in 6.7 million households who are officially counted as living below the federal poverty level. And that omits millions of illegal immigrants and other uncounted individuals who further crowd the dwindling lower-cost housing supply. In May 1995, the public housing authority of Washington, D.C. went into receivership and was placed under the administration of a court-appointed master for at least three years. Despite a waiting list of 15,000 low-income applicants, the authority holds several thousand vacant and delapidated units that it has failed to render habitable. A month later, the federal Department of Housing and Urban Development assumed legal control of the long-troubled Chicago Housing Authority.

3. Federal subsidies for new construction and rehabilitation of *affordable housing*, which flourished briefly during President Johnson's "War on Poverty," have since lacked vision, commitment, and often funding. Similarly, state programs such as the New York Urban Development Commission, which offered much promise two decades ago, have fallen far short of meeting the demand for lower-cost units, a situation that will surely worsen if the economies of urban states such as New York, Massachusetts, and New Jersey weaken in the late 1990s. In 1988, New Jersey required 145,000 new affordable units to comply with *Mount Laurel*–related mandates for communities, and a housing panel estimated that Connecticut needed 169,000 such units. But only a few thousand units priced below $100,000 were then under construction in those states. The median price of a home in the New York metropolitan region was then $192,000, affordable by only the upper 20 percent of the region's households.

4. Inevitably, the growing scarcity of affordable housing has precipitated a rapid increase in the *homeless* population, which has been estimated to amount to some 3 million people nationally (Rowe and Wolch 1990). Paradoxically, since the homeless take up "residence" in the public spaces of mainstream urban America, they have attracted more public attention than the more numerous but less visible occupants of ghettos and slum districts. To date, however, public awareness has not translated into public action to alleviate homelessness. According to Rowe and Wolch (p. 202): "The current lack

of homeless political power leads policymakers away from meeting their needs for greater assistance, such as additional low-cost housing, social services, job training and employment." The phenomenon has perhaps been regarded more as a pathetic but benign spectacle rather than a threat to the larger society. Lacking evidence of significant externalities, little public response has been forthcoming.

5. Public *infrastructure* of many kinds is displaying widespread evidence of inadequate capacity, lack of maintenance, and obsolescence. For instance, the Massachusetts Special Commission on Infrastructure Finance (undated) estimated that repair and replacement of public infrastructure (transportation, environmental management, state buildings and grounds, public housing, and so on) in that state would require expenditures totaling $37.4 billion during the 1990s. According to the National Academy of Engineering (1988, 4): "We do not know well the condition of our infrastructure. Simple, partial inventories are available for some components of the infrastructure. For many key systems, and for many cities, we are unable to specify much at all. Our diagnosis of the vital systems of cities and the nation remains primitive. . . ."

6. A closely related concern is the reliability of vital *lifeline* systems, such as transportation facilities, electrical power, water and sewage service, and other utilities in the face of natural or technological disaster. The major source of prolonged disruption resulting from the 1989 Loma Prieta earthquake was not the collapse of individual structures, which were built for the most part to seismic code standards, but the failure of the Oakland Bay Bridge and the Nimitz Expressway, both aging but vital links in the Bay Area highway system. Similar disruption followed the 1994 Northridge earthquake with the collapse of several freeways and other lifeline failures.

7. On the subject of *disasters*, American cities have achieved a measure of safety against some types of hazards while allowing the risks of others to be magnified. Urban conflagration, the scourge of wood-built cities from the colonial period until the San Francisco earthquake of 1906, has ceased to be the primary threat today, thanks to planning and building regulations, reliable water supply systems, and

modern fire-fighting technology. Urban flood disasters, however, have increased markedly during the 20th century due to the expansion of cities into their riverine and coastal floodplains. Smaller metropolitan streams flood more often and more dangerously as paving and development upstream contribute more runoff to natural drainage ways during storms. As discussed in Chapters 9 and 12, local floodplain management prompted by the National Flood Insurance Program since the mid-1970s has modified building practices for new or rebuilt structures in many floodplains. But millions of older buildings and their inhabitants remain at risk along rivers, lakes, and ocean shorelines. And in the wake of mass devastation, as along the South Carolina coast following Hurricane Hugo in 1989, governmental restrictions on rebuilding may be weakened out of sympathy for the victims.

8. The proliferation of new commercial malls, office parks, and condos that comprise the *mushburbs* or "Edge Cities" mentioned above is scarcely an unmitigated blessing. While internally planned for the comfort and convenience of their occupants (not always effectively), such developments inflict diverse adverse externalities on surrounding areas. These include traffic congestion (few are served by non-highway mass transit), air pollution, energy inefficiency, visual discord, and loss of natural habitat or agricultural land. Economically, such developments create large numbers of low-wage service jobs but do not provide affordable housing, schools, parks, medical clinics, and the other necessities of working class urban communities. In short, the people who qualify for jobs in such areas usually have to commute long distances, often by very inadequate public transportation from the inner city or lower-cost suburbs (Leinberger and Lockwood 1986). As documented by William H. Whyte (1988), a number of major New York corporations have moved their headquarters from Manhattan to affluent hinterland locations, which happened to be close to the estates of their chief executive officers but far from affordable communities for their employees. In the process, the central city loses not only jobs but corporate taxes as well. Despite all the lip-service given to regional planning since the 1920s, metropolitan growth in the 1980s continued to reflect the dominance of private capital and its handmaiden, local municipal

autonomy with regard to location, planning, and taxation of new development.

9. The private real estate development process was substantially distorted during the 1980s by *federal deregulation of mortgage lending*, particularly by savings and loan institutions (S & L's). By 1990, several dozen S & L's primarily in the South and Southwest had failed. Estimates of the potential liability of federal taxpayers to bail out the depositors of failed S & L's ranged up to $500 billion over several decades. Meanwhile the physical results of improvident speculation litter the American landscape. These include condominium projects, hotels and resorts, and office developments, often uncompleted or vacant. Arguably, many of these projects would have not been built if the investor had been prudent in terms of locational analysis— applying basic economic and marketing geography principles. The Reagan Administration deemed that federal restrictions on the soundness of S & L lending practices were obstructing economic growth, but S & L depositors continued to be insured by the federal government against loss. The availability of huge sums of investment funds untied to normal standards of economic soundness thus fueled the infamous S & L building binge. Far from restraining improper development through land use planning and regulation, the public sector actually managed to short-circuit even the normal caution of the private market with respect to financial risk-taking, with disastrous results.

10. *Solid and hazardous wastes*, as discussed in Chapter 12, pose a galaxy of unsolved land-related problems. Conventional solid waste management in 1990 is at a threshold: Land disposal sites are filling up and few new facilities are being established due to NIMBY objections, among other factors. Several new approaches are coming into wider usage, including source reduction, waste stream separation, recycling, incineration with energy recovery, composting, and other forms of land treatment. The political acceptability and economic feasibility of many of these approaches, however, depend on the isolation and safe disposal of toxic and hazardous substances that are commonly intermingled with conventional wastes. The number of substances deemed to be toxic or hazardous and estimates of the

total volume of such wastes have increased exponentially over the past two decades. Meanwhile, since the passage of the Resource Conservation and Recovery Act of 1976, ". . . not one state has succeeded in siting a hazardous waste disposal facility and few commercial facilities have obtained operating permits" due to intense local political opposition (Lake and Johns 1990). The U.S. Environmental Protection Agency has identified over 30,000 unsafe toxic and hazardous waste disposal sites, of which over 1800 have been placed on the National Priority List for eventual attention by the Superfund Program. The latter, however, has been mired in bureaucratic, scientific, and political difficulties and to date has only cleaned up a few dozen sites.

The foregoing chronicle of successes and failures comprises a crude "report card" on the status of several areas of land use policy in the United States. It is admittedly subjective and selective; other issues not mentioned here were discussed elsewhere in the book or have been omitted altogether. But this summary is meant to indicate areas of unfinished business, or even unstarted business, for professionals in the field of land use control over the next two or three decades.

Among the many techniques and approaches discussed in the latter half of this book, the most ubiquitous and least promising is, of course, old-fashioned Euclidean zoning. In the tradition of Reps and Delogu, I would agree that zoning has outlived its usefulness and probably causes more problems than it resolves. It legitimates and anoints the actions of the most geographically irrational unit of American land use management–the local government. However, like the premature reports of Mark Twain's death, proclamations of zoning's imminent demise have been greatly exaggerated. Zoning thrives, tenacious as a bittersweet vine, and about as useful in many cases.

The attempt to reform or overthrow zoning that occurred in the 1970s (for example, through the Model Land Development Code) succeeded chiefly in bringing states into the land use control process in certain locations and on certain issues. Meanwhile many local governments, despairing of zoning but unable to rid themselves of it, have resorted to a number of supplementary strategies under the broad rubric of "growth management." As considered in Chapter 9, devices such as transfer of development rights and impact fees attempt to "privatize" the provision of public needs through incentives or exactions directed at developers. The jury is still out as to how widely and effectively the "beyond zoning" techniques pioneered in the 1970s and 1980s will prove to be utilized, and what their external effects beyond the implementing municipality will be. The "rough proportionality test" set forth in the 1994 U.S. Supreme Court decision in *Dolan v. City of Tigard*, as discussed in Chapter 8, will be a major factor in how such measures fare in the near future.

The primary need for American land use planning is to get back to basics: protecting the public health, safety, and welfare, in light of the new political realities of the mid-1990s. In the 19th century, light, air, water, sanitation, and structural soundness were the goals of urban reformers who produced the modern city planning movement. Today, building and sanitary codes are virtually ubiquitous, although enforced unevenly for new construction and sometimes not at all for older buildings. Meanwhile, professionals in the field of land use control have long since left matters of health and safety to code enforcement officials and have concerned themselves increasingly with "quality of life" issues, particularly relating to more affluent sectors of the population who support planning. Amenities, not merely survival, have dominated much of the substance of public land use control since World War II.

There is, of course, nothing wrong with amenities, and this writer strongly maintains that aesthetics, historic preservation, billboard controls, and ecological protection are sufficiently related to the "public health, safety and (especially) welfare" to justify the use of public regulations with appropriate standards to achieve them. These efforts must continue.

But as small victories are gained in the areas listed above as "successes," social and economic disasters loom in the areas denoted as "failures." Since the end of President Johnson's "War on Poverty" in 1969, this country has ideologically abandoned its central cities. The federal government allocates $300 billion annually to defense while its Fiscal Year 1990 budget for the Department of Housing and Urban Development was $16.7 billion, much of which was earmarked for programs unrelated to central cities. The proliferation of homeless people, the deteriorating conditions in lower-income urban neighborhoods, and the costly, time-wasting, climate-altering scourge of long-distance highway commuting all relate to the absence of a national commitment to rational and equitable urban development. *How ironic that we are compelled to spend hundreds of billions of dollars to bail out S & L investors for financing ill-conceived development ventures while millions of people have little or no shelter because the government does not choose to support housing construction.*

In a sense, we stand where Chadwick stood in the 1830s, confronting a cesspool of public neglect that threatens to engulf the national society. Chadwick, Olmsted, Haussmann, Pullman, Howard, Riis, Marsh, Burnham, Bettmann, and their allies recognized the evils and dangers associated with urban conditions of their times. Each in diverse ways helped to initiate or promote new forms of public response to those conditions as recounted in Chapter 6.

As "sanitary reform" was the catalyzing issue in the 1840s, "congestion" in the first decade of this century, "open space" in the 1960s, and "environmental quality" in the 1970s–"urban sustainability" could be the focal issue of the 1990s. Cities and their metropolitan hinterlands are increasingly dysfunctional in light of social, economic, and ecological limitations. New perceptions, policies, doctrines, and institutions are required to address the interrelated issues of housing, transportation, economic growth, waste management, energy usage, and vulnerability to natural and technological disaster. A national commitment to the reexamination of these issues and the formulation of new expressions of public response requires a Presidential mandate and Congressional support comparable to the New Deal, the Manhattan Project, the Moon Program, or the Savings and Loan bailout.

While national objectives and fiscal resources are needed to mount remedial efforts, the national scale is too large for effective action, just as the municipal scale is too small. Sweeping reforms at the state or regional levels are required, with the help of federal funding and broad policy guidance. One precedent at the state level is the revolution in housing doctrine initiated in New Jersey through the *Mount Laurel* litigation. Given federal fiscal backing, this undertaking could yield significant levels of new affordable housing, widely distributed, as Justice Hall originally envisioned.

An example of "sweeping reform" at the regional scale is the recent plan to abate air pollution in metropolitan Los Angeles proposed by the California South Coast Air Quality Management district (Weisman 1989). This plan, published in 1989 in a 45-volume, 3-foot high stack of reports, apparently took literally Daniel Burnham's adage: "Make no little plans, for they have no magic to stir men's blood." If Angelenos are stirred to limit their use of cars and backyard barbecues as this plan urges, anything is possible.

*   *   *

The foregoing was written in 1990 to conclude the original edition of this book published by Prentice-Hall in 1991. In light of the wave of anti-government, pro-property rights rhetoric sweeping the nation since the 1994 Congressional elections, it sounds quixotic to say the least. As of this writing in June 1995, it is too early to assess what the impact of the "Contract with America" and the property rights movement will be. Some curtailment of the federal Endangered Species Act and the Section 404 wetlands program seem inevitable. State laws, if vigorously administered, could pick up much of the slack in those federal programs with perhaps benefits in terms of efficiency and avoidance of duplication of regulation. But since the same anti-regulation fervor is sweeping many states as well as Congress, the future of state efforts is also in doubt. Likewise, it is impossible at this time to assess the potential impact of federal and state proposed "takings" bills except to say that the language currently under consideration in the U.S. House and Senate far exceeds the traditional concepts of the Fifth Amendments by awarding compensation for regulatory "takings" *regardless of the purpose of the regulation.*

These proposals seem to disregard the fact that public land use controls and other police power regulations originated in the need to *protect property* from externalities that the common law of nuisance was incapable of controlling in modern metropolitan areas. It seems unlikely that the American public will turn the legal clock back to the 19th century as we approach the 21st century. But the current backlash could be a useful stimulus to reconsider more extreme forms of regulation, such as the Endangered Species Act, and to reaffirm the absolute necessity of those regulations that maintain public health, safety, and welfare, as we now recognize it in light of 20th century experience.

References

Easterbrook, G. 1995. "Here Comes the Sun." *The New Yorker* April 10, 1995.

Lake, R.W. and R.A. Johns. 1990. "Legitimation Conflicts: The Politics of Hazardous Waste Siting Law." Unpublished paper presented at the Annual Meeting of the Association of American Geographers, Toronto, Ontario, April 1990. Available from the authors at the Center for Urban Policy Research, Rutgers University, New Brunswick, NJ 08903.

Leinberger, C.B., and C. Lockwood. 1986. "How Business Is Reshaping America." *The Atlantic* 258(4): 43–52.

Massachusetts Special Commission on Infrastructure. Undated. *A Survey of Massachusetts Infrastructure Needs for the 1990s*. Boston: The Commission. Mimeo.

National Academy of Engineering. 1988. *Cities and Their Vital Systems: Infrastructure, Past, Present, and Future*. J.H. Ausubel and R. Herman, eds. Washington: National Academy Press.

Platt, R.H., R.A. Rowntree, and P.C. Muick, eds. 1994. *The Ecological City: Preserving and Restoring Urban Biodiversity*. Amherst: University of Massachusetts Press.

Rowe, S., and J. Wolch. 1990. "Social Networks in Time and Space: Homeless Women in Skid Row Los Angeles." *Annals of the Association of American Geographers* 80(2): 184–204.

Weisman, A. 1989. "L.A. Fights for Breath." *The New York Times Magazine*. July 30: 15 ff.

Whyte, W.H. 1988. *City: Rediscovering the Center*. New York: Doubleday.

Index

List of Cases Cited

Some Common Acronyms

BLM — Bureau of Land Management

CEQ — U.S. Council on Environmental Quality

CFR — Code of Federal Regulations

COE — Army Corps of Engineers

CZM — Coastal Zone Management

EIS — Environmental Impact Statement

EPA — U.S. Environmental Protection Agency

ESA — Endangered Species Act

FEMA — Federal Emergency Management Agency

FIRM — Flood Insurance Rate Map

FWS — U.S. Fish and Wildlife Service

HCP — Habitat Conservation Plan

LWCF — Land and Water Conservation Fund

NALS — National Agricultural Land Study

NEPA — National Environmental Policy Act

NFIP — National Flood Insurance Program

NPS — National Park Service

NRI — National Resources Inventory

NWI — National Wetlands Inventory

OCRM — Office of Ocean and Coastal Resource Management

PCS — Potential Cropland Study

SCS — Soil Conservation Service

SCORP — State Conservation Outdoor Recreation Plan

TVA — Tennessee Valley Authority

USC — U.S. Code

USCA — U.S. Code Annotated

USDA — U.S. Department of Agriculture

USFS — U.S. Forest Service

USGS — U.S. Geological Survey

About the Author

Rutherford H. Platt is a professor of geography and adjunct professor of regional planning at the University of Massachusetts at Amherst. He holds a B.A. in political science from Yale University and a law degree and Ph.D in geography from the University of Chicago and is a member of the Illinois Bar. Public policy issues of land and water resources, particularly the management of floodplains, wetlands, and coastal zones, have been the focus of his research, teaching, and consulting. He has served on several national panels, including six committees of the National Academy of Sciences/National Research Council. In addition to writing numerous articles and monographs, he wrote *Land Use Control* (1991, Prentice-Hall) and co-edited *The Ecological City* (1994, University of Massachusetts Press).

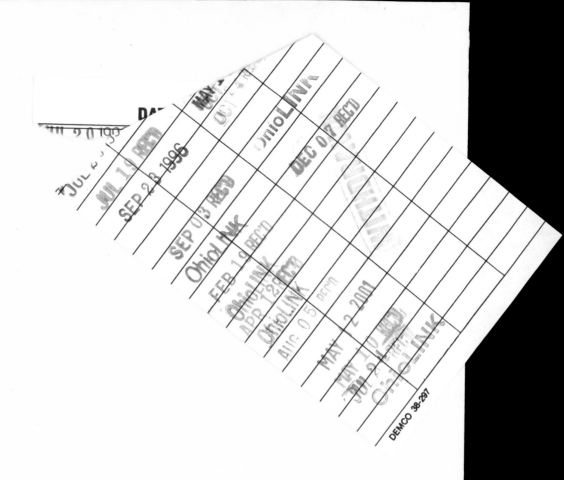